REA's Test Prep Books Are The Best!

(a sample of the <u>hundreds of letters</u> REA receives each year)

" The last formal English grammar class I had was more than 25 years ago, and I did not know how I was going to prepare for this [MTEL] test. Then I found [REA's MTEL] book! It was a very accurate representation of the test material. I would not take the test without using this to review—whether you graduated from college one year ago or 25 years ago. "

MTEL Test-Taker, Chelmsford, MA

" Your book was such a better value and was so much more complete than anything your competition has produced — and I have them all! "

Teacher, Virginia Beach, VA

" Compared to the other books that my fellow students had, your book was the most useful in helping me get a great score. "

Student, North Hollywood, CA

" Your book was responsible for my success on the exam, which helped me get into the college of my choice... I will look for REA the next time I need help. "

Student, Chesterfield, MO

" Just a short note to say thanks for the great support your book gave me in helping me pass the test... I'm on my way to a B.S. degree because of you! "

Student, Orlando, FL

(more on next page)

(continued from front page)

" I just wanted to thank you for helping me get a great score
on the AP U.S. History exam... Thank you for making great test preps! "
Student, Los Angeles, CA

" Your *Fundamentals of Engineering Exam* book was the absolute best
preparation I could have had for the exam, and it is one of the major
reasons I did so well and passed the FE on my first try. "
Student, Sweetwater, TN

" I used your book to prepare for the test and found that the advice and the
sample tests were highly relevant... Without using any other material, I earned
very high scores and will be going to the graduate school of my choice. "
Student, New Orleans, LA

" What I found in your book was a wealth of information sufficient to shore up
my basic skills in math and verbal... The section on analytical ability was
excellent. The practice tests were challenging and the answer explanations most
helpful. It certainly is the *Best Test Prep for the GRE*! "
Student, Pullman, WA

" I really appreciate the help from your excellent book. Please keep up
the great work. "
Student, Albuquerque, NM

" I am writing to thank you for your test preparation... your book helped me
immeasurably and I have nothing but praise for your *GRE* preparation."
Student, Benton Harbor, MI

(more on back page)

The Best Test Preparation for the

MTEL

Massachusetts Tests for Educator Licensure — Communication and Literacy Skills Test

Gail Rae, M.A.
Department of English
McKee Technical High School
Staten Island, NY

Ann Jenson-Wilson
Department of English
Southern Methodist University
Dallas, TX

Bernadette Brick
Department of English
University of Rochester
Rochester, NY

Brian Walsh
Department of English
Rutgers University
New Brunswick, NJ

And the Staff of Research and Education Association
Dr. M. Fogiel, Director

Research & Education Association
61 Ethel Road West
Piscataway, New Jersey 08854

The Best Test Preparation for the
MTEL: Massachusetts Tests for Educator Licensure
Communication and Literacy Skills Test

Printed in the United States of America

Library of Congress Control Number 2003095255

International Standard Book Number 0-87891-450-1

Research & Education Association
61 Ethel Road West
Piscataway, New Jersey 08854

REA supports the effort to conserve and
protect environmental resources by
printing on recycled papers.

Contents

CHAPTER 3

ABOUT RESEARCH & EDUCATION ASSOCIATION

Research & Education Association (REA) is an organization of educators, scientists, and engineers specializing in various academic fields. Founded in 1959 with the purpose of disseminating the most recently developed scientific information to groups in industry, government, high schools, and universities, REA has since become a successful and highly respected publisher of study aids, test preps, handbooks, and reference works.

REA's Test Preparation series includes study guides for all academic levels in almost all disciplines. Research & Education Association publishes test preps for students who have not yet completed high school, as well as high school students preparing to enter college. Students from countries around the world seeking to attend college in the United States will find the assistance they need in REA's publications. For college students seeking advanced degrees, REA publishes test preps for many major graduate school admission examinations in a wide variety of disciplines, including engineering, law, and medicine. Students at every level, in every field, with every ambition can find what they are looking for among REA's publications.

Unlike most test preparation books—which present only a few practice tests that bear little resemblance to the actual exams—REA's series presents tests that accurately depict the official exams in both degree of difficulty and types of questions. REA's practice tests are always based upon the most recently administered exams, and include every type of question that can be expected on the actual exams.

REA's publications and educational materials are highly regarded and continually receive an unprecedented amount of praise from professionals, instructors, librarians, parents, and students. Our authors are as diverse as the fields represented in the books we publish. They are well-known in their respective disciplines and serve on the faculties of prestigious high schools, colleges, and universities throughout the United States and Canada.

ACKNOWLEDGMENTS

In addition to our authors, we would like to thank Dr. Max Fogiel, President, for his overall guidance, which brought this publication to completion; Mike Sedelmaier, Editorial Assistant, for coordinating revisions; Ariana Baker, Project Manager, for coordinating development of the book; Anita Davis, Christopher Dickenson, Ellen Gong, Cheryl McQueen, Catherine Battos, Robert Coover, Kristin Rutkowski, and Alicia Shapiro for their editorial contributions; and Nancy Saxton and Michael Cote for typesetting the manuscript.

MTEL

*Massachusetts Tests for Educator Licensure —
Communication and Literacy Skills Test*

Chapter 1
Passing the Communication
and Literacy Skills Test

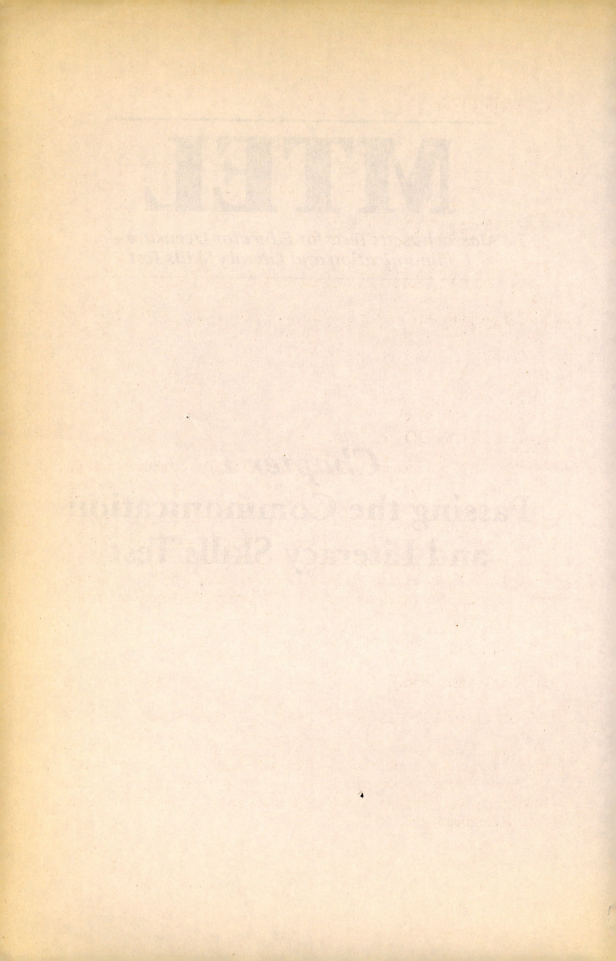

CHAPTER 1

Passing the Communication and Literacy Skills Test

ABOUT THIS BOOK

This REA test-preparation book is designed to help candidates pass the Communication and Literacy Skills Test section of the Massachusetts Tests for Educator Licensure. The Communication and Literacy Skills Test is composed of two subtests: reading and writing. Comprehensive review material for both subtests is available in this book, along with three practice tests. These practice tests contain the types of questions you can expect to encounter on the actual exam. Following each test, you will find an answer key with detailed explanations designed to help you more completely understand the test material.

ABOUT THE TEST

WHO TAKES THE TEST AND WHAT IS IT USED FOR?

The Massachusetts Tests for Educator Licensure must be taken by individuals seeking certification to teach in Massachusetts. Prospective teachers are required to take and pass two tests: a two-part test in communication and literacy skills and an additional test in the subject of the candidate's chosen area of certification.

WHO ADMINISTERS THE TEST?

The Massachusetts Tests for Educator Licensure are administered by the Massachusetts Department of Education. A comprehensive test development process was designed and implemented specifically to ensure that the content and difficulty level of the exam is appropriate.

WHEN AND WHERE IS THE TEST GIVEN?

The Massachusetts Tests for Educator Licensure are administered four times a year at six locations across the state. Specific information regarding test sites will be given upon registration for the tests. To receive information on upcoming test dates and locations, you may wish to contact the test administrator as follows:

Massachusetts Tests for Educator Licensure
National Evaluation Systems, Inc.
P.O. Box 660
Amherst, MA 01004-9013
Telephone: (413) 256-2892
Fax: (413) 256-8221
Website: www.doe.mass.edu/mtel

IS THERE A REGISTRATION FEE?

To take the Communication and Literacy Skills Test, you must pay a fee. A complete summary of the registration fees is included in your registration bulletin.

HOW TO USE THIS BOOK

WHEN SHOULD I START STUDYING?

An eight-week study schedule is provided in this text to assist you in preparing for the exam. This schedule can be adjusted to meet your unique needs. If your test date is only four weeks away, you can halve the time allotted to each section; keep in mind, however, that this is not the most effective way to study. If you have several months before your test date, you may wish to extend the time allotted to each section. Remember, the more time you spend studying, the better your chances of achieving your aim—a passing score on the MTEL.

FORMAT OF THE COMMUNICATION AND LITERACY SKILLS TEST

The subject area tests are designed to assess your knowledge of the subject for the certificate sought. The Communication and Literacy Skills Test is designed to ensure your ability to effectively convey that knowledge to a student.

The reading subtest of the Communication and Literacy Skills Test is composed of multiple-choice questions relating to reading passages and open-ended vocabulary questions, while the writing subtest consists of four sections: grammar and usage, written mechanics, written summary, and written composition.

ABOUT THE REVIEW SECTIONS

By using our review material in conjunction with our practice tests, you should be well prepared for the actual Communication and Literacy Skills Test. At some point in your educational experience, you have probably studied all the material that makes up this test. For many candidates, however, this may have been some time ago. REA's targeted reviews will serve to refresh your memory of these topics, and our practice tests will help you gauge which areas you need to work on.

SCORING THE COMMUNICATION AND LITERACY SKILLS TEST

HOW DO I SCORE MY PRACTICE TEST?

The Massachusetts Tests for Educator Licensure have a score range of 0-100 points for all tests. You must achieve a minimum of 70 to pass the exam. Your total score will derive from a combination of all test sections.

According to administrators of the MTEL, the reading subtest of the Communication and Literacy Skills Test contains approximately 30 multiple-choice items and six open-response items while the writing subtest contains approximately 14 multiple-choice items and six to nine open-response items. Our practice tests approximate the number of questions you will encounter on the actual exam. Because MTEL test forms vary, we cannot provide score conversions for the practice tests. It is safe to assume, however, that a score of 70 percent on each section equates with a passing score. It may be helpful to have a friend or colleague score your practice-test essays, since you will benefit from his or her ability to be more objective in judging the clarity and organization of your written responses.

If you do not achieve a passing score on your first practice test, don't worry. Review those sections with which you have had the most difficulty, and try the second practice test. With each practice test, you will sharpen the skills you need to pass the actual exam.

WHEN WILL I RECEIVE MY SCORE REPORT?

Your score report should arrive about five weeks after you take the test. No scoring information will be given via telephone or fax. Remember, the data on your score report will reflect your *scaled* score, *not* the number of questions you have answered correctly. All tests are reported on the same scale, and will not be compared to the score of any other examinees.

To receive a passing score on the Communication and Literacy Skills Test, you must attain a qualifying score on *both* the reading and writing subtests. If you do not pass one or both of the subtests, you will be able to register again for the necessary section(s).

STUDYING FOR THE COMMUNICATION AND LITERACY SKILLS TEST

There is no one correct way to study for the Communication and Literacy Skills Test. You must find the method that works best for you. Some test-takers prefer to set aside a few hours every morning to study, while others prefer to study at night before going to sleep. Only you can determine when and where your study time will be most effective. To help you budget your time, refer to the study schedule which appears at the end of this chapter.

When taking the practice tests you should try to duplicate the actual testing conditions as closely as possible. Keep in mind that the Communication and Literacy Skills Test is four hours long. It will be helpful to time yourself when you take the practice tests so you will have a better idea of how much time to spend on each section of the actual exam. A quiet, well-lit room, free from such distractions as the television or radio, is preferable. As you complete each practice test, thoroughly review the explanations. Keep track of the number of correct answers you receive on each test so you can gauge your progress accurately, and develop a clear sense of where you need improvement.

THE DAY OF THE TEST

Try to get a good night's rest, and wake up early on the day of the test. You should have a good breakfast so you will not be distracted by hunger. Dress in layers that can be removed or applied as the conditions of the testing center require. The Communication and Literacy Skills Test has a reporting time of 8:00 a.m.; plan to arrive early. This will allow you to become familiar with your surroundings in the testing center, and minimize the possibility of distraction during the test.

Before you leave for the testing center, make sure you have any admissions material you may need, including photo identification and sharpened No. 2 pencils. For the Communications and Literacy Skills subtests, a calculator is neither necessary nor permitted. No eating, drinking, or smoking will be permitted during the test, but if you are scheduled for both the morning and afternoon test sessions you may want to bring food to eat in the interim.

TEST-TAKING TIPS

Although you may have taken standardized tests like the Communication and Literacy Skills Test before, it is crucial that you become familiar with the format and content of each section of this exam. This will help to alleviate any anxiety about your performance. Following are several ways to help you become accustomed to the test.

➤ *Become comfortable with the format of the test.* The Communication and Literacy Skills Test covers a great deal of information, and the more comfortable you are with the format, the more confidence you will have when you take the actual exam. If you familiarize yourself with the requirements of each section individually, the whole test will be much less intimidating.

➤ *Read all of the possible answers.* Even if you believe you have found the correct answer, read all four options. Often answers that look right at first prove to be "magnet responses" meant to distract you from the correct choice.

➤ *Eliminate obviously incorrect answers.* In this way, even if you do not know the correct answer, you can make an educated guess.

➤ *Work quickly and steadily.* Remember, you will have to write a composition for the writing subtest. You need more time to compose a clear, concise, well-constructed essay than you need to answer a multiple-choice question, so don't spend too much time on any one item. Try to pace yourself. If you feel that you are spending too much time on any one question, mark the answer choice that you think is most likely the correct one, circle the item number in your test booklet, and return to it if time allows. Timing yourself while you take the practice tests will help you learn to use your time wisely.

➤ *Be sure that the circle you are marking corresponds to the number of the question in the test booklet.* The multiple-choice sections of the test are graded by a computer, which has no sympathy for clerical errors. One incorrectly placed response can upset your entire score.

COMMUNICATION AND LITERACY SKILLS TEST STUDY SCHEDULE

This study schedule allows for thorough preparation for the Communication and Literacy Skills Test. Although designed for eight weeks, it can be condensed into a four-week course by collapsing each two-week block into a one-week period. Be sure to set aside enough time—at least two or three hours each day—to study. No matter which study schedule works best for you, the more time you spend studying, the more prepared and relaxed you will feel on the day of the exam.

Week	Activity
1	Take your first exam as a diagnostic test. This will be an indication of your strengths and weaknesses. Carefully review the explanations for the items you answered incorrectly.
2	Study REA's review material and answer the drill questions provided. Highlight key terms and information. Take notes on the important theories and key concepts, since writing will aid in the retention of information.
3 & 4	Review your references and sources. Use any supplementary material that your education instructors recommend.
5	Condense your notes and findings. You should have a structured outline with specific facts. You may want to use index cards to help you memorize important information.
6	Test yourself using the index cards. You may want to have a friend or colleague quiz you on key facts and items. Take your second exam. Review the explanations for the items you answered incorrectly.
7	Study any areas you consider to be your weaknesses by using your study materials, references, and notes.
8	Take your third exam. Review the explanations for the items you answered incorrectly.

MTEL

*Massachusetts Tests for Educator Licensure —
Communication and Literacy Skills Test*

Chapter 2
Reading Subtest Review

CHAPTER 2

Reading Subtest Review

I. Vocabulary Review

II. Reading Review

I. VOCABULARY REVIEW

It is important to understand the meanings of all words—not just the ones you are asked to define. Possession of a good vocabulary is a strength that can help you perform well on all sections of this test. The following information will build your skills in determining the meanings of words.

SIMILAR FORMS AND SOUNDS

The complex nature of language sometimes makes reading difficult. Words often become confusing when they have similar forms and sounds. In fact, the author may have a correct meaning in mind, but an incorrect word choice can alter the meaning of the sentence or even make it totally illogical.

NO: Martha was always part of that *cliché.*

YES: Martha was always part of that *clique.*

(A *cliché* is a trite or hackneyed expression; a *clique* is an exclusive group of people.)

NO: The minister spoke of the soul's *immorality.*

YES: The minister spoke of the soul's *immortality.*

(*Immorality* means wickedness; *immortality* means imperishable or unending life.)

NO: Where is the nearest *stationary* store?

YES: Where is the nearest *stationery* store?

(*Stationary* means immovable; *stationery* is paper used for writing.)

Below are groups of words that are often confused because of their similar forms and sounds.

1. accent—*v.*—to stress or emphasize (You must *accent* the last syllable.)

   ascent—*n.*—a climb or rise (John's *ascent* of the mountain was dangerous.)

   assent—*n.*—consent; compliance (We need your *assent* before we can go ahead with the plans.)

2. accept—*v.*—to take something offered (She *accepted* the gift.)

   except—*prep.*—other than; but (Everyone was included in the plans *except* him.)

3. advice—*n.*—opinion given as to what to do or how to handle a situation (Her sister gave her *advice* on what to say at the interview.)

   advise—*v.*—to counsel (John's guidance counselor will *advise* him on where he should apply to college.)

4. affect—*v.*—to influence (Mary's suggestion did not *affect* me.)

   effect—1. *v.*—to cause to happen (The plan was *effected* with great success.); 2. *n.*—result (The *effect* of the medicine is excellent.)

5. allusion—*n.*—indirect reference (In the poem, there are many Biblical *allusions*.)

   illusion—*n.*—false idea or conception; belief or opinion not in accord with the facts (Greg was under the *illusion* that he could win the race after missing three weeks of practice.)

6. all ready—*adv. + adj.*—prepared (The family was *all ready* to leave on vacation.)

   already—*adv.*—previously (I had *already* read that novel.)

7. altar—*n.*—table or stand used in religious rites (The priest stood at the *altar.*)

alter—*v.*—to change (Their plans were *altered* during the strike.)

8. capital—*n.*—1. a city where the government meets (The senators had a meeting in Albany, the *capital* of New York.); 2. money used in business (They had enough *capital* to develop the industry.)

   capitol—*n.*—building in which the legislature meets (Senator Brown gave a speech at the *capitol* in Washington.)

9. choose—*v.*—to select (Which camera did you *choose*?)

   chose—past tense of *choose* (Susan *chose* to stay home.)

10. cite—*v.*—to quote (The student *cited* evidence from the text.)

    site—*n.*—location (They chose the *site* where the house would be built.)

11. clothes—*n.*—garments (Because she got caught in the rain, her *clothes* were wet.)

    cloths—*n.*—pieces of material (The *cloths* were used to wash the windows.)

12. coarse—*adj.*—rough; unrefined (Sandpaper is *coarse.*)

    course—*n.*—1. path of action (She did not know what *course* would solve the problem.); 2. passage (We took the long *course* to the lake.); 3. series of studies (We both enrolled in the physics *course.*); 4. part of a meal (She served a five-*course* meal.)

13. consul—*n.*—a person appointed by the government to live in a foreign city and represent the citizenry and business interests of his or her native country there (The *consul* was appointed to Naples, Italy.)

    council—*n.*—a group used for discussion, advisement (The *council* decided to accept his letter of resignation.)

    counsel—*v.*—to advise (Tom *counsels* Jerry on tax matters.)

14. decent—*adj.*—proper; respectable (He was very *decent* about the entire matter.)

    descent—*n.*—1. moving down (In Dante's *Inferno*, the *descent* into Hell was depicted graphically.); 2. ancestry (He is of Irish *descent.*)

15. device—*n.*—1. plan; scheme (The *device* helped her win the race.); 2. invention (We bought a *device* that opens the garage door automatically.)

    devise—*v.*—to contrive (He *devised* a plan so John could not win.)

16. emigrate—*v.*—to go away from a country (Many Japanese *emigrated* from Japan in the late 1800s.)

    immigrate—*v.*—to come into a country (Her relatives *immigrated* to the United States after World War I.)

17. eminent—*n.*—prominent (He is an *eminent* member of the community.)

    imminent—*adj.*—impending (The decision is *imminent.*)

    immanent—*adj.*—existing within (Maggie believed that religious spirit is *immanent* in human beings.)

18. fair—*adj.*—1. beautiful (She was a *fair* maiden.); 2. just (She tried to be *fair.*); 3. *n.*—festival (There were many games at the *fair.*)

    fare—*n.*—amount of money paid for transportation (The city proposed that the subway *fare* be raised.)

19. forth—*adv.*—onward (The soldiers moved *forth* in the blinding snow.)

    fourth—*n.*, *adj.*—4th (She was the *fourth* runner-up in the beauty contest.)

20. its—possessive form of *it* (Our town must improve *its* roads.)

    it's—contraction of *it is* (*It's* time to leave the party.)

21. later—*adj.*, *adv.*—at a subsequent date (We will take a vacation *later* this year.)

    latter—*n.*—second of the two (Susan can visit Monday or Tuesday. The *latter,* however, is preferable.)

22. lead—1. *n.*—[led] a metal (The handgun was made of *lead.*); 2. *v.*—[leed] to show the way (The camp counselor *leads* the way to the picnic grounds.)

    led—past tense of *lead* (#2 above) (The dog *led* the way.)

✓ 23. loose—*adj.*—free; unrestricted (The dog was let *loose* by accident.)

    lose—*v.*—to suffer the loss of (He was afraid he would *lose* the race.)

16

24. moral—1. *n.*—lesson taught by a story, incident, etc. (Most fables end with a *moral.*); 2. *adj.*—virtuous (She is a *moral* woman with high ethical standards.)

    morale—*n.*—mental condition (After the team lost the game, their *morale* was low.)

25. of—*prep.*—from (She is *of* French descent.)

    off—*adj.*—away; at a distance (The television fell *off* the table.)

26. passed—*v.*—having satisfied some requirement (He *passed* the test.)

    past—1. *adj.*—gone by or elapsed in time (His *past* deeds got him in trouble.); 2. *n.*—a period of time gone by (His *past* was shady.); 3. *prep.*—beyond (She ran *past* the house.)

27. personal—*adj.*—private (Jack was unwilling to discuss his childhood; it was too *personal.*)

    personnel—*n.*—staff (The *personnel* at the department store was primarily young adults.)

28. principal—1. *adj.*—first or highest in rank or value (Her *principal* reason for leaving was boredom.); 2. *n.*—head of a school (The *principal* addressed the graduating class.)

    principle—*n.*—the ultimate source, origin, or cause of something; a law, truth (The *principles* of physics were reviewed in class today.)

29. prophecy—*n.*—prediction of the future (His *prophecy* that he would become a doctor came true.)

    prophesy—*v.*—to declare or predict (He *prophesied* that we would win the lottery.)

30. quiet—*adj.*—still; calm (At night all is *quiet.*)

    quite—*adv.*—really; truly (She is *quite* a good singer.)

    quit—*v.*—to free oneself (Peter had little time to spare so he *quit* the chorus.)

31. respectfully—*adv.*—with respect, honor, esteem (He declined the offer *respectfully.*)

    respectively—*adv.*—in the order mentioned (Jack, Susan, and Jim, who are members of the club, were elected president, vice president, and secretary, *respectively.*)

32. straight—*adj.*—not curved (The road was *straight.*)

    strait—1. *adj.*—restricted; narrow; confined (The patient was put in a *strait* jacket.); 2. *n.*—narrow waterway (He sailed through the *Strait* of Magellan.)

33. than—*conj.*—used most commonly in comparisons (Maggie is older *than* I.)

    then—*adv.*—soon afterward (We lived in Boston; *then* we moved to New York.)

34. their—possessive form of *they* (That is *their* house on Tenafly Drive.)

    there—*adv.*—at that place (Who is standing *there* under the tree?)

    they're—contraction of *they are* (*They're* leaving for California next week.)

35. to—*prep.*—in the direction of; toward; as (She made a turn *to* the right on Norman Street.)

    too—*adv.*—1. more than enough (She served *too* much for dinner.); 2. also (He is going to Maine, *too.*)

    two—1. *n.*—the number 2; one plus one (The total number of guests is *two.*); 2. *adj.*—amounting to more than one (We have *two* pet rabbits.)

36. weather—*n.*—the general condition of the atmosphere (The *weather* is expected to be clear on Sunday.)

    whether—*conj.*—if it be a case or fact (We don't know *whether* the trains are late.)

37. who's—contraction of *who is* or *who has* (*Who's* willing to volunteer for the night shift?)

    whose—possessive form of *who* (*Whose* book is this?)

38. your—possessive form of *you* (Is this *your* seat?)

    you're—contraction of *you are* (I know *you're* going to do well on the test.)

MULTIPLE MEANINGS

In addition to words that sound alike, you must be careful when dealing with words that have multiple meanings. For example:

> The boy was thrilled that his mother gave him a piece of chew-
> ing *gum*.

> Dentists advise people to floss their teeth to help prevent *gum*
> disease.

As you can see, one word can have different meanings depending on the context in which it is used. For more examples of multiple meaning words, refer to *capital, course,* and *fair* on pages 15–16.

CONNOTATION AND DENOTATION

The English language can become even more complicated. Not only can a single word have numerous definitions and subtle meanings, but it may also take on added meanings through implication. The *connotation* is the idea suggested by its place near, or association with, other words or phrases. The *denotation* of a word is the direct, explicit meaning.

CONNOTATION

Sometimes you will be asked to tell the meaning of a word in the context of the paragraph. You may not have seen the word before, but from your understanding of the writer's intent you should be able to interpret the meaning. For example, read the following paragraph:

> Paris is a beautiful city, perhaps the most beautiful on earth.
> Long, broad avenues are lined with seventeenth- and eight-
> eenth-century apartments, office buildings, and cafes. Flow-
> ers give the city a rich and varied look. The bridges and the
> river lend an air of lightness and grace to the whole urban
> landscape.

1. In this paragraph, "rich" most nearly means

   (A) wealthy.

   (B) polluted.

   (C) colorful.

   (D) dull.

If you chose "colorful," you would be right. Although "rich" literally means "wealthy" (that is its denotation, or literal meaning), here the writer implies more than the word's literal meaning and seems to be highlighting the variety and color that the flowers add to the avenues. In this context, richness is used in a figurative sense.

The writer is using a nonliteral meaning, or connotation, that we associate with the word "rich" to show what he or she means. When we think of something "rich," we usually also think of abundance, variety, and color.

DENOTATION

Determining a word's denotation is different from determining its connotation. Read this paragraph:

> Many soporifics are on the market to help people sleep. Take a glass of water and two *Sleepeze* and you get the "zzzzz" you need. *Sominall* supposedly helps you get the sleep you need so you can go on working. With *Morpho,* your head hits the pillow and you're asleep before the light goes out.

1. From this paragraph, a "soporific" is probably a

   (A) drug that stimulates you to stay awake.

   (B) kind of sleeping bag.

   (C) kind of bed.

   (D) drug that helps you sleep.

What is a soporific? You can figure out what it means by looking at what is said around it. People take these "soporifics" to go to sleep, not to wake up, so it can't be (A). You can't take two beds and a glass of water to go to sleep, so it can't be (C) either. Soporifics must therefore be some sort of pill that you take to sleep. Because pills are usually drugs of some kind, the answer is (D).

VOCABULARY BUILDER

Although the context in which a word appears can help you determine the meaning of the word, one "sure-fire way" to know a definition is to learn it. By studying the following lists of words and memorizing their definition(s), you will be better equipped to answer Reading Section questions that deal with word meanings.

To get the most from this vocabulary list, study the words and their definitions and then answer all of the drill questions; make sure to check your answers with the answer key that appears at the end of this section.

WORDS FOR DRILL 1

abstract—*adj.*—not easy to understand; theoretical

acclaim—*n.*—loud approval; applause

acquiesce—*v.*—to agree or consent to an opinion

adamant—*adj.*—not yielding; firm

adversary—*n.*—an enemy; foe

advocate—1. *v.*—to plead in favor of; 2. *n.*—supporter; defender

aesthetic—*adj.*—showing good taste; artistic

alleviate—*v.*—to lessen or make easier

aloof—*adj.*—distant in interest; reserved; cool

altercation—*n.*—controversy; dispute

altruistic—*adj.*—unselfish

amass—*v.*—to collect together; to accumulate

ambiguous—*adj.*—not clear; uncertain; vague

ambivalent—*adj.*—undecided

ameliorate—*v.*—to make better; to improve

amiable—*adj.*—friendly

amorphous—*adj.*—having no determinate form

anarchist—*n.*—one who believes that a formal government is unnecessary

antagonism—*n.*—hostility; opposition

apathy—*n.*—lack of emotion or interest

appease—*v.*—to make quiet; to calm

apprehensive—*adj.*—fearful; aware; conscious

arbitrary—*adj.*—based on one's preference or whim

arrogant—*adj.*—acting superior to others; conceited

articulate—*v.*—1. to speak distinctly; 2. to hinge; to connect; 3. to convey; to express effectively; *adj.*—4. eloquent; fluent; 5. capable of speech

Drill 1

DIRECTIONS: Match each word in the left column with the word in the right column that is most *opposite* in meaning.

Word		Match	
1. __ articulate	6. __ abstract	A. hostile	F. disperse
2. __ apathy	7. __ acquiesce	B. concrete	G. enthusiasm
3. __ amiable	8. __ arbitrary	C. selfish	H. certain
4. __ altruistic	9. __ amass	D. reasoned	I. resist
5. __ ambivalent	10. __ adversary	E. ally	J. incoherent

DIRECTIONS: Match each word in the left column with the word in the right column that is most *similar* in meaning.

Word		Match	
11. __ adamant	14. __ antagonism	A. afraid	D. insistent
12. __ aesthetic	15. __ altercation	B. disagreement	E. hostility
13. __ apprehensive		C. tasteful	

Drill 1 Answers

1.	(J)	5.	(H)	9.	(F)	13.	(A)
2.	(G)	6.	(B)	10.	(E)	14.	(E)
3.	(A)	7.	(I)	11.	(D)	15.	(B)
4.	(C)	8.	(D)	12.	(C)		

WORDS FOR DRILL 2

assess—*v.*—to estimate the value of

astute—*adj.*—cunning; sly; crafty

atrophy—*v.*—to waste away through lack of nutrition

audacious—*adj.*—fearless; bold

augment—*v.*—to increase or add to; to make larger

austere—*adj.*—harsh; severe; strict

authentic—*adj.*—real; genuine; trustworthy

authoritarian—*adj.*—acting as a dictator; demanding obedience

banal—*adj.*—common; petty; ordinary

belittle—*v.*—to make small; to think lightly of

benefactor—*n.*—one who helps others; a donor

benevolent—*adj.*—kind; generous

benign—*adj.*—mild; harmless

biased—*adj.*—prejudiced; influenced; not neutral

blasphemous—*adj.*—irreligious; profane; impious; away from acceptable standards

blithe—*adj.*—happy; cheery; merry

brevity—*n.*—briefness; shortness

candid—*adj.*—honest; truthful; sincere

capricious—*adj.*—changeable; fickle

caustic—*adj.*—burning; sarcastic; harsh

censor—*v.*—to examine and delete objectionable material

censure—*v.*—to criticize or disapprove of

charlatan—*n.*—an imposter; fake

coalesce—*v.*—to combine or come together

collaborate—*v.*—to work together; to cooperate

Drill 2

DIRECTIONS: Match each word in the left column with the word in the right column that is most *opposite* in meaning.

Word		Match	
1. __ augment	6. __ authentic	A. permit	F. malicious
2. __ biased	7. __ candid	B. respectful	G. neutral
3. __ banal	8. __ belittle	C. praise	H. mournful
4. __ benevolent	9. __ blasphemous	D. diminish	I. unusual
5. __ censor	10. __ blithe	E. dishonest	J. fake

DIRECTIONS: Match each word in the left column with the word in the right column that is most *similar* in meaning.

Word		Match	
11. __ collaborate	14. __ censure	A. harmless	D. cooperate
12. __ benign	15. __ capricious	B. cunning	E. criticize
13. __ astute		C. changeable	

Drill 2 Answers

1.	(D)	5.	(A)	9.	(B)	13.	(B)
2.	(G)	6.	(J)	10.	(H)	14.	(E)
3.	(I)	7.	(E)	11.	(D)	15.	(C)
4.	(F)	8.	(C)	12.	(A)		

24

WORDS FOR DRILL 3

compatible—*adj.*—in agreement; harmonious

complacent—*adj.*—content; self-satisfied; smug

compliant—*adj.*—yielding; obedient

comprehensive—*adj.*—all-inclusive; complete; thorough

compromise—*v.*—to settle by mutual adjustment

concede—*v.*—1. to acknowledge; to admit; 2. to surrender; to abandon one's position

concise—*adj.*—in few words; brief; condensed

condescend—*v.*—to consciously come down from one's position or rank

condone—*v.*—to overlook; to forgive

conspicuous—*adj.*—easy to see; noticeable

consternation—*n.*—amazement or terror that causes confusion

consummation—*n.*—the completion; finish

contemporary—*adj.*—living or happening at the same time; modern

contempt—*n.*—scorn; disrespect

contrite—*adj.*—regretful; sorrowful

conventional—*adj.*—traditional; common; routine

cower—*v.*—to crouch down in fear or shame

defamation—*n.*—any harm to a name or reputation; slander

deference—*n.*—a yielding to the opinion of another

deliberate—1. *v.*—to consider carefully; to weigh in the mind; 2. *adj.*—intentional

denounce—*v.*—to speak out against; to condemn

depict—*v.*—to portray in words; to present a visual image

deplete—*v.*—to reduce; to empty

depravity—*n.*—moral corruption; badness

deride—*v.*—to ridicule; to laugh at with scorn

Drill 3

DIRECTIONS: Match each word in the left column with the word in the right column that is most *opposite* in meaning.

Word		Match	
1. __ deplete	6. __ condone	A. unintentional	F. support
2. __ contemporary	7. __ conspicuous	B. disapprove	G. beginning
3. __ concise	8. __ consummation	C. invisible	H. ancient
4. __ deliberate	9. __ denounce	D. respect	I. virtue
5. __ depravity	10. __ contempt	E. fill	J. verbose

DIRECTIONS: Match each word in the left column with the word in the right column that is most *similar* in meaning.

Word		Match	
11. __ compatible	14. __ comprehensive	A. portray	D. thorough
12. __ depict	15. __ complacent	B. content	E. common
13. __ conventional		C. harmonious	

Drill 3 Answers

1.	(E)	5.	(I)	9.	(F)	13.	(E)
2.	(H)	6.	(B)	10.	(D)	14.	(D)
3.	(J)	7.	(C)	11.	(C)	15.	(B)
4.	(A)	8.	(G)	12.	(A)		

WORDS FOR DRILL 4

desecrate—*v.*—to violate a holy place or sanctuary

detached—*adj.*—separated; not interested; standing alone

deter—*v.*—to prevent; to discourage; to hinder

didactic—*adj.*—1. instructive; 2. dogmatic; preachy

digress—*v.*—to stray from the subject; to wander from the topic

diligence—*n.*—hard work

discerning—*adj.*—distinguishing one thing from another

discord—*n.*—disagreement; lack of harmony

discriminate—*v.*—1. to distinguish one thing from another; 2. to demonstrate bias; 3. *adj.*—able to distinguish

disdain—1. *n.*—intense dislike; 2. *v.*—to look down upon; to scorn

disparage—*v.*—to belittle; to undervalue

disparity—*n.*—difference in form, character, or degree

dispassionate—*adj.*—lack of feeling; impartial

disperse—*v.*—to scatter; to separate

disseminate—*v.*—to circulate; to scatter

dissent—*v.*—to disagree; to differ in opinion

dissonance—*n.*—harsh contradiction

diverse—*adj.*—different; dissimilar

document—1. *n.*—official paper containing information; 2. *v.*—to support; to substantiate or verify

dogmatic—*adj.*—stubborn; biased; opinionated

dubious—*adj.*—doubtful; uncertain; skeptical; suspicious

eccentric—*adj.*—odd; peculiar; strange

efface—*v.*—to wipe out; to erase

effervescence—*n.*—1. liveliness; spirit; enthusiasm; 2. bubbliness

egocentric—*adj.*—self-centered

Drill 4

DIRECTIONS: Match each word in the left column with the word in the right column that is most *opposite* in meaning.

Word		Match	
1. __ detached	6. __ dubious	A. agree	F. respect
2. __ deter	7. __ diligence	B. certain	G. compliment
3. __ dissent	8. __ disdain	C. lethargy	H. sanctify
4. __ discord	9. __ desecrate	D. connected	I. harmony
5. __ efface	10. __ disparage	E. assist	J. restore

DIRECTIONS: Match each word in the left column with the word in the right column that is most *similar* in meaning.

Word		Match	
11. __ effervescence	14. __ document	A. belittle	D. liveliness
12. __ disparage	15. __ eccentric	B. distribute	E. odd
13. __ disseminate		C. substantiate	

Drill 4 Answers

1.	(D)	5.	(J)	9.	(H)	13.	(B)
2.	(E)	6.	(B)	10.	(G)	14.	(C)
3.	(A)	7.	(C)	11.	(D)	15.	(E)
4.	(I)	8.	(F)	12.	(A)		

WORDS FOR DRILL 5

elaboration—*n.*—act of clarifying; adding details

eloquence—*n.*—the ability to speak well

elusive—*adj.*—hard to catch; difficult to understand

emulate—*v.*—to imitate; to copy

endorse—*v.*—to support; to approve of; to recommend

engender—*v.*—to create; to bring about

enhance—*v.*—to improve; to complement; to make more attractive

enigma—*n.*—mystery; secret; perplexity

ephemeral—*adj.*—temporary; brief; short-lived

equivocal—*adj.*—doubtful; uncertain

erratic—*adj.*—unpredictable; strange

erroneous—*adj.*—untrue; inaccurate; not correct

esoteric—*adj.*—incomprehensible; obscure

euphony—*n.*—pleasant sound

execute—*v.*—1. to put to death; to kill; 2. to carry out or fulfill

exemplary—*adj.*—serving as an example; outstanding

exhaustive—*adj.*—thorough; complete

expedient—*adj.*—helpful; practical; worthwhile

expedite—*v.*—to speed up

explicit—*adj.*—specific; definite

extol—*v.*—to praise; to commend

extraneous—*adj.*—irrelevant; not related; not essential

facilitate—*v.*—to make easier; to simplify

fallacious—*adj.*—misleading

fanatic—*n.*—enthusiast; extremist

Drill 5

DIRECTIONS: Match each word in the left column with the word in the right column that is most *opposite* in meaning.

Word		Match	
1. __ extraneous	6. __ erratic	A. incomplete	F. eternal
2. __ ephemeral	7. __ explicit	B. delay	G. abridge
3. __ exhaustive	8. __ euphony	C. dependable	H. relevant
4. __ expedite	9. __ elusive	D. comprehensible	I. indefinite
5. __ erroneous	10. __ elaborate	E. dissonance	J. accurate

DIRECTIONS: Match each word in the left column with the word in the right column that is most *similar* in meaning.

Word		Match	
11. __ endorse	14. __ fallacious	A. enable	D. worthwhile
12. __ expedient	15. __ engender	B. recommend	E. deceptive
13. __ facilitate		C. create	

Drill 5 Answers

1.	(H)	5.	(J)	9.	(D)	13.	(A)
2.	(F)	6.	(C)	10.	(G)	14.	(E)
3.	(A)	7.	(I)	11.	(B)	15.	(C)
4.	(B)	8.	(E)	12.	(D)		

WORDS FOR DRILL 6

fastidious—*adj.*—fussy; hard to please

fervor—*n.*—passion; intensity

fickle—*adj.*—changeable; unpredictable

fortuitous—*adj.*—accidental; happening by chance; lucky

frivolity—*n.*—giddiness; lack of seriousness

fundamental—*adj.*—basic; necessary

furtive—*adj.*—secretive; sly

futile—*adj.*—worthless; unprofitable

glutton—*n.*—overeater

grandiose—*adj.*—extravagant; flamboyant

gravity—*n.*—seriousness

guile—*n.*—slyness; deceit

gullible—*adj.*—easily fooled

hackneyed—*adj.*—commonplace; trite

hamper—*v.*—to interfere with; to hinder

haphazard—*adj.*—disorganized; random

hedonistic—*adj.*—pleasure seeking

heed—*v.*—to obey; to yield to

heresy—*n.*—opinion contrary to popular belief

hindrance—*n.*—blockage; obstacle

humility—*n.*—lack of pride; modesty

hypocritical—*adj.*—two-faced; deceptive

hypothetical—*adj.*—assumed; uncertain

illuminate—*v.*—to make understandable

illusory—*adj.*—unreal; false; deceptive

Drill 6

DIRECTIONS: Match each word in the left column with the word in the right column that is most *opposite* in meaning.

Word		Match	
1. __ heresy	6. __ fervent	A. predictable	F. beneficial
2. __ fickle	7. __ fundamental	B. dispassionate	G. orthodoxy
3. __ illusory	8. __ furtive	C. simple	H. organized
4. __ frivolity	9. __ futile	D. extraneous	I. candid
5. __ grandiose	10. __ haphazard	E. real	J. seriousness

DIRECTIONS: Match each word in the left column with the word in the right column that is most *similar* in meaning.

Word		Match	
11. __ glutton	14. __ hackneyed	A. hinder	D. overeater
12. __ heed	15. __ hindrance	B. obstacle	E. obey
13. __ hamper		C. trite	

Drill 6 Answers

1.	(G)	5.	(C)	9.	(F)	13.	(A)
2.	(A)	6.	(B)	10.	(H)	14.	(C)
3.	(E)	7.	(D)	11.	(D)	15.	(B)
4.	(J)	8.	(I)	12.	(E)		

WORDS FOR DRILL 7

immune—*adj.*—protected; unthreatened by

immutable—*adj.*—unchangeable; permanent

impartial—*adj.*—unbiased; fair

impetuous—*adj.*—1. rash; impulsive; 2. forcible; violent

implication—*n.*—suggestion; inference

inadvertent—*adj.*—not on purpose; unintentional

incessant—*adj.*—constant; continual

incidental—*adj.*—extraneous; unexpected

inclined—*adj.*—1. apt to; likely to; 2. angled

incoherent—*adj.*—illogical; rambling

incompatible—*adj.*—disagreeing; disharmonious

incredulous—*adj.*—unwilling to believe; skeptical

indifferent—*adj.*—unconcerned

indolent—*adj.*—lazy; inactive

indulgent—*adj.*—lenient; patient

inevitable—*adj.*—sure to happen; unavoidable

infamous—*adj.*—having a bad reputation; notorious

infer—*v.*—to form an opinion; to conclude

initiate—1. *v.*—to begin; to admit into a group; 2. *n.*—a person who is in the process of being admitted into a group

innate—*adj.*—natural; inborn

innocuous—*adj.*—harmless; innocent

innovate—*v.*—to introduce a change; to depart from the old

insipid—*adj.*—uninteresting; bland

instigate—*v.*—to start; to provoke

intangible—*adj.*—incapable of being touched; immaterial

Drill 7

DIRECTIONS: Match each word in the left column with the word in the right column that is most *opposite* in meaning.

Word		Match	
1. __ immutable	6. __ innate	A. intentional	F. changeable
2. __ impartial	7. __ incredulous	B. articulate	G. avoidable
3. __ inadvertent	8. __ inevitable	C. gullible	H. harmonious
4. __ incoherent	9. __ intangible	D. material	I. learned
5. __ incompatible	10. __ indolent	E. biased	J. energetic

DIRECTIONS: Match each word in the left column with the word in the right column that is most *similar* in meaning.

Word		Match	
11. __ impetuous	14. __ instigate	A. lenient	D. conclude
12. __ incidental	15. __ indulgent	B. impulsive	E. extraneous
13. __ infer		C. provoke	

Drill 7 Answers

1. (F)	5. (H)	9. (D)	13. (D)
2. (E)	6. (I)	10. (J)	14. (C)
3. (A)	7. (C)	11. (B)	15. (A)
4. (B)	8. (G)	12. (E)	

WORDS FOR DRILL 8

ironic—*adj.*—contradictory; inconsistent; sarcastic

irrational—*adj.*—not logical

jeopardy—*n.*—danger

kindle—*v.*—to ignite; to arouse

languid—*adj.*—weak; fatigued

laud—*v.*—to praise

lax—*adj.*—careless; irresponsible

lethargic—*adj.*—lazy; passive

levity—*n.*—silliness; lack of seriousness

lucid—*adj.*—1. shining; 2. easily understood

magnanimous—*adj.*—forgiving; unselfish

malicious—*adj.*—spiteful; vindictive

marred—*adj.*—damaged

meander—*v.*—to wind on a course; to travel or wander aimlessly

melancholy—*n.*—depression; gloom

meticulous—*adj.*—exacting; precise

minute—*adj.*—extremely small; tiny

miser—*n.*—penny-pincher; stingy person

mitigate—*v.*—to alleviate; to lessen; to soothe

morose—*adj.*—moody; despondent

negligence—*n.*—carelessness

neutral—*adj.*—impartial; unbiased

nostalgic—*adj.*—longing for the past; filled with bittersweet memories

novel—*adj.*—new and different

Drill 8

DIRECTIONS: Match each word in the left column with the word in the right column that is most *opposite* in meaning.

Word		Match	
1. __ irrational	6. __ magnanimous	A. extinguish	F. ridicule
2. __ kindle	7. __ levity	B. jovial	G. kindly
3. __ meticulous	8. __ minute	C. selfish	H. sloppy
4. __ malicious	9. __ laud	D. logical	I. huge
5. __ morose	10. __ novel	E. seriousness	J. stale

DIRECTIONS: Match each word in the left column with the word in the right column that is most *similar* in meaning.

Word		Match	
11. __ ironic	14. __ jeopardy	A. lessen	D. carelessness
12. __ marred	15. __ negligence	B. damaged	E. danger
13. __ mitigate		C. sarcastic	

Drill 8 Answers

1. (D)	5. (B)	9. (F)	13. (A)
2. (A)	6. (C)	10. (J)	14. (E)
3. (H)	7. (E)	11. (C)	15. (D)
4. (G)	8. (I)	12. (B)	

WORDS FOR DRILL 9

nullify—*v.*—to cancel; to invalidate

objective—1. *adj.*—open-minded; impartial; 2. *n.*—goal

obscure—*adj.*—not easily understood; dark

obsolete—*adj.*—out of date; passé

ominous—*adj.*—threatening

optimist—*n.*—person who hopes for the best; sees the good side

orthodox—*adj.*—traditional; accepted

pagan—1. *n.*—polytheist; 2. *adj.*—polytheistic

partisan—1. *n.*—supporter; follower; 2. *adj.*—biased; one-sided

perceptive—*adj.*—full of insight; aware

peripheral—*adj.*—marginal; outer

pernicious—*adj.*—dangerous; harmful

pessimism—*n.*—seeing only the gloomy side; hopelessness

phenomenon—*n.*—1. miracle; 2. occurrence

philanthropy—*n.*—charity; unselfishness

pious—*adj.*—religious; devout; dedicated

placate—*v.*—to pacify

plausible—*adj.*—probable; feasible

pragmatic—*adj.*—matter-of-fact; practical

preclude—*v.*—to inhibit; to make impossible

predecessor—*n.*—one who has occupied an office before another

prodigal—*adj.*—wasteful; lavish

prodigious—*adj.*—exceptional; tremendous

profound—*adj.*—deep; knowledgeable; thorough

profusion—*n.*—great amount; abundance

Drill 9

DIRECTIONS: Match each word in the left column with the word in the right column that is most *opposite* in meaning.

Word		Match	
1. __ objective	6. __ plausible	A. scarcity	F. minute
2. __ obsolete	7. __ preclude	B. assist	G. anger
3. __ placate	8. __ prodigious	C. superficial	H. pessimism
4. __ profusion	9. __ profound	D. biased	I. modern
5. __ peripheral	10. __ optimism	E. improbable	J. central

DIRECTIONS: Match each word in the left column with the word in the right column that is most *similar* in meaning.

Word		Match	
11. __ nullify	14. __ pernicious	A. invalidate	D. threatening
12. __ ominous	15. __ prodigal	B. follower	E. harmful
13. __ partisan		C. lavish	

Drill 9 Answers

1.	(D)	5.	(J)	9.	(C)	13.	(B)
2.	(I)	6.	(E)	10.	(H)	14.	(E)
3.	(G)	7.	(B)	11.	(A)	15.	(C)
4.	(A)	8.	(F)	12.	(D)		

WORDS FOR DRILL 10

prosaic—*adj.*—tiresome; ordinary

provincial—*adj.*—regional; unsophisticated

provocative—*adj.*—1. tempting; 2. irritating

prudent—*adj.*—wise; careful; prepared

qualified—*adj.*—experienced; indefinite

rectify—*v.*—to correct

redundant—*adj.*—repetitious; unnecessary

refute—*v.*—to challenge; to disprove

relegate—*v.*—to banish; to put to a lower position

relevant—*adj.*—of concern; significant

remorse—*n.*—guilt; sorrow

reprehensible—*adj.*—wicked; disgraceful

repudiate—*v.*—to reject; to cancel

rescind—*v.*—to retract; to discard

resignation—*n.*—1. quitting; 2. submission

resolution—*n.*—proposal; promise; determination

respite—*n.*—recess; rest period

reticent—*adj.*—silent; reserved; shy

reverent—*adj.*—respectful

rhetorical—*adj.*—having to do with verbal communication; concerned with style and effect

rigor—*n.*—severity

sagacious—*adj.*—wise; cunning

sanguine—*adj.*—1. optimistic; cheerful; 2. red

saturate—*v.*—to soak thoroughly; to drench

scanty—*adj.*—inadequate; sparse

Drill 10

DIRECTIONS: Match each word in the left column with the word in the right column that is most *opposite* in meaning.

Word

1. __ provincial
2. __ reticent
3. __ prudent
4. __ qualified
5. __ relegate
6. __ remorse
7. __ repudiate
8. __ sanguine
9. __ relevant
10. __ prosaic

Match

A. inexperienced
B. joy
C. pessimistic
D. unrelated
E. careless
F. affirm
G. extraordinary
H. sophisticated
I. forward
J. promote

DIRECTIONS: Match each word in the left column with the word in the right column that is most *similar* in meaning.

Word

11. __ provocative
12. __ rigor
13. __ saturate
14. __ rescind
15. __ reprehensible

Match

A. drench
B. tempting
C. retract
D. severity
E. blameworthy

Drill 10 Answers

1. (H)	5. (J)	9. (D)	13. (A)
2. (I)	6. (B)	10. (G)	14. (C)
3. (E)	7. (F)	11. (B)	15. (E)
4. (A)	8. (C)	12. (D)	

WORDS FOR DRILL 11

scrupulous—*adj.*—honorable; exact

scrutinize—*v.*—to examine closely; to study

servile—*adj.*—slavish; groveling

skeptic—*n.*—doubter

slander—*v.*—to defame; to maliciously misrepresent

solemnity—*n.*—seriousness

solicit—*v.*—to ask; to seek

stagnant—*adj.*—motionless; uncirculating

stanza—*n.*—group of lines in a poem having a definite pattern

static—*adj.*—inactive; changeless

stoic—*adj.*—detached; unruffled; calm

subtlety—*n.*—1. understatement; 2. propensity for understatement; 3. sophistication; 4. cunning

superficial—*adj.*—on the surface; narrow-minded; lacking depth

superfluous—*adj.*—unnecessary; extra

surpass—*v.*—to go beyond; to outdo

sycophant—*n.*—flatterer

symmetry—*n.*—correspondence of parts; harmony

taciturn—*adj.*—reserved; quiet; secretive

tedious—*adj.*—time-consuming; burdensome; uninteresting

temper—*v.*—to soften; to pacify; to compose

tentative—*adj.*—not confirmed; indefinite

thrifty—*adj.*—economical; pennywise

tranquility—*n.*—peace; stillness; harmony

trepidation—*n.*—apprehension; uneasiness

trivial—*adj.*—unimportant; small; worthless

Drill 11

DIRECTIONS: Match each word in the left column with the word in the right column that is most *opposite* in meaning.

Word		Match	
1. __ scrutinize	6. __ tentative	A. frivolity	F. skim
2. __ skeptic	7. __ thrifty	B. enjoyable	G. turbulent
3. __ solemnity	8. __ tranquility	C. prodigal	H. active
4. __ static	9. __ solicit	D. chaos	I. believer
5. __ tedious	10. __ stagnant	E. give	J. confirmed

DIRECTIONS: Match each word in the left column with the word in the right column that is most *similar* in meaning.

Word		Match	
11. __ symmetry	14. __ subtle	A. understated	D. fear
12. __ superfluous	15. __ trepidation	B. unnecessary	E. flatterer
13. __ sycophant		C. balance	

Drill 11 Answers

1.	(F)	5.	(B)	9.	(E)	13.	(E)
2.	(I)	6.	(J)	10.	(G)	14.	(A)
3.	(A)	7.	(C)	11.	(C)	15.	(D)
4.	(H)	8.	(D)	12.	(B)		

WORD FOR DRILL 12

tumid—*adj.*—swollen; inflated

undermine—*v.*—to weaken; to ruin

uniform—*adj.*—consistent; unvaried; unchanging

universal—*adj.*—concerning everyone; existing everywhere

unobtrusive—*adj.*—inconspicuous; reserved

unprecedented—*adj.*—unheard of; exceptional

unpretentious—*adj.*—simple; plain; modest

vacillation—*n.*—fluctuation

valid—*adj.*—acceptable; legal

vehement—*adj.*—intense; excited; enthusiastic

venerate—*v.*—to revere

verbose—*adj.*—wordy; talkative

viable—*adj.*—1. capable of maintaining life; 2. possible; attainable

vigor—*n.*—energy; forcefulness

vilify—*v.*—to slander

virtuoso—*n.*—highly skilled artist

virulent—*adj.*—deadly; harmful; malicious

vital—*adj.*—important; spirited

volatile—*adj.*—changeable; undependable

vulnerable—*adj.*—open to attack; unprotected

wane—*v.*—to grow gradually smaller

whimsical—*adj.*—fanciful; amusing

wither—*v.*—to wilt or shrivel; to humiliate

zealot—*n.*—believer; enthusiast; fan

zenith—*n.*—point directly overhead in the sky

Drill 12

DIRECTIONS: Match each word in the left column with the word in the right column that is most *opposite* in meaning.

Word		Match	
1. __ uniform	6. __ vigorous	A. amateur	F. support
2. __ virtuoso	7. __ volatile	B. trivial	G. constancy
3. __ vital	8. __ vacillation	C. visible	H. lethargic
4. __ wane	9. __ undermine	D. placid	I. wax
5. __ unobtrusive	10. __ valid	E. unacceptable	J. varied

DIRECTIONS: Match each word in the left column with the word in the right column that is most *similar* in meaning.

Word		Match	
11. __ wither	14. __ vehement	A. intense	D. possible
12. __ whimsical	15. __ virulent	B. deadly	E. shrivel
13. __ viable		C. amusing	

Drill 12 Answers

1.	(J)	5.	(C)	9.	(F)	13.	(D)
2.	(A)	6.	(H)	10.	(E)	14.	(A)
3.	(B)	7.	(D)	11.	(E)	15.	(B)
4.	(I)	8.	(G)	12.	(C)		

ADDITIONAL VOCABULARY

The following words comprise additional vocabulary terms that may be found on the Communication and Literacy Skills Test.

abandon—*v.*—1. to leave behind; 2. to give something up; *n.*—3. freedom; enthusiasm; impetuosity

abase—*v.*—to degrade; to humiliate; to disgrace

abbreviate—*v.*—to shorten; to compress; to diminish

aberrant—*adj.*—abnormal

abhor—*v.*—to hate

abominate—*v.*—to loathe; to hate

abridge—*v.*—1. to shorten; 2. to limit; to take away

absolve—*v.*—to forgive; to acquit

abstinence—*n.*—self-control; abstention; chastity

accede—*v.*—to comply with; to consent to

accomplice—*n.*—co-conspirator; partner; partner-in-crime

accrue—*v.*—to collect; to build up

acrid—*adj.*—sharp; bitter; foul-smelling

adept—*adj.*—skilled; practiced

adverse—*adj.*—negative; hostile; antagonistic; inimical

affable—*adj.*—friendly; amiable; good-natured

aghast—*adj.*—1. astonished; amazed; 2. horrified; terrified; appalled

alacrity—*n.*—1. enthusiasm; fervor; 2. liveliness; sprightliness

allocate—*v.*—to set aside; to designate; to assign

allure—1. *v.*—to attract; to entice; 2. *n.*—attraction; temptation; glamour

amiss—1. *adj.*—wrong; awry; 2. *adv.*—wrongly; mistakenly

analogy—*n.*—similarity; correlation; parallelism; simile; metaphor

anoint—*v.*—1. to crown; to ordain; 2. to smear with oil

anonymous—*adj.*—nameless; unidentified

arduous—*adj.*—difficult; burdensome

awry—*adj., adv.*—1. crooked(ly); uneven(ly); 2. wrong; askew

baleful—*adj.*—sinister; threatening; evil; deadly

baroque—*adj.*—extravagant; ornate

behoove—*v.*—to be advantageous; to be necessary

berate—*v.*—to scold; to reprove; to reproach; to criticize

bereft—*adj.*—hurt by someone's death

biennial—1. *adj.*—happening every two years; 2. *n.*—a plant that blooms every two years

blatant—*adj.*—1. obvious; unmistakable; 2. crude; vulgar

bombastic—*adj.*—pompous; wordy; turgid

burly—*adj.*—strong; bulky; stocky

cache—*n.*—1. stockpile; store; heap; 2. hiding place for goods

calamity—*n.*—disaster

cascade—1. *n.*—waterfall; 2. *v.*—to pour; to rush; to fall

catalyst—*n.*—anything that creates a situation in which change can occur

chagrin—*n.*—distress; shame

charisma—*n.*—appeal; magnetism; presence

chastise—*v.*—to punish; to discipline; to admonish; to rebuke

choleric—*adj.*—cranky; cantankerous

cohesion—*n.*—the act of holding together

colloquial—*adj.*—casual; common; conversational; idiomatic

conglomeration—*n.*—mixture; collection

connoisseur—*n.*—expert; authority (usually refers to a wine or food expert)

consecrate—*v.*—to sanctify; to make sacred; to immortalize

craven—*adj.*—cowardly; fearful

dearth—*n.*—scarcity; shortage

debilitate—*v.*—to deprive of strength

deign—*v.*—to condescend; to stoop

delineate—*v.*—to outline; to describe

demur—1. *v.*—to object; 2. *n.*—objection; misgiving

derision—*n.*—ridicule; mockery

derogatory—*adj.*—belittling; uncomplimentary

destitute—*adj.*—poor; poverty-stricken

devoid—*adj.*—lacking; empty

dichotomy—*n.*—branching into two parts

disheartened—*adj.*—discouraged; depressed

diverge—*v.*—to separate; to split

docile—*adj.*—manageable; obedient

duress—*n.*—force; constraint

ebullient—*adj.*—showing excitement

educe—*v.*—to draw forth

effervescence—*n.*—bubbliness; enthusiasm; animation

emulate—*v.*—to follow the example of

ennui—*n.*—boredom; apathy

epitome—*n.*—model; typification; representation

errant—*adj.*—wandering

ethnic—*adj.*—native; racial; cultural

evoke—*v.*—to call forth; to provoke

exotic—*adj.*—unusual; striking

facade—*n.*—front view; false appearance

facsimile—*n.*—copy; reproduction; replica

fathom—*v.*—to comprehend; to uncover

ferret—*v.*—to drive or hunt out of hiding

figment—*n.*—product; creation

finite—*adj.*—measurable; limited; not everlasting

fledgling—*n.*—inexperienced person; beginner

flinch—*v.*—to wince; to draw back; to retreat

fluency—*n.*—smoothness of speech

flux—*n.*—current; continuous change

forbearance—*n.*—patience; self-restraint

foster—*v.*—to encourage; to nurture; to support

frivolity—*n.*—lightness; folly; fun

frugality—*n.*—thrift

garbled—*adj.*—mixed up

generic—*adj.*—common; general; universal

germane—*adj.*—pertinent; related; to the point

gibber—*v.*—to speak foolishly

gloat—*v.*—to brag; to glory over

guile—*n.*—slyness; fraud

haggard—*adj.*—tired looking; fatigued

hiatus—*n.*—interval; break; period of rest

hierarchy—*n.*—body of people, things, or concepts divided into ranks

homage—*n.*—honor; respect

hubris—*n.*—arrogance

ideology—*n.*—set of beliefs; principles

ignoble—*adj.*—shameful; dishonorable

imbue—*v.*—to inspire; to arouse

impale—*v.*—to fix on a stake; to stick; to pierce

implement—*v.*—to begin; to enact

impromptu—*adj.*—without preparation

inarticulate—*adj.*—speechless; unable to speak clearly

incessant—*adj.*—uninterrupted

incognito—*adj.*—unidentified; disguised; concealed

indict—*v.*—to charge with a crime

inept—*adj.*—incompetent; unskilled

innuendo—*n.*—hint; insinuation

intermittent—*adj.*—periodic; occasional

invoke—*v.*—to ask for; to call upon

itinerary—*n.*—travel plan; schedule; course

jovial—*adj.*—cheery; jolly; playful

juncture—*n.*—critical point; meeting

juxtapose—*v.*—to place side by side

knavery—*n.*—rascality; trickery

knead—*v.*—to mix; to massage

labyrinth—*n.*—maze

laggard—*n.*—a lazy person; one who lags behind

larceny—*n.*—theft; stealing

lascivious—*adj.*—indecent; immoral

lecherous—*adj.*—impure in thought and act

lethal—*adj.*—deadly

liaison—*n.*—connection; link

limber—*adj.*—flexible; pliant

livid—*adj.*—1. black-and-blue; discolored; 2. enraged; irate

lucrative—*adj.*—profitable; gainful

lustrous—*adj.*—bright; radiant

malediction—*n.*—curse; evil spell

mandate—*n.*—order; charge

manifest—*adj.*—obvious; clear

mentor—*n.*—teacher

mesmerize—*v.*—to hypnotize

metamorphosis—*n.*—change of form

mimicry—*n.*—imitation

molten—*adj.*—melted

motif—*n.*—theme

mundane—*adj.*—ordinary; commonplace

myriad—*adj.*—innumerable; countless

narcissistic—*adj.*—egotistical; self-centered

nautical—*adj.*—of the sea

neophyte—*n.*—beginner; newcomer

nettle—*v.*—to annoy; to irritate

notorious—*adj.*—infamous; renowned

obdurate—*adj.*—stubborn; inflexible

obligatory—*adj.*—mandatory; necessary

obliterate—*v.*—to destroy completely

obsequious—*adj.*—slavishly attentive; servile

obstinate—*adj.*—stubborn

occult—*adj.*—mystical; mysterious

opaque—*adj.*—dull; cloudy; nontransparent

opulence—*n.*—wealth; fortune

ornate—*adj.*—elaborate; lavish; decorated

oust—*v.*—to drive out; to eject

painstaking—*adj.*—thorough; careful; precise

pallid—*adj.*—sallow; colorless

palpable—*adj.*—tangible; apparent

paradigm—*n.*—model; example

paraphernalia—*n.*—equipment; accessories

parochial—*adj.*—religious; narrow-minded

passive—*adj.*—submissive; unassertive

pedestrian—*adj.*—mediocre; ordinary

pensive—*adj.*—reflective; contemplative

percussion—*n.*—the striking of one object against another

perjury—*n.*—the practice of lying

permeable—*adj.*—porous; allowing to pass through

perpetual—*adj.*—enduring for all time

pertinent—*adj.*—related to the matter at hand

pervade—*v.*—to occupy the whole of

petty—*adj.*—unimportant; of subordinate standing

phlegmatic—*adj.*—without emotion or interest

phobia—*n.*—morbid fear

pittance—*n.*—small allowance

plethora—*n.*—condition of going beyond what is needed; excess; overabundance

potent—*adj.*—having great power or physical strength

privy—*adj.*—private; confidential

progeny—*n.*—children; offspring

provoke—*v.*—to stir action or feeling; to arouse

pungent—*adj.*—sharp; stinging

quaint—*adj.*—old-fashioned; unusual; odd

quandary—*n.*—dilemma

quarantine—*n.*—isolation of a person to prevent spread of disease

quiescent—*adj.*—inactive; at rest

quirk—*n.*—peculiar behavior; startling twist

rabid—*adj.*—furious; with extreme anger

rancid—*adj.*—having a bad odor

rant—*v.*—to speak in a loud, pompous manner; to rave

ratify—*v.*—to make valid; to confirm

rationalize—*v.*—to offer reasons for; to account for

raucous—*adj.*—disagreeable to the sense of hearing; harsh

realm—*n.*—an area; sphere of activity

rebuttal—*n.*—refutation

recession—*n.*—withdrawal; depression

reciprocal—*n.*—mutual; having the same relationship to each other

recluse—*n.*—solitary and shut off from society

refurbish—*v.*—to make new

regal—*adj.*—royal; grand

reiterate—*v.*—to repeat; to state again

relinquish—*v.*—to let go; to abandon

render—*v.*—to deliver; to provide; to give up a possession

replica—*n.*—copy; representation

resilient—*adj.*—flexible; capable of withstanding stress

retroaction—*n.*—an action elicited by a stimulus

reverie—*n.*—the condition of being unaware of one's surroundings; trance

rummage—*v.*—to search thoroughly

rustic—*adj.*—plain and unsophisticated; homely

saga—*n.*—a legend; story

salient—*adj.*—noticeable; prominent

salvage—*v.*—to rescue from loss

sarcasm—*n.*—ironic, bitter humor designed to wound

satire—*n.*—a novel or play that uses humor or irony to expose folly

saunter—*v.*—to walk at a leisurely pace; to stroll

savor—*v.*—to receive pleasure from; to enjoy

seethe—*v.*—to be in a state of emotional turmoil; to become angry

serrated—*adj.*—having a sawtoothed edge

shoddy—*adj.*—of inferior quality; cheap

skulk—*v.*—to move secretly

sojourn—*n.*—temporary stay; visit

solace—*n.*—hope; comfort during a time of grief

soliloquy—*n.*—a talk one has with oneself (especially on stage)

somber—*adj.*—dark and depressing; gloomy

sordid—*adj.*—filthy; base; vile

sporadic—*adj.*—rarely occurring or appearing; intermittent

stamina—*n.*—endurance

steadfast—*adj.*—loyal

stigma—*n.*—a mark of disgrace

stipend—*n.*—payment for work done

stupor—*n.*—a stunned or bewildered condition

suave—*adj.*—effortlessly gracious

subsidiary—*adj.*—subordinate

succinct—*adj.*—consisting of few words; concise

succumb—*v.*—to give in; to yield; to collapse

sunder—*v.*—to break; to split in two

suppress—*v.*—to bring to an end; to hold back

surmise—*v.*—to draw an inference; to guess

susceptible—*adj.*—easily imposed; inclined

tacit—*adj.*—not voiced or expressed

tantalize—*v.*—to tempt; to torment

tarry—*v.*—to go or move slowly; to delay

taut—*adj.*—stretched tightly

tenacious—*adj.*—persistently holding to something

tepid—*adj.*—lacking warmth, interest, enthusiasm; lukewarm

terse—*adj.*—concise; abrupt

thwart—*v.*—to prevent from accomplishing a purpose; to frustrate

timorous—*adj.*—fearful

torpid—*adj.*—lacking alertness and activity; lethargic

toxic—*adj.*—poisonous

transpire—*v.*—to take place; to come about

traumatic—*adj.*—causing a violent injury

trek—*v.*—to make a journey

tribute—*n.*—expression of admiration

trite—*adj.*—commonplace; overused

truculent—*adj.*—aggressive; eager to fight

turbulence—*n.*—condition of being physically agitated; disturbance

turmoil—*n.*—unrest; agitation

tycoon—*n.*—wealthy leader

tyranny—*n.*—absolute power; autocracy

ubiquitous—*adj.*—ever present in all places; universal

ulterior—*adj.*—buried; concealed

uncanny—*adj.*—of a strange nature; weird

uncouth—*adj.*—1. awkward; ungainly; 2. crude; uncultured

unequivocal—*adj.*—clear; definite

unique—*adj.*—without equal; incomparable

unruly—*adj.*—not submitting to discipline; disobedient

unwonted—*adj.*—not ordinary; unusual

urbane—*adj.*—cultured; suave

usurpation—*n.*—act of taking something for oneself; seizure

usury—*n.*—the act of lending money at illegal rates of interest

utopia—*n.*—imaginary land with perfect social and political systems

vacuous—*adj.*—containing nothing; empty

vagabond—*n.*—wanderer; one without a fixed place

vagrant—1. *n.*—homeless person; 2. *adj.*—rambling; wandering; transient valance—*n.*—short drapery hanging over a window frame

valor—*n.*—bravery

vantage—*n.*—position giving an advantage

vaunted—*adj.*—boasted of

velocity—*n.*—speed

vendetta—*n.*—feud

venue—*n.*—location

veracious—*adj.*—conforming to fact; accurate

verbatim—*adj.*—employing the same words as another; literal

versatile—*adj.*—having many uses; multifaceted

vertigo—*n.*—dizziness

vex—*v.*—to trouble the nerves; to annoy

vindicate—*v.*—to free from charge; to clear

vivacious—*adj.*—animated; gay

vogue—*n.*—modern fashion

voluble—*adj.*—fluent

waft—*v.*—to move gently by wind or breeze

waive—*v.*—to give up possession or right

wanton—*adj.*—unruly; excessive

warrant—*v.*—to justify; to authorize

wheedle—*v.*—to try to persuade; to coax

whet—*v.*—to sharpen

wrath—*n.*—violent or unrestrained anger; fury

wry—*adj.*—mocking; cynical

xenophobia—*n.*—fear of foreigners

yoke—*n.*—harness; collar; bond

yore—*n.*—former period of time

zephyr—*n.*—a gentle wind; breeze

II. READING REVIEW

UNDERSTANDING THE MEANINGS OF WORDS AND PHRASES THROUGH CONTEXT CLUES

Many times a reader will come across unfamiliar words but seldom take the time to look up the definitions. The reading passage often will provide the necessary information to let the reader determine the definition. The following techniques can assist the reader in defining unfamiliar words.

CONTEXT DEFINITION

The context of a passage may give the definition of the new word, using other wording to explain it. The definition may come as an appositive, a word or group of words that follow a word and restate its meaning.

> Where can I find a specialist in *graphology,* the study of handwriting to reveal character?

> Harry hoped to *appease* his grandmother by taking her some flowers for missing her birthday. (definition: make happy)

CONTRASTING WORDS

Certain words or phrases indicate that the unknown word is opposite in meaning to other wording in the passage. Some words or phrases that indicate contrast are the following: *however, but, although, nevertheless, despite, not, even though,* and *on the other hand.*

> Although the voters *impugn* the idea of a tax increase, they accept all other legislative changes. (definition: reject or criticize)

WORDS OF COMPARISON

Words or phrases, like *also, moreover, in addition to, likewise, like,* and *as,* are signals that the new word is similar in meaning to the words in the comparison phrase.

> The coach often started arguments or challenged rulings of the referee; moreover, his *bellicose* outbursts embarrassed his team members. (definition: eager to fight)

USE OF EXAMPLES

An example of the unfamiliar word may reveal its meaning.

The list of *errata* included grammatical problems, misspellings, and capitalization errors. (definition: errors and corrections)

CAUSE AND EFFECT

Signal words or phrases for a cause-and-effect relationship between a new word and other wording in the passage include the following: *because, therefore, thus, since,* and *for that reason.*

Because the *megaliths* had been standing for several thousand years, the local people thought little of the giant rocks. (definition: large stones, often used in ancient constructions)

TONE OF THE PASSAGE

The general tone of the passage can indicate something about the unfamiliar word. For instance, whether the word is positive or negative can often be deduced by tone clues.

His speech *ostracized* his audience, who found his sarcastic, mordant, and rude comments disturbing. (definition: to exclude willingly. The reader can not miss the heavy negative tone of the words in the passage.)

Drill 1

> **DIRECTIONS**: Determine a working meaning for the underlined word in each of the following passages.

1. Romeyn de Hooghe, the first <u>limner</u> to limit his work to narrative strips, used his talent to create pictorial criticism of the persecution of the Huguenots under Louis XIV.

2. The somber clouds and the dreary rain caused the child to <u>mope</u> about the house.

3. The <u>veracity</u> of the witness's testimony, revealed through his eye-to-eye contact with the jury and lack of stumbling over words, was not doubted.

4. Why isn't the evening sun described as <u>moribund</u>, not setting; after all, it is coming to the day's end?

5. As president, state warden, and security chief, the leader described in Gilbert and Sullivan's "The Mikado" is a <u>poohbah</u>.

6. Robin Hood's <u>audacious</u> actions included conducting dangerous rescues of Maid Marian and visiting enemy territory disguised as a local.

7. Among common household health products are <u>St. John's Wort</u> and <u>Echinacea</u>, herbs from the garden.

8. My father is a <u>numismatist</u>; he spends several hours each week studying his coins from other countries and time periods.

Drill 1 Answers

1. artist; line drawer

2. unhappily move about

3. truthfulness

4. dying or dead

5. leader who holds several offices

6. daring

7. herbs used for good health

8. coin collector

PURPOSE, AUDIENCE, AND POINT OF VIEW

PURPOSE AND AUDIENCE

With any writing assignment, the author must first select a subject. Next the writer must decide the following:

1. Why am I writing about this subject? What do I want to achieve with what I write; that is, what is my purpose?

2. For whom or to whom am I writing? Who will be reading my words?

   The writer's intended meaning, or purpose, can be any of the following:

to entertain	to classify
to explain	to compare or contrast
to describe	to prove
to inform	to negate

to persuade   to contradict

to define   to restate

Often two or more of these purposes will control the writer's choice of wording and method of organizing thoughts. For instance, the writer may wish to explain his or her fear of high places and, at the same time, entertain his or her readers; the writer may wish, at another time, to explain the fear of high places and to compare this feeling to another's fear of open areas.

After establishing the purpose of writing, the author must then determine the audience—to whom he or she is addressing his or her comments. For example, in writing for his or her grandparents, the writer will probably be writing for a sympathetic reader. However, if the audience is a group of strangers the tone of the writing may be more effective if the writer chooses to explain the reason for this fear.

These two major considerations—purpose and audience—control other aspects of tone, persona, voice, and word choice.

POINT OF VIEW

The point of view refers to the person. With the first person point of view, the viewpoint is that of the speaker or writer. The pronouns *I, me, my, mine, myself, we, us, our, ours,* and *ourselves* will be used, referring to the "speaker"—the persona or voice of the piece of writing. This type of writing is subjective, strongly influenced by the speaker's personal feelings and beliefs. With the second person point of view, the writer uses the pronoun *you*. Some sentences may have the word *you* understood. (An example of this is *Read the passage carefully.*)

Third person point of view is identified by the lack of first person or second person pronouns, unless such pronouns are used in conversation. The pronoun forms identifying the third person are *he, she, him, her, his, hers, himself, herself, they, them, their, theirs,* and *themselves*. The third person point of view is objective and makes no direct reference to the writer.

Drill 2

DIRECTIONS: Read the passages and answer the questions that follow.

Passage 1

I have just spent another four hours in the yard. Creating an English garden à la Arkansas is neither an easy nor fast endeavor. My fourth pickax is now attacking the granite mountainside, more successfully than the previous three. (Slinging my sledge, I often feel like John Henry!) Beneath the scant ground cover—a true trail mix of acorn shells, gravel, natural compost from leaf decay, and small gravel—surprises await each hefty swing. Most common are the small, hairlike roots of nonexistent plants; equally common are the small rocks that sometimes include a tiny piece of crystal. The giant relatives of these two finds create the greatest problem I encounter. Big rocks are often heavier than I can maneuver out of the hole I've started. Real trouble occurs when the boulder begins widening as I dig down around its edges. Wisdom tells me to cover it back up and set a potted plant atop. The equally troublesome roots call for a Paul Bunyan remedy. Chop!

Nevertheless, every day I spend time pursuing my dream of a mountainside covered with perennial loveliness. Signs of possible success, after two years of never failing effort (and ever flailing pickaxes), are showing. Next spring, a blaze of blooms will encourage another season of palm blisters and a sun-burnt neck.

Passage 2

Creating an English garden on a mountainside in the Ouachita Mountains in central Arkansas may sound like an impossible endeavor, but after two years the dream is becoming reality. Digging up the rocks and replacing them with bags of top soil, humus, and peat, the persistent gardener now has sprouts that are not all weeds. Gravel paths meander through the beds of shasta daisies, marigolds, lavender, valerian, iris, day lilies, Mexican heather, and other flowers. Ornamental grasses, dogwood trees, and shrubs back up the flowers. Along the periodic waterway created by an underground spring, swamp hibiscus, helenium, hosta, and umbrella plants display their colorful and seasonal blooms. The flower beds are outlined by large rocks dug up by a pickax.

Blistered hands are worth the effort when people stop by to view the mountainside beauty.

1. The author probably wrote Passage 1 with the following audience in mind:

   (A) a reader of a gardening magazine.

   (B) a young child.

   (C) a close, literate friend or relative.

   (D) a neighbor gardener.

2. The author probably wrote Passage 2 with the following audience in mind:

   (A) a young child.   (C) a close friend.

   (B) an experienced gardener.   (D) a relative.

3. Passage 1 is written in the point of view known as

   (A) first person.   (C) third person.

   (B) second person.   (D) fourth person.

4. Not appearing in Passage 1 is/are the following:

   (A) a humorous tone.   (C) step-by-step directions.

   (B) literary allusions.   (D) word play examples.

5. The writer of Passage 2 is

   (A) unfamiliar with gardening.

   (B) a lazy gardener.

   (C) interested in changing the natural mountainside.

   (D) using only native plants to create a natural setting.

6. The point of view of Passage 2 is

   (A) first person.   (C) third person.

   (B) second person.   (D) first and third person.

7. Not found in both passages is/are

   (A) a reference to the rocky ground of the gardens.

   (B) literary allusions.

(C) the use of a pickax to dig.

(D) a feeling of success in gardening.

Passage 3

My daughter Marie has two cats. The older cat is named Annie. She is white with large black spots. Annie has long hair and sheds constantly in warm weather. Cinnamon is a two-year-old male tabby. He loves to chase squirrels in the backyard, but he probably would be very surprised to catch one. Cinnamon prefers to stay outside all night unless it is extremely cold. In the morning, Cinnamon wants to come into the house and sleep. Annie seldom goes outside. She prefers to sit on the table or a chair where she can look outside through the windows. Marie has cared for both of the cats since they were kittens. She is very fond of both of them.

8. The audience intended for this passage is

   (A) the daughter Marie.

   (B) a relative.

   (C) an unspecified person, probably somewhat young.

   (D) Marie's father.

9. A major purpose of this passage is to

   (A) explain Marie's sense of responsibility.

   (B) contrast the two cats.

   (C) explain how cats are good pets.

   (D) persuade the reader to get a cat as a pet.

10. The point of view used in this passage is

   (A) first person.   (C) third person.

   (B) second person.   (D) first and third person.

Passage 4

House fires result in the deaths of dozens of people every year. Smoke inhalation is the cause of death in most cases. Tragically, most house fires could easily be prevented. Many more house fires occur during cold winter months than during the summer. Unreliable space heaters account for the difference. Woodburning fire-places, especially those that do not have screens to prevent igniting nearby objects, are another cause of house fires. The third most common cause of house fires is untended pans left cooking on the stove. A pan of food can burn dry in a very short period of time. This situation creates so much heat that the cabinets and surrounding objects can burst into flames.

11. The audience for whom this passage is written is

    (A) older people who live alone.

    (B) people who have small children.

    (C) people who have fireplaces.

    (D) All of the above.

12. The author's purpose in writing this passage is to

    (A) describe fires in the kitchen.

    (B) persuade people to be more careful of fireplaces.

    (C) explain the major reasons for house fires.

    (D) prove that smoke inhalation is the major cause of deaths with house fires.

13. According to this passage, which of the following is NOT true?

    (A) Smoke causes many deaths in house fires.

    (B) Space heaters cause some house fires.

    (C) Household fires in the kitchen can be avoided if glassware pots are used on the stove.

    (D) More house fires occur in the winter than in the summer.

Passage 5

Representatives of the world's seven richest and most industrialized nations held a three-day economic summit in London, England, on July 14–16, 1991. On the second day of the summit, Mikhail Gorbachev of Russia appealed for help. The seven leaders offered him support for his economic reforms and his "new thinking" regarding political reforms. Because the allies were split on giving Gorbachev a big financial aid package, the seven leaders decided to provide help in the form of technical assistance in fields such as banking and energy, rather than hard cash.

14. Which one of the following statements best synthesizes the author's purpose in writing?

    (A) To announce that an economic summit was held in London

    (B) To announce that an economic summit of the world's seven richest nations was held in London in July 1991

    (C) To report that Mikhail Gorbachev appealed for financial help and that the seven leaders expressed support for his economic reforms

    (D) To report that the leaders of the world's seven richest and most industrialized nations met July 14–16, 1991, at an economic summit in London and agreed to provide technical support to Gorbachev

15. This passage is written for the following audience:

    (A) financial leaders throughout the world.

    (B) those throughout the world interested in the economic business decisions of the seven richest and most industrialized nations in the world.

    (C) Russian political leaders.

    (D) the citizens of the seven nations represented at the meeting.

16. Of the purposes for writing, which one is most prominent in this passage?

    (A) To entertain   (C) To prove

    (B) To persuade   (D) To inform

Drill 2 Answers

1. (C)	5. (C)	9. (B)	13. (C)
2. (B)	6. (C)	10. (A)	14. (D)
3. (A)	7. (B)	11. (D)	15. (B)
4. (C)	8. (C)	12. (C)	16. (D)

Detailed Explanations of Answers

1. **(C)** Although choice (A) is tempting, the presence of literary allusions such as John Henry and Paul Bunyan make choice (C) the better answer. Choice (B) is inappropriate due to the word choice and content, too advanced for a young child. Choice (D) is possible if the better response is not present; however, logic tells us the neighboring gardener would already be aware of the two years of work.

2. **(B)** The specific references to many plants are subject matter only for an informed reader. Choice (A) is inappropriate because the content and vocabulary are not addressing a young child. Choices (C) and (D) have equal drawing power without more information about the gardening background of the friend or the relative.

3. **(A)** The use of first-person pronouns as well as the sense of humor expressed indicates the correct choice. No fourth person point of view exists.

4. **(C)** Although the writer mentions several details about the gardening process, they are not organized in a step-by-step manner. Thus, choice (C) is best. Choices (A), (B), and (D) add to the writer's creative expression.

5. **(C)** The writer's evident knowledge of gardening and the hard work that created blisters rule out choices (A) and (B). No reference to native plants is made; therefore, choice (D) cannot be correct.

6. **(C)** The third person point of view is the correct answer. The point of view is objective and makes no direct reference to the writer.

7. **(B)** The literary allusions to John Henry and Paul Bunyan occur only in Passage 1. Both passages use (A), (C), and (D).

8. **(C)** The simple sentence structure, word choice, and subject matter indicate a younger person as the intended audience. There is no reason given to explain why it would have been written to Marie. (More personalization should occur between a mother and daughter passage.) Choices (B) and (D) are similar to one another. Without more information, neither could be selected over the other.

9. **(B)** The two cats are contrasted in both physical appearance and behavior. Although choice (A) may be implied, it is not the focus of the passage. Neither choice (C) nor (D) is addressed by the writer.

10. **(A)** The use of first-person pronouns indicates the point of view.

11. **(D)** Choices (A), (B), and (C) could be the audience; therefore, none alone could be the only answer.

12. **(C)** The writer refers to the content of choices (A), (B), and (D); however, no one of these is the major purpose of writing. The type of writing in each of these wrong answers—to describe, to persuade, or to prove—is also incorrect.

13. **(C)** No mention of glassware cooking utensils is given in this passage. (It would be faulty information anyway.) Choices (A), (B), and (D) all include information given in the passage.

14. **(D)** Only this response gives a thorough overview of the passage. Choices (A) and (B) are very vague, missing the main point and result of the summit meeting. Choice (C) does not clarify the decision made about the type of support that will be given to Gorbachev.

15. **(B)** Choices (A), (C), and (D) are all equally good answers. The information in choice (B) includes all three of the other answers as well as other interested persons.

16. **(D)** Information about the meeting is given with no attempt to entertain, persuade, or express feelings.

EVALUATING AN ARGUMENT IN WRITTEN MATERIAL

In making or evaluating an argument, be aware of the three types of supporting evidence: facts, examples, and opinions. A *fact* is verifiable. However, be aware that the same fact can be interpreted differently. For example, it could be a fact that unemployment decreased by two percent in the last year. One person might interpret this fact as a sign of a strong economy; another person might read the statistic as reflecting how the growing number of low-paying service jobs outweighs the shrinking number of high-paying professional jobs. Facts are also constantly changing with new research; this makes it crucial to use the most recent authoritative texts available to support your argument. In the same vein, you should be suspicious of any current argument that uses only outdated sources for support.

An *example* is a specific instance of the generalized argument. If the argument is that children are better prepared for school when they attend prekindergarten, a good example would be to compare two children from the same kindergarten class: one who had attended pre-kindergarten and one who hadn't. If the child who had gone to pre-kindergarten does better in school than the one who hadn't, the example supports the generalized argument.

An *opinion* is an interpretation of a fact. Pay particular attention to how well an opinion is supported in the written material. In your own writing, be sure to support your opinion with the opinions of experts who agree with you. For example, if it is your opinion that a recent rise in traffic accidents in the United States is due to the increasing use of cell phones in the car, it would help your argument if you could find experts who interpret the increase in accidents the same way you do.

Arguments are usually based on appeals to authority, logic, or emotion. To be effective, appeals to authority should use recognized authorities in the field in which the argument is being made. Again, be suspicious of quotations from unknown or outdated sources. Appeals to emotion attempt to convince the reader to place the same importance on the topic that the writer does, and usually try to motivate the reader to do something about the situation.

Arguments based on logic usually follow certain lines of argument, such as generalization, causation, sign, and parallel case. Arguments of generalization depend upon a wide enough sample experience from which a generalization could be drawn. In other words, if every time you buy milk at a certain store it turns out to be sour, you can argue that the store tends to sell sour milk. Arguments of causation have been reviewed in their own section in this book. Arguments of sign depend upon a correlation between two factors, so that if one occurs, the argument can be made that the other is present as well. A well-known example of this type of argument is the saying, "Where there's smoke, there's fire." Parallel case arguments are made about two similar cases: because it worked a certain way for the first case, the second case should work the same way. For this argument to work, the two cases must be closely related.

SCANNING FOR BASIC FEATURES

If the literature is a textbook, read the *introduction*, scan the *chapter titles*, and quickly review any *subheadings, charts, pictures, appendices,* and *indexes* that the book includes. If it is an article, read the first and last paragraphs. These are the most likely places to find the writer's *main point* or *thesis*.

Note that there is a significant difference between a thesis and a main point. Here is an example of a *main point*:

> The Rocky Mountains have three important geological features: abundant water, gold- and silver-bearing ore, and oil-bearing shale.

Notice that this statement is not a matter of the writer's opinion. It is a fact. Now, notice the following *thesis*:

> The Rocky Mountains are the most important source of geological wealth in the United States.

What is the difference? The second statement offers an arguable conclusion or informed opinion. It may be an informed opinion on the part of the writer, but it is still an opinion. A thesis, then, is a statement offered by a writer as true or correct, although it is actually a matter of opinion.

In the first statement, whether the author has an opinion about it or not, these features are an important part of the makeup of the Rocky Mountains. In the second statement, the author may have contrary evidence to offer about Alaska or the Everglades. The second statement bears proving; the first is self-evident. The writer would go on to show the existence of these features, not—as in the second case—the quality or value of those features. The writer of a main point paper is reporting to or informing his or her audience; the writer of a thesis is attempting to sway the audience to his or her point of view.

KEY SECTIONS TO RECOGNIZE

In reading a particular passage, you want to identify what portions or sections of a whole essay you confront. Depending upon which section of an essay is offered, you may decide whether you are reading the writer's main point, thesis, purpose, or evidence.

Introduction: The introductory paragraph usually shows the writer's point of view, or thesis, and introduces that position with some lead-in or general data to support it. The thesis of an essay is the writer's stated or implied position on a particular issue or idea. Identify the writer's purpose and point of view.

Development: This part consists of three or more middle paragraphs that prove the writer's position from different angles, using evidence from real-life experience and knowledge. Evidence may take the form of facts, examples, statistics, illustrations, opinions, or analogies.

In addition, each paragraph within the development section will have a stated or implied main point used to support the thesis of the whole passage. For example, a thesis might be "Dogs are better than cats." Having said that, a whole paragraph might be written with supporting examples to show a main point in support of that idea. The main point of the paragraph that needs support, then, might be as follows:

First of all, dogs are more loyal than cats.

The evidence that is summoned to support that point which, in turn, supports the overall thesis would therefore have to be facts, statistics, expert testimony, or anecdotal knowledge that shows that dogs are indeed more loyal than cats. For example: "The A.S.P.C.A. reports that 99 out of 100 dogs cannot adjust to new owners after the death of their original masters, while only 2 out of 100 cats cannot adjust in the same situation."

Conclusion: The last paragraph usually (but not always) sums up the writer's position and may add some final reminder of what the issue is, some speculation, or some call to action that the writer suggests.

EVIDENCE

While reading, make a distinction between key ideas and the evidence for those ideas. *Evidence* is anything used to prove that an idea is true, real, correct, or probable.

TYPES OF EVIDENCE

Only a few forms of evidence are available to the writer. The kinds of evidence that a writer can summon to support his or her position or point are as follows: (1) facts and statistics, (2) the testimony of an authority, (3) personal anecdote, (4) hypothetical illustrations, and (5) analogy. Strictly speaking, the last two in this list are not true evidence but only offer common sense probability to the support of an argument. In fact, there is a hierarchy for evidence similar to that of purpose. The most powerful evidence is fact, supported by statistics; the least powerful is analogy. The following table suggests the relationship:

Hierarchy of Validity of Evidence

Most Valid	Documented Facts and Statistics
	Expert Testimony
	Personal Experience and Anecdote
	Hypothetical Illustrations
Least Valid	Analogies

Documented facts and statistics are the most powerful evidence a writer can bring to bear on proving an idea or supporting a main thesis. Documented facts and statistics must be used fairly and come from reliable sources. For example, *Funk and Wagnall's Encyclopedia* is a reliable source but Joe the plumber's *Guide to Waterfowl in Hoboken* is not. This is true because, first of all, Joe is a plumber, not an ornithologist (a bird scientist), and second, no one has ever heard of Joe the plumber as an expert. Reliable sources for facts and statistics are the best information that can be offered.

Expert testimony is the reported positions, theses, or studies of people who are recognized experts in the field under discussion in the literature. A writer may use books, articles, essays, interviews, and so on by trained scientists and other professionals to support a thesis or position. Most often, this testimony takes the form of quotations from the expert or a paraphrasing of his or her important ideas or findings.

Personal anecdote is the evidence of a writer's own personal experience, or a "little story" about an event, person, or idea that exemplifies the point he or she is trying to make. It holds weight if the reader trusts the writer, and it is valuable; it is not as powerful or as conclusive as documented facts or the testimony of experts (unless the writer is a recognized authority in the field about which he or she has written).

Hypothetical illustrations are examples that suggest probable circumstances in which something would be true. Strictly speaking, a hypothetical illustration is not "hard" evidence, but rather evidence of probability. For example, to demonstrate that "people will do whatever they can get away with," a writer might bring up the hypothetical illustration of someone at a ticket counter who gets back more change than he or she paid for the ticket. The chances are, the writer might point out, that the person would pocket the extra money rather than be honest and return it. In this case, the writer is not naming anybody in particular or citing statistics to make the point, but rather is pointing to *a situation that is likely but is not an actual documented case.* This situation has either the weight of common sense for the reader or none at all.

Analogy is the last and weakest form of evidence. It is not actually evidence at all. An analogy is simply a comparison between items that are different but that also have some striking similarities. Analogies often use the term "like" to show the relationship of ideas. For example, the writer might say, "Life is like a tree: we start out struggling in the dirt, grow into the full bloom of youth, and become deeply rooted in our ways, until, in the autumn of our years, we lose our hair like leaves, and succumb ultimately to the bare winter of death."

While reading, determine what sort of evidence the writer is using and how effective it is in proving his or her point.

REASONS FOR EVIDENCE

To prove any thesis that the writer maintains is true, he or she may employ any one of the following seven strategies:

1. *show* that a process or a procedure does or should work step by step in time;

2. *compare or contrast* two or more things or ideas to show important differences or similarities;

3. *identify* a problem and then explain how to solve it;

4. *analyze* into its components, or *classify* by its types or categories, an idea or thing to show how it is put together, how it works, or how it is designed;

5. *explain* why something happens to produce a particular result or set of results;

6. *describe* the particular individual characteristics of a place, person, time, or idea;

7. *define* what a thing is or what an idea means.

CAUSE AND EFFECT

Most people agree that conditions that exist have causes and that if factors are changed, it will result in some new effects. Cause-and-effect arguments are, however, difficult to prove because the exact relationship between two events is often difficult to establish.

Looking out for the use of such words as 'consequently,' 'therefore,' and 'thus' will help you recognize when a cause and effect argument is being made.

IDEAS IN OPPOSITION

To analyze the relationship between ideas in opposition (pro and con), first identify the claim each side is making. (Of course, in many situations there are more than two sides.) Pay attention to the intricacies of the position; many arguments are not simply for or against something, but instead are qualified positions with exceptions. For example, the claim that Medicare should pay for standard prescriptions is different from the claim that Medicare should pay for prescriptions. The word 'standard' qualifies the argument; perhaps experimental drugs or preventative treatments are excluded from the proposal. In analyzing an argument, be sure to find the edges of the argument, where the arguer would not want to press the argument further.

After analyzing the argument, locate and evaluate the reasons that the author uses to support the claim. Ask yourself, "Why is the author's claim important?" Then examine the reasons the author gives: are they good reasons and are they connected to the claim? Finally, examine the evidence the author uses to support the reasons. The evidence should come from reliable sources and be pertinent to the reasons and claim. In examining two or more opposing arguments you will judge which best supports its claim. However, the best argument may fail to convince its reader, especially on politically volatile topics such as abortion rights.

LOGIC

INDUCTION, DEDUCTION, AND FALLACIES

In formulating critical evaluations of a piece of writing, it is important to understand the problems, if any, with the logic of the piece that has been read. Does it make sense? If not, why doesn't it? It is up to the reader to find the errors in any piece of writing he or she reads. Of course, if the writer is effective, the reader won't find these fallacies. Be on the lookout for them because it is often a good way to refute, criticize, or counterargue if called upon to respond critically to any author's central idea, thesis, or main point. Make sure the evidence proves the writer's point and not something else.

Pay special attention to conclusions. The writer may not have proved the point. An essay is essentially a *syllogism* that proves something by *induction* or *deduction*. The *syllogism* is that *basic form of deductive reasoning* that is the cornerstone of most logic. It consists of a *major premise*, a *minor premise*, and a *conclusion*. Note how they are used in the discussion below. *Induction* is the sort of reasoning that arrives at a general conclusion based on the relationship among the contributing elements of an idea.

For example, a writer may observe under experimental conditions that whenever a spider begins to spin a web, it first rubs its back legs over its silk gland. The author may have observed 100,000 different species of spiders display this behavior. He or she may have also observed that they never rub their hind legs over the gland at any other time, only when they are about to put out silk to start a web. He or she may then *induce* from these observations that spiders must rub their hind legs over their silk glands in order to begin the production of silk to spin a web. Another individual may prove this theory wrong later because new evidence shows up to invalidate the induction. Until that happens, this will be the conclusion drawn from observations of the behavior of spiders.

Deduction, by way of contrast, reasons from the general to the particular. For example, an author may assert that all trees grow upward from the earth, not downward from the sky. Until someone finds a tree that grows from the sky to the earth, an individual will assume that every tree started growing out of the earth and base all other conclusions about the growth and flowering of trees upon this *deduction* as well.

Occasionally, however, the *premises* of a deductive argument are false or unprovable. The *premises* of an argument are those *definitions* or *assumptions* that are givens (concepts that do not stand in need of proof but are either self-evident, common knowledge, or agreed upon as terms between the writer and the reader). For example,

Major Premise: All goats have beards.

Minor Premise: Harry Jones has a beard.

Conclusion: Therefore, Harry is a goat.

The conclusion is incorrect. It could be true if only goats have beards, but this is not the case; male human beings may have beards as well. Therefore, the conclusion is insupportable. In this example, we lack sufficient information to draw a conclusion about who or what Harry is.

TYPICAL LOGICAL FALLACIES

Below is a list of typical logical errors that weak writers commit. The list is not exhaustive. Know how they occur and practice finding them in others' arguments, either in conversation or in essays they may have written.

1. *Either/or:* The writer assumes only two opposing possibilities: "Either we abolish cars, or the environment is doomed." This argument is weak because other factors may contribute to the destruction of the environment as well.

2. *Oversimplification:* Here the author might first state, "Only motivated athletes become champions." Perhaps not; though unfortunate, unmotivated athletes who use enhancing steroids occasionally become champions, too.

3. *Begging the question:* The writer assumes he or she has proved something that has not been proven. "He is unintelligent because he is stupid." A lack of intelligence is almost synonymous with being stupid. It cannot be proven that he is stupid by saying he is unintelligent; that "he" is either or both of these is exactly what needs to be proved.

4. *Ignoring the issue:* An argument against the truth of a person's testimony in court shifts from what the witness observed to how the witness's testimony is inadmissible. "The witness is obviously unkempt and homeless." One has nothing to do with the other.

5. *Arguing against a person, not an idea:* The writer argues that somebody's idea has no merit because he or she is immoral or unintelligent: "John can't prove anything about dogs being faithful; he can't even understand basic mathematics."

6. *"It does not follow…"* or *non sequitur:* The writer leaps to a wrong conclusion: "John is tall; he must know a lot about mountains."

7. *Drawing the wrong conclusion from a sequence:* "He trained, read, then trained some more and, therefore, won the match." It is quite possible that other factors led to his winning the match.

Drill 3

DIRECTIONS: Read the passages and answer the questions that follow.

Passage 1

The Mitsushita Electric Industrial Company of Japan has developed a computer program that can use photographs of faces to predict the aging process and, also, how an unborn child may look. The system can show how a couple may look after 40 years of marriage and how newlyweds' future children may look. The computer analyzes facial characteristics from a photograph, based on shading and coloring differences, and then creates a three-dimensional model in its memory. The system consists of a personal computer with a program and circuit board. It will be marketed soon by the Mitsushita Company.

1. This passage is written in the point of view called

   (A) first person.

   (B) second person.

(C) third person.

(D) a combination of first and third person.

2. The intended purpose of this passage is to

(A) persuade a couple to send in their photographs to use to predict their children's appearance.

(B) explain how the aging process of adults and the appearance of their children can be predicted by a computer.

(C) express an opinion about the technology of the future in Japan.

(D) describe one way a computer uses photographs.

Passage 2

As a farmer from Conrad, Montana, I might be the last person expected to invent and patent a motorcycle helmet. (No, I don't wear a helmet while I am driving my tractor.) The law in the United States requires that all cars sold must carry a third, high-mounted brake light on the rear of the vehicle. If cars need this light, I thought, how much safer life would be for motorcyclists if they, too, had such a light. The problem, however, was to install it "high-mounted." I have designed a helmet with a brake light in the rear. Thus, motorcyclists wearing a helmet like mine are much safer on the road.

3. The intended purpose of the passage is to

(A) tell about a farmer in Montana.

(B) explain a safety requirement for cars in the United States.

(C) describe a man's motorcycle helmet invention that makes riding motorcycles safer.

(D) show the versatility of some people.

4. The point of view of this passage is

(A) first person.

(C) third person.

(B) second person.

(D) first and third person.

Drill 3 Answers

1. (C)   2. (B)   3. (C)   4. (A)

Detailed Explanations of Answers

1. **(C)** Choice (C) is the correct answer because the passage employs the point of view of an outsider through the use of pronouns such as *he, she,* and *it.*

2. **(B)** The intended purpose is to explain. Although couples might be interested in sending in their photographs to see what their children may look like, choice (A), the passage is not encouraging this reaction from those who read it. Choice (C) is much too broad a response; also, the passage is not expressing an opinion. Choice (D) is too vague, although what it says is incomplete truth.

3. **(C)** The focus of the passage is the motorcycle helmet, and the intended purpose is to explain why and how the helmet was invented. Choice (A) is a fact about the inventor—he is a farmer. Choice (B) is a true statement as well, but it is what prompted the writer's idea for a helmet. (D) is a general statement that is unrelated to this passage.

4. **(A)** The personality of the speaker is revealed along with his ideas and actions. Notice also the use of the pronoun *I.* Choice (D) will attract some test-takers, but the first person point of view often uses third person pronouns along with first person pronouns.

STRATEGIES FOR CRITICAL READING OF PASSAGES

Critical reading is a demanding process. Linguists and language philosophers speak passionately of the importance of true literacy in human affairs. It is not enough to merely comprehend; true literacy lies in the ability to make critical judgments, to analyze, and to evaluate. It is with this end in mind—true literacy—that any reader should approach a text.

WHAT CRITICAL READERS DO

If you can summarize the main points of an essay, that's a start. If you can recall the plot twists in a short story or articulate the line of reasoning in an argument, that's a start. But if you are able to offer an informed opinion about the purpose and merits of a text, then you are on the road to true literacy.

The Communication and Literacy Skills Test seeks to identify critical readers who not only can describe *what* happened in a text they've read, but *why* it happened and *how* it happened. As a critical reader, you will be an active participant, not a passive recipient. It may help to envision yourself in a dialogue with the author and other critical readers. As rhetorician and critic Mikhail Bahktin argues, language operates in a dialogic mode, where receivers are just as essential as senders to the effective transmission of messages.

There are six strategies a critical reader can employ to participate fully in the "re-creative act" that is reading.

1. Get the facts straight.

2. Analyze the argument.

3. Identify basic features of style.

4. Explore your personal response.

5. Evaluate the text overall and determine its significance.

6. Compare and contrast related texts.

1. Get the Facts Straight

Listen and read actively, pencil in hand, underlining important phrases or noting key points in the margin. Briefly record your reactions, questions, and conclusions. Though you may not have time to annotate thoroughly during a test, if you rigorously practice annotating beforehand, you'll begin to do it less laboriously and with less written back-up.

Your first task as a critical reader is to learn everything you can about the text. You can begin by scrutinizing the implications of the title, trying to identify the author and general time period in which the text was written, and identifying the thesis. In short, a good reader looks for the main ideas, but also looks for other information (author, era, form) that may help him or her determine the slant of those ideas.

Once you have identified the essence of a passage, try to jot it down in your own words in a single sentence. This will help you focus on the meaning and purpose—useful information when the detailed multiple-choice questions present you with "blind alleys" or slightly off-base interpretation of text.

There are really four activities you perform in order to "get the facts straight":

    a. **Previewing**—looking over a text to learn all you can *before* you start reading (This is, of course, much more difficult with excerpts.)

b. **Annotating**—marking up the text to record reactions, questions, and conclusions (Hint: It's especially useful to underline what you think the thesis is.)

c. **Outlining**—identifying the sequence of main ideas, often by *numbering* key phrases

d. **Summarizing**—stating the purpose and main idea of the passage

Once you have the facts straight, you are ready to tackle the analytic and evaluative aspects of critical reading. Before addressing those, let's test your ability to get the facts.

Following is an essay titled "Education of Women" by William Hazlitt, an essayist and scholar who wrote during the early nineteenth century. Try your hand at previewing, annotating, outlining, and summarizing it. Then look at the following pages, where a proficient critical reader has done those operations for you. Compare your responses and see where you can improve. Remember, you don't have to take copious notes to get to the essence of a text.

"Education of Women"

We do not think a classical education proper for women. It may pervert their minds, but it cannot elevate them. It has been asked, Why a woman should not learn the dead languages as well as the modern ones? For this plain reason, that the one are still spoken, and may have immediate associations connected with them, and the other not. A woman may have a lover who is a Frenchman, or an Italian, or a Spaniard; and it is well to be provided against every contingency in that way. But what possible interest can she feel in those old-fashioned persons, the Greeks and Romans, or in what was done two thousand years ago? A modern widow would doubtless prefer Signor Tramezzani to Aeneas, and Mr. Conway would be a formidable rival to Paris.[1] No young lady in our days, in conceiving an idea of Apollo, can go a step beyond the image of her favorite poet: nor do we wonder that our old friend, the Prince Regent,[2] passes for a perfect Adonis in the circles of beauty and fashion. Women in general have no ideas, except personal ones. They are mere egoists. They have no passion for truth, nor any love of what is purely ideal. They hate to think, and they hate every one who seems to think of anything but themselves. Everything is to them a perfect nonentity which does not touch their senses, their vanity, or their interest. Their poetry, their criticism, their politics, their morality, and their divinity, are downright affectation. That line in Milton is very striking—

"He for God only, she for God in him."

Such is the order of nature and providence; and we should be sorry to see any fantastic improvements on it. Women are what they were meant to be; and we wish for no alteration in their bodies or their minds. They are the creatures of the circumstances in which they are placed, of sense, of sympathy and habit. They are exquisitely susceptible of the passive impressions of things: but to form an idea of pure understanding or imagination, to feel an interest in the true and the good beyond themselves, requires an effort of which they are incapable. They want principle, except that which consists in an adherence to established custom; and this is the reason of the severe laws which have been set up as a barrier against every infringement of decorum and propriety in women. It has been observed by an ingenious writer of the present day, that women want imagination. This requires explanation. They have less of that imagination which depends on intensity of passion, on the accumulation of ideas and feelings round one object, on bringing all nature and all art to bear on a particular purpose, on continuity and comprehension of mind; but for the same reason, they have more fancy, that is greater flexibility of mind, and can more readily vary and separate their ideas at pleasure. The reason of the greater presence of mind which has been remarked in women is, that they are less in the habit of speculating on what is best to be done, and the first suggestion is decisive. The writer of this article confesses that he never met with any woman who could reason, and with but one reasonable woman. There is no instance of a woman having been a great mathematician or metaphysician or poet or painter: but they can dance and sing and act and write novels and fall in love, which last quality alone makes more than angels of them. Women are no judges of the characters of men, except as men. They have no real respect for men, or they never respect them for those qualities, for which they are respected by men. They in fact regard all such qualities as interfering with their own pretensions, and creating a jurisdiction different from their own. Women naturally wish to have their favourites all to themselves, and flatter their weaknesses to make them more dependent on their own good opinion, which, they think, is all they want. We have, indeed, seen instances of men, equally respectable and amiable, equally admired by the women and esteemed by the men, but who have been ruined by an excess of virtues and accomplishments.

—William Hazlitt (1815)

1. Hazlitt was a theatre critic and had accused a popular Italian tenor, Tramezzani, of overacting in his love scenes. He also criticized actor William Conway in the role of Romeo.

2. The Prince Regent was George, Prince of Wales.

A. Previewing "Education of Women"

A quick look over the text of "Education of Women" reveals a few items worth mentioning. This short essay is probably most closely related to an Op-Ed (Opinion-Editorial) piece written in a newspaper. Published in the *Examiner* in 1815, the essay begins with a proclamation, "We do not think a classical education proper for women." The term "we" suggests the assurance of numbers and power. It's safe to assume Hazlitt believes he speaks for a significant group (perhaps educated men?). The year 1815 is relevant to our reading because it suggests a time when women did not enjoy the rights and privileges that are commonplace in the twenty-first century, at least in most of the major industrialized cultures. If the year were not stated, you could infer from the debate over educating women that the piece was written before the present time.

B. Annotating "Education of Women"

An annotation records reactions, questions, and conclusions. Underlining key phrases may help you find the theme. Here is Hazlitt's essay with underlining and annotations alongside to facilitate easy reference.

"Education of Women"

We do not think a classical education proper for women. It may pervert their minds, but it cannot elevate them. It has been asked, Why a woman should not learn the dead languages as well as the modern ones? For this plain reason, that the one are still spoken, and may have immediate associations connected with them, and the other not. A woman may have a lover who is a Frenchman, or an Italian, or a Spaniard; and it is well to be provided against every contingency in that way. But what possible interest can she feel in those old-fashioned persons, the Greeks and Romans, or in what was done two thousand years ago? A modern widow would doubtless prefer Signor Tramezzani to Aeneas, and Mr. Conway would be a formidable rival to Paris.[1] No young lady in our days, in conceiving an idea of Apollo, can go a step beyond the image of her favorite poet: nor do we wonder that our old friend, the Prince Regent[2], passes for a perfect Adonis in the circles of beauty and fashion. Women in general have no ideas, except personal ones. They are mere egoists. They have no passion for truth, nor any love of what is purely ideal. They hate to think, and they hate every one who seems to think of anything but themselves. Everything is to them a perfect nonentity which does not touch their senses, their vanity, or their interest. Their poetry, their criticism, their politics, their morality, and their divinity, are downright

1. The Thesis! But what was a "classical" education in 1815? Probably Latin and Greek, philosophy, and the "classics" of literature.

2. Perversion, not elevation, is the result of education of women; learning "taints" women.

3. Women learn modern languages only to be able to speak to their lovers; women have a shallow purpose for education.

4. Allusion to "poor" actors of the day (see footnote) who are preferable to historical figures (Aeneas, Paris); women have little interest in history or politics, only romantic self-gratification.

5. Women don't think; they are selfish and frivolous.

affectation. That line in Milton is very striking—

"He for God only, she for God in him."

Such is the order of nature and providence; and we should be sorry to see any fantastic improvements on it. Women are what they were meant to be; and we wish for no alteration in their bodies or their minds. They are the creatures of the circumstances in which they are placed, of sense, of sympathy and habit. They are exquisitely susceptible of the passive impressions of things: but to form an idea of pure understanding or imagination, to feel an interest in the true and the good beyond themselves, requires an effort of which they are incapable. They want principle, except that which consists in an adherence to established custom; and this is the reason of the severe laws which have been set up as a barrier against every infringement of decorum and propriety in women. It has been observed by an ingenious writer of the present day, that women want imagination. This requires explanation. They have less of that imagination which depends on intensity of passion, on the accumulation of ideas and feelings round one object, on bringing all nature and all art to bear on a particular purpose, on continuity and comprehension of mind; but for the same reason, they have more fancy, that is greater flexibility of mind, and can more readily vary and separate their ideas at pleasure. The reason of that

6. Women's destiny; they are creatures of circumstance, habit. Women can't change.

7. They have impressions, not ideas. So women only feel, can't think? They aren't interested in any truths beyond what is true for them.

8. They "want" principle... They "want" imagination... "Want" means lack, not desire.

greater presence of mind which has been remarked in women is, that they are <u>less in the habit of speculating on what is best to be done, and the first suggestion is decisive. The writer of this article confesses that he never met with any woman who could reason, and with but one reasonable woman. There is no instance of a woman having been a great mathematician or metaphysician or poet or painter: but they can dance and sing and act and write novels and fall in love,</u> which last quality alone makes more than angels of them. <u>Women are no judges of the characters of men, except as men. They have no real respect for men, or they never respect them for those qualities, for which they are respected by men.</u> They in fact regard all such qualities as interfering with their <u>own pretensions,</u> and creating a jurisdiction different from their own. Women naturally wish to have their favourites all to themselves, and flatter their weaknesses to make them more dependent on their own good opinion, which, they think, is all they want. We have, indeed, seen instances of <u>men,</u> equally respectable and amiable, equally admired by the women and esteemed by the men, but <u>who have been ruined by an excess of virtues and accomplishments.</u>

9. They don't synthesize ideas but rather "separate" them. Does this mean they can't compare issues and see things only in isolation?

10. Women go with the first idea and don't reason through alternatives. Where is his evidence?

11. Oh, here's the proof: he's met only one reasonable woman.

12. Women have accomplished little. Falling in love is their greatest skill. The double-standard is in action; women are restricted to "noncognitive" activity. The most they can aspire to is performing arts and romance.

13. Women ruin men.

As these annotations illustrate, a reader approaching Hazlitt's text would have several questions and perhaps express surprise at Hazlitt's opinionated judgments. Your notes should, as the sample annotations do, reflect your reactions as the text progresses. Make sure you include any conclusions you have drawn as well as the questions that occur to you. The lines you underline or highlight and the places where the text makes statement of "fact" will help you identify the main ideas later.

C. Outlining "Education of Women"

Go back to the statements you have underlined. Paraphrase and list them in numerical order, with supporting statements subsumed under key statements. Hazlitt's essay could be said to have the following key points, extrapolated from the underlining and written in outline form.

1. Classical education is not proper for women.

   a. Modern language study better suits their romances.

   b. Women have no interest in history.

2. Education is wasted on them.

   a. Women have no ideas.

   b. Women have no passion for truth.

   c. Women hate to think.

3. Women are what they are meant to be: frivolous and superficial.

   a. They are creatures of circumstance, sympathy, and habit.

   b. They can't form ideas of understanding or imagination.

   c. They lack principle.

   d. They have fancy and flexibility of mind.

   e. They can't synthesize ideas but see ideas separately.

   f. They take the first suggestion rather than speculate on what's best.

   g. Women can't reason.

4. There are no examples of great women thinkers.

5. Women are frivolous creatures.

   a. Women are able only to dance, sing, act, write novels, and fall in love.

    b.   Women cannot judge character.

    c.   Women don't respect men for qualities considered good in women themselves. (They're hypocrites.)

D. Summarizing "Education of Women"

Read in this outline form, Hazlitt's essay is clearly an opinionated discussion of why women are not suited to education. Women are "born to" certain frivolous qualities of mind and behavior and lack the mental capacity to reason, particularly in any principled fashion. The outline of key points and supporting statements leads the reader rather pointedly to this conclusion. Though at first Hazlitt's essay seems a disjointed litany of complaints, a sequence of reasons becomes more apparent after annotating and outlining the essay. It also becomes clearer how much Hazlitt relies on "accepted" opinion and his own experience rather than demonstrable proof.

We have just undertaken previewing, annotating, outlining, and summarizing the elements of "Get the Facts Straight." Very often at the conclusion of this stage of critical reading, the reader begins to get a handle on the text. The remaining five strategies after "Get the Facts Straight" seem to flow readily and speedily. Let's apply these remaining five strategies to Hazlitt's "Education of Women."

2. Analyze the Argument

An analysis examines a whole as the sum of its parts. Another brief look at the outline of "Education of Women" reveals the parts of Hazlitt's argument. In short, women should not be educated because they lack the qualities education enhances. They lack the capacity to entertain ideas because they have no passion for truth and hate to think. Women are naturally predisposed to acting precipitously rather than thoughtfully, with the use of reasoning. Evidence for these statements may be found in the lack of female contributions to human knowledge. Women can "perform," write novels (a less-than-respectable literary endeavor in 1815), and fall in love, but can do little else. In short, things that require judgment are not suitable activities for women.

Hazlitt's essay has a rather simple argumentative structure. He asserts that women are not educable and then provides "reasons" why. Hazlitt's "reasons" are primarily opinions, offered without any backing except the assertion that women have achieved little. The essay concludes with a final comment on the ability of women to ruin men, chiefly through flattery.

Analysis reveals that Hazlitt's essay has little to offer in support of the opinion it presents. Further, its statements seem more an emotional outpouring than a reasonable explanation. (The careful reader will also make note of how difficult it is to view Hazlitt's remarks in an unprejudiced fashion—the twenty-first century reader will, in all probability, find his assertions a bit ridiculous.)

3. Identify Basic Features of Style

Stylistically, Hazlitt's essay may be described as a series of blunt statements followed by reflection on how the statement is manifested in his culture. Hazlitt draws on anecdotal support—his observations of the women of his day, a line from Milton, and his own knowledge of the absence of women's accomplishments. Hazlitt's essay seems a collection of accepted or common knowledge: he writes as though his "reasons" are generally agreed upon, undisputed statements of fact. This structure suggests that because something is widely believed, readers should accept it. In all probability, readers in 1815 did. Thus, the tone is both authoritative and perhaps a bit annoyed—annoyed with the problems women present.

Hazlitt's diction is largely straightforward, more plain than flowery. A few of the words and phrases he chooses have powerful or dramatic connotations, such as "pervert," "mere egoists," "perfect nonentity," "downright affectation," "hate to think," and "no passion for truth." But he relies largely on ordinary language and sentence structure. Only occasionally does he indulge in a syntactic permutation. For example, in the sentence "The writer of this article confesses that he never met with any woman who could reason, and with but one reasonable woman," Hazlitt shifts the modal verb "could reason" to the adjective "reasonable" with memorable effect. By and large, however, his sentences are simple declaratives, not difficult to read or interpret and not especially memorable stylistically.

4. Explore Your Personal Response

While nineteenth-century readers would probably have nodded in agreement as Hazlitt offered reasons why women shouldn't be educated, contemporary readers are probably surprised, dismayed, and perhaps even angry. Review your responses in the annotations to the text. They will help recreate your personal reactions and the causes for those reactions. Do not always expect to agree with, or even appreciate, a writer's point of view. You will find yourself disagreeing with texts rather regularly. The important thing is to be certain you can account for the sources and causes of your disagreement. Much of reader disagreement with Hazlitt's essay rests in what we would consider a more enlightened, modern perspective on the abilities of women. An awareness of historical context does help explain "Education of Women," but probably doesn't increase twenty-first century sympathy for Hazlitt's position.

5. Evaluate the Text Overall and Determine Its Significance

Hazlitt's essay "Education of Women" was a product of early nineteenth-century sensibilities. Its chief significance today is as a representative of its time, an indicator of a social and intellectual climate much different from our own. As a citizen of the Romantic period preceding the Victorian age, Hazlitt expresses an understanding of women that today we would deem, at the very least, incomplete.

6. Compare and Contrast Related Texts

A complete analysis of Hazlitt's essay would include a comparison of other essays of his, if available, on the subject of women and education. It would also be useful to examine other early nineteenth-century essays on this subject and, lastly, to contrast Hazlitt's essay with contemporary essays that argue for and against the education of women. Through such comparison, a more complete understanding of Hazlitt's essay is possible. On the Communication and Literacy Skills Test, you might be asked to contrast opposing (or similar) views on a single subject, but only within very narrow parameters. For instance, you might be questioned about two distinct styles used to approach the same subject and the resulting effects.

Although you may experience certain points of departure from the previous discussion, most skilled readers will agree, in general, with its broad conclusions. This is because the text has been kept in mind and referred to throughout the discussion. If you read attentively, that is, if you attend to the text carefully, you are much more likely to reflect judiciously upon it. Thus, the components of our good reading definition—to read attentively, reflectively, and judiciously—are all present in the six broad strategies described and employed.

The very *active* reading strategies employed on Hazlitt's essay "Education of Women" can be used with any text to help you "re-create" it with optimal effectiveness. That is to say, you as a reader should be able to very closely approximate the original authorial intentions, as well as understand the general audience response and your more particular individual response. Remember to work with the six strategies in sequence.

Drill 4

DIRECTIONS: Read the passages and answer the questions that follow.

Passage 1

1   We laymen have always been intensely curious to know—like the cardinal who put a similar question to Ariosto—from what sources that strange being, the creative writer, draws his material, and how he manages to make such an impression on us with
5   it and to arouse in us emotions of which, perhaps, we had not even thought ourselves capable. Our interest is only heightened the more by the fact that, if we ask him, the writer himself gives us no explanation, or none that is satisfactory, and it is not at all weakened by our knowledge that not even the clearest insight into the
10   determinants of his choice of material and into the nature of the art of creating imaginative form will ever help to make creative writers of us.

    If we could at least discover in ourselves or in people like ourselves an activity which was in some way akin to creative writ-
15   ing! An examination of it would then give us a hope of obtaining the beginnings of an explanation of the creative work of writers. And, indeed, there is some prospect of this being possible. After all, creative writers themselves like to lessen the distance between their kind and the common run of humanity; they so often assure
20   us that every man is a poet at heart and that the last poet will not perish till the last man does.

    Should we not look for the first traces of imaginative activity as early as in childhood? The child's best-loved and most intense occupation is with his play or games. Might we not say that every
25   child at play behaves like a creative writer, in that he creates a world of his own, or, rather, rearranges the things of his world in a new way which pleases him? It would be wrong to think he does not take that world seriously; on the contrary, he takes play very seriously and he expends large amounts of emotion on it. The op-
30   posite of play is not what is serious but what is real. In spite of all the emotion with which he cathects his world of play, the child distinguishes it quite well from reality; and he likes to link his imagined objects and situations to the tangible and visible things of the real world. This linking is all that differentiates the child's "play" from
35   "fantasying."

1. What is the effect of the speaker's use of "we"?

    (A) It separates the speaker and his or her colleagues from the reader.

    (B) It involves the reader in the search for, yet distinguishes him or her from, the creative writer.

    (C) It creates a royal and authoritative persona for the speaker.

    (D) It makes the speaker the stand-in for all men.

2. What is the antecedent of "it" (line 8)?

    (A) "explanation"   (C) "interest"

    (B) "fact"   (D) "impression"

3. Which one of the following statements would the speaker be most likely to DISAGREE with?

    (A) A lay person cannot become a creative writer by studying the writer's methods.

    (B) All men are writers at heart.

    (C) Creative writers are fundamentally different from nonwriters.

    (D) Children understand the distinction between imagination and reality.

4. "Cathects" (line 31) can best be defined as

    (A) constructs.   (C) fantasizes.

    (B) distances.   (D) discourages.

5. The structure of the passage can best be described as

    (A) an initial paragraph that introduces an idea and two paragraphs that digress from that idea.

    (B) a series of paragraphs that answer the questions with which they begin.

    (C) a series of questions ascending in their inability to be answered.

    (D) paragraphs whose brevity parallels their narrowness of inquiry.

6. It can be inferred that the speaker believes that creative writing is

    (A) an opposite of childhood play.

    (B) unrelated to childhood play.

(C) a continuation of childhood play.

(D) similar to the fantasizing of childhood play.

Passage 2

1   Under the strange nebulous envelopment, wherein our Professor has now shrouded himself, no doubt but his spiritual nature is nevertheless progressive, and growing: for how can the "Son of Time," in any case, stand still? We behold him, through those
5   dim years, in a state of crisis, of transition: his mad Pilgrimings, and general solution into aimless Discontinuity, what is all this but a mad Fermentation; wherefrom, the fiercer it is, the clearer product will one day evolve itself.

      Such transitions are ever full of pain: thus the Eagle when he
10   moults is sickly; and, to attain his new beak, must harshly dash-off the old one upon rocks. What Stoicism soever our Wanderer, in his individual acts and motions, may affect, it is clear that there is a hot fever of anarchy and misery raging within; coruscations of which flash out: as, indeed, how could there be other? Have we
15   not seen him disappointed, bemocked of Destiny, through long years? All that the young heart might desire and pray for has been denied; nay, as in the last worst instance, offered and then snatched away. Ever an "excellent Passivity"; but of useful, reasonable Activity, essential to the former as Food to Hunger, noth-
20   ing granted: till at length, in this wild Pilgrimage, he must forcibly seize for himself an Activity, though useless, unreasonable. Alas, his cup of bitterness, which had been filling drop by drop, ever since that first "ruddy morning" in the Hinterschlag Gymnasium, was at the very lip; and then with that poison drop, of the
25   Towngood-and-Blumine business, it runs over, and even hisses over in a deluge of foam.

      He himself says once, with more justice than originality: "Man is, properly speaking, based upon Hope, he has no other possession but Hope; this world of his is emphatically the Place of Hope."
30   What, then, was our Professor's possession? We see him, for the present, quite shutout from Hope; looking not into the golden orient, but vaguely all round into a dim copper firmament, pregnant with earthquake and tornado.

7. All of the following name the main character of the passage EXCEPT

(A) our Wanderer.   (C) he/him.

(B) the Eagle.   (D) our Professor.

8. Which phrase best summarizes the speaker's intent in examining this stage of the main character's life?

   (A) "Such transitions are ever full of pain" (line 9)

   (B) "Have we not seen him disappointed, bemocked of Destiny, through long years" (lines 14–16)

   (C) "there is a hot fever of anarchy and misery raging within" (lines 12–13)

   (D) "what is all this but a mad Fermentation; wherefrom, the fiercer it is, the clearer product will one day evolve itself" (lines 6–7)

9. "Emphatically" (line 29) can best be defined as

   (A) surprisingly.   (C) originally.

   (B) unimportantly.   (D) unequivocally.

10. What is the function of the clause introduced by "nay" in line 17?

   (A) It negates the clause that precedes it.

   (B) It contradicts the clause that precedes it.

   (C) It intensifies the clause that precedes it.

   (D) It restates the clause that precedes it.

Drill 4 Answers

1.	(B)	4.	(A)	7.	(B)	10.	(C)
2.	(C)	5.	(B)	8.	(D)		
3.	(C)	6.	(D)	9.	(D)		

Detailed Explanations of Answers

1. **(B)** The term "we" is used to separate the speaker and his or her audience from creative writers. Rather than to create "a royal and authoritative persona" (C), the speaker uses the term "we" to relate to ordinary people, or "laymen."

2. **(C)** The speaker is referring to "our interest," as shown at the beginning of the sentence (line 6).

3. **(C)** This statement is contradicted in the second paragraph, in which the speaker discusses his or her hopes of finding similarities between "people like ourselves" and creative writers.

4. **(A)** Cathects means "to construct." Children are not distanced or discouraged from play, and in lines 34-35 we are told that "child's play" is different from "fantasying."

5. **(B)** Choice (A) cannot be correct because the writer builds upon, rather than digresses from, the idea. Only one question is asked, and it is, at least partially, answered at the conclusion of the passage. Finally, the supporting paragraphs are in no way either brief or narrow.

6. **(D)** The speaker finds "the first traces of imaginative activity" in childhood play, making choices (A) and (B) incorrect. Creative writing is more than a continuation of childhood play (choice C); it is imagination without a link to the "real world"—fantasizing.

7. **(B)** The main character is repeatedly referred to as he/him. The use of the word "our" before "Wanderer" and "Professor" lets the reader know that "Wanderer" and "Professor" are two names given to the main character. The main character is compared to "the Eagle," but they are not the same person.

8. **(D)** The "Discontinuity" and "mad Fermentation" mentioned in this sentence imply the speaker's intentions for the rest of the passage.

9. **(D)** This answer can be determined from the context of the sentence: "…he has no other possession but Hope; this world of his is emphatically the Place of Hope." It must mean "undoubtedly," or "unequivocally."

10. **(C)** The audience is told that the main character's desires are not only denied, but are actually offered and then taken away. The word "nay" thus initiates the intensification of the situation.

Following is another reading passage. Remember to use the four activities discussed on pages 77–78 to "get the facts straight."

Step 1: Preview

A preview of the reading passage will give you a purpose and a reason for reading; previewing is a good strategy to use in test-taking. Before beginning to read the passage (usually a four-minute activity if you preview and review), you should take about 30 seconds to look over the passage and questions. An effective way to preview the passage is to read quickly the first sentence of each paragraph, the concluding sentence of the passage, and the questions — but not the answers—following the passage. A passage is given below. Practice previewing the passage by reading the first sentence of each paragraph and the last line of the passage.

That the area of obscenity and pornography is a difficult one for the Supreme Court is well documented. The Court's numerous attempts to define obscenity have proven unworkable; they left the decision to the subjective preferences of the justices. Perhaps Justice Stewart put it best when, after refusing to define obscenity, he declared, "But I know it when I see it." Does the Court literally have to see it to know it? Specifically, what role does the fact-pattern, including the materials' medium, play in the Court's decision?

Several recent studies employ fact-pattern analysis in modeling the Court's decision making. These studies examine the fact-pattern or case characteristics, often with ideological and attitudinal factors, as a determinant of the decision reached by the Court. In broad terms, these studies owe their theoretical underpinnings to attitude theory. As the name suggests, attitude theory views the Court's attitudes as an explanation of its decisions.

These attitudes, however, do not operate in a vacuum. As Spaeth explains, "the activation of an attitude involves both an object and the situation in which that object is encountered." The objects to which the court directs its attitudes are litigants. The situation—the subject matter of the case—can be defined in broad or narrow terms. One may define the situation as an entire area of the law (e.g., civil liberties issues). On an even broader scale the situation may be defined as the decision to grant certiorari or whether to defect from a minimum-winning coalition.

Defining the situation with such broad strokes, however, does not allow one to control for case content. In many specific issue areas, the cases present strikingly similar patterns. In examining the Court's search and seizure decisions, Segal found that a relatively small number of situational and case characteristic variables explain a high proportion of the Court's decisions.

Despite Segal's success, verification of the applicability of fact-pattern analysis in other issue areas has been slow in forthcoming. Renewed interest in obscenity and pornography by federal and state governments, the academic community, and numerous antipornography interest groups indicates the Court's decisions in this area deserve closer examination.

The Court's obscenity and pornography decisions also present an opportunity to study the Court's behavior in an area where the Court has granted significant decision-making authority to the states. In *Miller v. California* (1973) the Court announced the importance of local community standards in obscenity determinations. The Court's subsequent behavior may suggest how the Court will react in other areas where it has chosen to defer to the states (e.g., abortion).

Questions

1. The main idea of the passage is best stated in which of the following?

   (A) The Supreme Court has difficulty convicting those who violate obscenity laws.

   (B) The current definitions for obscenity and pornography provided by the Supreme Court are unworkable.

   (C) Fact-pattern analysis is insufficient for determining the attitude of the Court toward the issues of obscenity and pornography.

   (D) Despite the difficulties presented by fact-pattern analysis, Justice Segal found the solution in the patterns of search and seizure decisions.

2. The main purpose of the writer in this passage is to

   (A) convince the reader that the Supreme Court is making decisions about obscenity based on their subjective views only.

   (B) explain to the reader how fact-pattern analysis works with respect to cases of obscenity and pornography.

   (C) define obscenity and pornography for the layperson.

   (D) demonstrate the role fact-pattern analysis plays in determining the Supreme Court's attitude about cases in obscenity and pornography.

3. Of the following, which fact best supports the writer's contention that the Court's decisions in the areas of obscenity and pornography deserve closer scrutiny?

(A) The fact that a Supreme Court Justice said, "I know it when I see it."

(B) The fact that recent studies employ fact-pattern analysis in modeling the Court's decision-making process

(C) The fact that attitudes do not operate in a vacuum

(D) The fact that federal and state governments, interest groups, and the academic community show renewed interest in the obscenity and pornography decisions made by the Supreme Court

4. Among the following statements, which states an opinion rather than a fact expressed by the writer?

(A) The area of obscenity and pornography is a difficult one for the Supreme Court and is well documented.

(B) The objects to which a court directs its attitudes are the litigants.

(C) In many specific issue areas, the cases present strikingly similar patterns.

(D) The Court's subsequent behavior may suggest how the Court will react in other legal areas.

5. The list of topics below that best reflects the organization of the topics of the passage is

(A) I.   The difficulties of the Supreme Court

II.   Several recent studies

III. Spaeth's definition of "attitude"

IV.   The similar patterns of cases

V.   Other issue areas

VI.   The case of *Miller v. California*

(B) I.   The Supreme Court, obscenity, and fact-pattern analysis

II.   Fact-pattern analyses and attitude theory

III. The definition of "attitude" for the Court

IV.   The definition of "situation"

V.   The breakdown in fact-pattern analysis

VI.   Studying Court behavior

(C) I.   Justice Stewart's view of pornography

     II.   Theoretical underpinnings

     III.   A minimum-winning coalition

     IV.   Search and seizure decisions

     V.   Renewed interest in obscenity and pornography

     VI.   The importance of local community standards

(D) I.   The Court's numerous attempts to define obscenity

     II.   Case characteristics

     III.   The subject matter of cases

     IV.   The Court's proportion of decisions

     V.   Broad-based factors

     VI.   Obscenity determination

6. Which paragraph below is the best summary of the passage?

(A) The Supreme Court's decision-making process with respect to obscenity and pornography has become too subjective. Fact-pattern analyses, used to determine the overall attitude of the Court, reveal only broad-based attitudes on the part of the Court toward the situations of obscenity cases. These patterns cannot fully account for the Court's attitudes toward case content. Research is not conclusive that fact-pattern analyses work when applied to legal areas. Renewed public and local interest suggests continued study and close examination of how the Court makes decisions. Delegating authority to the states may reflect patterns for Court decisions in other socially sensitive areas.

(B) Though subjective, the Supreme Court's decisions are well documented. Fact-pattern analyses reveal the attitude of the Supreme Court toward its decisions in cases. Spaeth explains that an attitude involves both an object and a situation. For the Court, the situation may be defined as the decision to grant certiorari. Cases present strikingly similar patterns, and a small number of variables explain a high proportion of the Court's decisions. Segal has made an effort to verify the applicability of fact-pattern analysis with some success. The Court's decisions on obscenity and pornography suggest weak Court behavior, such as in *Miller v. California*.

(C) To determine what obscenity and pornography mean to the Supreme Court, we must use fact-pattern analysis. Fact-pattern analysis reveals the ideas that the Court uses to operate in a vacuum. The litigants and the subject matter of cases are defined in broad terms (such as an entire area of law) to reveal the Court's decision-making process. Search and seizure cases reveal strikingly similar patterns, leaving the Court open to grant certiorari effectively. Renewed public interest in the Court's decisions proves how the Court will react in the future.

(D) Supreme Court decisions about pornography and obscenity are under examination and are out of control. The Court has to see the case to know it. Fact-pattern analyses reveal that the Court can only define cases in narrow terms, thus revealing individual egotism on the part of the Justices. As a result of strikingly similar patterns in search and seizure cases, the Court should be studied further for its weakness in delegating authority to state courts, as in the case of *Miller v. California*.

7. Based on the passage, the rationale for fact-pattern analyses arises out of what theoretical groundwork?

   (A) Subjectivity theory

   (B) The study of cultural norms

   (C) Attitude theory

   (D) Cybernetics

8. Based on data in the passage, what would most likely be the major cause for the difficulty in pinning down the Supreme Court's attitude toward cases of obscenity and pornography?

   (A) The personal opinions of the Court Justices

   (B) The broad nature of the situations of the cases

   (C) The ineffective logistics of certiorari

   (D) The inability of the Court to resolve the variables presented by individual case content

9. In the context of the passage, *subjective* (Sentence 2) might be most nearly defined as

   (A) personal.   (C) focused.

   (B) wrong.   (D) objective.

By previewing the passage, you should have read the following:

- The fact that the area of obscenity and pornography is a difficult one for the Supreme Court is well documented.

- Several recent studies employ fact-pattern analysis in modeling the Court's decision making.

- These attitudes, however, do not operate in a vacuum.

- Defining the situation with such broad strokes, however, does not allow one to control for case content.

- Despite Segal's success, verification of the applicability of fact-pattern analysis in other issue areas has been slow in forthcoming.

- The Court's obscenity and pornography decisions also present an opportunity to study the Court's behavior in an area where the Court has granted significant decision-making authority to the states.

- The Court's subsequent behavior may suggest how the Court will react in other areas where it has chosen to defer to the states (e.g., abortion).

These few sentences tell you much about the entire passage.

As you begin to examine the passage, you should first determine the main idea and underline it so that you can easily refer to it if a question requires you to do so (see Question 1). The main idea should be found in the first paragraph of the passage and may even be the first sentence. From what you have read thus far, you know that the main idea of this passage is that the Supreme Court has difficulty in making obscenity and pornography decisions.

In addition, you know that recent studies have used fact-pattern analysis in modeling the Court's decisions. You have learned also that attitudes do not operate independently and that case content is important. The feasibility of using fact-pattern analysis in other issue areas has not been quickly verified. To study the behavior of the Court in an area in which they have granted significant decision-making authority to the states, one only has to consider the obscenity and pornography decisions. In summary, the author suggests that the Court's subsequent behavior may suggest how the Court will react in those other areas in which decision-making authority has previously been granted to the states. As you can see, having this information will make the reading of the passage much easier.

Step 2: Annotate

After you preview, you will be ready to read actively. This means that as you read, you will be engaged in such things as underlining important words, topic sentences, main ideas, and words denoting tone of the passage.

Read carefully the first sentence of each paragraph since this often contains the topic of the paragraph. You may wish to underline each topic sentence.

During this stage, you should also determine the writer's purpose in writing the passage (see Question 2), as this will help you focus on the main points and the writer's key points in the organization of a passage. You can determine the author's purpose by asking yourself, "Does *the relationship* between the writer's main idea plus evidence the writer uses answer one of four questions?":

• What is the writer's overall primary goal or objective?

• Is the writer trying primarily to persuade you by proving or using facts to make a case for an idea?

• Is the writer trying primarily to inform and enlighten you about an idea, object, or event?

• Is the writer attempting primarily to amuse you? Keep you fascinated? Laughing?

Make sure you examine all of the facts that the author uses to support his or her main idea. This will allow you to decide whether the writer has made a case and what sort of purpose he or she supports. Look for supporting details—facts, examples, illustrations, the testimony or research of experts—that are about the topic in question and that *show* what the writer *says* is so. In fact, paragraphs and theses consist of *show* and *tell*. The writer *tells* you something is so or not so and then *shows* you facts, illustrations, expert testimony, or experience to back up what he or she says is or is not so. As you determine where the author's supporting details are, you may want to label them so that you can refer to them easily when answering questions.

Step 3: Outline

There may not be enough time for you to write a detailed outline for this test. However, you can organize the key points and ideas by numbering them in the text.

As you read, you should note the structure of the passage. There are several common structures for passages, some of which are described below.

Main Types of Paragraph Structures

1. The structure is a main idea plus supporting arguments (examples).

2. The structure includes comparisons or contrasts.

3. There is a pro and a con structure.

4. The structure is chronological.

5. The structure has several different aspects of one idea.

By understanding the *relationship* among the main point, transitions, and supporting information, you may more readily determine the structure of organization and the writer's purpose in a given piece of writing.

Step 4: Summarize

After you finish annotating and outlining, take 10 or 20 seconds to look over the main idea, the topic sentences that you have underlined, and the key words and phrases you have marked. At this point you have gathered enough information from the passage to answer questions dealing with main idea, purpose, support, fact vs. opinion, organization, summarization, recall, cause and effect, and definition. Let's look again at these questions.

Main Idea Questions

Looking back at the questions that follow the passage, you see that Question 1 is a "main idea" question. In answering the question, you see that answer choice (C) is correct. The writer uses the second, third, fourth, and fifth paragraphs to show how fact-pattern analysis is an ineffective determinant of the attitude of the Court toward obscenity and pornography.

Answer (A) is incorrect. Nothing is ever said directly about "convicting" persons accused of obscenity, only that the Court has difficulty defining it.

Choice (B) is also incorrect. Though it is stated as a fact by the writer, it is used only as an effect that leads the writer to examine how fact-pattern analysis does or does not work to reveal the "cause" or attitude of the Court toward obscenity and pornography.

Finally, answer choice (D) is incorrect. The statement is contrary to what Segal found when he examined search and seizure cases.

Purpose Questions

In examining Question 2, you see that you must determine the author's purpose in writing the passage. Looking at the answer choices, you see that choice (D) is correct. Though the writer never states it directly, he or she summons data consistently to show that fact-pattern analysis gives us only part of the picture; it cannot account for the attitude toward individual cases.

Choice (A) is incorrect. The writer doesn't try to convince us of this fact but merely states it as an opinion resulting from the evidence derived from the "well-documented" background to the problem.

(B) is also incorrect. The writer does not just explain the role of fact-pattern analysis but rather shows how it cannot fully apply.

The passage is about the Court's difficulty in defining these terms rather than what the definition is. Nowhere do definitions for these terms appear. Therefore, choice (C) is incorrect.

Support Questions

Question 3 requires you to analyze the author's supporting details. To answer this question, let's look at the answer choices. Choice (D) must be correct. In the fifth paragraph, the writer states that the "renewed interest"— a real and observable fact—from these groups "indicates the Court's decisions...deserve closer examination," which is another way of saying scrutiny.

Answer (A) is incorrect. The writer uses this remark to show how the Court cannot effectively define obscenity and pornography but must rely on "subjective preferences" to resolve issues.

In addition, choice (B) is incorrect because the writer points to the data in (D), not fact-pattern analyses, to prove this.

(C), too, is incorrect. Although the statement is true, the writer makes this point to show how fact-pattern analysis doesn't help clear up the real-world "situation" in which the Court must make its decisions.

Fact vs. Opinion Questions

By examining Question 4, you can see that you are required to know the difference between fact and opinion. Keeping in mind that an opinion is something that cannot be proven to hold true in all circumstances, you can determine that choice (D) is correct. It is the only statement among the four for which the evidence is yet to be gathered. It is the writer's opinion that this may be a way to predict the Court's attitudes.

(A), (B), and (C) are all taken from data or documentation already in existence in the world and are, therefore, incorrect.

Organization Questions

Question 5 asks you to organize given topics to reflect the organization of the passage. After examining all of the choices, you will determine that choice (B) is the correct response. These topical areas lead directly to the implied thesis that the "role" of fact-pattern analysis is insufficient for determining the attitude of the Supreme Court in the areas of obscenity and pornography.

Answer (A) is incorrect because the first topic stated in the list is not the topic of the first paragraph. It is too global. The first paragraph is about the difficulties the Court has with defining obscenity and how fact-pattern analysis might be used to determine the Court's attitude and clear up the problem.

(C) is incorrect because each of the items listed in this topic list is supporting evidence or data for the real topic of each paragraph. [See the list in (B) for correct topics.] For example, Justice Stewart's statement about pornography is cited only to indicate the nature of the problem with obscenity for the Court. It is not the focus of the paragraph itself.

Finally, (D) is incorrect. As with choice (C), these are all incidental pieces of information or data used to make broader points.

Summarization Questions

To answer Question 6, you must be able to summarize the passage. The paragraph that best and most accurately reports what the writer demonstrated based on the implied thesis is answer choice (C).

Choice (A) is incorrect. While it reflects some of the evidence presented in the passage, the passage does not imply that all Court decisions are subjective, just the ones about pornography and obscenity.

Response (B) is also incorrect. The writer repeatedly summons information to show how fact-pattern analysis cannot pin down the Court's attitude toward case content. Similarly, the writer does not suggest that delegating authority to the states, as in *Miller v. California*, is a sign of some weakness, but merely that it is worthy of study as a tool for predicting or identifying the Court's attitude.

(D) is incorrect. Nowhere does the writer say or suggest that the justice system is "out of control" or that the justices are "egotists," only that they are liable to make "subjective" decisions rather than decisions based on an identifiable shared standard.

At this point, the three remaining question types (recall questions, cause/effect questions, and definition questions) must be discussed. (See numbers 7, 8, and 9 on pages 95 and 96).

Recall Questions

To answer Question 7, you must be able to recall information from the passage. The easiest way to answer this question is to refer to the passage. In the second paragraph, the writer states that recent studies using fact-pattern analyses "owe their theoretical underpinnings to attitude theory." Therefore, we can conclude that response (C) is correct.

Answer choices (A), (B), and (D) are incorrect, as they are never discussed or mentioned by the writer.

Cause/Effect Questions

Question 8 requires you to analyze a cause-and-effect relationship. Choice (D) is correct because it is precisely what fact-pattern analyses cannot resolve.

Response (A) is incorrect because no evidence is presented for this; it is stated that they do make personal decisions but not how these decisions cause difficulty.

Answer choice (B) is incorrect because this is one way in which fact-pattern analysis can be helpful.

Finally, (C) is only a statement about certiorari being difficult to administer, but this was never claimed by the writer.

Definition Questions

In question 9, choice (A) is best. By noting the example of Justice Stewart, we can see that Justice Stewart's comment is not an example of right or wrong. (He doesn't talk about right or wrong. He uses the verb "know"—whose root points to *know*ledge, primarily understanding or insight, not ethical considerations.) He probably doesn't mean "focused" by this because the focus is provided by the appearance or instance of the case itself. By noting the same word ending and the appearance of the root "object"—meaning an observable thing existing outside of ourselves in time and space, and comparing it with the root of subjective, "subject"—often pointing to something personally studied, we can begin to rule out "objective" as perhaps the opposite of "subjective." Most of the time if we are talking about people's "preferences," we are talking about taste or quality. These preferences are usually not a result of scientific study or clear reasoning, but they arise out of a combination of personal taste and idiosyncratic intuitions. Thus, (A) becomes the best choice.

Answer (B) is incorrect. Nothing is implied or stated about the rightness or wrongness of the decisions themselves. Rather, it is the definition of obscenity that seems "unworkable."

(C) is incorrect because the Court's focus is already in place: on obscenity and pornography.

(D) is also incorrect. *Objective* is the direct opposite of *subjective*. Reasoning based on the object of study (objective) is the opposite of reasoning based upon the beliefs, opinions, or ideas of the one viewing the object (subjective).

You may not have been familiar with the word subjective, but from your understanding of the writer's intent you should have been able to figure out what he or she was after. Surrounding words and phrases almost always offer you some clues in determining the meaning of a word. In addition, any examples that appear in the text may also provide some hints.

INTERPRETATION OF GRAPHIC INFORMATION QUESTIONS

Although graphs, charts, and tables may not play a large part on the Communication and Literacy Skills Test, you should be familiar with them. You will likely encounter at least one passage that is accompanied by some form of graphic information. You will then be required to answer any question(s) based on the information presented in the graph, chart, or table.

Graphs are used to produce visual aids for given sets of information. Often, the impact of numbers and statistics is diminished by an overabundance of tedious numbers. A graph helps a reader visualize rapid or irregular information, as well as trace long periods of decline or increase. The following is a guide to reading the three principal graphic forms that you may encounter when taking the Communication and Literacy Skills Test.

LINE GRAPHS

Line graphs, like the one that follows, are used to track two elements of one or more subjects. One element is usually a time factor, over whose span the other element increases, decreases, or fluctuates. The lines that make up such a graph are composed of connected points that follow the chart through each integral stage. For example, look at the following graph.

Immigration to the United States, 1820–1930

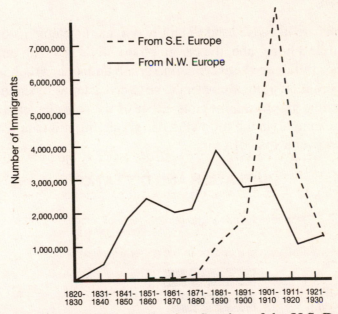

Source: Immigration and Naturalization Service of the U.S. Dept. of Justice

The average number of immigrants from 1820–1830 is represented at one point; the average number of immigrants from 1831–1840 is represented at the next. The line that connects these points is used only to ease the visual gradation between the points. It is not meant to give an accurate degree for every year between the two decades. If this were so, the line would hardly represent a straight, even progression from year to year. The sharp directness of the lines reveals otherwise. The purpose of the graph is to plot the average increases or decreases from point to point. When dealing with more than one subject, the line graph must use either different color lines or different types of lines. In the graph above, the dark bold line represents immigration from Northwestern Europe; the broken line represents immigration from Southeastern Europe.

To read a line graph, find the point of change that interests you. For example, if you want to trace immigration from Northwestern Europe from

1861–1870, you would find the position of the dark line on that point. Next, trace the position to the vertical information on the chart. In this instance, one would discover that approximately 2,000,000 immigrants arrived from Northwestern Europe in the period of time from 1861–1870. If you wish to discover when the number of immigrants reached 4,000,000, you would read across from 4,000,000 on the vertical side of the graph and see that this number was reached in 1881–1890 from Northwestern Europe and in 1891–1910 from Southeastern Europe.

BAR GRAPHS

Bar graphs are likewise used to plot two dynamic elements of a subject. However, unlike a line graph, the bar graph usually deals with only one subject. The other difference between a line graph and a bar graph is that a bar graph usually calls for a single element to be traced in terms of another, whereas a reader of a line graph usually plots either of the two elements with equal interest. For example, in the following bar graph, inflation and deflation are being marked over a span of years.

INFLATION AND DEFLATION

Inflation is a rise in the general level of prices.

Deflation is a decline in the general level of prices.

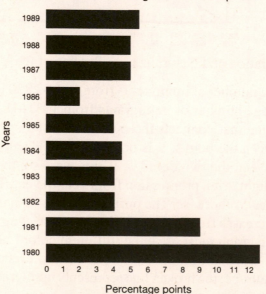

Percentage points are assigned to each year's level of prices, and that percentage decreases (deflation) from 1980 to 1981, and from 1981 to 1982. The price level is static from 1982 to 1983. The price level then increases (inflation) from 1983 to 1984. Therefore, it is obvious that the bar graph is read strictly in terms of the changes exhibited over a period of time. A line graph, conversely, is used to plot two dynamic elements of equal interest to the reader (e.g., either number of immigrants or the particular decade in question).

To read a bar graph, simply begin at the element at the base of a bar, and trace the bar its full length. Once reaching its length, cross-reference the other element of information that matches the length of the bar.

PIE CHARTS

Pie charts differ greatly from line or bar graphs. Pie charts are used to help a reader visualize percentages of information with many elements to the subject. An entire "pie" represents 100% of a given quantity of information. The pie is then sliced into measurements that correspond to their respective shares of the whole. For example, in the following pie chart Myrna's rent occupies a slice greater than any other in the pie, because no other element equals or exceeds 25% of Myrna's monthly budget.

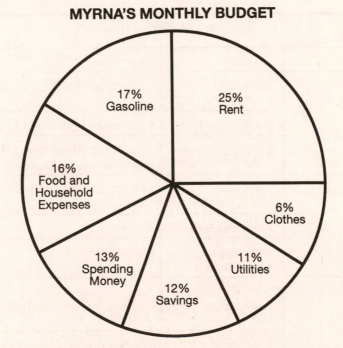

MYRNA'S MONTHLY BUDGET

Another aspect of pie charts is that the smaller percentage elements are moved consecutively to the larger elements. Therefore, the largest element in the chart will necessarily be adjacent to the smallest element in the chart, and the line that separates them is the beginning or endpoint of the chart. From this point the chart fans out to the other elements of the chart, going from the smallest percentages to the largest.

To read a pie chart, choose the element of the subject that interests you, and compare its size to those of the other elements. In cases where the elements are similar in size, do not assume they are equal. The exact percentage of the element will be listed within that slice of the chart. For example, Myrna's utilities, savings, and spending money are all similar in size, but it is clear when reading the chart that each possesses a different value.

READING TABLES

Tables such as the one below are useful because they relate to large bodies of information within a confined area. To read a table, cross index the headings that run horizontally across the top of the table with the headings that run vertically down the left side of the table. Scanning the table for the overall information within is usually done by reading line by line as if reading regular text, although with a table the reader is constantly referring to the appropriate headings at the top of the table to interpret the information listed.

Summary of Plant Tissues		
Tissue	Location	Functions
Epidermal	Root	Protection; Increases absorption area
	Stem	Protection; Reduces H_2O loss
	Leaf	Protection; Reduces H_2O loss; Regulates gas exchange
Parenchyma	Root, stem, leaf	Storage of food and H_2O
Sclerenchyma	Stem and leaf	Support
Chlorenchyma	Leaf and young stems	Photosynthesis
Vascular a. Xylem	Root, stem, leaf	Upward transport of fluid
b. Phloem	Leaf, stem, root	Downward transport of fluid
Meristematic	Root and stem	Growth; Formation of xylem, phloem, and other tissues

To use the table on the previous page, simply choose a particular plant tissue and then find the appropriate information needed about that tissue through the headings listed at the top of the table. For example, the one function of chlorenchyma tissue is photosynthesis.

HELPFUL HINTS

You should approach any graphic information you encounter as a key to a larger body of information in abbreviated form. Be sure to use the visual aids of the graphics (e.g., the size of slices on pie charts) as aids only; do not ignore the written information listed on the graph, table, etc. Note especially the title and headings so that you know exactly at what you are looking. Also, be aware of the source of the information, where applicable. Know what each element of the graphic information represents; this will help you compare how drastic or subtle any changes are, and over what span of time they take place. Be sure you realize what the actual numbers represent, whether they be dollars, thousands of people, millions of shares, etc. Finally, note the way in which the graphic information relates to the text it seeks to illustrate; know in what ways the graphic information supports the arguments of the author of the given passage.

Drill 5

DIRECTIONS: Read the passage and answer the questions that follow.

Immigration

The influx of immigrants that America had been experiencing slowed during the conflicts with France and England, but the flow increased between 1815 and 1837, when an economic downturn sharply reduced their numbers. Thus, the overall rise in population during these years was due more to incoming foreigners than to natural increase. Most of the newcomers were from Britain, Germany, and southern Ireland. The Germans usually fared best because they brought more money and more skills. Discrimination, primarily directed against the Catholics, was common in the job market. "Irish Need Not Apply" signs were common. However, the persistent labor shortage prevented the natives from totally excluding the foreign elements. These newcomers huddled in ethnic neighborhoods in the cities, or those who could moved out West to try their hands at farming.

In 1790, 5% of the U.S. population lived in cities of 2,500 or more. By 1860, that figure had risen to 25%. This rapid urbanization created an array of problems.

The rapid growth in urban areas was not matched by the growth of services. Clean water, trash removal, housing, and public transportation all lagged behind, and the wealthy got them first. Bad water and poor sanitation produced poor health, and epidemics of typhoid fever, typhus, and cholera were common. Police and fire protection were usually inadequate and the development of professional forces was resisted because of the cost and the potential for political patronage and corruption.

Rapid growth helped to produce a wave of violence in the cities. In New York City in 1834, the Democrats fought the Whigs with such vigor that the state militia was summoned. New York and Philadelphia witnessed race riots in the mid-1830s, and a New York mob sacked a Catholic convent in 1834. In the 1830s, 115 major incidents of mob violence were recorded. Street crime was common in all the major cities.

SOURCES OF IMMIGRATION, 1820 – 1840

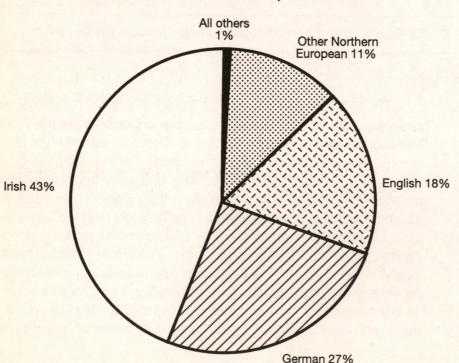

All others 1%

Other Northern European 11%

English 18%

German 27%

Irish 43%

1. The author's purpose for writing this essay is

   (A) to bring to light the poor treatment of immigrants.

   (B) to show the violent effects of overpopulation.

   (C) to trace the relation of immigration to the problems of rapid urban growth.

   (D) to dissuade an active life in big cities.

2. Which of the following best defines the word *sacked* as it is used in the last paragraph?

   (A) Robbed

   (B) Carried

   (C) Trespassed on

   (D) Vandalized

3. Which of the following statements best summarizes the main idea of the fourth paragraph?

   (A) Racial tensions caused riots in New York City and Philadelphia.

   (B) The rapid growth in urban population sowed the seeds of violence in U.S. cities.

   (C) Street crimes were far worse in urban areas than race riots and political fights.

   (D) The state militia was responsible for curbing urban violence.

4. Ideas presented in the passage are most influenced by which of the following assumptions?

   (A) Urban life was more or less controllable before the flow of immigration in 1820.

   (B) The British had more skills than the Irish.

   (C) Ethnic neighborhoods had always been a part of American society.

   (D) France and England often held conflicts.

5. According to the graph, from 1820–1840

   (A) there were more Irish immigrants than all other nationalities combined.

   (B) the combined number of immigrants from England and Germany exceeded those from Ireland.

   (C) 1% of the immigrants were from Italy.

   (D) there was an equal number of English and German immigrants.

Drill 5 Answers

1. (C)	3. (B)	5. (B)
2. (D)	4. (A)	

Detailed Explanations of Answers

1. **(C)** While the author does mention poor treatment (such as discrimination) and violence, those examples are used only as support for his or her purpose, which is to trace the relation of immigration to the problems of rapid urban growth. The author makes no attempt to dissuade an active life in big cities.

2. **(D)** Choices (A), (C), and (D) have similar meanings, but only "vandalized," choice (D), is a synonym of "sacked."

3. **(B)** Choices (A), (C), and (D) each account for only one issue. Choice (B) summarizes the problems discussed throughout the entire paragraph.

4. **(A)** The issues presented in this passage are not dependent on (B) the skill-level of immigrants, (C) the history of ethnic neighborhoods in America, or (D) conflict between France and England.

5. **(B)** Although this answer is not immediately clear from visually interpreting the graph, (B) is proven to be the correct answer when the numbers are added. The number of English and German immigrants at this time were 18% and 27%, respectively. The total from these two countries is 45%, 2% more than were from Ireland.

MTEL

*Massachusetts Tests for Educator Licensure —
Communication and Literacy Skills Test*

Chapter 3
Writing Subtest Review

CHAPTER 3

Writing Subtest Review

    I. **Written Mechanics**

    II. **Grammar and Usage**

    III. **Written Composition**

I. WRITTEN MECHANICS

SENTENCE ORDER AND SEQUENCE OF IDEAS IN A PARAGRAPH

The order of sentences within a paragraph is important. The sentences should be ordered so that the writer presents ideas logically and effectively. Several patterns of organizing sentences and ideas are available for the writer's use.

Chronological Order presents events in the order in which they occurred. This type of order is also called time order.

Emphatic Order moves from least important to most important or most important to least important. This type of order is also known as order of importance.

Spatial Order is used to describe a person, object, or place. This type of order is also called space order because the subject is being described from top to bottom or from left to right.

Drill 1

DIRECTIONS: Read the following sentences and determine the sequence you think would be best.

(1) The computer can be a great help in planning a trip. (2) The best routes to drive to the area are mapped for the traveler. (3) Once a traveler selects a destination, information about the area chosen is available. (4) The major attractions of the area are described. (5) Where to eat and sleep as well as the history of the area is provided. (6) Alternate routes for driving to the area can be the most rapid or the most scenic. (7) Sometimes discounts to special sites are offered in the form of computer print-outs. (8) The computer as a "travel agent" provides all of these services without cost.

Drill 1 Answer

The recommended sequence of the sentences is 1, 3, 2, 6, 5, 4, 7, and 8.

TRANSITIONS

As you review the passage a second time, look for and circle transitions that reveal the connections among the writer's ideas. Transitions show how the writer is reasoning to get to the point—perhaps it is a cause/effect pattern or a problem/solution discussion in which the writer provides the solution. He or she may use transitions either at the beginnings of paragraphs or to show connections among ideas within a single paragraph.

Here are some typical transitional words and phrases:

LINKING SIMILAR IDEAS

For explanation, analogy, and accruing factual evidence or opinions for a point of view.

again	besides	further
also	equally important	furthermore
and	for example	in addition
another	for instance	in like manner

| likewise | nor | similarly |
| moreover | of course | too |

> EXAMPLE: Neither Emerson *nor* any of the others were real observers of the moral life.

LINKING DISSIMILAR/CONTRADICTORY IDEAS

To show comparison or contrast among similar or opposing notions.

although	however	on the other hand
and yet	in spite of	otherwise
as if	instead	provided that
but	nevertheless	still
conversely	on the contrary	yet

> EXAMPLE: *Although* he did not mention Hawthorne by name, the reference was unmistakable.

INDICATING CAUSE, PURPOSE, OR RESULT

Causes may be immediate or remote: The immediate cause for my spilling the glass of water was that I knocked it over with my hand. The remote cause might be that I was trying to put on my hat, and in the process I lost my focus on the glass of water in line with my sweeping hand, which was reaching for my hat across the table.

To show the solutions to a problem or the outcome of a certain series of causes.

as a result	for this reason	then
as for	hence	therefore
because	since	thus
consequently	so	

> EXAMPLE: *As a result* of the romantic movement, we have almost forgotten that poetry can deal with epistemology.

INDICATING TIME OR POSITION

Used in process and procedure explanations or chronological narratives to show a sequence in time or place.

above	before	meanwhile
across	beyond	next
afterward	eventually	presently
around	finally	second
at once	first	thereafter
at the present time	here	thereupon

EXAMPLE: At first clearly symbolizing Hester's adulterousness, the scarlet letter *eventually* represents multiple meanings for the townspeople.

INDICATING AN EXAMPLE OR SUMMARY

Used to point to supporting evidence or explanatory material and to complete an idea within a paragraph or within a whole essay.

as a result	in any event	in other words
as I have said	in brief	in short
for example	in conclusion	on the whole
for instance	in fact	to sum up
in any case		

EXAMPLE: *In other words,* he must devise a structure that can combine the story of whaling, Ahab's tragedy, and his own speculations on human destiny.

II. GRAMMAR AND USAGE

The requirements for informal spoken English are much more relaxed than the rigid rules for "standard written English." While slang, colloquialisms, and other informal expressions are acceptable and sometimes very appropriate in casual speech, they are inappropriate in academic and business writing. More often than not, writers do not make a distinction between the two; they use, albeit unsuccessfully, the same words, grammar, and sentence structure from their everyday speech in their college papers.

WORD CHOICE SKILLS

DENOTATIVE AND CONNOTATIVE MEANINGS

The *denotative* meaning of a word is its literal, dictionary definition: what the word denotes or "means." The *connotative* meaning of a word is what the word connotes or "suggests"; it is a meaning apart from what the word literally means. A writer should choose a word based on the tone and context of the sentence; this ensures that a word bears the appropriate connotation while still conveying some exactness in denotation. For example, a gift might be described as "cheap," but the directness of this word has a negative connotation—something cheap is something of little or no value. The word "inexpensive" has a more positive connotation, though "cheap" is a synonym for "inexpensive." Decisions of this type require you to determine the appropriateness of words and phrases for the context of a sentence.

WORDINESS AND CONCISENESS

Effective writing is concise. Wordiness, on the other hand, decreases the clarity of expression by cluttering sentences with unnecessary words.

Effective writing demands that you avoid redundancies (unnecessary repetitions), circumlocution (failure to get to the point), and padding with loose synonyms.

Notice the difference in impact between the first and second sentences in the following pairs:

INCORRECT: The medical exam that he gave me was entirely complete.

CORRECT: The medical exam he gave me was complete.

INCORRECT:	Larry asked his friend John, who was a good, old friend, if he would join him and go along with him to see the foreign film made in Japan.
CORRECT:	Larry asked his good, old friend John if he would join him in seeing the Japanese film.

INCORRECT:	I was absolutely, totally happy with the present that my parents gave to me at 7 a.m. on the morning of my birthday.
CORRECT:	I was happy with the present my parents gave me on the morning of my birthday.

Drill 2

DIRECTIONS: Read each sentence and replace the underlined words with the appropriate answer.

1. His <u>principal</u> reasons for resigning were his <u>principles</u> of right and wrong.

    (A) principal . . . principals   (C) principle . . . principles

    (B) principle . . . principals   (D) No change is necessary.

2. The book tells about Alzheimer's disease—how it <u>affects</u> the patient and what <u>effect</u> it has on the patient's family.

    (A) effects . . . affect   (C) effects . . . effects

    (B) affects . . . affect   (D) No change is necessary.

3. The <u>amount</u> of homeless children we can help depends on the <u>number</u> of available shelters.

    (A) number . . . number   (C) number . . . amount

    (B) amount . . . amount   (D) No change is necessary.

4. All students are <u>suppose to</u> pass the test before <u>achieving</u> upper-division status.

    (A) supposing to . . . achieving

    (B) suppose to . . . being achieved

(C) supposed to . . . achieving

(D) No change is necessary.

5. The reason he <u>succeeded</u> is <u>because</u> he worked hard.

(A) succeeded . . . that

(C) succede . . . because of

(B) seceded . . . that

(D) No change is necessary.

DIRECTIONS: Select the sentence that clearly and effectively states the idea and has no structural errors.

---

6. (A) South of Richmond, the two roads converge together to form a single highway.

(B) South of Richmond, the two roads converge together to form an interstate highway.

(C) South of Richmond, the two roads converge to form an interstate highway.

(D) South of Richmond, the two roads converge to form a single interstate highway.

7. (A) The student depended on his parents for financial support.

(B) The student lacked the ways and means to pay for his room and board, so he depended on his parents for this kind of money and support.

(C) The student lacked the ways and means or the wherewithal to support himself, so his parents provided him with the financial support he needed.

(D) The student lacked the means to pay for his room and board, so he depended on his parents for financial support.

8. (A) Vincent van Gogh and Paul Gauguin were close personal friends and companions who enjoyed each other's company and frequently worked together on their artwork.

(B) Vincent van Gogh and Paul Gauguin were friends who frequently painted together.

(C) Vincent van Gogh was a close personal friend of Paul Gauguin's, and the two of them often worked together on their artwork because they enjoyed each other's company.

(D) Vincent van Gogh, a close personal friend of Paul Gauguin's, often worked with him on their artwork.

9. (A) A college education often involves putting away childish thoughts, which are characteristic of youngsters, and concentrating on the future, which lies ahead.

(B) A college education involves putting away childish thoughts, which are characteristic of youngsters, and concentrating on the future.

(C) A college education involves putting away childish thoughts and concentrating on the future.

(D) A college education involves putting away childish thoughts and concentrating on the future which lies ahead.

10. (A) I had the occasion to visit an Oriental pagoda while I was a tourist on vacation and visiting in Kyoto, Japan.

(B) I visited a Japanese pagoda in Kyoto.

(C) I had occasion to visit a pagoda when I was vacationing in Kyoto, Japan.

(D) On my vacation, I visited a Japanese pagoda in Kyoto.

Drill 2 Answers

1.	(D)	4.	(C)	7.	(A)	10.	(B)
2.	(D)	5.	(A)	8.	(B)		
3.	(A)	6.	(C)	9.	(C)		

In order to better understand the role of grammar in sentence structure, it is necessary to know and be able to define grammatical terms. For this reason, one section of the Communication and Literacy Skills Test will ask you to define selected grammatical terms. Study the following list of words and their definitions; knowledge of these terms will help you not only in this section but throughout the entire test.

absolute phrase – a phrase that is related to a sentence in meaning, though it has no grammatical relationship to the sentence

abstract noun – a noun that names a quality or mental concept; something intangible that exists only in our minds

active voice sentence – a sentence in which the subject performs the action

adjective – a word that describes or modifies a noun or pronoun

adjective clause – a clause that functions as an adjective and usually begins with a relative pronoun that is often omitted

antecedent – the noun, usually before the pronoun, that the pronoun replaces

case – groupings of nouns and pronouns that tell how the words in question are related to the other words used with them

clause – a group of related words containing both a subject and a predicate

collective noun – a noun that describes a group of people or things that are considered a single unit

comma splice – an incorrect sentence construction in which two independent clauses are fused together with a comma

common noun – a noun that does not name a specific person, place, thing, or idea.

comparative adjective – compares two persons, places, things, or ideas

complement – a word often used to complete the meaning of an intransitive verb without receiving the intransitive verb's action and with copulative (linking) verbs to describe state of being

compound sentence – a sentence with at least two verbs and two subjects

concrete noun – a noun that names a member of a class; a group of people, places, or things that is physical, visible, and tangible

conjunction – a word that connects other words to each other

countable noun – a noun that can be made plural via changing the ending, usually by adding "s"

declarative statement – a sentence that makes a statement

demonstrative pronoun – a pronoun that points to or identifies a noun without explicitly naming it

dependent clause – a group of connected words that have both a predicate and a subject but still cannot stand alone

direct object – a word that receives a direct action from the subject of a sentence

elliptical clause – an instance in which clause elements are omitted if the context makes clear what is being indicated exclamatory statement – a sentence that communicates a strong emotion or surprise.

first person – indicates an "I" or "we" as the subject of the sentence

future tense – an expression of action that takes place in a time to follow the present

idiom – an expression that is characteristic of a particular language

imperative – a verb used as a command

imperative statement – a sentence that makes a command

indefinite pronoun – a pronoun that has an unknown or ambiguous antecedent

independent (or main) clause – a clause that can stand by itself as a simple sentence

indicative mood – a verb used to state a fact or ask a question

indirect object – a word that receives the action of the subject of the sentence indirectly

infinitive – the basic form of the verb, usually preceded by the preposition "to"

interjection – used to express strong emotion or surprise

interrogative pronoun – a pronoun that poses a question

interrogative statement – a sentence that asks a question

intransitive verb – a verb that does not take an object

misplaced modifier – a modifier that is not placed near the word it modifies

mood – indicates the tone of a verb

nominal of a sentence – a word or group of words that can function as a noun

nominative case – when a noun or pronoun is the subject of the verb

noncountable noun – a noun that cannot be made plural via changing the ending, usually by adding "s"

noun – a person, place, thing, animal, action, or quality

noun compound – a group of words (usually two) that functions as a single part of speech

object of the preposition – the noun after the preposition

objective case – when a noun or pronoun is used as the direct object, indirect object, or object of a preposition

participial phrase – a phrase that contains a participle and its modifiers, which is used as an adjective to modify a noun or pronoun

passive voice sentence – a sentence in which the subject receives the action

past tense – an expression of action that is completed at a definite moment before the present

person – indicates who is speaking and whether the subject is singular or plural

personal pronoun – a pronoun that refers to beings and objects. The basic personal pronouns are *I, you, he, she, we, they*

phrase – a group of connected words without a subject or predicate

positive adjective – describes a noun or pronoun on its own terms, without comparing it to anything else

possessive case – a noun or pronoun used to show ownership

predicate – the action of the sentence or what is said about the subject

preposition – a word that demonstrates the relationship between its object and another word in the sentence

prepositional phrase – a phrase that begins with a preposition and contains a noun and its modifiers

present tense – an expression of action that goes on in the current time or with regularity

pronoun – a word that replaces a noun

proper noun – the official name of a particular person, place, or thing

regular verb – a verb that forms the past tense by adding "ed" to the basic verb

relative pronoun – a pronoun that relates one part of a sentence to a word in another part of the sentence

run-on sentence – two complete sentences, totally fused

second person – indicates a "you" singular or "you" plural as the subject of the sentence

sentence – a group of words that contains a subject and a predicate and ends with a period, exclamation point, or question mark sentence fragment – part of a sentence; usually missing a predicate or a subject

split infinitive – an instance in which the words that make up an infinitive are separated by one or more words

subject of the sentence – the part of a sentence about which something is said

subjunctive – an uncommon construction used to express with exactitude how a verb usage is to be interpreted

superlative – compares three or more persons, places, or things

third person – indicates "he," "she," "it," or "they" as the subject of the sentence

transitive verb – a verb that takes an object to complete its meaning

verb – a word showing action or state of being

SENTENCE STRUCTURE SKILLS

PARALLELISM

Parallel structure is used to express matching ideas. It refers to the grammatical balance of a series of any of the following:

Phrases:

> The squirrel ran *along the fence, up the tree,* and *into his burrow* with a mouthful of acorns.

Adjectives:

> The job market is flooded with *very talented, highly motivated,* and *well-educated* young people.

Nouns:

> You will need a *notebook, pencil,* and *dictionary* for the test.

Clauses:

> The children were told to decide *which toy they would keep* and *which toy they would give away.*

Verbs:

> The farmer *plowed, planted,* and *harvested* his corn in record time.

Verbals:

> *Reading, writing,* and *calculating* are fundamental skills that all of us should possess.

Correlative Conjunctions:

> *Either* you will do your homework *or* you will fail.

Repetition of Structural Signals:

Structural signals include articles, auxiliaries, prepositions, and conjunctions.

> INCORRECT: I have quit my job, enrolled in school, and am looking for a reliable babysitter.

> CORRECT: I *have quit* my job, *have enrolled* in school, and *am looking* for a reliable babysitter.

Note: Repetition of prepositions is considered formal and is unnecessary.

> You can travel *by car, by plane, or by train*; it's all up to you.

>   OR

> You can travel *by car, plane, or train*; it's all up to you.

When a sentence contains items in a series, check for both punctuation and sentence balance. When you check for punctuation, make sure the commas are used correctly. When you check for parallelism, make sure that the conjunctions connect similar grammatical constructions, such as all adjectives or all clauses.

MISPLACED AND DANGLING MODIFIERS

A misplaced modifier is one that is in the wrong place in the sentence. Misplaced modifiers come in all forms—words, phrases, and clauses. Sentences containing misplaced modifiers are often very comical: *Mom made me eat the spinach instead of my brother*. Misplaced modifiers, like the one in this sentence, are usually too far away from the word or words they modify. This sentence should read: *Mom made me, instead of my brother, eat the spinach*.

Modifiers like *only, nearly,* and *almost* should be placed next to the word they modify and not in front of some other word, especially a verb, that they are not intended to modify.

A modifier is misplaced if it appears to modify the wrong part of the sentence or if we cannot be certain what part of the sentence the writer intended it to modify. To correct a misplaced modifier, move the modifier next to the word it describes.

INCORRECT: She served hamburgers to the men on paper plates.

CORRECT: She served hamburgers on paper plates to the men.

Split infinitives also result in misplaced modifiers. Infinitives consist of the marker *to* plus the plain form of the verb. The two parts of the infinitive make up a grammatical unit that should not be split. Splitting an infinitive is placing an adverb between the *to* and the verb.

INCORRECT: The weather service expects temperatures to not rise.

CORRECT: The weather service expects temperatures not to rise.

Sometimes a split infinitive may be natural and preferable, and though it may still bother some readers, it has become acceptable in formal writing.

EXAMPLE: Several U.S. industries expect *to* more than *triple* their use of robots within the next decade.

A squinting modifier is one that may refer to either a preceding or a following word, leaving the reader uncertain about what it is intended to modify. Correct a squinting modifier by moving it next to the word it is intended to modify.

INCORRECT: Snipers who fired on the soldiers often escaped capture.

CORRECT: Snipers who often fired on the soldiers escaped capture.

OR Snipers who fired on the soldiers escaped capture often.

A dangling modifier is a modifier or verb in search of a subject: the modifying phrase (usually an *-ing* word group, an *-ed* or *-en* word group, or a *to* + *a verb* word group—participle phrase or infinitive phrase respectively) either appears to modify the wrong word or has nothing to modify. It is literally dangling at the beginning or the end of a sentence. The sentences often look and sound correct: *To be a student government officer, your grades must be above average.* (However, the verbal modifier has nothing to describe. Who is *to be a student government officer*? Your grades?) Questions of this type require you to determine whether a modifier has a headword or whether it is dangling at the beginning or the end of the sentence.

To correct a dangling modifier, reword the sentence by either: 1) changing the modifying phrase to a clause with a subject or 2) changing the subject of the sentence to the word that should be modified. The following are examples of a dangling participle and a dangling infinitive:

INCORRECT: Shortly after leaving home, the accident occurred.

      Who is <u>leaving home</u>, the accident?

CORRECT: Shortly after we left home, the accident occurred.

INCORRECT: To get up on time, a great effort was needed.

      <u>To get up</u> needs a subject.

CORRECT: To get up on time, I made a great effort.

FRAGMENTS

A fragment is an incomplete construction that may or may not have a subject and a verb. Specifically, a fragment is a group of words pretending to be a sentence. Not all fragments appear as separate sentences, however. Often, fragments are separated by semicolons.

INCORRECT: Traffic was stalled for ten miles on the freeway. Because repairs were being made on potholes.

CORRECT: Traffic was stalled for ten miles on the freeway because repairs were being made on potholes.

INCORRECT: It was a funny story; one that I had never heard before.

CORRECT: It was a funny story, one that I had never heard before.

RUN-ON/FUSED SENTENCES

A run-on/fused sentence is not necessarily a long sentence or a sentence that the reader considers too long; in fact, a run-on may be two short sentences: *Dry ice does not melt it evaporates.* A run-on results when the writer fuses or runs together two separate sentences without using any correct mark of punctuation to separate them.

INCORRECT: Knowing how to use a dictionary is no problem each dictionary has a section in the front of the book telling how to use it.

CORRECT: Knowing how to use a dictionary is no problem. Each dictionary has a section in the front of the book telling how to use it.

Even if one or both of the fused sentences contains internal punctuation, the sentence is still a run-on.

INCORRECT: Bob bought dress shoes, a suit, and a nice shirt he needed them for his sister's wedding.

CORRECT: Bob bought dress shoes, a suit, and a nice shirt. He needed them for his sister's wedding.

COMMA SPLICES

A comma splice is the unjustifiable use of only a comma to combine what really is two separate sentences.

INCORRECT: One common error in writing is incorrect spelling, the other is the occasional use of faulty diction.

CORRECT: One common error in writing is incorrect spelling; the other is the occasional use of faulty diction.

Both run-on sentences and comma splices may be corrected in one of the following ways:

RUN-ON: Neal won the award he had the highest score.

COMMA SPLICE: Neal won the award, he had the highest score.

Separate the sentences with a period:

Neal won the award. He had the highest score.

Separate the sentences with a comma and a coordinating conjunction such as *and, but, or, nor, for, yet,* or *so:*

Neal won the award for he had the highest score.

Separate the sentences with a semicolon:

Neal won the award; he had the highest score.

Separate the sentences with a subordinating conjunction such as *although, because, since,* or *if:*

Neal won the award because he had the highest score.

SUBORDINATION, COORDINATION, AND PREDICATION

Suppose, for the sake of clarity, you wanted to combine the information in these two sentences to create one statement:

I studied a foreign language. I found English quite easy.

How you decide to combine this information should be determined by the relationship you'd like to show between the two facts. *I studied a foreign language, and I found English quite easy* seems rather illogical. The **coordination** of the two ideas (connecting them with the coordinating conjunction *and*) is ineffective. Using **subordination** instead (connecting the sentences with a subordinating conjunction) clearly shows the degree of relative importance between the expressed ideas:

After I studied a foreign language, I found English quite easy.

When using a conjunction, be sure that the sentence parts you are joining are in agreement.

INCORRECT: She loved him dearly but not his dog.

CORRECT: She loved him dearly, but she did not love his dog.

A common mistake that is made is to forget that each member of the pair must be followed by the same kind of construction.

INCORRECT: They complimented them both for their bravery and they thanked them for their kindness.

CORRECT: They both complimented them for their bravery and thanked them for their kindness.

While refers to time and should not be used as a substitute for *although, and,* or *but.*

INCORRECT: While I'm usually interested in Fellini movies, I'd rather not go tonight.

CORRECT: Although I'm usually interested in Fellini movies, I'd rather not go tonight.

Where refers to a place and should not be used as a substitute for *that.*

INCORRECT: We read in the paper where they are making great strides in DNA research.

CORRECT: We read in the paper that they are making great strides in DNA research.

After words like *reason* and *explanation*, use *that*, not *because*.

INCORRECT: His explanation for his tardiness was because his alarm did not go off.

CORRECT: His explanation for his tardiness was that his alarm did not go off.

Drill 3

DIRECTIONS: Select the sentence that clearly and effectively states the idea and has no structural errors.

1. (A) Many gases are invisible, odorless, and they have no taste.

   (B) Many gases are invisible, odorless, and have no taste.

   (C) Many gases are invisible, odorless, and tasteless.

2. (A) Everyone agreed that she had neither the voice or the skill to be a speaker.

   (B) Everyone agreed that she had neither the voice nor the skill to be a speaker.

   (C) Everyone agreed that she had either the voice nor the skill to be a speaker.

3. (A) The mayor will be remembered because he kept his campaign promises and because of his refusal to accept political favors.

   (B) The mayor will be remembered because he kept his campaign promises and because he refused to accept political favors.

   (C) The mayor will be remembered because of his refusal to accept political favors and he kept his campaign promises.

4. (A) While taking a shower, the doorbell rang.

   (B) While I was taking a shower, the doorbell rang.

   (C) While taking a shower, someone rang the doorbell.

5. (A) He swung the bat while the runner stole second base.

   (B) The runner stole second base while he swung the bat.

   (C) While he was swinging the bat, the runner stole second base.

DIRECTIONS: Choose the correct replacement for the underlined words.

---

6. Nothing grows as well in Mississippi as <u>cotton. Cotton</u> being the state's principal crop.

    (A) cotton, this

    (B) cotton; cotton

    (C) cotton cotton

    (D) No change is necessary.

7. It was a heartwrenching <u>movie; one</u> that I had never seen before.

    (A) movie and

    (B) movie, one

    (C) movie. One

    (D) No change is necessary.

8. Traffic was stalled for three miles on the <u>bridge. Because</u> repairs were being made.

    (A) bridge because

    (B) bridge; because

    (C) bridge, because

    (D) No change is necessary.

9. The ability to write complete sentences comes with <u>practice writing</u> run-on sentences seems to occur naturally.

    (A) practice, writing

    (B) practice. Writing

    (C) practice and

    (D) No change is necessary.

10. Even though she had taken French classes, she could not understand native French <u>speakers they</u> all spoke too fast.

    (A) speakers, they

    (B) speakers. They

    (C) speaking

    (D) No change is necessary.

Drill 3 Answers

1. (C)	4. (B)	7. (B)	10. (B)
2. (B)	5. (A)	8. (A)	
3. (B)	6. (A)	9. (B)	

EFFECTIVE USE OF NEGATIVES IN A SENTENCE

The use of negative words and phrases in forming effective sentences falls into two categories: the avoidance of common nonstandard uses of negative words and the use of negative wording to achieve a special purpose in a sentence.

COMMON NONSTANDARD NEGATIVE EXPRESSIONS

The most common error in forming sentences with negative words and phrases is the use of a *double negative*, or two negative terms used for the same purpose. A double negative is nonstandard English. The following are examples of double negatives:

1. The adverbs, such as *never* and *nowhere*, combined with a verb and the negative word *not* to form a contraction.

   INCORRECT: Marty *don't never* listen to all of the directions before he starts a project.

   CORRECT: Marty *doesn't ever* listen to all of the directions before he starts a project.

   Marty *never* listens to all of the directions before he starts a project.

   The sentences are made correct by removing one of the negative words.

2. The pronouns, such as *no one, none, nobody, nothing,* or *neither,* combined with a verb and the negative word *not* to form a contraction.

   INCORRECT: We *don't* know *nobody* who can do the task.

   CORRECT: We *don't* know *anybody* who can do the task.

   We know *nobody* who can do the task.

   The sentences are made correct by removing one of the negative words.

3. The words *hardly, scarcely,* or *barely* combined with a verb and the negative word *not* to form a contraction.

   INCORRECT: Surely the hot temperature *can't hardly* last much longer.

   CORRECT: Surely the hot temperature *can't* last much longer.

   Surely the hot temperature *can hardly* last much longer.

The sentence is made correct in the second example by changing the first negative (*can't*) to a positive (*can*).

INCORRECT: The travelers became lost when they *couldn't barely* see the road.

CORRECT: The travelers became lost when they *could barely* see the road.

The travelers became lost when they *couldn't* see the road.

The sentence is made correct by removing one of the negative words.

4. The words *only* or *but* combined with a verb and the negative word *not*.

INCORRECT: The astronaut *can't help but try* to avert the accident.

CORRECT: The astronaut *can't help trying* to avert the accident

The astronaut *must try* to avert the accident.

The sentence is made correct by removing the word *but* and changing the negative to a positive.

Drill 4

DIRECTIONS: Underline the double negative in the following sentences.

1. The neighbors didn't see nobody parked in the driveway.

2. A series of thunderstorms can't help but bring relief after the long drought.

3. Neither of the programs won't be held at a time when most of us can attend.

4. Listening for the doorbell, Irene don't never fall alseep.

5. The science lesson can't barely cover all of the material in the assignment.

6. A few witnesses didn't give no possible cause for the accident.

7. The students in the class don't like no change in the daily routine.

8. The club members do not allow no one to be late to a meeting.

9. The principal can't do nothing about the required fire drills.

10. The Broadway play doesn't have no more tickets for tonight's performance.

Drill 4 Answers

1. The neighbors <u>didn't</u> see <u>nobody</u> parked in the driveway.

2. A series of thunderstorms <u>can't</u> help <u>but</u> bring relief after the long drought.

3. <u>Neither</u> of the programs <u>won't</u> be held at a time when most of us can attend.

4. Listening for the doorbell, Irene <u>don't never</u> fall alseep.

5. The science lesson <u>can't barely</u> cover all of the material in the assignment.

6. A few witnesses <u>didn't</u> give <u>no</u> possible cause for the accident.

7. The students in the class <u>don't</u> like <u>no</u> change in the daily routine.

8. The club members do <u>not</u> allow <u>no</u> one to be late to a meeting.

9. The principal <u>can't</u> do <u>nothing</u> about the required fire drills.

10. The Broadway play <u>doesn't</u> have <u>no</u> more tickets for tonight's performance.

EFFECTIVE NEGATIVE WORDING FOR SENTENCE VARIETY

Some special sentence structures using negative wording can be quite effective. Of course, no double negative expressions occur in these sentence patterns.

1. Provide a definition by giving examples of what a term is not.

   EXAMPLE: The speaker's special technique of appealing to his audience—*not* by using meaningless examples, *not* by providing boring details, *not* by trying to impress with his experience—centered on his awareness of their interests and career goals.

2. Use a series of negative introductory phrases.

> EXAMPLE: *Never* late to class, *never* poorly prepared for the day's lesson, *never* unresponsive to his students' interests, the teacher easily involved them in the class focus.

3. Use two or more negatives that do not create a double negative within the sentence because each refers to a separate verb or serves another purpose in the sentence.

> EXAMPLES: A loud chorus of *nays* indicated the senators did *not* favor the amendment.
>
> (*Nays* is a noun, the subject of *indicated; did not favor* is a verb, the predicate of the noun *senators.*)
>
> *Never* resisting the array of desserts, Joey could *not* lose weight.
>
> (*Never resisting* is a participial phrase modifying the subject *Joey; could not lose* is the predicate verb of *Joey.*)
>
> A problem *never* before encountered did *not* interfere with the results of the race.
>
> (The participial phrase *never before encountered* describes *problem; did not interfere* is the predicate verb for the subject *problem.*)

VERBS

VERB FORMS

This section covers the principal parts of some irregular verbs including *lie* and *lay*. The use of regular verbs like *look* and *receive* poses no real problem to most writers because the past and past participle forms end in *-ed*; it is the irregular forms that pose the most serious problems—for example, *seen*, *written*, and *begun*.

REGULAR VERBS

Regular verbs form the past tense by adding -ed to the present tense.

Present	Past	Past Perfect
walk	walked	had walked
study	studied	had studied

EXAMPLES: I *walk* to school.

Yesterday, I *walked* to the store.

Yesterday I *had walked* to school before I *walked* to the store.

IRREGULAR VERBS

Irregular verbs form the past tense in a number of different ways. Many commonly used verbs are irregular, such as the verb *to be*.

Present	Past	Past Perfect
am	was	had been
begin	began	had begun
choose	chose	had chosen
drink	drank	had drunk
see	saw	had seen
write	wrote	had written

The commonly used verbs above are probably familiar to you. Most errors in usage result from a confusion of the past and past perfect forms.

EXAMPLES: She *sees* stars.

We *saw* a new film.

After we *had seen* the film, we *went* out to dinner.

I *drink* eight glasses of water a day.

Yesterday I *drank* ten glasses of Perrier.

After I *had drunk* ten glasses of water, I *was* no longer thirsty.

TRANSITIVE AND INTRANSITIVE VERBS

The verbs *lay* and *lie*, *set* and *sit*, and *raise* and *rise* are often confused. This is probably because the verbs in each pair have similar meanings; however, one takes a direct object (transitive) to complete its meaning, and the other stands alone (intransitive). Some of the verbs are regular and some irregular. The only way to be sure to use them correctly is to memorize them. The present progressive tense is also given below because students often find this form confusing as well. (The present progressive tense signals an ongoing action in the present.)

Present	Past	Past Perfect	Present Progressive
lay (to place something)	laid	had laid	is laying
lie (to rest)	lay	had lain	is lying

to lay (transitive)

Please *lay* the books on the table.

She is *laying* the table for dinner.

He *laid* the books on the floor.

After he *had laid* the books on the floor, he *was told* to clean his room.

to lie (intransitive)

Go *lie* down.

Whose books *are lying* on the floor?

His books *lay* on the floor all day.

After the books *had lain* on the floor all day he *picked* them up.

Present	Past	Past Perfect
set (to place something)	set	had set
sit (to be seated)	sat	had sat

to set (transitive)

Just *set* that down anywhere.

I *set* the table yesterday.

Because I *had set* the table, you *had to do* the dishes.

---

to sit (intransitive)

Please *sit* down.

They *sat* down to dinner.

After they *had sat* down to dinner, they *realized* that the glasses were not crystal clear.

Present	**Past**	**Past Perfect**
raise (to move something to a higher position)	raised	had raised
rise (to stand up, to ascend)	rose	had risen

to raise (transitive)

I *raise* the flag every morning.

I *raised* my hand in class yesterday.

After I *had raised* my hand, the teacher *called* on me.

---

to rise (intransitive)

I *rise* at eight.

The price of milk *rose* by eight percent last year.

After the dough *had risen*, I *baked* it.

Remember: *Lay*, *set*, and *raise* are transitive verbs. They transfer their action to an object, which is present in the sentence. *Lie*, *sit*, and *rise* are intransitive verbs. Their action is limited to the subject of the sentence.

VERB TENSES

Tense sequence indicates a logical time sequence.

Use Present Tense

in statements about the present:

I *am* tired.

in statements about habitual conditions:

I go to bed at 10:30 *every night*.

in statements of universal truth:

I learned that the sun *is* 90 million miles from the earth.

in statements about the contents of literature and other published works:

In this book, Sandy *becomes* a nun and *writes* a book on psychology.

Use Past Tense

in statements of the finished past:

He *wrote* his first book in 1949, and it was *published* in 1952.

Use Future Tense

in statements to indicate an action or condition expected in the future:

I *will graduate* next year.

Use Present Perfect Tense

for an action that began in the past but continues into the future:

I *have lived* here all my life.

Use Past Perfect Tense

for an earlier action that is mentioned in a later action:

Cindy ate the apple that she *had picked*.

(First she picked it; then she ate it.)

Use Future Perfect Tense

for an action that will have been completed at a specific future time:

By May, I *shall have graduated*.

Use a Present Participle

for action that occurs at the same time as the verb:

Speeding down the interstate, I saw a cop's flashing lights.

Use a Perfect Participle

for action that occurred before the main verb:

Having read the directions, I started the test.

Use the Subjunctive Mood

to express a wish or state a condition contrary to fact:

If it were not raining, we could have a picnic.

in *that* clauses after verbs like *request, recommend, suggest, ask, require,* and *insist* and after such expressions as *it is important* and *it is necessary*:

It is necessary that all papers *be submitted* on time.

SUBJECT-VERB AGREEMENT

Agreement is the grammatical correspondence between the subject and the verb of a sentence: *I do; we do; you do; they do; he, she, it does.*

Every English verb has five forms, two of which are the bare form (plural) and the *-s* form (singular). Usually, singular verb forms end in *-s;* plural forms do not.

RULES GOVERNING SUBJECT-VERB AGREEMENT

A verb must agree with its subject, not with any additive phrase in the sentence such as a prepositional or verbal phrase. Ignore such phrases.

Your *copy* of the rules *is* on the desk.

Ms. Craig's *record* of community service and outstanding teaching *qualifies* her for a promotion.

In an inverted sentence beginning with a prepositional phrase, the verb still agrees with its subject.

At the end of the summer *come* the best *sales.*

Under the house *are* some old Mason *jars.*

Prepositional phrases beginning with compound prepositions such as *along with, together with, in addition to,* and *as well as* should be ignored because they do not affect subject-verb agreement.

> *Gladys Knight,* as well as the Pips, *is* riding the midnight train to Georgia.

A verb must agree with its subject, not its subject complement.

> *Taxes are* a problem.

> A *problem is* taxes.

When a sentence begins with an expletive such as *there, here,* or *it,* the verb agrees with the subject, not the expletive.

> Surely, there *are* several *alumni* who would be interested in forming a group.

> There *are* 50 *students* in my English class.

> There *is* a horrifying *study* on child abuse in *Psychology Today.*

Indefinite pronouns such as *each, either, one, everyone, everybody,* and *everything* are singular.

> *Somebody* in Detroit *loves* me.

> *Does either* [one] of you have a pencil?

> *Neither* of my brothers *has* a car.

Indefinite pronouns such as *several, few, both,* and *many* are plural.

> *Both* of my sorority sisters *have* decided to live off campus.

> *Few seek* the enlightenment of transcendental meditation.

Indefinite pronouns such as *all, some, most,* and *none* may be singular or plural depending on their referents.

> *Some* of the food *is* cold.

> *Some* of the vegetables *are* cold.

> I can think of some retorts, but *none seem* appropriate.

> *None* of the children *is* as sweet as Sally.

Fractions such as *one-half* and *one-third* may be singular or plural depending on the referent.

> *Half* of the mail *has* been delivered.

Half of the letters *have* been read.

Subjects joined by *and* take a plural verb unless the subjects are thought to be one item or unit.

Jim and *Tammy were* televangelists.

Simon and Garfunkel is my favorite group.

In cases when the subjects are joined by *or, nor, either…or,* or *neither…nor,* the verb must agree with the subject closer to it.

Either the teacher or the *students are* responsible.

Neither the students nor the *teacher is* responsible.

Relative pronouns such as *who, which,* or *that,* which refer to plural antecedents, require plural verbs. However, when the relative pronoun refers to a singular subject, the pronoun takes a singular verb.

She is one of the girls *who cheer* on Friday nights.

She is the only cheerleader *who has* a broken leg.

Subjects preceded by *every, each,* and *many a* are singular.

Every man, woman, and child *was* given a life preserver.

Each undergraduate *is* required to pass a proficiency exam.

Many a tear *has* to fall before one matures.

A collective noun, such as *audience, faculty, jury,* etc., requires a singular verb when the group is regarded as a whole, and a plural verb when the members of the group are regarded as individuals.

The *jury has* made its decision.

The *faculty are* preparing their grade rosters.

Subjects preceded by *the number of* or *the percentage of* are singular, while subjects preceded by *a number of* or *a percentage of* are plural.

The number of vacationers in Florida *increases* every year.

A number of vacationers *are* young couples.

Titles of books, companies, name brands, and groups are singular or plural depending on their meaning.

Great Expectations is my favorite novel.

The *Rolling Stones are* performing in the Super Dome.

Certain nouns of Latin and Greek origin have unusual singular and plural forms.

Singular	Plural
criterion	criteria
alumnus	alumni
datum	data
medium	media

The *data are* available for inspection.

The only *criterion* for membership *is* a high GPA.

Some nouns, such as *deer*, *shrimp*, and *sheep,* have the same spellings for both their singular and plural forms. In these cases, the meaning of the sentence will determine whether they are singular or plural.

Deer are beautiful animals.

The spotted *deer is* licking the sugar cube.

Some nouns, like *scissors*, *jeans*, and *wages,* have plural forms but no singular counterparts. These nouns almost always take plural verbs.

The *scissors are* on the table.

My new *jeans fit* me like a glove.

Words used as examples, not as grammatical parts of the sentence, require singular verbs.

Can't is the contraction for "cannot."

Cats is the plural form of "cat."

Mathematical expressions of subtraction and division require singular verbs, but expressions of addition and multiplication take either singular or plural verbs.

Ten divided by two equals five.

Five times two equals ten.

OR   Five times two equal ten.

Nouns expressing time, distance, weight, and measurement are singular when they refer to a unit and plural when they refer to separate items.

Fifty yards is a short distance.

Ten years have passed since I finished college.

Expressions of quantity are usually plural.

Nine out of ten dentists *recommend* that their patients floss.

Some nouns ending in *-ics,* such as *economics* and *ethics*, take singular verbs when they refer to principles or a field of study; however, when they refer to individual practices, they usually take plural verbs.

Ethics is being taught in the spring.

His unusual business *ethics are* what got him into trouble.

Some nouns, like *measles*, *news*, and *calculus,* appear to be plural but are actually singular in number. These nouns require singular verbs.

Measles is a very contagious disease.

Calculus requires great skill in algebra.

A verbal noun (infinitive or gerund) serving as a subject is treated as singular, even if the object of the verbal phrase is plural.

Hiding your mistakes *does* not make them go away.

To run five miles *is* my goal.

A noun phrase or clause acting as the subject of a sentence requires a singular verb.

What I need is to be loved.

Whether there is any connection between them is unknown.

Clauses beginning with *what* may be singular or plural depending on the meaning, that is, whether *what* means "the thing" or "the things."

What I want for Christmas is a new motorcycle.

What matters are his ideas.

A plural subject followed by a singular appositive requires a plural verb; similarly, a singular subject followed by a plural appositive requires a singular verb.

When the girls throw a party, *they* each *bring* a gift.

The *board,* all ten members, *is* meeting today.

Drill 5

DIRECTIONS: Choose the correct replacement for the underlined words.

---

1. If you <u>had been concerned</u> about Marilyn, you <u>would have went</u> to greater lengths to ensure her safety.

   (A) had been concern . . . would have gone

   (B) was concerned . . . would have gone

   (C) had been concerned . . . would have gone

   (D) No change is necessary.

2. Susan <u>laid</u> in bed too long and missed her class.

   (A) lays   (C) lied

   (B) lay   (D) No change is necessary.

3. The Great Wall of China <u>is</u> fifteen hundred miles long; it <u>was built</u> in the third century B.C.

   (A) was . . . was built   (C) has been . . . was built

   (B) is . . . is built   (D) No change is necessary.

4. The professor <u>was retiring</u> in February.

   (A) is retiring   (C) is retired

   (B) has retired   (D) No change is necessary.

5. The ceiling of the Sistine Chapel <u>was</u> painted by Michelangelo; it <u>depicted</u> scenes from the Creation in the Old Testament.

   (A) was . . . depicts   (C) has been . . . depicting

   (B) is . . . depicts   (D) No change is necessary.

6. After Christmas <u>comes</u> the best sales.

   (A) has come   (C) is coming

   (B) come   (D) No change is necessary.

7. The bakery's specialty <u>are</u> wedding cakes.

   (A) is   (C) be

   (B) were   (D) No change is necessary.

8. Every man, woman, and child <u>were given</u> a life preserver.

    (A) have been given   (C) was given

    (B) had gave   (D) No change is necessary.

9. Hiding your mistakes <u>don't</u> make them go away.

    (A) doesn't   (C) have not

    (B) do not   (D) No change is necessary.

10. The Board of Regents <u>has recommended</u> a tuition increase.

    (A) have recommended   (C) had recommended

    (B) has recommend   (D) No change is necessary.

Drill 5 Answers

1.	(C)	4.	(A)	7.	(A)	10.	(D)
2.	(B)	5.	(A)	8.	(C)		
3.	(D)	6.	(B)	9.	(A)		

PRONOUNS

PRONOUN CASE

Appropriate pronoun case is essential to effective, understandable essay writing. Pronoun case can either be nominative or objective.

Nominative Case	Objective Case
I	me
he	him
she	her
we	us
they	them
who	whom

This review section answers the most frequently asked grammar questions: when to use *I* and when to use *me*; when to use *who* and when to use *whom*.

Some writers avoid *whom* altogether, and instead of distinguishing between *I* and *me*, many writers incorrectly use *myself*.

Use the Nominative Case (Subject Pronouns)

for the subject of a sentence:

> *We* students studied until early morning for the final.

> Alan and *I* "burned the midnight oil," too.

for pronouns in apposition to the subject:

> Only two students, Alex and *I*, were asked to report on the meeting.

for the predicate nominative/subject complement:

> The actors nominated for the award were *she* and *I*.

for the subject of an elliptical clause:

> Molly is more experienced than *he*.

for the subject of a subordinate clause:

> Robert is the driver *who* reported the accident.

for the complement of an infinitive with no expressed subject:

> I would not want to be *he*.

Use the Objective Case (Object Pronouns)

for the direct object of a sentence:

> Mary invited *us* to her party.

for the object of a preposition:

> The books that were torn belonged to *her*.

> Just between you and *me*, I'm bored.

for the indirect object of a sentence:

> Walter gave a dozen red roses to *her*.

for the appositive of a direct object:

> The committee elected two delegates, Barbara and *me*.

for the object of an infinitive:

> The young boy wanted to help *us* paint the fence.

for the object of a gerund:

Enlisting *him* was surprisingly easy.

for the object of a past participle:

Having called the other students and *us,* the secretary went home for the day.

for a pronoun that precedes an infinitive (the subject of an infinitive):

The supervisor told *him* to work late.

for the complement of an infinitive with an expressed subject:

The fans thought the best player to be *him.*

for the object of an elliptical clause:

Susan writes Shawn oftener than *me.*

When a conjunction connects two pronouns or a pronoun and a noun, remove the "and" and the other pronoun or noun to determine the correct pronoun form:

Mom gave ~~Tom and~~ myself a piece of cake.

Mom gave ~~Tom and~~ I a piece of cake.

Mom gave ~~Tom and~~ me a piece of cake.

Removal of these words reveals what the correct pronoun should be:

Mom gave *me* a piece of cake.

The only pronouns that are acceptable after *between* and other prepositions are *me, her, him, them,* and *whom.* When deciding between *who* and *whom,* try substituting *he* for *who* and *him* for *whom;* then follow these easy transformation steps:

1. Isolate the *who* clause or the *whom* clause:

   whom we can trust

2. Invert the word order, if necessary. Place the words in the clause in the natural order of an English sentence, with the subject followed by the verb:

   we can trust whom

3. Read the final form with the *he* or *him* inserted:

> We can trust ~~whom~~ him.

When a pronoun follows a comparative conjunction like *than* or *as*, complete the elliptical construction to help you determine which pronoun is correct.

> EXAMPLE: She has more credit hours than me [do].
>
> She has more credit hours than I [do].

PRONOUN-ANTECEDENT AGREEMENT

Using the appropriate pronoun antecedent is very important to the effective essay. Pronouns must agree with their antecedent in number, gender, and person. An antecedent is a noun or pronoun to which another noun or pronoun refers.

Here are the two basic rules for pronoun reference-antecedent agreement:

1. Every pronoun must have a conspicuous antecedent.

2. Every pronoun must agree with its antecedent in number, gender, and person.

When an antecedent is one of dual gender, like *student*, *singer*, *artist*, *person*, *citizen*, etc., use *his or her*. Some careful writers change the antecedent to a plural noun to avoid using the sexist, singular masculine pronoun *his*:

> INCORRECT: Everyone hopes that he will win the lottery.
>
> CORRECT: Most people hope that they will win the lottery.

Ordinarily, the relative pronoun *who* is used to refer to people, *which* and *that* to refer to things and places, and *where* to refer to places. The distinction between *that* and *which* is a grammatical distinction. When differentiating something from a larger class of which it is a member, use 'that." When the subject is not being distinguished from a larger class, use "which."

> EXAMPLE: I bought the sweater *that* was on sale.
>
> EXAMPLE: There were many sweaters, all of *which* were on sale.

Many writers prefer to use *that* to refer to collective nouns.

> EXAMPLE: A family *that* traces its lineage is usually proud of its roots.

Many writers are not sure when to use the reflexive case pronoun and when to use the possessive case pronoun. The rules governing the usage of the reflexive case and the possessive case are quite simple.

Use the Possessive Case

before a noun in a sentence:

Our friend moved during the semester break.

My dog has fleas, but *her* dog doesn't.

before a gerund in a sentence:

Her running helps to relieve stress.

His driving terrified her.

as a noun in a sentence:

Mine was the last test graded that day.

to indicate possession:

Karen never allows anyone else to drive *her* car.

Brad thought the book was *his,* but it was someone else's.

Use the Reflexive Case

as a direct object to rename the subject:

I kicked *myself.*

as an indirect object to rename the subject:

Henry bought *himself* a tie.

as an object of a prepositional phrase:

Tom and Lillie baked the pie for *themselves.*

as a predicate pronoun:

She hasn't been *herself* lately.

Do not use the reflexive in place of the nominative pronoun:

INCORRECT: Both Randy and *myself* plan to go.

CORRECT: Both Randy and *I* plan to go.

INCORRECT: *Yourself* will take on the challenges of college.

CORRECT: *You* will take on the challenges of college.

INCORRECT: Either James or *yourself* will paint the mural.

CORRECT: Either James or *you* will paint the mural.

Watch out for careless use of the pronoun form:

INCORRECT: George *hisself* told me it was true.

CORRECT: George *himself* told me it was true.

INCORRECT: They washed the car *theirselves*.

CORRECT: They washed the car *themselves*.

Notice that reflexive pronouns are not set off by commas:

INCORRECT: Mary, *herself*, gave him the diploma.

CORRECT: Mary *herself* gave him the diploma.

INCORRECT: I will do it, *myself*.

CORRECT: I will do it *myself*.

PRONOUN REFERENCE

Pronoun reference requires you to determine whether the antecedent is conspicuously written in the sentence or whether it is remote, implied, ambiguous, or vague, none of which results in clear writing. Make sure that every italicized pronoun has a conspicuous antecedent and that one pronoun substitutes only for another noun or pronoun, not for an idea or a sentence.

Pronoun Reference Problems Occur

when a pronoun refers to either of two antecedents:

INCORRECT: Joanna told Kim that *she* was getting fat.

CORRECT: Joanna told Kim, "I'm getting fat."

when a pronoun refers to a remote antecedent:

INCORRECT: A strange car followed us closely, and *he* kept blinking his lights at us.

CORRECT: A strange car followed us closely, and its driver kept blinking his lights at us.

when *this*, *that*, and *which* refer to the general idea of the preceding clause or sentence rather than the preceding word:

INCORRECT: The students could not understand the pronoun reference handout, *which* annoyed them very much.

CORRECT: The students could not understand the pronoun reference handout, a fact which annoyed them very much.

OR The students were annoyed because they could not understand the pronoun reference handout.

when a pronoun refers to an unexpressed but implied noun:

INCORRECT: My husband wants me to knit a blanket, but I'm not interested in *it*.

CORRECT: My husband wants me to knit a blanket, but I'm not interested in knitting.

when *it* is used as something other than an expletive to postpone a subject:

INCORRECT: *It* says in today's paper that the newest shipment of cars from Detroit, Michigan, seems to include outright imitations of European models.

CORRECT: Today's paper says that the newest shipment of cars from Detroit, Michigan, seems to include outright imitations of European models.

INCORRECT: The football game was canceled because *it* was bad weather.

CORRECT: The football game was canceled because the weather was bad.

when *they* or *it* is used to refer to something or someone indefinitely, and there is no definite antecedent:

INCORRECT: At the job placement office, *they* told me to stop wearing ripped jeans to my interviews.

CORRECT: At the job placement office, the interviewer told me to stop wearing ripped jeans to my interviews.

when the pronoun does not agree with its antecedent in number, gender, or person:

INCORRECT: Any graduate student, if *they* are interested, may attend the lecture.

CORRECT: Any graduate student, if he or she is interested, may attend the lecture.

OR   All graduate students, if they are interested, may attend the lecture.

INCORRECT: Many Americans are concerned that the overuse of slang and colloquialisms is corrupting *the* language.

CORRECT: Many Americans are concerned that the overuse of slang and colloquialisms is corrupting their language.

INCORRECT: The Board of Regents will not make a decision about tuition increase until *their* March meeting.

CORRECT: The Board of Regents will not make a decision about tuition increase until its March meeting.

when a noun or pronoun has no expressed antecedent:

INCORRECT: In the President's address to the union, *he* promised no more taxes.

CORRECT: In his address to the union, the President promised no more taxes.

Drill 6

DIRECTIONS: Choose the correct replacement for the underlined words.

1. My friend and <u>myself</u> bought tickets for *Cats*.

(A) I

(B) me

(C) us

(D) No change is necessary.

2. Alcohol and tobacco are harmful to <u>whomever</u> consumes them.

   (A) whom   (C) whoever

   (B) who   (D) No change is necessary.

3. Everyone is wondering <u>whom</u> her successor will be.

   (A) who   (C) who'll

   (B) whose   (D) No change is necessary.

4. Rosa Lee's parents discovered that it was <u>her who</u> wrecked the family car.

   (A) she who   (C) her whom

   (B) she whom   (D) No change is necessary.

5. A student <u>who</u> wishes to protest <u>his or her</u> grades must file a formal grievance in the Dean's office.

   (A) that . . . their   (C) whom . . . their

   (B) which . . . his   (D) No change is necessary.

6. One of the best things about working for this company is that <u>they pay</u> big bonuses.

   (A) it pays   (C) they paid

   (B) they always pay   (D) No change is necessary.

7. Every car owner should be sure that <u>their</u> automobile insurance is adequate.

   (A) your   (C) its

   (B) his or her   (D) No change is necessary.

8. My mother wants me to become a teacher, but I'm not interested in <u>it</u>.

   (A) this   (C) that

   (B) teaching   (D) No change is necessary.

9. Since I had not paid my electric bill, <u>they</u> sent me a delinquent notice.

   (A) the power company   (C) it

   (B) he   (D) No change is necessary.

10. Margaret seldom wrote to her sister when <u>she</u> was away at college.

    (A) who   (C) her sister

    (B) her   (D) No change is necessary.

Drill 6 Answers

1. (A)		4. (A)		7. (B)		10. (C)
2. (C)		5. (D)		8. (B)		
3. (A)		6. (A)		9. (A)		

ADJECTIVES AND ADVERBS

CORRECT USAGE

Adjectives are words that modify nouns or pronouns by defining, describing, limiting, or qualifying those nouns or pronouns.

Adverbs are words that modify verbs, adjectives, or other adverbs. They express ideas such as time, place, manner, cause, and degree. Use adjectives as subject complements with linking verbs; use adverbs with action verbs.

EXAMPLE:	The old man's speech was *eloquent*.	ADJECTIVE
	Mr. Brown speaks *eloquently*.	ADVERB
	Please be *careful*.	ADJECTIVE
	Please drive *carefully*.	ADVERB

Good or Well

Good is an adjective; its use as an adverb is colloquial and nonstandard.

INCORRECT:	He plays *good*.
CORRECT:	He looks *good* for an octogenarian.
	The quiche tastes very *good*.

Well may be either an adverb or an adjective. As an adjective, *well* means "in good health."

CORRECT:	He plays *well*.	ADVERB
	My mother is not *well*.	ADJECTIVE

Bad or Badly

Bad is an adjective used after sense verbs such as *look, smell, taste, feel,* or *sound,* or after linking verbs such as *is, am, are, was,* or *were.*

INCORRECT: I feel *badly* about the delay.

CORRECT: I feel *bad* about the delay.

Badly is an adverb used after all other verbs.

INCORRECT: It doesn't hurt very *bad.*

CORRECT: It doesn't hurt very *badly*.

Real or Really

Real is an adjective; its use as an adverb is colloquial and nonstandard. It means "genuine."

INCORRECT: He writes *real* well.

CORRECT: This is *real* leather.

Really is an adverb meaning "very."

INCORRECT: This is *really* diamond.

CORRECT: Have a *really* nice day.

EXAMPLE: This is *real* amethyst.   ADJECTIVE

This is *really* difficult.   ADVERB

This is a *real* crisis   ADJECTIVE

This is *really* important.   ADVERB

Sort Of and Kind Of

Sort of and *kind of* are often misused in written English by writers who actually mean *rather* or *somewhat.*

INCORRECT: Jan was *kind of* saddened by the results of the test.

CORRECT: Jan was *somewhat* saddened by the results of the test.

Drill 7

1. Although the band performed <u>badly</u>, I feel <u>real bad</u> about missing the concert.

   (A) badly . . . real badly

   (B) bad . . . badly

   (C) badly . . . very bad

   (D) No change is necessary.

2. These reports are <u>relative simple</u> to prepare.

   (A) relatively simple

   (B) relative simply

   (C) relatively simply

   (D) No change is necessary.

3. He did <u>very well</u> on the test although his writing skills are not <u>good</u>.

   (A) real well . . . good

   (B) very good . . . good

   (C) good . . . great

   (D) No change is necessary.

4. Shake the medicine bottle <u>good</u> before you open it.

   (A) very good

   (B) real good

   (C) well

   (D) No change is necessary.

5. Though she speaks <u>fluently</u>, she writes <u>poorly</u> because she doesn't observe <u>closely</u> or think <u>clear</u>.

   (A) fluently . . . poorly . . . closely . . . clearly

   (B) fluent . . . poor . . . close . . . clear

   (C) fluently . . . poor . . . closely . . . clear

   (D) No change is necessary.

Drill 7 Answers

1.	(C)	4.	(C)
2.	(A)	5.	(A)
3.	(D)		

FAULTY COMPARISONS

Most problems with adjectives and adverbs concern what is commonly called the use of degrees of comparison. There are three forms of modifiers: positive, comparative, and superlative.

Positive	Comparative	Superlative
good	better	best
old	older	oldest
friendly	friendlier	friendliest
lonely	lonelier	loneliest
talented	more talented	most talented
beautiful	more beautiful	most beautiful

The *positive* form of a modifier describes a thing, action, or quality without comparing it to another.

EXAMPLES: Jan and her mother have a *close* relationship.

Kurt is a *talented* musician.

A professional mountaineer always climbs *carefully*.

The *comparative* form of a modifier compares a thing, action, or quality to one other thing, action, or quality.

EXAMPLES: The relationship between Jan and her sister is *closer* than the relationship between Jan and her mother.

Kurt is a *more talented* musician than Frank.

A professional mountaineer climbs *more carefully* than a typical weekend mountain climber.

The *superlative* form of a modifier compares a thing, quality, or action to two or more other things, qualities, or actions. Often the comparison is indicated by the words "of all."

EXAMPLES: The *closest* relationship *of all* between siblings often occurs with twins.

The *most talented* artists still have difficulty making a living by selling their work.

Anthony is the *most experienced* in the Piedmont Mountain Climbing Club.

Most adjectives and adverbs of one- and two-syllable words add "-er" or "-est" to form the comparative and superlative forms. Modifiers of three syllables or more use "more" or "less" for the comparative form and "most" or "least" for the superlative form.

Common errors occur when a speaker or writer uses both methods of forming the comparative or superlative forms for a description or uses the wrong method to form the appropriate degree.

INCORRECT: Jack is *more taller* than Gordon. (As a one-syllable adjective, *tall* forms the comparative degree by adding only *-er.*)

CORRECT: Jack is *taller* than Gordon.

INCORRECT: The fall leaves are *beautifuler* this year than last. (As a three-syllable word, *beautiful* forms the comparative degree with *more* or *less.*)

CORRECT: The fall leaves are *more beautiful* this year than last.

INCORRECT: The *most shortest* poem is the one I want to memorize. (*Short*, a one-syllable word, forms the superlative degree with *-er* or *-est.*)

CORRECT: The *shortest* poem is the one I want to memorize.

A few adjectives and adverbs have irregular forms for the comparative and superlative degrees. The descriptive word changes to a new word for the following:

Adjective/Adverb	Comparative	Superlative
good or well	better	best
many or much	more	most
ill, bad, or badly	worse	worst
far	farther or further	farthest or furthest
little	less or littler	least or littlest

A dictionary indicates the correct formation of comparative and superlative degrees of words and the occasion for the use of each.

EXAMPLES: We must walk *far* to get enough exercise.

We must walk *farther* than we have already to lose a pound this week.

Whoever reads *furthest* in the novel tonight will lead the class discussion tomorrow.

Some adjectives and adverbs cannot be used in comparative or superlative forms. These words are called *absolutes*. The meaning of an absolute has no potential for comparison or superlative. Frequently used absolute modifiers are "dead," "empty," "full," "perfect," "unique," "false," "final," and "true." Sometimes, however, an absolute can be used with "nearly."

EXAMPLE: A *nearly empty* gas tank caused Jorge to be late.

Drill 8

DIRECTIONS: Correct any error in the form of adjective or adverb used in the following sentences.

1. The recent tornado caused the most dreadfulest damage of any recent storm.

2. The new machine works goodest for me than for other employees.

3. A last minute change made the hike further than we had expected.

4. Your feeling worst today than yesterday concerns me.

5. Who is the best informed, Beth or Ricky?

6. The most warmest weather of all the months occurs often in August.

DIRECTIONS: Put the following words into the appropriate comparative and superlative forms.

7. high

8. much

9. courteous

10. smoothly

Drill 8 Answers

1. The recent tornado caused the <u>most dreadful</u> damage of any recent storm.

2. The new machine works <u>better</u> for me than for other employees.

3. A last minute change made the hike <u>farther</u> than we had expected.

4. Your feeling <u>worse</u> today than yesterday concerns me.

5. Who is the <u>better</u> informed, Beth or Ricky?

6. The <u>warmest</u> weather of all the months occurs often in August.

	Positive	Comparative	Superlative
7.	high	higher	highest
8.	much	more	most
9.	courteous	more or less courteous	most or least courteous
10.	smoothly	more or less smoothly	most or least smoothly

PUNCTUATION

COMMAS

Commas should be placed according to standard rules of punctuation for purpose, clarity, and effect. The proper use of commas is explained in the following rules and examples.

In a series, when more than one adjective describes a noun, use a comma to separate and emphasize each adjective. The comma takes the place of the word "and" in the series.

> the long, dark passageway
>
> another confusing, sleepless night
>
> an elaborate, complex, brilliant plan
>
> the old, gray, crumpled hat

Some adjective-noun combinations are thought of as one word. In these cases, the adjective in front of the adjective-noun combination needs no comma. If you inserted *and* between the adjective-noun combination, it would not make sense.

a stately oak tree

an exceptional wine glass

my worst report card

a china dinner plate

The comma is also used to separate words, phrases, and whole ideas (clauses); it still takes the place of *and* when used this way.

an apple, a pear, a fig, and a banana

a lovely lady, an elegant dress, and many admirers

She lowered the shade, closed the curtain, turned off the light, and went to bed.

The only question that exists about the use of commas in a series is whether or not one should be used before the final item. It is standard usage to do so although many newspapers and magazines have stopped using the final comma. Occasionally, the omission of the comma can be confusing.

INCORRECT: He got on his horse, tracked a rabbit and a deer and rode on to Canton.

CORRECT: He got on his horse, tracked a rabbit and a deer, and rode on to Canton.

INCORRECT: We planned the trip with Mary and Harold, Susan, Dick and Joan, Gregory and Jean and Charles.

CORRECT: We planned the trip with Mary and Harold, Susan, Dick and Joan, Gregory and Jean, and Charles.

Usually if a dependent clause or a phrase of more than five or six words precedes the subject at the beginning of a sentence, a comma is used to set it off.

After last night's fiasco at the disco, she couldn't bear the thought of looking at him again.

Whenever I try to talk about politics, my wife leaves the room.

Provided you have said nothing, they will never guess who you are.

It is not necessary to use a comma with a short sentence.

In January she will go to Switzerland.

After a rest I'll feel better.

During the day no one is home.

If an introductory phrase includes a verb form that is being used as another part of speech (a verbal), it must be followed by a comma.

INCORRECT:	When eating Mary never looked up from her plate.
CORRECT:	When eating, Mary never looked up from her plate.

INCORRECT:	Because of her desire to follow her faith in James wavered.
CORRECT:	Because of her desire to follow, her faith in James wavered.

INCORRECT:	Having decided to leave Mary James wrote her a letter.
CORRECT:	Having decided to leave Mary, James wrote her a letter.

To separate sentences with two main ideas, you need to be able to recognize compound sentences. When a sentence contains more than two subjects and verbs (clauses) and when the two clauses are joined by a conjunction (*and, but, or, nor, for,* or *yet*), use a comma before the conjunction to show that another clause is coming.

I thought I knew the poem by heart, but he showed me three lines I had forgotten.

Are we really interested in helping the children, or are we more concerned with protecting our good names?

He is supposed to leave tomorrow, but he is not ready to go.

Jim knows you are disappointed, and he has known it for a long time.

If the two parts of the sentence are short and closely related, it is not necessary to use a comma.

He threw the ball and the dog ran after it.

Jane played the piano and Michael danced.

Be careful not to confuse a sentence that has a compound verb and a single subject with a compound sentence. If the subject is the same for both verbs, there is no need for a comma.

INCORRECT:	Charles sent some flowers, and wrote a long letter explaining why he had not been able to attend.
CORRECT:	Charles sent some flowers and wrote a long letter explaining why he had not been able to attend.

INCORRECT:	Last Thursday we went to the concert with Julia, and afterwards dined at an old Italian restaurant.
CORRECT:	Last Thursday we went to the concert with Julia and afterwards dined at an old Italian restaurant.

INCORRECT:	For the third time, the teacher explained that the literacy level for high school students was much lower than it had been in previous years, and this time wrote the statistics on the board for everyone to see.
CORRECT:	For the third time, the teacher explained that the literacy level for high school students was much lower than it had been in previous years and this time wrote the statistics on the board for everyone to see.

In general, words and phrases that stop the flow of the sentence or are unnecessary for the main idea are set off by commas. This includes

Abbreviations after Names:

Did you invite John Paul, Jr., and his sister?

Martha Harris, Ph.D., will be the speaker tonight.

Interjections (an Exclamation Without Added Grammatical Connection):

Oh, I'm so glad to see you.

I tried so hard, alas, to do it.

Hey, let me out of here.

Direct Address:

Roy, won't you open the door for the dog?

I can't understand, Mother, what you are trying to say.

May I ask, Mr. President, why you called us together?

Hey, lady, watch out for that car!

Tag Questions:

I'm really hungry, aren't you?

Jerry looks like his father, doesn't he?

Geographical Names and Addresses:

The concert will be held in Chicago, Illinois, on August 12.

The letter was addressed to Mrs. Marion Heartwell, 1881 Pine Lane, Palo Alto, California 95824.

(Note: No comma is needed before the zip code because it is already clearly set off from the state name.)

Transitional Words and Phrases:

On the other hand, I hope he gets better.

In addition, the phone rang constantly this afternoon.

I am, nevertheless, going to the beach on Sunday.

You'll find, therefore, that no one is more loyal than I am.

Parenthetical Words and Phrases:

You will become, I believe, a great statesman.

We know, of course, that this is the only thing to do.

The Mannes affair was, to put it mildly, a surprise.

Unusual Word Order:

The dress, new and crisp, hung in the closet.

Intently, she stared out the window.

Nonrestrictive Elements:

Parts of a sentence that modify other parts are sometimes essential to the meaning of the sentence and sometimes not. When a modifying word or group of words is not vital to the meaning of the sentence, it is set off by commas. Since it does not restrict the meaning of the words it modifies, it is called "nonrestrictive." Modifiers that are essential to the meaning of the sentence are called "restrictive" and are not set off by commas.

ESSENTIAL:	The girl *who wrote the story* is my sister.
NONESSENTIAL:	My sister, *the girl who wrote the story*, has always loved to write.

ESSENTIAL:	John Milton's *Paradise Lost* tells a remarkable story.
NONESSENTIAL:	Dante's greatest work, *The Divine Comedy,* marked the beginning of the Renaissance.

ESSENTIAL:	The cup *that is on the piano* is the one I want.
NONESSENTIAL:	The cup, *which my brother gave me last year*, is on the piano.

ESSENTIAL:	The people *who arrived late* were not seated.
NONESSENTIAL:	George, *who arrived late*, was not seated.

Direct Quotations:

Most direct quotes or quoted materials are set off from the rest of the sentence by commas.

"Please read your part more loudly," the director insisted.

"I won't know what to do," said Michael, "if you leave me."

The teacher said sternly, "I will not dismiss this class until I have silence."

Who was it who said, "Do not ask for whom the bell tolls; it tolls for thee"?

Note: Commas always go inside the closing quotation mark, even if the comma is not part of the material being quoted.

Be careful not to set off indirect quotes or quotes that are used as subjects or complements.

She said she would never come back. (indirect quote)

"To be or not to be" is the famous beginning of a soliloquy in Shakespeare's *Hamlet.* (subject)

Back then my favorite poem was "Evangeline." (complement)

Contrasting Elements:

Her intelligence, not her beauty, got her the job.

Your plan will take you a little further from, rather than closer to, your destination.

It was a reasonable, though not appealing, idea.

He wanted glory, but found happiness instead.

Dates:

Both forms of the date are acceptable.

She will arrive on April 6, 1998.

He left on 5 December 1980.

In January 1967, he handed in his resignation.

On October 22, 1992, Frank and Julie were married.

Usually, when a subordinate clause is at the end of a sentence, no comma is necessary preceding the clause. However, when a subordinate clause introduces a sentence, a comma should be used after the clause.

Some common subordinating conjunctions are

after	even though	till
although	if	unless
as	inasmuch as	until
as if	since	when
because	so that	whenever
before	though	while

SEMICOLONS

Correct semicolon usage requires you to be able to distinguish between the semicolon, the comma, and the colon. This review section covers the basic uses of the semicolon: to separate independent clauses not joined by a coordinating conjunction, to separate independent clauses separated by a conjunctive adverb, and to separate items in a series containing internal commas. It is important to be consistent; if you use a semicolon between *any* of the items in the series, you must use semicolons to separate *all* of the items in the series.

Usually a comma follows the conjunctive adverb. Note also that a period can be used to separate two sentences joined by a conjunctive adverb. Some common conjunctive adverbs are

accordingly	indeed	now
besides	in fact	on the other hand
consequently	moreover	otherwise
finally	nevertheless	perhaps
furthermore	next	still
however	nonetheless	therefore

Then is also used as a conjunctive adverb, but it is not usually followed by a comma.

Use the Semicolon

to separate independent clauses that are not joined by a coordinating conjunction:

I understand how to use commas; the semicolon I have not yet mastered.

to separate two independent clauses connected by a conjunctive adverb:

He took great care with his work; *therefore,* he was very successful.

to combine two independent clauses connected by a coordinating conjunction if either or both of the clauses contain other internal punctuation:

Success in college, some maintain, requires intelligence, industry, and perseverance; *but* others, fewer in number, assert that only personality is important.

to separate items in a series when each item has internal punctuation:

I bought an old, dilapidated chair; an antique table which was in beautiful condition; and a new, ugly, blue and white rug.

Call our customer service line for assistance: Arizona, 1-800-555-6020; New Mexico, 1-800-555-5050; California, 1-800-555-3140; or Nevada, 1-800-555-3214.

Do Not Use the Semicolon

to precede an explanation or summary of the first clause:

> WEAK: The first week of camping was wonderful; we lived in cabins instead of tents.

> BETTER: The first week of camping was wonderful: we lived in cabins instead of tents.

Note: Although the sentences above are punctuated correctly, the use of the semicolon provides a miscue, suggesting that the second clause is merely an extension, not an explanation, of the first clause. The colon provides a better clue.

to separate a dependent and an independent clause:

> INCORRECT: You should not make such statements; even though they are correct.

> CORRECT: You should not make such statements even though they are correct.

to separate an appositive phrase or clause from a sentence:

> INCORRECT: His immediate aim in life is centered around two things; becoming an engineer and learning to fly an airplane.

> CORRECT: His immediate aim in life is centered around two things: becoming an engineer and learning to fly an airplane.

to substitute for a comma:

> INCORRECT: My roommate also likes sports; particularly football, basketball, and baseball.

> CORRECT: My roommate also likes sports, particularly football, basketball, and baseball.

to set off other types of phrases or clauses from a sentence:

> INCORRECT: Being of a cynical mind; I should ask for a recount of the ballots.

> CORRECT: Being of a cynical mind, I should ask for a recount of the ballots.

> INCORRECT: The next meeting of the club has been postponed two weeks; inasmuch as both the president and vice president are out of town.

CORRECT: The next meeting of the club has been postponed two weeks, inasmuch as both the president and vice president are out of town.

Note that the semicolon is not a terminal mark of punctuation; therefore, it should not be followed by a capital letter unless the first word in the second clause ordinarily requires capitalization.

COLONS

While it is true that a colon is used to precede a list, one must also make sure that a complete sentence precedes the colon. The colon signals the reader that a list, explanation, or restatement of the preceding will follow. It is like an arrow, indicating that something is to follow. The difference between the colon and the semicolon and between the colon and the period is that the colon is an introductory mark, not a terminal mark. Look at the following examples:

The Constitution provides for a separation of powers among the three branches of government.

government. The period signals a new sentence.

government; The semicolon signals an interrelated sentence.

government, The comma signals a coordinating conjunction followed by another independent clause.

government: The colon signals a list.

The Constitution provides for a separation of powers among the three branches of government: executive, legislative, and judicial.

Observe the following rules to ensure that a complete sentence precedes a colon.

Use the colon to introduce a list (one item may constitute a list):

I hate this one course: English.

Three plays by William Shakespeare will be presented in repertory this summer at the University of Michigan: *Hamlet, Macbeth,* and *Othello.*

To introduce a list preceded by *as follows* or *the following*:

The reasons he cited for his success are as follows: integrity, honesty, industry, and a pleasant disposition.

To separate two independent clauses, when the second clause is a restatement or explanation of the first:

> All of my high school teachers said one thing in particular: college is going to be difficult.

To introduce a word or word group that is a restatement, explanation, or summary of the first sentence:

> These two things he loved: an honest man and a beautiful woman.

To introduce a formal appositive:

> I am positive there is one appeal that you can't overlook: money.

To separate the introductory words from a quotation that follows, if the quotation is formal, long, or paragraphed separately:

> The actor then stated: "I would rather be able to adequately play the part of Hamlet than to perform a miraculous operation, deliver a great lecture, or build a magnificent skyscraper."

The colon should be used only after statements that are grammatically complete.

Do *not* use a colon after a verb:

> INCORRECT: My favorite holidays are: Christmas, New Year's Eve, and Halloween.
>
> CORRECT: My favorite holidays are Christmas, New Year's Eve, and Halloween.

Do *not* use a colon after a preposition:

> INCORRECT: I enjoy different ethnic foods such as: Greek, Chinese, and Italian.
>
> CORRECT: I enjoy different ethnic foods such as Greek, Chinese, and Italian.

Do *not* use a colon interchangeably with a dash:

> INCORRECT: Mathematics, German, English: These gave me the greatest difficulty of all my studies.
>
> CORRECT: Mathematics, German, English—these gave me the greatest difficulty of all my studies.

Information preceding the colon should be a complete sentence regardless of the explanatory information following the clause.

Do *not* use the colon before the words *for example, namely, that is,* or *for instance* even though these words may be introducing a list.

INCORRECT: We agreed to it: namely, to give him a surprise party.

CORRECT: We agreed to it, namely, to give him a surprise party.

Colon-usage questions test your knowledge of the colon preceding a list, restatement, or explanation. These questions also require you to be able to distinguish between the colon and the period, the colon and the comma, and the colon and the semicolon.

APOSTROPHES

Apostrophes require you to know when an apostrophe has been used appropriately to make a noun possessive, not plural. Remember the following rules when considering how to show possession.

Add *'s* to singular nouns and indefinite pronouns:

> Tiffany's flowers
>
> a dog's bark
>
> everybody's computer
>
> at the owner's expense
>
> today's paper

Add *'s* to singular nouns ending in *s,* unless this distorts the pronunciation:

> Delores's paper
>
> the boss's pen
>
> for righteousness' sake
>
> Dr. Evans's office OR Dr. Evans' office

Add *an apostrophe* to plural nouns ending in *s* or *es:*

> two cents' worth
>
> ladies' night
>
> thirteen years' experience
>
> two weeks' pay

Add *'s* to plural nouns not ending in *s:*

> men's room
>
> children's toys

Add *'s* to the last word in compound words or groups:

> brother-in-law's car
>
> someone else's paper

Add *'s* to the last name when indicating joint ownership:

> Joe and Edna's home
>
> Julie and Kathy's party
>
> women and children's clinic

Add *'s* to both names if you intend to show ownership by each person:

> Joe's and Edna's trucks
>
> Julie's and Kathy's pies
>
> Ted's and Jane's marriage vows

Possessive pronouns change their forms *without* the addition of an apostrophe:

> her, his, hers
>
> your, yours
>
> their, theirs
>
> it, its

Use the possessive form of a noun preceding a gerund:

> His driving annoys me.
>
> My bowling a strike irritated him.
>
> Do you mind our stopping by?
>
> We appreciate your coming.

Add *'s* to letters, numbers, words referred to as words, and abbreviations with periods to show that they are plural:

> no if's, and's, or but's
>
> the do's and don't's of dating

three A's

Ph.D.'s are granted by universities.

Add *s* to decades, symbols, and abbreviations without periods to show that they are plural:

TVs

VCRs

the 1800s

the returning POWs

QUOTATION MARKS

It is important to have an understanding of the proper use of quotation marks with other marks of punctuation, with titles, and with dialogue.

The most common use of double quotation marks (") is to set off quoted words, phrases, and sentences.

"If everybody minded their own business," said the Duchess in a hoarse growl, "the world would go round a great deal faster than it does."

"Then you would say what you mean," the March Hare went on.

"I do," Alice hastily replied: "at least—at least I mean what I say—that's the same thing, you know."

—from Lewis Carroll's *Alice in Wonderland*

Single quotation marks are used to set off quoted material within a quote.

"Shall I bring 'Rime of the Ancient Mariner' along with us?" she asked her brother.

Mrs. Green said, "The doctor told me, 'Go immediately to bed when you get home!'"

"If she said that to me," Katherine insisted, "I would tell her, 'I never intend to speak to you again! Goodbye, Susan!'"

When writing dialogue, begin a new paragraph each time the speaker changes.

"Do you know what time it is?" asked Jane.

"Can't you see I'm busy?" snapped Mary.

"It's easy to see that you're in a bad mood today!" replied Jane.

Use quotation marks to enclose words used as words. (Sometimes italics are used for this purpose.)

"Judgment" has always been a difficult word for me to spell.

Do you know what "abstruse" means?

"Horse and buggy" and "bread and butter" can be used either as adjectives or as nouns.

If slang is used within more formal writing, the slang words or phrases should be set off with quotation marks.

Harrison's decision to leave the conference and to "stick his neck out" by flying to Jamaica was applauded by the rest of the conference attendees.

When words are meant to have an unusual or specific significance to the reader, for instance irony or humor, they are sometimes placed in quotation marks.

For years, women were not allowed to buy real estate in order to "protect" them from unscrupulous dealers.

The "conversation" resulted in one black eye and a broken nose.

To set off titles of TV shows, poems, stories, and book chapters, use quotation marks. (Book, motion picture, newspaper, and magazine titles are underlined when handwritten.)

The article "Moving South in the Southern Rain," by Jergen Smith in the *Southern News*, attracted the attention of our editor.

The assignment is "Childhood Development," Chapter 18 of *Human Behavior.*

My favorite essay by Montaigne is "On Silence."

"Happy Days" led the TV ratings for years, didn't it?

You will find Keats' "Ode on a Grecian Urn" in Chapter 3, "The Romantic Era," in Lastly's *Selections from Great English Poets.*

Errors to Avoid

Be sure to remember that quotation marks always come in pairs. Do not make the mistake of using only one set.

INCORRECT:	"You'll never convince me to move to the city, said Thurman. I consider it an insane asylum."
CORRECT:	"You'll never convince me to move to the city," said Thurman. "I consider it an insane asylum."

INCORRECT:	"Idleness and pride tax with a heavier hand than kings and parliaments," Benjamin Franklin is supposed to have said. If we can get rid of the former, we may easily bear the latter."
CORRECT:	"Idleness and pride tax with a heavier hand than kings and parliaments," Benjamin Franklin is supposed to have said. "If we can get rid of the former, we may easily bear the latter."

When a quote consists of several sentences, do not put the quotation marks at the beginning and end of each sentence; put them at the beginning and end of the entire quotation.

INCORRECT:	"It was during his student days in Bonn that Beethoven fastened upon Schiller's poem." "The heady sense of liberation in the verses must have appealed to him." "They appealed to every German."—John Burke
CORRECT:	"It was during his student days in Bonn that Beethoven fastened upon Schiller's poem. The heady sense of liberation in the verses must have appealed to him. They appealed to every German."—John Burke

Instead of setting off a long quote with quotation marks, if it is longer than five or six lines, you may want to indent and single space it. If you do indent, do not use quotation marks.

In his *First Inaugural Address,* Abraham Lincoln appeals to the war-torn American people:

> We are not enemies, but friends. We must not be enemies. Though passion may have strained, it must not break, our bonds of affection. The mystic chords of memory, stretching from every battlefield and patriot grave to every living heart and hearthstone all over this broad land, will yet swell the chorus of the Union when again touched, as surely they will be, by the better angels of our nature.

Be careful not to use quotation marks with indirect quotations.

INCORRECT: Mary wondered "if she would get over it."

CORRECT: Mary wondered if she would get over it.

INCORRECT: The nurse asked "how long it had been since we had visited the doctor's office."

CORRECT: The nurse asked how long it had been since we had visited the doctor's office.

When you quote several paragraphs, it is not sufficient to place quotation marks at the beginning and end of the entire quote. Place quotation marks at the *beginning of each paragraph* but only at the *end of the last paragraph.* Here is an abbreviated quotation for an example:

"Here begins an odyssey through the world of classical mythology, starting with the creation of the world...

"It is true that themes similar to the classical may be found in any corpus of mythology...Even technology is not immune to the influence of Greece and Rome...

"We need hardly mention the extent to which painters and sculptors...have used and adapted classical mythology to illustrate the past, to reveal the human body, to express romantic or antiromantic ideals, or to symbolize any particular point of view."

Remember that commas and periods are *always* placed inside the quotation marks even if they are not actually part of the quote.

INCORRECT: "Life always gets colder near the summit", Nietzsche is purported to have said, "—the cold increases, responsibility grows".

CORRECT: "Life always gets colder near the summit," Nietzsche is purported to have said, "—the cold increases, responsibility grows."

INCORRECT: "Get down here right away", John cried. "You'll miss the sunset if you don't."

CORRECT: "Get down here right away," John cried. "You'll miss the sunset if you don't."

INCORRECT: "If my dog could talk", Mary mused, "I'll bet he would say, 'Take me for a walk right this minute'".

CORRECT: "If my dog could talk," Mary mused, "I'll bet he would say, 'Take me for a walk right this minute'."

Other marks of punctuation, such as question marks, exclamation points, colons, and semicolons, go inside the quotation marks if they are part of the quoted material. If they are not part of the quotation, however, they go outside the quotation marks. Be careful to distinguish between the guidelines for the comma and period, which always go inside the quotation marks, and those for other marks of punctuation.

INCORRECT: "I'll always love you"! he exclaimed happily.

CORRECT: "I'll always love you!" he exclaimed happily.

INCORRECT: Did you hear her say, "He'll be there early?"

CORRECT: Did you hear her say, "He'll be there early"?

INCORRECT: She called down the stairs, "When are you going"?

CORRECT: She called down the stairs, "When are you going?"

INCORRECT: "Let me out"! he cried. "Don't you have any pity"?

CORRECT: "Let me out!" he cried. "Don't you have any pity?"

Remember to use only one mark of punctuation at the end of a sentence ending with a quotation mark.

INCORRECT: She thought out loud, "Will I ever finish this paper in time for that class?".

CORRECT: She thought out loud, "Will I ever finish this paper in time for that class?"

INCORRECT: "Not the same thing a bit!", said the Hatter. "Why, you might just as well say that 'I see what I eat' is the same thing as 'I eat what I see'!".

CORRECT: "Not the same thing a bit!" said the Hatter. "Why, you might just as well say that 'I see what I eat' is the same thing as 'I eat what I see'!"

Drill 9

DIRECTIONS: Choose the correct replacement for the underlined words.

1. Indianola, <u>Mississippi, where B.B. King and my father grew up,</u> has a population of less than 50,000 people.

   (A) Mississippi where, B.B. King and my father grew up,

   (B) Mississippi where B.B. King and my father grew up,

   (C) Mississippi; where B.B. King and my father grew up,

   (D) No change is necessary.

2. John Steinbeck's best known novel *The Grapes of Wrath* is the story of the <u>Joads an Oklahoma family</u> who were driven from their dust-bowl farm and forced to become migrant workers in California.

   (A) Joads, an Oklahoma family

   (B) Joads, an Oklahoma family,

   (C) Joads; an Oklahoma family

   (D) No change is necessary.

3. All students who are interested in student teaching next <u>semester, must submit an application to the Teacher Education Office.</u>

   (A) semester must submit an application to the Teacher Education Office.

   (B) semester, must submit an application, to the Teacher Education Office.

   (C) semester: must submit an application to the Teacher Education Office.

   (D) No change is necessary.

4. Whenever you travel by <u>car, or plane, you</u> must wear a seatbelt.

   (A) car or plane you   (C) car or plane, you

   (B) car, or plane you   (D) No change is necessary.

5. Wearing a seatbelt is not just a good <u>idea, it's</u> the law.

   (A) idea; it's
   (B) idea it's
   (C) idea. It's
   (D) No change is necessary.

6. Senators and representatives can be reelected <u>indefinitely; a</u> president can only serve two terms.

   (A) indefinitely but a
   (B) indefinitely, a
   (C) indefinitely a
   (D) No change is necessary.

7. Students must pay a penalty for overdue library <u>books, however, there</u> is a grace period.

   (A) books; however, there
   (B) books however, there
   (C) books: however, there
   (D) No change is necessary.

8. Among the states that seceded from the Union to join the Confederacy in 1860–1861 <u>were:</u> Mississippi, Florida, and Alabama.

   (A) were
   (B) were;
   (C) were.
   (D) No change is necessary.

9. The art exhibit displayed works by many famous <u>artists such as:</u> Dali, Picasso, and Michelangelo.

   (A) artists such as;
   (B) artists such as
   (C) artists. Such as
   (D) No change is necessary.

10. The National Shakespeare Company will perform <u>the following plays:</u> *Othello*, *Macbeth*, *Hamlet*, and *As You Like It*.

   (A) the following plays,
   (B) the following plays;
   (C) the following plays
   (D) No change is necessary.

Drill 9 Answers

1. (D)	4. (C)	7. (A)	10. (D)
2. (A)	5. (A)	8. (A)	
3. (A)	6. (D)	9. (B)	

CAPITALIZATION

When a word is capitalized, it calls attention to itself. This attention should be for a good reason. There are standard uses for capital letters. In general, capitalize (1) all proper nouns, (2) the first word of a sentence, and (3) the first word of a direct quotation.

You Should Also Capitalize

Names of ships, aircraft, spacecraft, and trains:

Apollo 13	*Mariner IV*
DC-10	*S.S. United States*
Sputnik II	Boeing 707

Names of deities:

God	Jupiter
Allah	Holy Ghost
Buddha	Venus
Jehovah	Shiva

Geological periods:

Neolithic age	Cenozoic era
late Pleistocene times	Ice Age

Names of astronomical bodies:

Mercury	Big Dipper
the Milky Way	Halley's comet
Ursa Major	North Star

Personifications:

Reliable Nature brought her promised Spring.

Bring on Melancholy in his sad might.

She believed that Love was the answer to all her problems.

Historical periods:

Middle Ages	World War I
Reign of Terror	Great Depression
Christian Era	Roaring Twenties
Age of Louis XIV	Renaissance

Organizations, associations, and institutions:

Girl Scouts	North Atlantic Treaty Organization
Kiwanis Club	League of Women Voters
Boston Red Sox	Unitarian Church
Smithsonian Institution	Common Market
Library of Congress	Franklin Glen High School
New York Philharmonic	Harvard University

Government and judicial groups:

Senate	United States Court of Appeals
Parliament	Committee on Foreign Affairs
Peace Corps	Boston City Council
Census Bureau	Massachusetts Supreme Court
Department of State	House of Representatives

A general term that accompanies a specific name is capitalized if it follows the specific name. If it stands alone or comes before the specific name, it is usually (but not always), put in lowercase:

Washington State	the state of Washington
Senator Dixon	the senator from Illinois
Central Park	the park
Golden Gate Bridge	the bridge
President Clinton	the president of the United States
Pope John XXIII	the pope
Queen Elizabeth I	the queen of England
Tropic of Capricorn	the tropics

Monroe Doctrine	the doctrine of expansion
Mississippi River	the river
Easter Day	the day
Treaty of Versailles	the treaty
Webster's Dictionary	the dictionary
Equatorial Current	the equator

Use a capital letter to start a sentence:

Our car would not start.

When will you leave? I need to know right away.

Never!

Let me in! Please!

When a sentence appears within a sentence, start it with a capital letter:

We had only one concern: When would we eat?

My sister said, "I'll find the Monopoly game."

He answered, "We can only stay a few minutes."

The most important words of titles are capitalized. Those words not capitalized are conjunctions *(and, or, but)* and short prepositions *(of, on, by, for)*. The first and last word of a title must always be capitalized:

A Man for All Seasons	*Crime and Punishment*
Of Mice and Men	*Rise of the West*
Strange Life of Ivan Osokin	"Sonata in G Minor"
"Let Me In"	"Ode to Billy Joe"
"Rubaiyat of Omar Khayyam"	"All in the Family"

Capitalize newspaper and magazine titles:

U.S. News & World Report

National Geographic

The New York Times

The Boston Globe

Capitalize radio and TV station call letters:

ABC	NBC
WNEW	WBOP
CNN	HBO

Do not capitalize compass directions or seasons:

west	north
east	south
spring	winter
autumn	summer

Capitalize regions:

the South	the Northeast
the West	Eastern Europe

BUT: the south of France

the east part of town

Capitalize specific military units:

the U.S. Army

the 7th Fleet

the German Navy

the 1st Infantry Division

Capitalize political groups and philosophies:

Democratic party	Communist party
Marxist party	Nazi party
Whig party	Federalist party
Existentialism	Transcendentalism

BUT do not capitalize systems of government or individual adherents to a philosophy:

democracy	communism
fascist	agnostic
existentialist	transcendentalist

Drill 10

DIRECTIONS: Choose the correct replacement for the underlined words.

1. Mexico is the southernmost country in <u>North America</u>. It borders the United States on the north; it is bordered on the <u>south</u> by Belize and Guatemala.

   (A) north America . . . South
   (C) North america . . . south
   (B) North America . . . South
   (D) No change is necessary.

2. The <u>Northern Hemisphere</u> is the half of the <u>earth</u> that lies north of the <u>Equator.</u>

   (A) Northern hemisphere . . . earth . . . equator
   (B) Northern hemisphere . . . Earth . . . Equator
   (C) Northern Hemisphere . . . earth . . . equator
   (D) No change is necessary.

3. Aphrodite (<u>Venus in Roman Mythology</u>) was the <u>Greek</u> goddess of love.

   (A) Venus in Roman mythology . . . greek
   (B) venus in roman mythology . . . Greek
   (C) Venus in Roman mythology . . . Greek
   (D) No change is necessary.

4. The <u>Koran</u> is considered by <u>Muslims</u> to be the holy word.

   (A) koran . . . muslims
   (C) Koran . . . muslims
   (B) koran . . . Muslims
   (D) No change is necessary.

5. At the <u>spring</u> graduation ceremonies, the university awarded over 2,000 <u>bachelor's</u> degrees.

   (A) Spring . . . Bachelor's
   (C) Spring . . . bachelor's
   (B) spring . . . Bachelor's
   (D) No change is necessary.

6. The fall of the <u>Berlin wall</u> was an important symbol of the collapse of <u>Communism</u>.

    (A) berlin Wall . . . communism   (C) Berlin Wall . . . Communism

    (B) Berlin Wall . . . communism   (D) No change is necessary.

7. A photograph of <u>mars</u> was printed in <u>The *New York Times*</u>.

    (A) Mars . . . *The New York Times*

    (B) mars . . . *The New York times*

    (C) mars . . . *the New York Time*s

    (D) No change is necessary.

DIRECTIONS: Select the sentence that clearly and effectively states the idea and has no structural errors.

---

8. (A) Until 1989, Tom Landry was the only Coach the Dallas cowboys ever had.

    (B) Until 1989, Tom Landry was the only coach the Dallas Cowboys ever had.

    (C) Until 1989, Tom Landry was the only Coach the Dallas Cowboys ever had.

9. (A) My favorite works by Ernest Hemingway are "The Snows of Kilamanjaro," *The Sun Also Rises,* and *For Whom the Bell Tolls.*

    (B) My favorite works by Ernest Hemingway are "The Snows Of Kilamanjaro," *The Sun Also Rises,* and *For Whom The Bell Tolls.*

    (C) My favorite works by Ernest Hemingway are "The Snows of Kilamanjaro," *The Sun also Rises,* and *For whom the Bell Tolls.*

10. (A) The freshman curriculum at the community college includes english, a foreign language, Algebra I, and history.

    (B) The freshman curriculum at the community college includes English, a foreign language, Algebra I, and history.

    (C) The Freshman curriculum at the Community College includes English, a foreign language, Algebra I, and History.

Drill 10 Answers

1.	(D)	4.	(D)	7.	(A)	10.	(B)
2.	(C)	5.	(D)	8.	(B)		
3.	(C)	6.	(B)	9.	(A)		

SPELLING

Spelling questions test your ability to recognize misspelled words. This section reviews spelling tips and rules to help you spot incorrect spellings. Problems such as the distinction between "to" and "too" and "lead" and "led" are covered in the vocabulary review at the beginning of this book.

- Remember, "i" before "e" except after "c," or when sounded as "a" as in "neighbor" and "weigh."

- There are only three words in the English language that end in "-ceed":

    proceed, succeed, exceed

- There are several words that end in "-cede":

    secede, recede, concede, precede

- There is only one word in the English language that ends in "-sede":

    supersede

Many people learn to read English phonetically; that is, by sounding out the letters of the words. However, many English words are not pronounced the way they are spelled, and those who try to spell English words phonetically often make spelling "errors." It is better to memorize the correct spelling of English words rather than to rely on phonetics to spell correctly.

Frequently Misspelled Words

The following is a list of frequently misspelled words. Study the spelling of each word by having a friend or teacher drill you on the words. Then mark down the words that you misspelled and study those select ones again. (The words appear in their most popular spellings.)

a lot	advertisement	annual
ability	advice	another
absence	advisable	answer
absent	advise	antiseptic
abundance	advisor	anxious
accept	aerial	apologize
acceptable	affect	apparatus
accident	affectionate	apparent
accommodate	again	appear
accompanied	against	appearance
accomplish	aggravate	appetite
accumulation	aggressive	application
accuse	agree	apply
accustomed	aisle	appreciate
ache	all right	appreciation
achieve	almost	approach
achievement	already	appropriate
acknowledge	although	approval
acquaintance	altogether	approve
acquainted	always	approximate
acquire	amateur	argue
across	American	arguing
address	among	argument
addressed	amount	arouse
adequate	analysis	arrange
advantage	analyze	arrangement
advantageous	angel	article
advertise	angle	artificial

ascend	being	campaign
assistance	believe	capital
assistant	benefit	capitol
associate	benefited	captain
association	between	career
attempt	bicycle	careful
attendance	board	careless
attention	bored	carriage
audience	borrow	carrying
August	bottle	category
author	bottom	ceiling
automobile	boundary	cemetery
autumn	brake	cereal
auxiliary	breadth	certain
available	breath	changeable
avenue	breathe	characteristic
awful	brilliant	charity
awkward	building	chief
bachelor	bulletin	choose
balance	bureau	chose
balloon	burial	cigarette
bargain	buried	circumstance
basic	bury	citizen
beautiful	bushes	clothes
because	business	clothing
become	cafeteria	coarse
before	calculator	coffee
beginning	calendar	collect

college

colonel

column

comedy

comfortable

commitment

committed

committee

communicate

company

comparative

compel

competent

competition

compliment

conceal

conceit

conceivable

conceive

concentration

conception

condition

conference

confident

congratulate

conquer

conscience

conscientious

conscious

consequence

consequently

considerable

consistency

consistent

continual

continuous

controlled

controversy

convenience

convenient

conversation

cooperate

corporal

corroborate

council

counsel

counselor

courage

courageous

course

courteous

courtesy

criticism

criticize

crystal

curiosity

curriculum

cylinder

daily

daughter

daybreak

death

deceive

December

deception

decide

decision

decisive

deed

definite

delicious

dependent

deposit

derelict

descend

descent

describe

description

desert

desirable

despair

desperate

dessert

destruction

determine	dollar	entrance
develop	doubt	envelope
development	dozen	environment
device	earnest	equipment
dictator	easy	equipped
died	ecstasy	especially
difference	ecstatic	essential
different	education	evening
dilemma	effect	evident
dinner	efficiency	exaggerate
direction	efficient	exaggeration
disappear	eight	examine
disappoint	either	exceed
disappointment	eligibility	excellent
disapproval	eligible	except
disapprove	eliminate	exceptional
disastrous	embarrass	exercise
discipline	embarrassment	exhausted
discover	emergency	exhaustion
discriminate	emphasis	exhilaration
disease	emphasize	existence
dissatisfied	enclosure	exorbitant
dissection	encouraging	expense
dissipate	endeavor	experience
distance	engineer	experiment
distinction	English	explanation
division	enormous	extreme
doctor	enough	facility

factory	governor	hurrying
familiar	grammar	ignorance
fascinate	grateful	imaginary
fascinating	great	imbecile
fatigue	grievance	imitation
February	grievous	immediately
financial	grocery	immigrant
financier	guarantee	incidental
flourish	guess	increase
forcibly	guidance	independence
forehead	half	independent
foreign	hammer	indispensable
formal	handkerchief	inevitable
former	happiness	influence
fortunate	healthy	influential
fourteen	heard	initiate
fourth	heavy	innocence
frequent	height	inoculate
friend	heroes	inquiry
frightening	heroine	insistent
fundamental	hideous	instead
further	himself	instinct
gallon	hoarse	integrity
garden	holiday	intellectual
gardener	hopeless	intelligence
general	hospital	intercede
genius	humorous	interest
government	hurried	interfere

interference	leisure	measure
interpreted	length	medicine
interrupt	lesson	millennium
invitation	library	million
irrelevant	license	miniature
irresistible	light	minimum
irritable	lightning	miracle
island	likelihood	miscellaneous
its	likely	mischief
it's	literal	mischievous
itself	literature	misspelled
January	livelihood	mistake
jealous	loaf	momentous
journal	loneliness	monkey
judgment	loose	monotonous
kindergarten	lose	moral
kitchen	losing	morale
knew	loyal	mortgage
knock	loyalty	mountain
know	magazine	mournful
knowledge	maintenance	muscle
labor	maneuver	mysterious
laboratory	marriage	mystery
laid	married	narrative
language	marry	natural
later	match	necessary
latter	material	needle
laugh	mathematics	negligence

neighbor	oscillate	perpendicular
neither	ought	perseverance
newspaper	ounce	persevere
newsstand	overcoat	persistent
niece	paid	personal
noticeable	pamphlet	personality
o'clock	panicky	personnel
obedient	parallel	persuade
obstacle	parallelism	persuasion
occasion	particular	pertain
occasional	partner	pianist
occur	pastime	picture
occurred	patience	piece
occurrence	peace	plain
ocean	peaceable	playwright
offer	pear	pleasant
often	peculiar	please
omission	pencil	pleasure
omit	people	pocket
once	perceive	poison
operate	perception	policeman
opinion	perfect	political
opportune	perform	population
opportunity	performance	portrayal
optimist	perhaps	positive
optimistic	period	possess
origin	permanence	possession
original	permanent	possessive

possible	professional	recipe
post office	professor	recognize
potatoes	profitable	recommend
practical	prominent	recuperate
prairie	promise	referred
precede	pronounce	rehearsal
preceding	pronunciation	reign
precise	propeller	relevant
predictable	prophet	relieve
prefer	prospect	remedy
preference	psychology	renovate
preferential	pursue	repeat
preferred	pursuit	repetition
prejudice	quality	representative
preparation	quantity	requirements
prepare	quarreling	resemblance
prescription	quart	resistance
presence	quarter	resource
president	quiet	respectability
prevalent	quite	responsibility
primitive	raise	restaurant
principal	realistic	rhythm
principle	realize	rhythmical
privilege	reason	ridiculous
probably	rebellion	right
procedure	recede	role
proceed	receipt	roll
produce	receive	roommate

sandwich	similarity	sudden
Saturday	sincerely	superintendent
scarcely	site	suppress
scene	soldier	surely
schedule	solemn	surprise
science	sophomore	suspense
scientific	soul	sweat
scissors	source	sweet
season	souvenir	syllable
secretary	special	symmetrical
seize	specified	sympathy
seminar	specimen	synonym
sense	speech	technical
separate	stationary	telegram
service	stationery	telephone
several	statue	temperament
severely	statute	temperature
shepherd	stockings	tenant
sheriff	stomach	tendency
shining	straight	tenement
shoulder	strength	therefore
shriek	strenuous	thorough
siege	stretch	through
sight	striking	title
signal	studying	together
significance	substantial	tomorrow
significant	succeed	tongue
similar	successful	toward

tragedy	vacuum	waist
transferred	valley	waste
treasury	valuable	weak
tremendous	variety	wear
tries	vegetable	weather
truly	vein	Wednesday
twelfth	vengeance	week
twelve	versatile	weigh
tyranny	vicinity	weird
undoubtedly	vicious	whether
United States	view	which
university	village	while
unnecessary	villain	whole
unusual	visitor	wholly
useful	voice	whose
usual	volume	wretched

Drill 11

DIRECTIONS: Identify the misspelled word in each set.

1. (A) probly
   (B) accommodate
   (C) acquaintance

2. (A) auxiliary
   (B) atheletic
   (C) beginning

3. (A) environment
   (B) existence
   (C) Febuary

4. (A) ocassion
   (B) occurrence
   (C) omitted

5. (A) perspiration
   (B) referring
   (C) priviledge

DIRECTIONS: Choose the correct replacement for the underlined words.

6. Preceding the business session, lunch will be served in a separate room.
   (A) preceeding . . . business . . . seperate
   (B) proceeding . . . bussiness . . . seperate
   (C) proceeding . . . business . . . seperite
   (D) No change is necessary.

7. Monte inadvertently left several of his libary books in the cafeteria.
   (A) inadverdently . . . serveral . . . libery
   (B) inadvertently . . . several . . . library

(C) inadvertently . . . several . . . librery

(D) No change is necessary.

8. Sam wished he had more <u>liesure</u> time so he could <u>persue</u> his favorite hobbies.

(A) leisure . . . pursue

(C) leisure . . . persue

(B) Liesure . . . pursue

(D) No change is necessary.

9. One of my <u>favrite charecters</u> in <u>litrature</u> is Bilbo from *The Hobbit*.

(A) favrite . . . characters . . . literature

(B) favorite . . . characters . . . literature

(C) favourite . . . characters . . . literature

(D) No change is necessary.

10. Even <u>tho</u> Joe was badly hurt in the <u>accidant</u>, the company said they were not <u>lible</u> for damages.

(A) though . . . accidant . . . libel

(B) though . . . accident . . . liable

(C) though . . . acident . . . liable

(D) No change is necessary.

Drill 11 Answers

1.	(A)	4.	(A)	7.	(B)	10.	(B)
2.	(B)	5.	(C)	8.	(A)		
3.	(C)	6.	(D)	9.	(B)		

III. WRITTEN COMPOSITION

PRE-WRITING/PLANNING

Before you begin to write, there are certain preliminary steps you should take. A few minutes spent planning pay off—your final essay will be more focused, better-developed, and clearer. For a 30-minute essay, you should spend about five minutes on the pre-writing process.

UNDERSTAND THE QUESTION

Read the essay question very carefully and ask yourself the following questions:

- What is the meaning of the topic statement?

- Is the question asking me to persuade the reader of the validity of a certain opinion?

- Do I agree or disagree with the statement? What will be my thesis?

- What kinds of examples can I use to support my thesis? Explore personal experiences, historical evidence, current events, and literary subjects.

CHOOSING A TOPIC

You may be assigned a topic to write about or you may be able to choose your own. A *topic* is any subject of study, inquiry, or discussion that is addressed for the sake of an audience. A topic, however, is not a main point or a thesis. Remember that a *topic* is the subject about which the author writes. Books, cars, people, sports, rainbows, fish, potato chips—*anything* can be a topic of inquiry, study, or discussion. The point is to choose one and begin to focus on writing about it.

Some topics are too broad to deal with in a short 500-word essay, so you may be asked to narrow the topic. Narrowing a topic means limiting it and becoming more specific about what is to be discussed in the paper, making it a manageable length and scope. For example, suppose the chosen topic is "books." Before writing, decide on the *purpose* in writing and the *audience* that is going to read the work. Decide on some relevant characteristics that the reader(s) may have.

GETTING IDEAS ON PAPER QUICKLY

Often the most difficult question in writing is how to begin. Several techniques for becoming *fluent* are recommended by experts. This section explores some of the major ones available. In the reading process, the reader must determine what his or her purpose for reading is and what the writer's purpose for writing is.

Similarly, in the writing process, the writer must decide what the purpose for writing is going to be. This technique will help the writer get started and, at the same time, will help narrow down the topic. What does the author want to explain when writing about "books"? Does the author wish to describe (that is, talk about what physical qualities the books possess), explain what they are, inform readers about some issue or quality about them, or persuade readers about something in relation to "books"?

More often than not, the writer is asked to *persuade* the reader(s) of something about the topic. This calls for the use of *argumentation*, or persuasive composition, to make the point.

Suppose the writer wants to persuade the reader that books are difficult to read. *Audience* is the next important consideration. The writer must decide on the person or group of people that would, or should, be persuaded by the argument. Once the author determines the audience, his or her focus for persuasion changes. *Audience awareness often determines the direction and content of writing.* If a student attempts to persuade his or her professors that books are difficult to read, then he or she will have to summon a great deal of information because most professors would disagree. On the other hand, if the audience consists of students, the writer may be able to limit his or her evidence and convince them using fewer examples.

It would be impossible, however, to discuss in a 500-word essay, or even in a short research paper, how all the books on the whole earth are difficult to read. The writer needs to narrow the subject of discussion even further. The way to do this is to use specific adjectives to condense the field of thinking and discussion. Thus, instead of claiming that books are difficult to read and leaving open an encyclopedia of trouble, narrow the field.

History textbooks are difficult for first-year college students to read.

Admittedly, however, *some* first-year students will not find reading history textbooks difficult. Therefore, do not claim that this statement is true for all by not *qualifying the thesis*. Instead, narrow the topic even further:

Many history textbooks are difficult to read for selected first-year college students.

Obviously, this topic can be narrowed even further.

Freewriting

Through a technique called *freewriting*, the writer can also begin the writing process. Freewriting is putting down on paper whatever comes to mind at the time. When utilizing this technique, be sure not to worry about technical matters such as spelling, punctuation, paragraphing, etc. The writer often develops interesting and novel ideas during this stage. The important aspect about freewriting is the "flow" of the writing, however imperfect the technical aspects of sentence structure and grammar may be at the moment. Correcting these errors comes later in the process.

Brainstorming

Brainstorming is the technique by which the author takes a few minutes to list, in random order, all the ideas and thoughts he or she has about a topic. When brainstorming a topic, the writer acts as a reporter would act and uses the *reporter's heuristic* for getting the "lead" to the story. A good reporter asks key questions of any event in order to write the "lead" or beginning to a story: What happened? Who was there? When did it happen? How did it happen? Where did it happen? Why did it happen? When confronting a topic, the writer asks similar related questions of the topic and writes down the answers to the relevant questions as quickly as he or she thinks of them. The author must simply write down ideas as they come out and not censor them. By the end of this process, the writer will have conceived many ideas and concepts.

Clustering

Clustering involves writing a topic in the center of a piece of blank, unlined paper around which the writer writes down all the things about the topic that he or she can think of, thus creating little "rays" of thought that stem from the topic. Following is an illustration of how this might look.

Clustering: A Pre-writing Technique

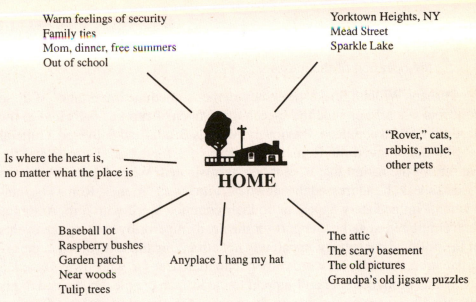

Warm feelings of security
Family ties
Mom, dinner, free summers
Out of school

Yorktown Heights, NY
Mead Street
Sparkle Lake

Is where the heart is,
no matter what the place is

"Rover," cats,
rabbits, mule,
other pets

HOME

Baseball lot
Raspberry bushes
Garden patch
Near woods
Tulip trees

Anyplace I hang my hat

The attic
The scary basement
The old pictures
Grandpa's old jigsaw puzzles

CONSIDER YOUR AUDIENCE

Essays would be pointless without an audience. Why write an essay if no one wants or needs to read it? Why add evidence, organize your ideas, or correct bad grammar? The reason to do any of these things is because someone out there needs to understand what you mean or say.

What does the audience need to know to believe you or to come over to your position? Imagine someone you know listening to you declare your position or opinion and then saying, "Oh, yeah? Prove it!" This is your audience—write to them. Ask yourself the following questions so that when you are confronted by a person who says "Prove it," you will have a well thought-out response.

- What evidence do I need to prove my idea to this skeptic?

- What would he or she disagree with me about?

- What does he or she share with me as common knowledge? What do I need to tell the reader?

WRITING FOR A SPECIFIC AUDIENCE, PURPOSE, AND OCCASION

For effective communication, a writer or speaker must consider three factors:

1. the audience addressed (for whom or to whom the message is being sent);

2. the purpose of the message; and

3. the occasion of the message.

Perhaps William Shakespeare best demonstrated the importance of these concepts when he created the speech that Marcus Antonius delivered to the aroused Roman populace. Previously, Marcus Brutus had delivered a funeral oration that assured the Romans that it was for their best interests and the welfare of the nation that Caesar was assassinated. When Marcus Antonius rose to speak, he addressed the crowd of Romans as "friends, Romans, countrymen," immediately appealing to their common spirit with him. Antonius then continued to gather support for the dead emperor by reciting the events of the political conspiracy, apparently not criticizing those involved in the assassination. Actually his words brought honor to Caesar, who always acted in a way that brought honor and support to the Roman people. By the end of his clever address, the crowd was ready to chase the conspirators from Rome.

Shakespeare realized that the audience listening to Marcus Antonius's speech could not be immediately and directly brought to support Caesar and, in turn, brought to attack Marcus Brutus and other assassins. First, they must be exposed to a list of supposed "faults" of the emperor and then be led to view his shortcomings as positive traits, functioning always to bring benefits to the Romans. Finally, the occasion of the speech, immediately after Marcus Brutus's funeral oration, involved a volatile gathering. The Romans' attitudes toward Caesar must be brought into alignment with Marcus Antonius's for the clever spokesman to convert the people.

Not so dramatic an occasion or so clever a style of expression affects the typical writer today. Awareness of the audience addressed, the purpose of one's words, and the occasion for the words are all important. A communicator must know the audience and the individual attitudes, opinions, fears, and concerns that motivate.

Drill 1

DIRECTIONS: Read the following short essay. Then answer the questions.

Mankind has always attempted to assess the time. Ancient man used the position of the sun to determine the time of day.

During the night, a water clock was used, working much like an hour glass. The sundial today is primarily an attractive garden item, no longer used to tell time.

Probably the Chinese designed the first mechanical time pieces in the eighth century. Europeans did not begin using them until the twelfth or thirteenth century. Early clocks were created to get people to the church on time. Church bells rang each hour, but there were no numbers on the face of the clock for the hour. Hence, the name for the time device was the French word *cloche*, meaning "bell." People were not too concerned about the exact time. Today many people want to have an accurate time awareness.

When hands were added to the face of a clock, they did not move although the face of the clock did sometimes, circling for the 12-hour period. Hands, which move, often appear on the face of the clock although many modern clocks and watches have numerals displayed digitally.

Early clocks were only approximately accurate. Today's atomic clocks are accurate to within one second each 60,000 years. Check the various clocks and watches in your household. Are all showing the same time?

1. The purpose of this essay is to

   (A) convince the reader of the importance of exact time.

   (B) suggest that people not pay so much attention to exact timing.

   (C) explain some of the steps in the development of time pieces.

   (D) show how much more useful modern clocks are.

2. The intended audience of the essay is

   (A) historians.

   (B) a reasonably well-educated group of young adults and adults.

   (C) collectors of old clocks.

   (D) educators.

WRITING YOUR ESSAY

Once you have considered your position on the topic and thought of several examples to support it, you are ready to begin writing.

ORGANIZING YOUR ESSAY

Decide how many paragraphs you will write. In a timed exercise, you will probably have time for no more than four or five paragraphs. In such a format, the first paragraph should be the introduction, the next two or three should develop your thesis with specific examples, and the final paragraph should be a strong conclusion.

Introduction

The focus of your introduction should be the thesis statement. This statement allows your reader to understand the point and direction of your essay. The statement identifies the central idea of your essay and should clearly state your attitude about the subject. It will also dictate the basic content and organization of your essay. If you do not state your thesis clearly, your essay will suffer.

The thesis is the heart of the essay. Without it, readers won't know what your major message or central idea is in the essay.

The thesis must be something that can be argued or needs to be proven, not just an accepted fact. For example, "Animals are used every day in cosmetic and medical testing" is a fact—it needs no proof. But if the writer says, "Using animals for cosmetic and medical testing is cruel and should be stopped," we have a point that must be supported and defended by the writer.

The thesis can be placed in any paragraph of the essay, but in a short essay, especially one written for evaluative exam purposes, the thesis is most effective when placed in the last sentence of the opening paragraph.

Consider the following sample question:

> **ESSAY TOPIC:** "That government is best which governs least."
>
> **ASSIGNMENT:** Do you agree or disagree with this statement? Choose a specific example from current events, personal experience, or your reading to support your position.

After reading the topic statement, decide if you agree or disagree. If you agree with this statement, your thesis statement could be the following:

> "Government has the right to protect individuals from interference but no right to extend its powers and activities beyond this function."

This statement clearly states the writer's opinion in a direct manner. It also serves as a blueprint for the essay. The remainder of the introduction should give two or three brief examples that support your thesis.

Supporting Paragraphs

The next two or three paragraphs of your essay will elaborate on the supporting examples you gave in your introduction. Each paragraph should discuss only one idea. Like the introduction, each paragraph should be coherently organized with a topic sentence and supporting details.

The topic sentence is to each paragraph what the thesis statement is to the essay as a whole. It tells the reader what you plan to discuss in that paragraph. It has a specific subject and is neither too broad nor too narrow. It also establishes the author's attitude and gives the reader a sense of the direction in which the writer is going. An effective topic sentence also arouses the reader's interest.

Although it may occur in the middle or at the end of the paragraph, the topic sentence usually appears at the beginning of the paragraph. Placing it at the beginning is advantageous because it helps you stay focused on the main idea.

The remainder of each paragraph should support the topic sentence with examples and illustrations. Each sentence should progress logically from the previous one and be centrally connected to your topic sentence. Do not include any extraneous material that does not serve to develop your thesis.

Organizing and Reviewing the Paragraphs

The unit of work for revising is the paragraph. After you have written what you wanted to say based on your prewriting list, spend some time revising your draft by looking to see if you need to indent for paragraphs anywhere. If you do, make a little proofreader's mark (¶) to indicate to the reader that you think a paragraph should start here. Check to see if you want to add anything that would make your point of view more convincing. Be sure to supply useful transitions to keep up the flow and maintain the focus of your ideas. If you don't have room on the paper, or if your new paragraph shows up out of order, add that paragraph and indicate with a number or some other mark where you want it to go. Check to *make sure* that you gave examples or illustrations for your statements. In the examples below, two paragraphs are offered: one without concrete evidence and one with evidence for its idea. Study each. Note the topic sentence and how that sentence is or is not supported with evidence.

Paragraphing with No Evidence

Television is bad for people. *Watching television takes time away from other things.* Programs on television are often stupid and depict crimes that people later copy. Television takes time away from loved ones, and it often becomes addictive. So, television is bad for people because it is no good.

In this example, the author has not given any concrete evidence for any of the good ideas presented. He or she just declares them to be so. Any one of the sentences above might make a good opening sentence for a whole paragraph.

Paragraphing with Evidence

Watching television takes time away from other things. For example, all those hours people spend sitting in front of the tube could be spent working on building a chair or fixing the roof. *(first piece of evidence)* Maybe the laundry needs to be done, but because people watch television, they may end up not having time to do it. Then Monday comes around again and they have no socks to wear to work—all because they couldn't stand to miss that episode of "The Simpsons." *(second piece of evidence)* Someone could be writing a letter to a friend in Boston who hasn't been heard from or written to for months. *(third piece of evidence)* Or maybe someone misses the opportunity to take in a beautiful day in the park because he or she had to see "The View." They'll repeat "The View," but this beautiful day only comes around once. Watching television definitely keeps people from getting things done.

The primary evidence the author uses here is that of probable illustrations taken from life experience, largely anecdotal. Always *supply evidence.* Three examples or illustrations of your idea per paragraph is a useful number. Four is OK, but stop there. Don't go on and on about a single point. You don't have time.

Conclusion

Your conclusion should briefly restate your thesis and explain how you have shown it to be true. Because you want to end your essay on a strong note, your conclusion should be concise and effective.

Do not introduce any new topics that you cannot support. If you were watching a movie that suddenly shifted plot and characters at the end, you would be disappointed or even angry. Similarly, conclusions must not drift away from the major focus and message of the essay. Make sure your conclusion is clearly on the topic and represents your perspective without any confusion about what you really mean and believe. The reader will respect you for staying true to your intentions.

The conclusion is your last chance to grab and impress the reader. You can even use humor, if appropriate, but a dramatic close will remind the reader you are serious, even passionate, about what you believe.

EFFECTIVE USE OF LANGUAGE

Clear organization, while vitally important, is not the only factor the graders of your essay consider. You must also demonstrate that you can express your ideas clearly, using correct grammar, diction, usage, spelling, and punctuation.

Point of View

An important way to maintain unity in writing is to maintain consistency in the point of view selected by the writer. The writer has three choices, each of which has a special role in the writing process. Once selected, the point of view may not be switched back and forth without adversely affecting the unity of the piece of writing.

First person point of view

The first person point of view method used in most personal writing—autobiographical, memories of feelings or experiences, viewpoints that are the writer's own beliefs—is identified by the use of *I*, *me*, *we*, *us*, *my*, *mine*, *our*, and *ours*.

> EXAMPLE: I often wondered about my childhood friend, Freddy. Freddy was my shadow when I was eight years old. We played the same games, read the same books,

hiked the same paths, and fished the same streams. Then suddenly, Freddy's parents moved. I never even said good-bye to him. Where is Freddy today?

ANALYSIS: This childhood memory is told by a narrator, recalling when he was eight years of age. Now, older, he wonders about his constant companion in those days. The narrator may use the pronoun *him* to refer to Freddy without changing the point of view since the narrator still refers to himself as *I*.

Second person point of view

The second person point of view uses the pronouns *you* and *your*. They are correctly used when someone is addressing a person in direct dialogue.

EXAMPLE: The judge addressed the witness, "Are you sure of the time you saw the accident?

One of the most common errors in writing, however, is using *you* (or *your*) in the midst of a passage that is written in first or third person point of view. The corrected passage uses a noun naming the person(s) addressed to maintain a consistent point of view.

INCORRECT: The group of tourists entered the mosque, removing their shoes as requested. Several had difficulty finding their shoes later. How would *you* have left *your* shoes so that *you* could find them easily?

CORRECT: The group of tourists entered the mosque, removing their shoes as requested. Several had difficulty finding their shoes later. How can *visitors* leave *their* shoes so that *they* can find them easily?

Third person point of view

Most writing uses the third person point of view. Fiction, explanatory writing, persuasive writing, journalistic expression, and similar forms use this point of view. The pronouns identifying third person are *he, him, she, her, his, hers, them, their, theirs,* and *they.*

EXAMPLE: Many people believe that Christopher Columbus was the first to visit the land that became known as North America. Actually, over 500 years earlier than Columbus, a Norseman named Biarni Heriulfson sighted

Labrador when he missed his intended destination, Greenland. A few years after Heriulfson's voyage, Leif Ericson bought Heriulfson's ship and made the return journey to the new land in 1002. He and his shipmates probably landed at Cape Cod. They also explored Labrador and Nova Scotia. Remains of other early Viking settlements have been discovered. Since this was a hostile area for settlement, however, the northern explorers gave up ideas of living there by 1025.

Drill 2

DIRECTIONS: Rewrite the following passage so that the point of view is consistent.

The stranger walked into the room with obvious intent. Stopping in the center, he slowly looked around, his eyes moving from person to person. If you had been the one for whom he searched, you would have moved rapidly for the nearest exit.

Drill 2 Answers

The answers may vary from the following. The last sentence must remove the second person pronouns, however.

The stranger walked into the room with obvious intent. Stopping in the center, he slowly looked around, his eyes moving from person to person. Anyone fearing the stranger was searching for him would have moved rapidly for the nearest exit.

Tone

A writer's tone results from his or her attitude toward the subject and the reader. If the essay question requires you to take a strong stand, the tone of your essay should reflect this.

Your tone should also be appropriate for the subject matter. A serious topic demands a serious tone. For a more light-hearted topic, you may wish to inject some humor into your essay. Whatever tone you choose, be consistent. Do not make any abrupt shifts in tone in the middle of your essay.

Verb Tense

Make sure to remain in the same verb tense in which you began your essay. If you start in the past, make sure all verbs are past tense. Staying in the same verb tense improves the continuity and flow of ideas. Avoid phrases such as "now was," a confusing blend of present and past. Consistency of time is essential to the reader's understanding.

COMMON WRITING ERRORS

The four writing errors most often made by beginning writers are run-ons (also known as fused sentences), fragments, lack of subject-verb agreement, and incorrect use of the object:

1. **Run-ons**: "She swept the floor it was dirty" is a run-on. A period or semicolon is needed after "floor."

2. **Fragments**: "Before Jimmy learned how to play baseball" is a fragment. The word "before" fragmentizes the clause.

3. **Problems with subject-verb agreement**: A singular subject requires a singular verb; a plural subject or a compound subject requires a plural verb. If the separate parts of a subject are connected by *either—or*, *neither—nor*, or *or*, the verb agrees in number with the nearer part of the subject. "Either Maria or Robert are going to the game" is incorrect because one of them is going, but not both. The sentence should say, "Either Maria or Robert is going to the game."

4. **Incorrect object**: An objective case pronoun serves as the direct or indirect object of a verb, as the object of a preposition, and in apposition with an object of a verb or preposition; the nominative case serves as the subject of a verb, as a predicate pronoun, in apposition with the subject or with a predicate noun, in direct address, and in the nominative absolute construction. For example, "between you and I" sounds correct, but isn't. "Between" is a preposition that takes the objective case "me." The correct usage is "between you and me."

Other writing problems that may occur on the Communication and Literacy Skills Test are lack of thought and development, misspellings, and use of incorrect pronouns or antecedents. Keep in mind that clear, coherent handwriting always works to your advantage. Readers will appreciate an essay they can read with ease.

FIVE WORDS WEAK WRITERS OVERUSE

Weak and inexperienced writers overuse the vague pronouns *you*, *we*, *they*, *this*, and *it* often without telling exactly who or what is represented by the pronoun.

1. Beginning writers often shift to second person *you*, when the writer means "a person." This shift confuses readers and weakens the flow of the essay. Although *you* is commonly accepted in creative writing, journalism, and other arenas, in a short, formal essay it is best to avoid *you* altogether.

2. *We* is another pronoun that should be avoided. If by *we* the writer means "Americans," "society," or some other group, then he or she should say so.

3. *They* is often misused in essay writing because it is overused in conversation: "I went to the doctor, and they told me to take some medicine." Identify *they* for the reader.

4. *This* is usually used incorrectly without a referent: "She told me she received a present. This sounded good to me." This what? This idea? This news? This present? Be clear—don't make your readers guess what you mean. The word *this* should be followed by a noun or referent.

5. *It* is a common problem among weak writers. To what does *it* refer? Your readers don't appreciate vagueness; take the time to be clear and complete in your expression of ideas.

USE YOUR OWN VOCABULARY

Is it a good idea to use big words that sound sophisticated in the dictionary or thesaurus, but that you don't really use or understand? No. So whose vocabulary should you use? Your own. You will be most comfortable with your own level of vocabulary.

This "comfort zone" doesn't give you license to be informal in a formal setting or to violate the rules of standard written English, but if you try to write in a style that is not yours, your writing will be awkward and lack a true voice.

You should certainly improve and build your vocabulary at every opportunity, but remember: you should not attempt to change your vocabulary level at this point.

AVOID THE PASSIVE VOICE

In much of your writing you will want to use the active voice in order to convey a sense of directness and immediacy. However, avoiding the passive voice completely is neither possible nor desirable. Both constructions have their proper uses: the active voice stresses the actor while the passive voice stresses the action. Use the passive voice when the action of the verb is more important than the doer or when the doer is unknown.

> ACTIVE: She kicked the winning field goal.

In this case, the active construction directly and clearly communicates to the reader. The passive construction (The winning field goal was kicked by her.) would be awkward and wordy.

> PASSIVE: She was arraigned and sentenced to ten years hard labor.

In this case, the passive construction is preferable because the actor (the court or the judge) is unimportant to the sense of the sentence.

PROOFREADING

Make sure to leave yourself enough time at the end to read over your essay for errors such as misspellings, omitted words, or incorrect punctuation. You will not have enough time to make large-scale revisions, but take this chance to make any small changes that will make your essay stronger. Consider the following when proofreading your work:

- Are all your sentences really sentences? Have you written any fragments or run-on sentences?

- Are you using vocabulary correctly?

- Did you leave out any punctuation? Did you capitalize correctly?

- Are there any misspellings, especially of difficult words?

If you have time, read your essay backwards from end to beginning. By doing so, you may catch errors that you missed reading forward only.

REVISING

Revising occurs each time a concept in the rough draft is changed, rearranged, or altered. Be sure to examine the *organization*, *paragraphing*, *scope and nature of the thesis*, and *format* (the appearance and layout of the paper). This is the step and time in the process when *transitions*, *flow*, and the *logic* of the paper are analyzed. Revise before editing, and remember to keep paragraphs short and concise. This may entail moving whole paragraphs from one place to another within the text, adding a transition, or cutting out whole paragraphs. Continue this process until the paper logically supports the thesis.

EDITING

Editing is the stage after revising in which *correct grammar*, *sentence style*, *diction*, *punctuation*, and *spelling* are inspected. When editing a paper, focus attention not on the concepts, content, or logic but on the clarity of sentences and the correctness of the grammar. If problems of organization and logic still exist, *revise* the paper more before *editing*. Editing should be strictly for grammar and individual sentence structure.

Drill 3

DIRECTIONS: You have 30 minutes to plan and write an essay on the topic below. You may write only on the assigned topic.

Make sure to give specific examples to support your thesis. Proofread your essay carefully and take care to express your ideas clearly and effectively.

ESSAY TOPIC: In the last 20 years, the deterioration of the environment has become a growing concern among both scientists and ordinary citizens.

ASSIGNMENT: Choose one pressing environmental problem, explain its negative impact, and discuss possible solutions.

Drill 3 Answer

This answer key provides three sample essays that represent possible responses to the essay topic. Compare your own response to those given on the next few pages. Allow the strengths and weaknesses of the sample essays to help you to critique your own essay and improve your writing skills.

ESSAY I (GOOD)

There are many pressing environmental problems facing both this country and the world today. Pollution, the misuse and squandering of resources, and the cavalier attitude many people express all contribute to the problem. But one of the most pressing problems this country faces is the apathetic attitude many Americans have toward recycling.

Why is recycling so imperative? There are two major reasons. First, recycling previously used materials conserves precious national resources. Many people never stop to think that reserves of metal ores are not unlimited. There is only so much gold, silver, tin, and other metals in the ground. Once it has all been mined, there will never be any more unless we recycle what has already been used.

Second, the United States generates more solid waste per day than any other country on earth. Our disposable consumer culture consumes fast food meals in paper or styrofoam containers, uses disposable diapers with plastic liners that do not biodegrade, receives pounds, if not tons, of unsolicited junk mail every year, and relies more and more on prepackaged rather than fresh food.

No matter how it is accomplished, increased recycling is essential. We have to stop covering our land with garbage, and the best ways to do this are to reduce our dependence on prepackaged goods and to minimize the amount of solid waste disposed of in landfills. The best way to reduce solid waste is to recycle it. Americans need to band together to recycle, to preserve our irreplaceable natural resources, reduce pollution, and preserve our precious environment.

ANALYSIS

This essay presents a clearly defined thesis, and the writer elaborates on this thesis in a thoughtful and sophisticated manner. Various aspects of the problem under consideration are presented and explored, along with possible solutions. The support provided for the writer's argument is convincing and logical. There are few usage or mechanical errors to interfere with the writer's ability to communicate effectively. This writer demonstrates a comprehensive understanding of the rules of written English.

ESSAY II (AVERAGE)

A pressing environmental problem today is the way we are cutting down too many trees and not planting any replacements for them. Trees are beneficial in many ways, and without them, many environmental problems would be much worse.

One of the ways trees are beneficial is that, like all plants, they take in carbon dioxide and produce oxygen. They can actually help clean the air this way. When too many trees are cut down in a small area, the air in that area is not as good and can be unhealthy to breath.

Another way trees are beneficial is that they provide homes for many types of birds, insects, and animals. When all the trees in an area are cut down, these animals lose their homes and sometimes they can die out and become extinct that way. Like the spotted owls in Oregon, that the loggers wanted to cut down the trees they lived in. If the loggers did cut down all the old timber stands that the spotted owls lived in, the owls would have become extinct.

But the loggers say that if they can't cut the trees down then they will be out of work, and that peoples' jobs are more important than birds. The loggers can do two things—they can either get training so they can do other jobs, or they can do what they should have done all along, and start replanting trees. For every mature tree they cut down, they should have to plant at least one tree seedling.

Cutting down the trees that we need for life, and that lots of other species depend on, is a big environmental problem that has a lot of long term consaquences. Trees are too important for all of us to cut them down without thinking about the future.

ANALYSIS

This essay has a clear thesis, which the author supports with good examples. However, the writer shifts between the chosen topic, which is that indiscriminate tree-cutting is a pressing environmental problem, and a list of the ways in which trees are beneficial and a discussion about the logging profession. Also, while there are few mistakes in usage and mechanics, the writer has some problems with sentence structure. The writing is pedestrian and the writer does not elaborate on the topic as much as he or she could have. The writer failed to provide the kind of critical analysis that the topic required.

ESSAY III (POOR)

The most pressing environmental problem today is that lots of people and companies don't care about the environment, and they do lots of things that hurt the environment.

People throw litter out car windows and don't use trash cans, even if their all over a park, soda cans and fast food wrappers are all over the place. Cigarette butts are the worst cause the filters never rot. Newspapers and junk mail get left to blow all over the neighborhood, and beer bottles too.

Companies pollute the air and the water. Sometimes the ground around a company has lots of toxins in it. Now companies can buy credits from other companies that let them pollute the air even more. They dump all kinds of chemicals into lakes and rivers that kill off the fish and causes acid rain and kills off more fish and some trees and small animals and insects and then noone can go swimming or fishing in the lake.

People need to respect the environment because we only have one planet, and if we keep polluting it pretty soon nothing will grow and then even the people will die.

ANALYSIS

The writer of this essay does not define his or her thesis. Because of this lack of a clear thesis, the reader is left to infer the topic from the body of the essay. It is possible to perceive the writer's intended thesis; however, the support for this thesis is very superficial. The writer presents a list of common complaints about polluters without any critical discussion of the problems and possible solutions. Many sentences are run-ons and the writer has made several spelling errors. While the author manages to communicate his or her position on the issue, he or she does so on such a superficial level and with so many errors in usage and mechanics that the writer fails to demonstrate an ability to communicate effectively.

Practice Test 1

PRACTICE TEST 1

(Answer sheets appear in the back of this book.)

Section 1 – Reading

MULTIPLE CHOICE

> **DIRECTIONS:** Read each passage and answer the questions that follow.

Passage A

Why is everybody here lying—every single man? I am convinced that I will be immediately stopped and that people will start shouting: "Oh, what nonsense, by no means everybody! You have no topic, and so you are inventing things in order to begin in a more imposing fashion." I have already been upbraided for the lack of themes. But the point is that now I am earnestly convinced of the universality of our lying. One lives 50 years with an idea, one perceives and feels it, and all of a sudden it appears in such an aspect as to make it seem that one had hitherto not known it at all.

Lately, I was suddenly struck by the thought that in Russia, among our educated classes, there cannot be even one man who wouldn't be addicted to lying. This is precisely because among us even quite honest people may be lying. I am certain that in other nations, in the overwhelming majority of them, only scoundrels are lying; they are lying for the sake of material gain, that is, with directly criminal intent.

Well, in our case, even the most esteemed people may be lying for no reason at all, and with most honorable aims. We are lying almost invariably for the sake of hospitality. One wishes to create in the listener an aesthetical impression, to give him pleasure, and so one lies even, so to speak, sacrificing oneself to the listener.

From Fyodor Dostoyevsky, "Something about Lying," 1873

1. The central idea of this passage is that

   (A) people all over the world lie for the sake of material gain.

   (B) only scoundrels lie; respectable people do not.

   (C) everybody in Russia is lying, almost always for the sake of the listener.

   (D) there can be nothing wrong with lying since everybody is doing it.

2. In developing the passage, the organizational pattern used by the author could be described as

   (A) definition.

   (B) statement and clarification.

   (C) cause and effect.

   (D) classification.

3. In this passage, what is the meaning of the word "upbraided" in the first paragraph?

   (A) Reprimanded   (C) Distinguished

   (B) Complimented   (D) Noticed

4. What is the relationship between the first two sentences of Paragraph 2?

   (A) Statement and clarification

   (B) Generalization and example

   (C) Comparison and contrast

   (D) Cause and effect

Passage B

The stranger who wanders through the great streets of London, and does not chance right into the regular quarters of the multitude, sees little or nothing of the fearful misery existing there. Only here and there at the mouth of some dark alley stands a ragged woman with a suckling babe at her weak breast, and begs with her eyes. Perhaps if those eyes are still beautiful, we glance into them, and are shocked at the world of wretchedness visible within. The common beggars are old people, generally blacks, who stand at the corners of the streets cleaning pathways—a very necessary thing in muddy London—and ask for "coppers" in reward. It is in the dusky twilight that Poverty with her mates Vice and Crime glide forth from their lairs. They shun daylight the more anxiously since their wretchedness there contrasts more cruelly with the pride of wealth which glitters everywhere; only Hunger sometimes drives them at noonday from their dens, and then they stand with silent, speaking eyes, staring beseechingly at the rich merchant who hurries along, busy and jingling gold, or at the lazy lord who, like a surfeited god, rides by on his high horse, casting now and then an aristocratically indifferent glance at the mob below, as though they were swarming ants, or rather a mass of baser beings, whose joys and sorrows have nothing in common with his feel-ings.

From Heinrich Heine, "London and the English," 1828

5. The author of this passage has created a tone that could be described as

   (A) apathetic.   (C) bitter.

   (B) arrogant.   (D) sympathetic.

6. What is the relationship between the second sentence ("Only here and there...") and the first sentence ("The stranger who...")?

   (A) Contrast

   (B) Statement and clarification

   (C) Addition

   (D) Generalization and example

7. Which statement below most accurately describes the main idea of this passage?

   (A) London is a marvelous city to visit if you avoid the shabby sections.

   (B) The wretchedness of London's poor is not obvious to the casual visitor.

   (C) In London the rich and the poor live side by side in harmony.

   (D) London should do something to hide the poor from the public eye.

Passage C

The effect of historical reading is analogous, in many respects, to that produced by foreign travel. The student, like the tourist, is transported into a new state of society. He sees new fashions. He hears new modes of expression. His mind is enlarged by contemplating the wide diversities of laws, of morals, and of manners. But men may travel far, and return with minds as contracted as if they had never stirred from their own market-town. In the same manner, men may know the dates of many battles and the genealogies of many royal houses, and yet be no wiser. Most people look at past times as princes look at foreign countries. More than one illustrious stranger has landed on our island amidst the shouts of a mob, has dined with the King, has hunted with the master of the stag-hounds, has seen the guards reviewed, and a knight of the garter installed, has cantered along Regent Street, has visited Saint Paul's, and noted down its dimensions; and has then departed, thinking that he has seen England. He has, in fact, seen a few public buildings, public men, and public ceremonies. But of the vast and complex system of society, of the fine shades of national character, of the practical operation of government and laws, he knows nothing. He who would understand these things rightly must not confine his observations to palaces and solemn days. He must see ordinary men as they appear in their ordinary business and in their ordinary pleasures. He must mingle in the crowds of the exchange and the coffee-house. He must obtain admittance to the convivial table and the domestic hearth. He must bear with vulgar expression. He must not shrink from exploring even the retreats of misery. He who wishes to understand the condition of mankind in former ages must proceed on the same principle. If he attends only to public transactions, to wars, congresses, and debates, his studies will be as unprofitable as the travels of those imperial, royal, and serene sovereigns who form their judgment of our island from having gone in state to a few fine sights, and from having held formal conferences with a few great officers.

From Thomas B. Macaulay, "History," 1828

8. In developing the paragraph, the organizational pattern used by the author could be described as

    (A) comparison.

    (C) cause and effect.

    (B) time order.

    (D) classification.

9. The sentence "But men may travel far, and return with minds as contracted as if they had never stirred from their own market-town" is a statement of

    (A) fact.

    (B) opinion.

10. This paragraph indicates that the author's purpose is to

    (A) describe what the typical visitor to England sees.

    (B) point out the differences between traveling and reading history.

    (C) show how the study of history is similar to foreign travel.

    (D) mock those who think they know England but do not.

Passage D

In democratic armies the desire of advancement is almost universal: it is ardent, tenacious, perpetual; it is strengthened by all other desires and extinguished only with life itself. But it is easy to see that, of all armies in the world, those in which advancement must be slowest in time of peace are the armies of democratic countries. As the number of commissions is naturally limited while the number of competitors is almost unlimited, and as the strict law of equality is over all alike, none can make rapid progress; many can make no progress at all. Thus the desire of advancement is greater and the opportunities of advancement fewer than elsewhere. All the ambitious spirits of a democratic army are consequently ardently desirous of war, because war makes vacancies and warrants the violation of that law of seniority which is the sole privilege natural to democracy.

We thus arrive at this singular consequence, that, of all armies, those most ardently desirous of war are democratic armies, and of all nations, those most fond of peace are democratic nations; and what makes these facts still more extraordinary is that these contrary effects are produced at the same time by the principle of equality.

From Alexis de Tocqueville, "Democracy in America," 1840

11. The central idea of this passage is that

    (A) democratic armies desire war, whereas democratic nations desire peace.

    (B) no one can be promoted in a democratic army because all are equal.

    (C) war is the only means by which an army can justify its existence.

    (D) in a democracy war is justified by the common will of the people.

12. The author of this passage has created a tone that could be described as

    (A) objective.   (C) malicious.

    (B) impassioned.   (D) depressed.

13. The author implies that

    (A) democracy is an inferior form of government.

    (B) the principle of equality has both good and bad effects.

    (C) armies everywhere should be abolished because they become corrupted.

    (D) democracy is the best form of government ever devised.

Passage E

People of every civilization throughout the relentless timeline of the ages have celebrated the transmutation of life from one state to another. Birth, the arrival of adulthood, completion of our education at various levels, birthdays, weddings, funerals—each of these significant stages is proclaimed in some ceremonial fashion, always public, verified by the witness of others, testifying to life's perpetualness of some natural sequence of human history. Validating the uniqueness of the rite of passage, its separateness from the day's other occurrences, these rituals, by the norm, demand pageantry, elaborate dress, the giving of gifts, and eating and drinking. Funerals ask for our dark apparel, christenings and birthdays ask for our gifts, wakes give us the right to get stoned, and bar mitzvahs make gluttons of us all. Yet, of fundamental birth, marriage, and death, oddly enough, only one can claim our actual attendance completely and fully: the wedding, mankind's most vital rite of passage. And so it is that this indelible imprint is found engraved in civilization's foundation.

The wedding ceremony itself, which prepares an individual's move from one stage in life to another, is organic to the society from which the individual comes. In certain African tribes, a young adolescent male finds himself hurled headlong into a wilderness where he is expected to kill a lion with nothing but his hands and intellect. His society judges his value as a man on the basis of his success in meeting that challenge. In an odd way, American newlyweds experience a similar rite as they enter a consumer society; therefore, the dynamics of wedding hoo-hah appropriately testify to commercial, mercantile values. Not only the "witnesses" buy presents. Brides buy for grooms, grooms for brides, brides for bridesmaids, ushers for grooms, and on the procedure goes. Rehearsal dinners, last-fling dinners, showers. The spiraling carnival of splish-splash around the wedding itself. The American wedding celebrates in a raucous epicurean fashion a frenzied, gluttonous revelry unparalleled by any future event in the life of an American couple.

From Martha Seligson, "The American Wedding"

14. Which of the following best describes the word "organic" as the writer uses the term in the second paragraph?

    (A) That which occurs naturally and spontaneously

    (B) Healthy

    (C) Artificial and contrived

    (D) Fundamental and basic

15. Which of the following statements best expresses the central idea of this passage?

    (A) The progression of humans from one stage in life to the next is marked by ceremony and ritual.

    (B) Weddings are frenzied affairs.

(C)   While the passage of an individual from one stage of life to another plays a vital role in civilization, the wedding is, of all such rituals, the most important.

(D)   Weddings are important affairs in all cultures.

16.   The selection includes the made-up word "hoo-hah." Which describes its most probable meaning as the writer uses it?

(A)   The crass commercialism surrounding a wedding

(B)   Bustling excitement surrounding the wedding

(C)   Chaotic and meaningless

(D)   Laughter and mirth

Passage F

Cold is a negative condition, and depends on the absence, or privation, of heat. Intense artificial cold may be produced by the rapid absorption of heat during the conversion of solids into liquids. Dr. Black long since discovered the principle, that when bodies pass from a denser to a rarer state, heat is absorbed and becomes latent in the body so transformed, and consequently cold is produced. And also that when bodies pass from a rarer to a denser state, their latent heat is evolved, and becomes sensible.

It is known to almost everyone, that dissolving common salt in water, particularly if the salt is fine, will render the water so cold, even in summer, as to be painful to the hand. The salt, as it passes from the solid to the liquid state, absorbs caloric from the water, and thus the heat that was before sensible, becomes latent, and cold is produced.

On the contrary, when a piece of lead, or iron, is beaten smartly with a hammer, it becomes hot, because the metal, in consequence of the hammering, has its capacity for caloric reduced, and thus the heat which was before latent, now becomes sensible. For the same reason, when air is compressed forcibly in a tube, or as it is sometimes called, in a *fire-pump*, the heat, which was before latent, becomes sensible, because the condensation lessens its capacity for caloric.

The principle on which all freezing mixtures act is therefore the change of state which one or more of the articles employed undergo, during the process, and this change consists in an enlarged capacity for caloric. The degree of cold will then depend on the quantity of caloric which passes from a free to a latent state, and this again will depend on the quantity of substance liquefied, and the rapidity of the liquefaction.

The substances most commonly employed for this purpose are those originally used by Fahrenheit, to produce the zero of his thermometric scale; viz. common salt and snow, or pounded ice. For this purpose the salt should be fine, and the ice, which must always be used in summer, is to be reduced to small particles in a cold mortar.

The vessel to contain the substance to be frozen may be made of tin. It is simply a tall vessel, holding a few pints, with a close cover, and a rim round the top, for the convenience of handling it. For common purposes, this may be set into any convenient wooden vessel (having first introduced the substance to be frozen) and then surrounded by the freezing mixture. The only care to be taken in this part of the process is to see that the freezing mixture in the outside vessel reaches as high as the contents of the internal one. With two or three pounds of fine common salt, and double this weight of pounded ice, three or four pints of iced cream may be made in this way, during the warmest days of summer. The process requires two or three hours, and while it is going on, the vessel should be set in a cellar, or covered with a flannel cloth, as a bad conductor of the external heat.

From J.L. Comstack, "Elements of Chemistry"

17. After reading the above passage, the reader could correctly infer that dissolving sugar in hot tea will

    (A) lower the temperature of the hot tea.

    (B) cause the temperature of the tea to become even warmer just as beating a piece of lead with a hammer will raise its temperature.

    (C) lower the temperature of hot tea so that if it were placed about cream in a tin container, the cream would freeze within two to three hours.

    (D) reduce the temperature of the hot tea to such a low temperature as to be painful to the hand.

18. The drop in temperature which occurs when sugar is added to coffee is the result of

    I.   sugar passing from a solid to a liquid state.

    II.   sugar absorbing caloric from the water.

    III. heat becoming latent when it was sensible.

    (A) I only.   (C) I, II, and III.

    (B) I and II.   (D) I and III.

19. Which is the best example of Dr. Black's discovery as outlined in the article?

    (A) To gargle with warm salt water, one should start with water cooler than one desires and then add the salt.

    (B) To gargle with warm salt water, one should start with salt and then pour water which is cooler than that desired over the salt.

    (C) To gargle with warm salt water, one should adjust the temperature of the tap water to the temperature desired and then add fine salt; the fineness of the salt will prevent any change in the water temperature.

    (D) To gargle with warm salt water, one should start with water warmer than desired and then add the salt.

20. The narrator seems to base this article on

    (A) a sociological study.   (C) scientific procedures.

    (B) trial-and-error methods.   (D) historical research.

21. The word "mortar" (Paragraph 5) as used in this article can be best interpreted to mean

    (A) that which can fix or hold together, as mortar holds bricks.

    (B) a weapon, a piece of artillery, or a small cannon.

    (C) a container used for grinding or mixing.

    (D) a mixture.

22. The writer does not make use of

    (A) descriptions.   (C) mathematics.

    (B) interviews.   (D) experiments.

23. In pumping up a basketball, one can infer from this article that the metal needle going into the ball

    (A) will become warm.

    (B) will not be affected by the process since metal is strong.

    (C) will become cooler.

    (D) will quickly reach a freezing temperature.

24. The writer can be best described as

    (A) concerned with literary form and stylistic devices.

    (B) subjective in his writing.

    (C) objective.

    (D) presenting facts which are new to most scientists in the twenty-first century.

25. A positive condition depending on the absence of cold is

    (A) Fahrenheit.

    (B) intense artificial cold.

    (C) heat.

    (D) a rarer state, according to Black.

26. Black found that when bodies pass from a rarer to a denser state, their latent heat is evolved, and becomes sensible. "Sensible" can be interpreted to mean

    (A) knowledgeable, making sense.

    (B) logical.

    (C) evolving.

    (D) perceptible.

Passage G

   "Good evening to you, honored sir," said he, making a low bow, and still retaining his hold of the skirt. "I pray you tell me whereabouts is the dwelling of my kinsman, Major Molineux."

The youth's question was uttered very loudly; and one of the barbers, whose razor was descending on a well-soaped chin, and another who was dressing a Ramillies wig, left their occupations, and came to the door. The citizen, in the meantime, turned a long-favored countenance upon Robin, and answered him in a tone of excessive anger and annoyance. His two sepulchral hems, however, broke into the very centre of his rebuke, with most singular effect, like a thought of the cold grave obtruding among wrathful passions.

"Let go my garment, fellow! I tell you, I know not the man you speak of. What! I have authority, I have—hem, hem—authority; and if this be the respect you show for your betters, your feet shall be brought acquainted with the stocks by daylight, tomorrow morning!"

Robin released the old man's skirt, and hastened away, pursued by an ill-mannered roar of laughter from the barber's shop. He was at first considerably surprised by the result of his question, but, being a shrewd youth, soon thought himself able to account for the mystery.

"This is some country representative," was his conclusion, "who has never seen the inside of my kinsman's door, and lacks the breeding to answer a stranger civilly. The man is old, or verily—I might be tempted to turn back and smite him on the nose. Ah, Robin, Robin! even the barber's boys laugh at you for choosing such a guide! You will be wiser in time, friend Robin."

He now became entangled in a succession of crooked and narrow streets, which crossed each other, and meandered at no great distance from the waterside. The smell of tar was obvious to his nostrils, the masts of vessels pierced the moonlight above the tops of the buildings, and the numerous signs, which Robin paused to read, informed him that he was near the centre of business. But the streets were empty, the shops were closed, and lights were visible only in the second stories of a few dwelling-houses. At length, on the corner of a narrow lane, through which he was passing, he beheld the broad countenance of a British hero swinging before the door of an inn, whence proceeded the voices of many guests. The casement of one of the lower windows was thrown back, and a very thin curtain permitted Robin to distinguish a party at supper, round a well-furnished table. The fragrance of the good cheer steamed forth into the outer air, and the youth could not fail to recollect that the last remnant of his travelling stock of provision had yielded to his morning appetite, and that noon had found and left him dinnerless.

"Oh, that a parchment three-penny might give me a right to sit down at yonder table!" said Robin, with a sigh. "But the Major will make me welcome to the best of his victuals; so I will even stop boldly in, and inquire my way to his dwelling."

He entered the tavern, and was guided by the murmur of voices and the fumes of tobacco in the public-room. It was a long and low apartment, with oaken walls, grown dark in the continual smoke, and a floor which was thickly sanded, but of no immaculate purity. A number of persons—the larger part of whom appeared to be mariners, or in some way connected with the sea—occupied the wooden benches, or leather-bottomed chairs, conversing on various matters, and occasionally lending their attention to some topic of general interest. Three or four little groups were draining as many bowls of punch, which the West India trade had long since made a familiar drink in the colony. Others, who had the appearance of men who lived by regular and laborious handicraft, preferred the insulated bliss of an unshared potation, and became more taciturn under its influence. Nearly all, in short, evinced a predilection for the Good Creature in some of its various shapes, for this is a vice to which, as Fast Day sermons of a hundred years ago will testify, we have a long hereditary claim. The only guests to whom Robin's sympathies inclined him were two or three sheepish countrymen, who were using the inn somewhat after the fashion of a Turkish caravansary; they had gotten themselves into the darkest corner of the room, and heedless of the Nicotian atmosphere, were supping on the bread of their own ovens, and the bacon cured in their own chimney-smoke. But though Robin felt a sort of brotherhood with these strangers, his eyes were attracted from them to a person who stood near the door, holding whispered conversation with a group of ill-dressed associates. His features were separately striking almost to grotesqueness, and the whole face left a deep impression on the memory. The forehead bulged out into a double prominence, with a vale between; the nose came boldly forth in an irregular curve, and its bridge was of more than a finger's breadth; the eyebrows were deep and shaggy, and the eyes glowed beneath them like fire in a cave.

While Robin deliberated of whom to inquire respecting his kinsman's dwelling, he was accosted by the innkeeper, a little man in a stained white apron, who had come to pay his professional welcome to the stranger. Being in the second generation from a French Protestant, he seemed to have inherited the courtesy of his parent nation; but no variety of circumstances was ever known to change his voice from the one shrill note in which he now addressed Robin.

"From the country, I presume, sir?" said he, with a profound bow. "Beg leave to congratulate you on your arrival, and trust you intend a long stay with us. Fine town here, sir, beautiful buildings, and much that may interest a stranger. May I hope for the honor of your commands in respect to supper?"

"The man sees a family likeness! the rogue has guessed that I am related to the Major!" thought Robin, who had hitherto experienced little superfluous civility.

All eyes were now turned on the country lad, standing at the door, in his worn three-cornered hat, gray coat, leather breeches, and blue yarn stockings, leaning on an oaken cudgel, and bearing a wallet on his back.

From Nathaniel Hawthorne, "My Kinsman, Major Molineux"

27. Of all the people in the room, Robin would be most inclined to strike up a conversation with the

   (A)   mariners.   (C)   countrymen.

   (B)   day laborers.   (D)   persons standing near the door.

28. From all indications, which of the following is probably true of the men eating their home-cooked food?

   I.   They are from the countryside.

   II.   They are uncomfortable being in the tavern.

   III.   They are resented by the rest of the men in the tavern.

   (A)   I only.   (C)   III only.

   (B)   II only.   (D)   I and II only.

29. Taken in context of the passage, the best interpretation of "Nearly all, in short, evinced a predilection for the Good Creature" (Paragraph 8) is that nearly all the

    (A) mariners are celebrating a successful voyage to the West Indies.

    (B) people in the tavern are drinking an alcoholic beverage.

    (C) people in the tavern had been reformed by turning to religion.

    (D) men in the tavern were known for seeking out the enjoyable things in life.

30. To what does the author say "we have a long hereditary claim"?

    (A) Seafaring   (C) Smoking

    (B) Drinking   (D) Gossiping

STOP

The following additional multiple-choice questions have been provided to help you sharpen your skills. This section will not appear on the actual MTEL test. Please turn to "Vocabulary" on page 240 to resume the timed practice test.

31. The tone of the citizen in the barber's shop who responded to Robin can best be described as

    (A) jovial and light-hearted   (C) interested and helpful.

    (B) disdainful and aloof.   (D) passionate and gloomy.

32. The statements "your feet shall be brought acquainted with the stocks" can be interpreted as

    (A) first-hand contact with farm animals.

    (B) personal attention to investment.

    (C) punishment that could result from the youth's behavior.

    (D) a reference to a dance step familiar to the common people.

33. "As a result of drink, some of the tavern occupants became more taciturn"; this can be interpreted to mean that they were

    (A) unreticent.   (C) boisterous.

    (B) talkative.   (D) uncommunicative.

34. Compare and/or contrast the citizen at the barber shop and the innkeeper.

   (A)   The innkeeper and the citizen were courteous.

   (B)   The innkeeper and the citizen were inhospitable.

   (C)   The innkeeper was courteous; the citizen was inhospitable.

   (D)   The citizen was hospitable; the innkeeper was discourteous.

35. Which of the following quotations best indicates the reception Robin received?

   (A)   "…a predilection for the Good Creature…"

   (B)   "…after the fashion of a Turkish caravansary…"

   (C)   "…little superfluous civility…"

   (D)   "…insulated bliss of an unshared potation…"

36. Robin did not eat at the tavern because

   (A)   food was not served there.

   (B)   he expected to eat with the Major.

   (C)   the tavern keeper was inhospitable.

   (D)   no places were available.

Passage H

Economic Effects of the Depression

During the early months of the depression most people thought it was just an adjustment in the business cycle which would soon be over. Hoover repeatedly assured the public that prosperity was just around the corner. As time went on, the worst depression in American history set in, reaching its bottom point in early 1932. The gross national product fell from $104.6 billion in 1929 to $56.1 billion in 1933. Unemployment reached about 13 million in 1933, or about 25 percent of the labor force excluding farmers. National income dropped 54 percent from $87.8 billion to $40.2 billion. Labor income fell about 41 percent, while farm income dropped 55 percent, from $11.9 billion to $5.3 billion. Industrial production dropped about 51 percent. The banking system suffered as 5,761 banks—over 22 percent of the total—failed by the end of 1932.

UNEMPLOYMENT, 1929–1945

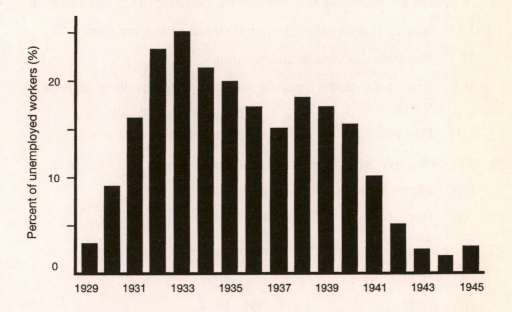

As the depression grew worse, more and more people lost their jobs or had their wages reduced. Many were unable to continue credit payments on homes, automobiles, and other possessions, and lost them. Families doubled up in houses and apartments. Both the marriage rate and the birth rate declined as people put off family formation. Hundreds of thousands became homeless and lived in groups of makeshift shacks called Hoovervilles in empty spaces around cities. Others traveled the country by foot and boxcar seeking food and work. State and local government agencies and private charities were overwhelmed in their attempts to care for those in need, although public and private soup kitchens and soup lines were set up throughout the nation. Malnutrition was widespread but few died of starvation, perhaps because malnourished people are susceptible to many fatal diseases.

37. The author's purpose for writing this passage was probably

    (A) to degrade Hoover's presidency.

    (B) to track the gross national product.

    (C) to link Depression statistics to their effects in everyday life.

    (D) to monitor the effects of the banking system.

38. Which of the following best explains the meaning of the last sentence?

    (A) Many diseases can make people immune to starvation.

    (B) Many diseases cause malnutrition.

    (C) Few malnourished people survived diseases long enough to starve.

    (D) Few died from the effects of malnutrition.

39. According to the bar graph, the unemployment rate was highest in

    (A) 1929.   (C) 1938.

    (B) 1933.   (D) 1944.

40. According to the graph, the unemployment rate was lowest in

    (A) 1929.   (C) 1938.

    (B) 1933.   (D) 1944.

VOCABULARY

DIRECTIONS: This section tests your vocabulary knowledge. Use the spaces below each word to write the definitions. Your responses will be marked as correct or incorrect based on the accuracy and adequacy of the definition provided.

1. Define *pungent*.

    _____

    _____

    _____

2. Define *condone*.

    _____

    _____

    _____

3. Define *finite*.

    _____

    _____

    _____

4. Define *ruminate*.

    _____

    _____

    _____

5. Define *facsimile*.

    _____

    _____

    _____

6. Define *enamored*.

    _____

    _____

    _____

7. Define *omniscient*.

    _____

    _____

    _____

8. Define *demise*.

_____

_____

_____

9. Define *pàlpable*.

_____

_____

_____

Section 2 – Writing

WRITTEN SUMMARY

Essay 1

Whatever may be thought of the evidence bearing upon the question of the former gaseous condition of our world, it is generally admitted that the evidence of former igneous fluidity is somewhat conclusive. Our earth was once a self-luminous star.

At the temperature which would fuse the mass of the rocks, all the more volatile substances could only exist in the form of an elastic vapor surrounding the earth. All the carbon in the world must have existed in the form of carbonic acid; all the water as an invisible elastic vapor, extending out beyond the limits of the present atmosphere. There could hence be upon the earth no vegetation, no animals, no salt, no water. All that we now behold must have been represented by a glowing, liquid nucleus, enveloped in a dense atmosphere of burning acrid vapors. This orb must have revolved upon its axis and performed its revolutions around the sun. The sun and moon (if the latter existed) must have raised the fiery ocean to a tidal wave which rolled around the globe. An ocean of fire sent up to the nocturnal heavens a glare that was more fearful than the poisoned ray of feebly-shining sun. Here was chaos. Here was the death and silence of the primeval ages, when the Uncreated alone looked on, and saw order, and beauty, and life germinating in the heart of universal discord.

In obedience to the law of thermal equilibrium, the high temperature of the earth gradually subsided through radiation into external space. A crystallization of the least fusible elements and simple compounds eventually took place in the superficial portions of the molten mass. This process continued till a crystalline crust had been formed, resting upon the liquid mass which still constituted the chief bulk of the globe.

It has sometimes been objected to this view that the solidified materials would possess superior density, and would, accordingly, sink into the liquid portions. If this were so, the solidification of such a molten mass would either commence at the center, or a uniform refrigeration would proceed till the whole world would suddenly be consolidated. It is the general belief that the central portions of the earth still remain in a molten condition, while the habitable exterior is but a comparatively thin crust. If this belief is well founded, the first solidified portions did not descend toward the centre. Moreover, we know that, in the case of water and several other substances, the newly-solidified parts are less dense, and float upon the liquid portions. This apparent exception to the law of expansion by heat is accounted for by supposing that, when the molecules of a solidifying fluid arrange themselves in a regular crystalline manner, they inclose certain minute spaces, so that the resulting crystal is a little more bulky than the unarranged molecules from which it was constructed. If this law applies to the refrigeration of water, iron, and other substances, we may reasonably infer it to be a general law of matter. We should expect, then, that crystals of quartz would float upon molten quartz, just as solid iron floats upon molten iron. We have, therefore, not only evidences of the fact of a forming crust, but also a probable means of accounting for it.

From Alexander Winchell, "Sketches of Creation"

Essay 2

While the influence of Theodore Roosevelt and other influential and empire-minded persons may have helped to persuade McKinley to enter the Spanish-American War, the weight of public opinion must be considered as a major factor in the president's decision.

The 1890s were the heyday of "Yellow Journalism." Named for "the Yellow Kid," a cartoon character regularly appearing in the mass circulation papers of the time, Yellow Journalism grew out of the competition for circulation between the mass-market papers of William Randolph Hearst and Joseph Pulitzer. In order to boost their circulation, the papers were not above sensationalizing, distorting, falsifying, or even creating news.

This had its most striking effect in helping to bring on the Spanish-American War. Newspapers gave sensationalized reports of Spanish attempts to suppress a rebellion in Cuba, making it appear that the Spaniards were guilty of extreme human rights violations. As public outrage grew, so too did pressure on the McKinley administration to take a hard line with Spain. Spain was conciliatory, but McKinley felt compelled to send the battleship U.S.S. *Maine* to the harbor of Havanna, Cuba, to show the flag and generally uphold American interests. While there the *Maine* was torn by an explosion and sank with heavy loss of life. The yellow press immediately roared its opinion that this was the doing of Spain, though the cause of the explosion was and remains unknown.

The public outcry raised by such reporting, coupled with the public's sincere but in part misled humanitarian desire to free the Cubans from Spanish tyranny and bestow on it the benefits of a free government, finally drove McKinley to decide for war with Spain. Though imperialists in high places in Washington may have helped him toward such a decision for reasons of their own, the primary reason must be viewed as the pressure of public opinion, artificially created by an irresponsible press, on an astute politician like William McKinley.

Essay 3

While it is true that other countries did away with slavery without the resort to civil war, this could have happened in the United States only had the South been willing to part with slavery under some other circumstances. Unfortunately, that was not the case.

Attempts to deal with the issue of slavery in the United States go back to the period of the Articles of Confederation. The Northwest Ordinance, drafted in 1787 by Virginia slaveholder Thomas Jefferson, prohibited slavery in what was to become the states of Ohio, Indiana, Illinois, Michigan, and Wisconsin. Jefferson believed slavery was evil and inconsistent with American ideals but that it could not be abolished suddenly in the areas where it already existed. He did not, however, desire its spread—an attitude reflected in the Northwest Ordinance and shared by most Southerners throughout the United States' first half-century of independence. The slave trade was abolished in 1808 without controversy, and various schemes were discussed for the gradual and compensated emancipation of the slaves, usually coupled with plans to repatriate them to Africa. In these, Northerners and Northern state legislatures offered their financial help, but little came of them as most slaveholders seemed more willing to confess the evil of slavery in principle than to part with their own valuable investments in human chattels.

As the 1830s began both anti-slavery rhetoric on the part of Northern opponents of the institution as well as the attitudes of the slaveholders themselves began to become more extreme. It is hard to say which phenomenon was caused by the other. They were mutually aggravating. Abolitionists denounced slavery as a national sin, and slaveholders began to defend it not as an unavoidable evil but now as a positive good for both white man and black.

The issue that finally led to civil war was that of slavery in the territories. Northerners, or at least the vast majority of them, freely conceded that the federal government had no right to prohibit slavery in the states where it existed, and repeatedly assured the South that they had no intention of doing so. They did, however, believe the federal government had the right to keep slavery from spreading into new territories and felt it their duty to achieve this. As expressed by Abraham Lincoln, their goal in this was to "place slavery where the public may rest assured that it is in the course of ultimate extinction." This was much the same attitude Thomas Jefferson had held with regard to the Northwest Ordinance, but by the mid-nineteenth century Southern attitudes had changed. Southerners too saw the limitation of slavery expansion as an indication that slavery would some day in the distant future cease to exist in their states as well, and as such they rejected it, determined to have slavery not only for the present but for the indefinite future as well.

Several attempts were made to limit the spread of slavery— the Missouri dispute of 1819-20 and the struggle over the Wilmott Proviso (1846-50)—but each ended in a compromise that gave more land to slavery. When in 1861 the Republican party came to power on a platform calling for no further spread of slavery and then refused to compromise away the results of the election, Southerners responded by seceding and setting up their own republic where slavery might never be threatened.

Thus, while it is possible to say that slavery could have been ended in the United States without a civil war—if the South would have agreed to give up its slaves on any other terms—Southern determination to preserve the institution at all costs made such a course impossible and war was the only means to rid the country of slavery.

WRITTEN COMPOSITION

DIRECTIONS: Read the following statements and passages, as well as each set of directions; then write your response. Your compositions will be scored according to the following characteristics: appropriateness, mechanical conventions, word usage, sentence structure, focus and unity, organization, and development.

Essay 1

Young people seem very conscious of wearing trendy or brand-name clothing, especially that worn by professional athletes and movie stars.

Does this statement reinforce the idea that "clothes make the man (or woman)"? Write an essay that presents your opinion on this subject.

Essay 2

The old saying "Experience is the best teacher" suggests to some people that they would benefit more from learning on the job or in the world than from continuing their formal education in the school or college class-room.

Write an essay in which you discuss the relative values of experiential and academic learning. Support your view with specific examples from literature, history, current events, or personal experience.

Essay 3

Think of a common misconception that has led to a derogatory stereo-type. Write an essay that presents your opinion on this subject.

GRAMMAR AND USAGE

> **DIRECTIONS:** Read each passage and answer the questions that follow.

Passage A

[1]Although most new homes across the United States are finished in brick, stucco is an old finish that is becoming in-creasingly popular. [2]Stucco finishes, applied with a trowel, <u>is</u> composed of sand, water, and a cementing mixture. [3]The first coat or two is thicker, about $3/8$ of an inch, with the final coat about $1/4$ to $1/8$ of an inch thick.

⁴Stucco has many advantages. ⁵One of the most attractive selling features is that stucco is energy efficient. ⁶In addition, a waterproof, low maintenance exterior is produced by coating the final application with a clear acrylic finish. ⁷Since stucco finishes are mixed with color homeowners and designers can select from a wide range of shades. ⁸Also, stucco is lightweight and quite inexpensive. ⁹By substituting stucco for brick veneer, the typical home gains about 200 square feet of living space.

1. Which of the following, if added between Sentences 2 and 3, is most consistent with the writer's purpose and audience.

    (A) Personally, I know people who think stucco is an ugly finish for a home.

    (B) Sometimes, Spanish and Indian style homes in the Southwest are finished with stucco on the interior walls.

    (C) Indeed, stucco creates a California ambiance many wish to emulate.

    (D) The plaster-like stucco is applied in two or three thin coats.

2. Which of the following is needed in the second paragraph?

    (A) Sentence 5: Delete the second "is."

    (B) Sentence 6: Move "in addition" after "finish."

    (C) Sentence 7: Place a comma after "color."

    (D) Sentence 8: Move "quite" after "is."

3. Which of the following should be used in place of the underlined verb in Sentence 2?

    (A) are   (C) being

    (B) will be   (D) should be

Passage B

¹There are more things to recycle than tin, plastic, aluminum, and newsprint. ²One type of recycling that is gaining in popularity is Christmas tree recycling. ³Most of the 34 million Christmas trees that Americans buy every year end up in landfills. ⁴This is an expensive waste of organic material and valu-

able space in the landfills. [5]Many communities have bought wood chippers so the trees can be turned into mulch for the garden. [6]Some areas dump the trees on the bottoms of lakes to supply habitat for fish and other organisms, and along the coast-lines, states are tying Christmas trees into large bundles for use in coastline reclamation projects. [7]Eventually covered by sand and coastal vegetation, the trees become dunes which keep valu-able beaches from being washed away.

[8]In Texas, along the Gulf Coast, there are people who re-cycle used oil rigs. [9]Following a master plan designed by a special advisory commission, this self-sustaining program en-couraged the use of petroleum rigs for the development of un-derwater recreational areas. [10]Because it is cheaper to topple a rig rather than tow it back to shore, participating companies topple their tall offshore petroleum drilling platforms and give half the money saved to the Artificial Reef Fund. [11]The state has an Artificial Reef Fund, a program which does not use the tax-payers' money. [12]These offshore rigs have already become un-derwater fish habitats because the rig's barnacle-encrusted legs provide protection against larger predators. [13]Often, undersea sport fishers and divers already know the locations of these plat-forms and come there even while drilling is in progress. [14]Once the rig is toppled, new organisms will inhabit the structure, and new types of fish will find a home there. [15]The toppled rigs become an artificial reef.

4. Which of the following, if added between Sentences 4 and 5, is most consistent with the writer's purpose and audience?

   (A) It makes more sense to recycle the trees.

   (B) Some people think the trees provide a useful function in the landfill by adding organic material.

   (C) A big problem is that people often don't take off the tinsel and artificial icicles.

   (D) How could anyone get out in the cold of late December?

5. Which of the following makes the sequence of ideas clearer in the second paragraph?

   (A) Delete Sentence 8.

(B)   Delete Sentence 10.

(C)   Reverse the order of Sentences 8 and 15.

(D)   Place Sentence 11 before Sentence 9.

6.   Which one of the following changes is needed?

(A)   Sentence 8: Change "who" to "which."

(B)   Sentence 9: Change "encouraged" to "encourages."

(C)   Sentence 10: Change "cheaper" to "cheapest."

(D)   Sentence 13: Add a comma after "platforms."

Passage C

[1]Dena may die soon. [2]For 21 years, all Dena has ever known is captivity. [3]How would you like to spend your entire life in captivity? [4]Even though Dena is not a human, but an orca, a killer whale, like in the movie *Orca,* don't you think Dena deserves to be released from her natural habitat? [5]Orcas are much too intelligent and too delicate to be confined in tanks. [6]Dena's owners claim, Sea Habitat, Inc., she is displaying geriatric signs normal for an orca 25 years old. [7]Orcas are not meant to be caged, no matter how kind the jailer who holds the keys.

[8]We don't know enough about orcas and how they interact. [9]Who are we to confine a species that may be as intelligent as humans? [10]True, Dena may be rejected by her original pod, members of which stayed together for life. [11]_____. [12]Maybe she is too old to live much longer. [13]However, we should at least allow Dena to die with dignity in her natural surroundings. [14]And, if Dena succeeds in surviving in the wild, maybe we can pressure other zoos and marine institutions around the world to release these beautiful animals back to the wild, where they can have longer, healthier lives. [15]I urge everyone to write a letter to their local senator and congressman demanding the return of all orcas to the oceans of the Earth.

7.   Which of the following, if added between Sentences 6 and 7, is most consistent with the writer's purpose and audience?

(A) Some say leave her where she is because there's no use in crying over spilled milk.

(B) People attempt to obfuscate the issue by ignoring the fact that orcas have no natural enemy other than man.

(C) Did you know that orcas have an average of 40–48 teeth?

(D) However, the high death rate of orcas in captivity clearly indicates that Dena may be sick from having been confined.

8. Which of the following displays nonstandard pronoun usage?

(A) Sentence 3   (C) Sentence 14

(B) Sentence 7   (D) Sentence 15

9. Which of the following phrases is unnecessary and should be eliminated?

(A) "For 21 years" in Sentence 2

(B) "like in the movie *Orca*" in Sentence 4

(C) "that may be as intelligent as humans" in Sentence 9

(D) "to the oceans of the Earth" in Sentence 15

10. Which of the following corrects the underlined portion of Sentence 4?

Even though Dena is not a human, but an orca, a killer whale, like in the movie *Orca*, don't you think <u>Dena deserves to be released from her natural habitat?</u>

(A) Dena deserved to be released from her natural habitat?

(B) Dena deserves from her natural habitat to be released?

(C) Dena deserves to be released under her natural habitat?

(D) Dena deserves to be released into her natural habitat?

11. Which of the following best corrects Sentence 6?

(A) Dena's owners, Sea Habitat, Inc., claim she is displaying geriatric signs normal for an orca 25 years old.

(B) Since they are Dena's owners, Sea Habitat, Inc. claim she is displaying geriatric signs normal for an orca 25 years old.

(C) Sea Habitat, Inc., Dena's owners, claim she is displaying geriatric signs normal for an orca 25 years old.

(D)   Choices (A) and (C) only.

12. Which of the following, if used between Sentences 10 and 12, best develops the main idea of the second paragraph?

(A)   Another problem to be overcome is training Dena to hunt live fish, instead of depending on being fed dead fish by her human captors.

(B)   As a matter of fact, it is now against the law to capture orcas in the wild and sell them to zoos.

(C)   As we all know, the breeding of captive orcas has not been successful.

(D)   This issue was made famous by the movie *Free Willy*.

13. Which of the following verbs are used incorrectly?

(A)   "deserves" in Sentence 4

(B)   "holds" in Sentence 7

(C)   "stayed" in Sentence 10

(D)   Choices (B) and (C) only.

14. Which of the following best punctuates Sentence 8?

(A)   We don't know enough, about orcas, and how they interact.

(B)   We don't know enough, about orcas and how they interact!

(C)   We don't know enough: about orcas and how they interact.

(D)   Best as is.

STOP

The following additional multiple-choice questions have been provided to help you sharpen your skills. This section will not appear on the actual MTEL test. Please turn to "Sentence Corrections" on page 263 to resume the timed practice test.

Passage D

[1]In 1840 Dickens came up with the idea of using a raven as a character in his new novel, *Barnaby Rudge*. [2]Soon, the word got out among his friends and neighbors that the famous author was interested in ravens and wanted to know more about them.

[3]When someone gave a raven as a pet, he was delighted. [4]The raven was named Grip by Dickens' children and became a successful member of his family. [5]Grip began to get his way around the household, and if he wanted something, he took it, and Grip would bite the children's ankles when he felt displeased. [6]The raven in *Barnaby Rudge* is depicted as a trickster who slept "on horseback" in the stable and "has been known, by the mere superiority of his genius, to walk off unmolested with the dog's dinner." [7]So we get an idea of what life with Grip was like.

[8]Poe, however, was dissatisfied. [9]This was a comical presentation of the raven. [10]Poe felt that the large black bird should have a more prophetic use. [11]So, about a year after *Barnaby Rudge* was published, Poe began work on his poem, "The Raven." [12]Any schoolchild can quote the famous line, "Quoth the Raven, 'Nevermore,'" but almost no one knows about Grip. [13]What happened to Grip? [14]Well, when he died, the Dickens family had become so attached to him that they had him stuffed and displayed him in the parlor.

15. Which of the following is the best revision of the underlined portion of Sentence 3 below?

   When <u>someone gave a raven as a pet, he was delighted</u>.

   (A)   giving someone a raven as a pet, he was delighted.

   (B)   someone gave Dickens a raven for a pet, the author was delighted.

   (C)   someone delightedly gave a raven for a pet to Dickens.

   (D)   someone gave Dickens a raven as a pet, the result was that the author was delighted with the gift.

16. Which of the following is the best revision of the underlined portion of Sentence 5 below?

   Grip began to get his way around the household, and <u>if he wanted something, he took it, and Grip would bite the children's ankles when he felt displeased</u>.

   (A)   if he wanted something, he took it; if he felt displeased, he bit the children's ankles.

   (B)   if wanting something, he would take, and if unhappy, he would bite.

(C)   when he wanted something, he would take it; being displeased, he would bite the children's ankles.

(D)   when taking something that he wanted, he would bite the children's ankles.

17. In the context of the sentences preceding and following Sentence 7, which of the following is the best revision of Sentence 7?

(A)   So, you can get an idea of what life with Grip was like.

(B)   Therefore, the challenges of living with Grip must have been numerous and varied.

(C)   So, an idea of the life with Grip can be gotten.

(D)   Life with Grip must have been entertaining.

18. Which of the following is the best way to combine Sentences 8, 9, and 10?

(A)   Poe, however, was dissatisfied with this comical presentation and thought that the large black bird should have a more prophetic use.

(B)   As a result of dissatisfaction, Poe thought the big black bird should be presented more prophetically than comically.

(C)   However, Poe felt the comical presentation was not as good as the prophetic one.

(D)   Poe, however, dissatisfied with the comical presentation of the big black bird, felt a more prophetic use would be better.

19. In relation to the passage as a whole, which of the following best describes the writer's intention in the first paragraph?

(A)   To provide background information

(B)   To provide a concrete example of a humorous episode

(C)   To arouse sympathy in the reader

(D)   To evaluate the effectiveness of the treatment of the subject

20. Which of the following is the best revision of the underlined portion of Sentence 4 below?

The raven was named Grip <u>by Dickens' children and became a successful member of his family</u>.

(A)   by the children and it became a successful member of his family.

(B)   by Dickens' children and was becoming a successful member of his family.

(C)   by Dickens' children and became a successful member of the family.

(D)   , Dickens' children named him that, and he became a successful member of the family.

Passage E

¹Medieval literature and art, throughout the predominance of religious themes, was greatly varied. ²In literature, for example, the chivalric tradition embodied in such works as the Arthurian legends, as well as the Anglo-Saxon epic *Beowulf* and the French epic *Song of Roland,* showed the richness of themes. ³Originating in France during the mid-1100s, the Gothic style spread to other parts of Europe. ⁴However, it was in Gothic architecture that the Medieval religious fervor best exhibited itself. ⁵Gothic cathedrals were the creation of a community, with many artisans and craftsman working over many generations. ⁶Most of the populace could not read or write, so donating funds or working on the building and its furnishings becomes a form of religious devotion as well as a means of impressing neighboring areas and attracting tourism. ⁷The first Gothic structures were parts of an abbey and a cathedral. ⁸Later during the twelfth and thirteenth centuries Gothic architecture reached its peak in the great cathedrals of Notre Dame in Paris, Westminster Abbey in England, and Cologne Cathedral in Germany.

⁹Gothic architecture strives to emphasize height and light. ¹⁰Characteristic internal structures are the ribbed vault and pointed arches. ¹¹Thick stone walls give way to stained glass windows depicting religious scenes, and the masonry is embellished with delicate tracery. ¹²Outside, slender beams called "flying buttresses" provide support for the height of the building. ¹³Great spires complete the illusion of rising to the sky.

21.   Which of the following would most appropriately replace "throughout" in Sentence 1?

    (A)   beyond   (C)   despite

    (B)   until   (D)   unless

22. Which of the following should be plural rather than singular?

    (A)   "art" in Sentence 1

    (B)   "architecture" in Sentence 4

    (C)   "craftsman" in Sentence 5

    (D)   "tracery" in Sentence 11

23. Which of the following would improve and clarify the structure of the first paragraph?

    (A)   Eliminate Sentence 5.

    (B)   Place Sentence 3 after Sentence 7.

    (C)   Reverse the order of Sentences 2 and 4.

    (D)   Place Sentence 1 after Sentence 13.

24. Which of the following words is used incorrectly in Sentence 6?

    (A)   populace   (C)   becomes

    (B)   donating   (D)   devotion

25. How would the following underlined portion of Sentence 8 be better clarified by punctuation?

    <u>Later during the twelfth and thirteenth centuries Gothic architecture reached its peak in the great cathedrals</u> of Notre Dame in Paris, Westminster Abbey in England, and Cologne Cathedral in Germany.

    (A)   Later during the twelfth and thirteenth centuries, Gothic architecture reached its peak, in the great cathedrals

    (B)   Later, during the twelfth and thirteenth centuries: Gothic architecture reached its peak in the great cathedrals

    (C)   Later, during the twelfth, and thirteenth centuries, Gothic architecture reached its peak, in the great cathedrals

    (D)   Later, during the twelfth and thirteenth centuries, Gothic architecture reached its peak in the great cathedrals

26. Which of the following would best fit between Sentences 10 and 11?

    (A)   Often, you can find gargoyles, grotesque demonic-looking creatures carved on the outside of the building.

(B)   Particularly impressive to me are the carvings of realistic animals and plants on the pulpits.

(C)   Tall, thin columns reach to the ceiling and help to support the roof.

(D)   These buildings were designed to impress everyone who saw them with the glory of God.

Passage F

[1]Using Indians to track down and fight other Indians was not a new idea during the conflict between the Whites and the Indians during the mid-1800 Indian Wars during the conquest of the Apaches. [2]The English and the French from early colonial times had exploited traditional intertribal rivalries to their own advantage.

[3]What was a novel idea of the U.S. Army during its war against the Apaches was using an Indian against members of his own tribe. [4]Gen. George Crook believed that the best work would be done by an Indian who had only just been fighting him. [5]Crook had learned that such a scout would know alot because he would know the fighting habits, the hiding places, and the personalities of the Indians being pursued. [6]This method worked well for Crook and by the end of his career he had used about 500 Apache scouts.

[7]Crook demanded trust from all his troops and, in turn, he gave them his trust. [8]He paid his scouts well and on time, two very important factors. [9]Most importantly, Crook treated all the personnel under his command with dignity and respect. [10]These were good qualities. [11]These qualities no doubt earned Crook the admiration and loyalty of his Indian soldiers. [12]Though, the man himself won their respect. [13]Crook was like few West Point trained officers, for he understood his enemy well. [14]He learned to fight the Indians on their terms, to use the land and terrain to his advantage, and to abandon the textbook examples. [15]He got on a trail, and with his Apache scouts to guide him, he followed his quarry relentlessly.

[16]Crook's faith in his scouts never wavered. [17]Moreover, they gave him no grounds for worry. [18]In the annals of the Indian Wars, the story of Crook and his scouts is unique.

27. Which of the following is the best revision of the underlined portion of Sentence 1 below?

Using Indians to track down and fight other Indians was not a new idea <u>during the conflict between Whites and the Indians during the mid-1800 Indian Wars during the conquest of the Apaches</u>.

(A)   during the mid-1800 Indian Wars between Whites and Apaches.

(B)   during the long years of conflict between Whites and Indians.

(C)   during the mid-1800s when Indians and Whites came into conflict in the Indian Wars.

(D)   when the Apaches and Whites were engaged in conflict.

28. Which of the following is the best revision of the underlined portion of Sentence 3 below?

<u>What was a novel idea of the U.S. Army during its war</u> against the Apaches was using an Indian against members of his own tribe.

(A)   The U.S. Army's novel idea during this war

(B)   What the U.S. Army had as a novel idea during its war

(C)   The U.S. Army had the novel idea during this war

(D)   During its war the U.S. Army's novelty

29. Which of the following is the best revision of the underlined portion of Sentence 5 below?

Crook had learned that such a scout <u>would know alot because he would know</u> the fighting habits, the hiding places, and the personalities of the Indians being pursued.

(A)   would know alot about

(B)   would know a lot about

(C)   would know

(D)   would have a great deal of useful knowledge concerning

30. Which of the following is the best way to combine Sentences 10, 11, and 12?

(A)   Admiring and loyal because of Crook's good qualities, the Indian soldiers gave him their respect.

(B)   Although earning the loyalty and admiration of the Indian soldiers, Crook won their respect.

(C)   Crook won the Indian soldier's respect, admiration, and loyalty
because of his good qualities.

(D)   Although these good qualities no doubt earned Crook the admiration and loyalty of his Indian soldiers, the man himself won their
respect.

31.   In relation to the passage as a whole, which of the following best
describes the writer's intention in Paragraph 4?

(A)   To narrate an important event

(B)   To describe the best features of the subject

(C)   To persuade readers to take a certain course of action

(D)   To provide a conclusion

32.   Which of the following would be the best way to revise Sentence 15?

(A)   He got on a trail, with his Apache scouts to guide him, he followed
his quarry relentlessly.

(B)   He would get on a trail, and with his Apache scouts to guide him,
would follow his quarry relentlessly.

(C)   He would get on a trail, and with his Apache scouts to guide him,
he followed his quarry relentlessly.

(D)   He got on a trail and he followed his quarry relentlessly, with his
Apache scouts to guide him.

Passage G

[1]Dr. Robert Goddard at one time a physics professor at Clark University, Worcester, Massachusetts was largely responsible for the sudden interest in rockets back in the twenties. [2]When Dr. Goddard first started his
experiments with rockets, no related technical information was available.
[3]He started a new science, industry, and field of engineering. [4]Through his
scientific experiments, he pointed the way to the development of rockets
as we know them today. [5]The Smithsonian Institute agreed to finance his
experiments in 1920. [6]From these experiments he wrote a paper titled "A
Method of Reaching Extreme Altitudes," in which he outlined a space

rocket of the step (multistage) principle, theoretically capable of reaching the moon.

[7]Dr. Goddard later was the first to fire a rocket that reached a speed faster than the speed of sound. [8]He was first to develop a gyroscopic steering <u>thing</u> for rockets. [9]The first to use vanes in the jet stream for rocket stabilization during <u>the initial phase</u> of a rocket flight. [10]He was also the first person to patent the idea of step rockets. [11]After proving on paper and in <u>actual</u> tests that a rocket can travel in a vacuum, he developed the mathematical theory of rocket propulsion and rocket flight, including basic designs for long-range rockets. [12]All of his information was available to military men before World War II, but evidently its immediate use did not seem applicable. [13]Near the end of World War II the United States started intense <u>work</u> on rocket-powered guided missiles, using the experiments and developments of Dr. Goddard and the American Rocket Society.

33. Which of the following should be changed to reflect correct punctuation in the first paragraph?

    (A)   Sentence 1: Put commas after "Goddard" and after "Massachusetts."

    (B)   Sentence 2: Remove the comma after "rockets."

    (C)   Sentence 4: Put a comma in after "rockets."

    (D)   Sentence 6: Remove the comma after "principle."

34. Which of the following parts of the third paragraph is a nonstandard sentence?

    (A)   Sentence 8   (C)   Sentence 10

    (B)   Sentence 9   (D)   Sentence 11

35. Which of the underlined words in the second paragraph should be replaced by more precise or appropriate words?

    (A)   thing   (C)   actual

    (B)   the initial phase (D)   work

Passage H

[1]We've grown accustomed to seeing this working woman hanging from the subway strap during commuting hours. [2]The woman who leaves her children to go to work in the morning is no longer a pariah in her

community or her family. ³Her paycheck is more than pin money; it buys essential family staples and often supports the entire family.

⁴The situation for men has also changed as a result of women's massive entry into the work force for the better. ⁵Men who would once have felt unrelenting pressure to remain with one firm and climb the career ladder are often enabled by a second income to change careers in midlife. ⁶They also enjoy greatest intimacy and involvement with their children.

⁷The benefits for business are also readily apparent. ⁸No senior manager in the country would deny that the huge generation of women who entered management seven or eight years ago has functioned superbly, often outperforming men.

⁹Yet the prevailing message from the media on the subject of women and business is one filled with pessimism. ¹⁰We hear about women leaving their employers in the lurch when they go on maternity leave. ¹¹Or we hear the flip side, that women are overly committed to their careers and neglectful of their families. ¹²And in fact, it is true that problems arising from women's new work force role do exist, side by side with the benefits.

¹³The problems hurt businesses as well as individuals and their families, affordable quality childcare is still a distant dream. ¹⁴Some women are distracted at work, and men who would have felt secure about their children when their wives were home are also anxious and distracted. ¹⁵Distraction also impedes the productivity of some high-achieving women with the birth of their first child and causes some to depart with the birth of their second.

36. Which of the following sentences displays a nonstandard placement of a modifying phrase?

  (A) Sentence 1   (C) Sentence 4

  (B) Sentence 3   (D) Sentence 5

37. Which of the following sentences displays a nonstandard use of a comparative form?

  (A) Sentence 3   (C) Sentence 8

  (B) Sentence 6   (D) Sentence 10

38. Which of the following sentences is a nonstandard sentence?

  (A) Sentence 9   (B) Sentence 13

(C) Sentence 14   (D)   Sentence 15

Passage I

[1]Alexander the Great was a general and ruler who changed the world. [2]His boyhood was shaped by two strong parents. [3]Alexander's father, King Philip of Macedonia, was an <u>excellent general</u> whose armies conquered Greece and made Macedonia a powerful force in the ancient world. [4]Taught before he was ten to read, sing, and debate in Greek, Alexander was later encouraged by the philosopher Aristotle to be curious about foreign lands.

[5]Alexander was <u>fearless and showed great promise</u>. [6]He observed a horse that no one had been able to touch, much less ride. [7]After noticing that the horse <u>shied</u> every time it saw its own shadow Alexander concluded that the horse was afraid. [8]He mounted the horse, rode it only into the sun at first, and thus tamed Bucephalus. [9]Alexander grew up in a military environment and became accustomed to the hardships of a soldier's life. [10]He enjoyed combat and at a <u>very early age</u> commanded some cavalry in battle, defeating the Greeks at Chaeronea. [11]However, his father seldom took Alexander with him on his campaigns. [12]News of his father's conquests prompted the ambitious son to complain that his father would leave nothing great for Alexander to do.

39. Which of the following, underlined in the passage, needs to be replaced by more precise words?

    (A)   excellent general

    (B)   fearless and showed great promise

    (C)   shied

    (D)   very early age

40. Which of the following is needed?

    (A)   Sentence 6: Change "that" to "who."

    (B)   Sentence 7: Place a comma after the phrase "every time it saw its own shadow."

    (C)   Sentence 11: Move "However" after the word "seldom."

    (D)   Sentence 12: Change "to complain" to "in complaining."

SENTENCE CORRECTIONS

> **DIRECTIONS:** The sentences in this section contain grammatical errors. Rewrite them using the correct grammatical form.

1. The new rule prohibits smoking by the employee's inside the building.

   _____

2. Australia is noted for their unique animals: koalas, platypus, kangaroo, and emu.

   _____

3. Economics can teach a person to effectively manage ~~their~~ his own affairs and be a contributing member of society.

   _____

4. Growth stocks are when stocks are expected to increase in market value over a period of years.

   _____

5. The woman who was the winner's voice had an excited tone, so it made her sound shrill.

   _____

6. The newspaper said on Monday that Paul Radous would receive a scholarship grant of $1,000.

   _____

GRAMMATICAL VOCABULARY

> **DIRECTIONS:** This section tests your knowledge of grammatical vocabulary. Use the space below each statement to provide the correct definitions. Your responses will be graded as correct or incorrect based on their accuracy and adequacy.

1. Define *antecedent*.

_____

2. What is a *compound sentence*?

_____

3. Define *independent clause*.

_____

4. Define *mood*.

_____

5. Define *predicate*.

_____

6. What is *passive voice*?

_____

WRITTEN MECHANICS

DIRECTIONS: This portion of the Communication and Literacy Skills Test will be dictated on audiotape. You will be expected to write down the passage exactly as it is spoken on the audiotape; use correct spelling, punctuation, and capitalization. Each passage will be read three times: the first time at a normal speed, the second time more slowly, and the third time, again at a normal speed. (There will be a two-minute break between the second and third readings in order to revise what you have written.) Your responses will be assigned a score based on the following scale:

4 6 or fewer errors

3 7 to 12 errors

2 13 to 18 errors

1 19 or more errors

For this practice test, we advise that you have someone read the passage out loud to you (three times as described above). Use the scale to determine your score and refer to this section in the Detailed Explanations of Answers, provided at the end of each practice test, for a review of potential problems.

Passage 1

Frank Lloyd Wright's architecture is characterized by its organic nature. His buildings and houses are in harmony with their surroundings and incorporate elements of nature in the design. For example, Wright built the house called Fallingwater in such a way that it mirrors the waterfall over which it is cantilevered. Fallingwater does not overwhelm its natural site, but on the contrary, accentuates the character of the landscape. Another famous work of Wright, the Guggenheim Museum in New York City, showcases Wright's creation of interior space that is open and harmonious. Instead of the box-like structure of separate floors and rooms, the Guggenheim is much like a spiral, so that the lines are curved and the floor is a continuous line. In his effort to integrate form and function, Wright designed not only buildings but the furnishings and landscaping that were to accompany them. In this way he ensured that his buildings portrayed the democratic inclusiveness he felt was part of the American lifestyle.

Passage 2

Meta Warrick Fuller's sculptures are most often viewed in light of the Harlem Renaissance although she had produced much work well before the period. It was through the exhibitions made possible by the patronage of Harlem Renaissance artists that her work was first introduced to a national audience. Fuller's bronze, *Ethiopia Awakening*, is a celebration of African heritage at the same time as it points to the self-conscious artistic and political awakening of African Americans in the early twentieth century. Another of her most famous sculptures is *Mary Turner (A Silent Protest Against Mob Violence)* commemorating the lynching of Mary Turner by a white mob. The figure of a woman struggling to free herself from the mass which encumbers her legs and feet symbolizes the struggle of African American women against racist society. Fuller's early work, in demonstrating the capability of African Americans to be artists, affected the generation of black artists which makes up the Harlem Renaissance.

Communication and Literacy Skills Test

PRACTICE TEST 1

ANSWER KEY

MULTIPLE CHOICE

1.	(C)	11.	(A)	21.	(C)	31.	(D)
2.	(B)	12.	(A)	22.	(B)	32.	(C)
3.	(A)	13.	(B)	23.	(A)	33.	(D)
4.	(A)	14.	(D)	24.	(C)	34.	(C)
5.	(D)	15.	(C)	25.	(C)	35.	(C)
6.	(A)	16.	(B)	26.	(D)	36.	(B)
7.	(B)	17.	(A)	27.	(C)	37.	(C)
8.	(A)	18.	(C)	28.	(D)	38.	(C)
9.	(B)	19.	(D)	29.	(B)	39.	(B)
10.	(C)	20.	(C)	30.	(B)	40.	(D)

GRAMMAR AND USAGE

1.	(D)	11.	(D)	21.	(C)	31.	(D)
2.	(C)	12.	(A)	22.	(C)	32.	(B)
3.	(A)	13.	(C)	23.	(B)	33.	(A)
4.	(A)	14.	(D)	24.	(C)	34.	(B)
5.	(D)	15.	(B)	25.	(D)	35.	(A)
6.	(B)	16.	(A)	26.	(C)	36.	(C)
7.	(D)	17.	(D)	27.	(A)	37.	(B)
8.	(D)	18.	(A)	28.	(A)	38.	(B)
9.	(B)	19.	(A)	29.	(C)	39.	(D)
10.	(D)	20.	(C)	30.	(D)	40.	(B)

DETAILED EXPLANATIONS OF ANSWERS

Section 1 – Reading

MULTIPLE CHOICE

1. **(C)** (C) is correct because the passage is specifically about lying in Russia. (A) contradicts reasons for lying given in the third paragraph; (B) contradicts material in the second paragraph; (D) is not implied by the passage.

2. **(B)** (B) is correct because the passage explains more fully the author's statement that everybody is lying. The passage does not work to show what conditions led to universal lying (C), does not divide the subject into categories (D), and does not seek to define any particular word or term (A).

3. **(A)** (A) is correct because lines 1– 4 suggest that the author expected a negative response to his topic and (A) has a negative connotation. (B) has a positive meaning; (C) and (D) are more neutral.

4. **(A)** (A) is the correct answer because the sentence beginning in line 13 seeks to explain the previous sentence more carefully. It does not provide a specific example of lying (B), show differences or similarities that relate to lies (C), or show a cause or effect of lying (D).

5. **(D)** (D) is correct because the author describes poor people with compassion; (C) is incorrect because while the author treats the rich people who ignore the poor with some bitterness, the general mood of the passage is sympathetic. The author shows no arrogance (B) towards anyone he describes, and his use of emotional language suggests that he is not at all apathetic (A).

6. **(A)** (A) is correct because the second sentence contrasts the reality of the ragged woman with the great streets which the stranger in the first sentence sees. The forcefulness of this contrast makes (C) incorrect because (C) suggests a weaker connection between the sentences. (B) is incorrect because the second sentence does not explain the first sentence more fully; (D) is

incorrect because the second sentence doesn't provide a specific example of what the stranger does see.

7. **(B)** (B) is correct because the passage mentions both the wretchedness of the poor and the visitor who doesn't see this wretchedness. While the author may imply (A), it is not the point he wants to make in this passage; (C) is incorrect because the author does not describe harmony between the rich and the poor; (D) contradicts the sympathetic tone of the passage.

8. **(A)** (A) is correct because the author is comparing traveling with reading history. Because there is no causal relationship suggested, (C) is incorrect. (D) is incorrect because the author does not seek to divide up one subject; (B) is incorrect because there is no narration of chronological events.

9. **(B)** This is a statement of opinion because it is not possible to check with any accuracy the contraction of minds as the author has described it.

10. **(C)** The correct response is (C) because throughout the passage the author compares history with foreign travel; (B) contradicts the author's first sentence. (A) and (D) are incorrect because the author uses travel in England as a detail supporting his main point about similarities between travel and reading history.

11. **(A)** (A) is correct because it contains important points made in each paragraph. While (B) is implied, it is not the central idea of the passage. (C) and (D) are incorrect because the author makes no statements justifying the existence of armies or of war itself.

12. **(A)** (A) is correct because the author's tone is very neutral. (B), (C), and (D) are incorrect because the author shows little evidence of any passion or emotion.

13. **(B)** (B) is correct because the passage describes both good and bad attributes of democracy, a political system based on equality. (A), (C), and (D) all take either an all-good or all-bad position; however, the author is careful to treat both good and bad effects.

14. **(D)** "Organic" means "of a fundamental nature"; the ceremony itself is fundamentally important, the writer says. (A) is incorrect; in the context of the selection, the ceremony does not have to occur, nor is it spontaneous. (B) is incorrect; neither physical nor mental health is implied by the term's usage here. (C) is incorrect; the term's meaning suggests the opposite, just as the opposite is suggested here in this article.

15. **(C)** The first paragraph establishes the first clause of this answer; the next-to-last sentence in that paragraph states the idea found in the main clause of the statement. (A) is incorrect; while this statement is true of the article, it does not constitute the main point of the writer. (B) is incorrect; again this statement is true and occurs in the selection; however, the article's meaning goes beyond the idea. (D) is incorrect; the point of the article is not so much a look at weddings around the world but rather an emphasis on weddings per se, especially in comparison to other rites of passage.

16. **(B)** The passage that follows the term pinpoints such bustling activity as buying, partying, etc. (A) is incorrect; the writer's tone is not necessarily demeaning. (C) is incorrect; the term may suggest chaos but not meaningless-ness. (D) is incorrect; mirth may be implicit in the passage, but the context in which the term appears does not focus on the mirth of the occasion but on the excitement of it.

17. **(A)** (A) is the best answer since, as stated in the third sentence of the passage, changing the solid to liquid will lower the temperature of the hot tea. Because changing the sugar to liquid will not raise, but rather lower, the temperature of the tea, (B) should not be selected. The temperature of the hot tea will not be lowered to such an extent that it will freeze cream (C) or cause the hand to be painful from the cold (D).

18. **(C)** The best answer is (C) since it includes three correct statements. The sugar does pass from a solid to a liquid state, the sugar does absorb caloric from the water, and the heat does become latent when it is sensible. Since I, II, and III are all causes of the drop of temperature when sugar is added to coffee, all three must be included when choosing an answer. (A) states that sugar passes from a solid to a liquid state (I), but no other information is given. (B) includes two true statements (I and II), but it does not include all the information since there is no mention of heat becoming latent when it was sensible (III). (D) is not a proper answer since it excludes statement II—that sugar absorbs caloric from the water. While (A), (B), and (D) each contain one or more of these statements, none contains all three; subsequently, each of these choices is incorrect.

19. **(D)** The best answer is (D). Answer (D) states that one should take into consideration that dissolving the salt in the water will lower the tempera-ture of the water and that one should start with water that is warmer than is desired. One should not start with water that is cooler than one desires; (A) is not the best answer. The order of adding the salt and the water will make little difference; the temperature will be lowered in both instances; (B) is not the

best answer. The salt will lower the temperature of the water; (C) suggests that this will not happen if the salt is fine, so (C) is not an acceptable choice.

20. **(C)**   The writing seems scientific since it refers to principles, causes and effects, and measures of heat and cold; (C) is the best answer. The writing is not sociological since there is no description of people and their relationships; consequently, (A) should not be chosen. Because the narrator reports scientific facts and there is no trial-and-error reporting, (B) is not the best answer. Since the information is not reported as historical research with references, footnotes, or dates of previous discoveries, (D) should not be chosen.

21. **(C)**   The best choice is (C); paragraph five shows that in this case a mortar is a container used for pounding, pulverizing, and/or mixing. As employed in the last sentence of the fifth paragraph, the use of the mortar is not to fix or hold together; (A) should not be chosen. A mortar can be a weapon (B), but that would not be used to reduce ice to small particles; therefore, (B) is not an acceptable choice. The word does not fit into the sentence in this context; choice (D) would not be practical.

22. **(B)**   The best choice is (B). The only device that the writer does not record is that of interviews. The other items—descriptions (A), mathematics (C), and experiments (D)—are used.

23. **(A)**   One can infer that the metal needle will become warm when the basketball is being pumped up by the air pump. The reason is that the article states, "...air is compressed forcibly in a tube...the heat, which was before latent, becomes sensible..."; (A) is the correct answer. Choice (B) states that the needle will not be affected; (B) should not be chosen since the quotation from the passage states that there will be an effect. (C) is also incorrect because it states that the needle will become cooler, not warmer. (D) is also an incorrect choice; it states that the needle will become freezing cold.

24. **(C)**   The writer is objective in his writing and offers no opinions of his own; (C) is the best answer. The writer's main concern is not literary form or stylistic devices; (A) is not acceptable. The writer is objective and does not offer his own opinions; since he is not subjective, (B) is not the best answer. Since the facts presented in the article are not new, (D) is not the best answer.

25. **(C)**   Since heat is a positive condition depending on the absence of cold, (C) is the best answer. Fahrenheit is a measure of temperature, not a condition; therefore, (A) is an incorrect choice. Heat is the opposite of intense artificial cold; (B) is not acceptable. Black states that it is "...when bodies pass from a rarer to a denser state that their latent heat is evolved..."; (D) is incorrect.

26. **(D)**   In this case, the word "sensible" means perceptible; (D) is the best answer. "Sensible" can mean knowledgeable (A), but the definition does not make sense in this case. The meaning of "sensible" can be logical (B), but that particular meaning does not fit the sentence or passage here. "Evolving" (C) is not an acceptable answer because it does not seem to fit the context.

27. **(C)**   The correct choice is (C) because the author states that the "two or three sheepish country men" are the "only guests to whom Robin's sympathies inclined him." The mariners (A) and the day laborers (B) would not interest Robin and they are incorrect. Although the man at the door does draw Robin's attention, he does not seem like the type of person to start a conversation with; choice (D) is incorrect.

28. **(D)**   Statements I and II best describe the diners, so choice (D) is correct. The author states that they are "countrymen" who are eating in the "darkest corner of the room"; that indicates that they do not wish to bring attention to themselves. There is no sign of hostility from the other men in the tavern; therefore, Statement III is invalid and cannot be a part of the correct answer; choice (C) is incorrect. Choices (A) and (B) are incorrect as they are incomplete.

29. **(B)**   Almost all the tavern's patrons are drinking an alcoholic beverage of some kind, making choice (B) the correct one. The "Good Creature" is the punch "long since made a familiar drink in the colony." Also, some men prefer the "insulated bliss of an unshared potation"; "potation" is an alcoholic beverage. Where the mariners have returned from is not mentioned, so choice (A) should not be selected. There is no reference to religion in the passage; choice (C) is incorrect. Although drinking alcohol was most likely considered an enjoyable activity for the patrons, it was not described as such within the text; choice (D) is also incorrect.

30. **(B)**   Choice (B) should be selected because we have already determined that the Good Creature to which "we have a long hereditary claim" is alcohol. Seafaring is hardly a vice; choice (A) is incorrect. Although smoking [choice (C)] and gossiping [choice (D)] could be considered vices, the author does not describe them as such and therefore these are incorrect selections.

31. **(D)**   Choice (D) is the best answer. The citizen was passionate in his response and threats to Robin. The citizen was also described as being "sepulchral"; passionate and gloomy best describe him. The citizen was not jovial and light-hearted but rather angry and annoyed; choice (A) is incorrect. The citizen, while disdainful, was not aloof; choice (B) should not be selected. The citizen was neither interested nor helpful, so choice (C) is also incorrect; he denied his knowledge of the kinsman.

32. **(C)** Choice (C) is the acceptable answer; this quote from the passage refers to feet being locked in a pillory for punishment—the threat issued when the youth clutches the citizen's clothing. Even though the word "stock" can refer to animals, that is not the meaning in this case; choice (A) is not the best answer. While the dictionary offers "stocks" as one definition of investments, that meaning does not fit this passage; choice (B) should not be chosen. Although feet are mentioned, it is not in relation to a dance step; choice (D) is incorrect.

33. **(D)** "Taciturn" means quiet, silent, and uncommunicative; choice (D) is correct. The tavern occupants were often reticent or reluctant to talk when they were under the influence of potation; therefore, they were not unreticent; choice (A) should not be chosen. The occupants were less talkative; choice (B), which states that they were talkative after drinking, should not be selected. Boisterous, choice (C) means rowdy and noisy, and is therefore incorrect.

34. **(C)** Choice (C) is the best answer because the innkeeper behaved in a hospitable manner but the citizen did not. The innkeeper and the citizen were not both courteous; choice (A) is incorrect. Since the innkeeper was not inhospitable and this choice states that BOTH the innkeeper and citizen were, choice (B) is incorrect. Choice (D) is incorrect since it reverses accurate descriptions of the characters' behavior; it was the citizen who was discourteous and the innkeeper who was hospitable.

35. **(C)** Choice (C) is the best answer since Robin certainly received little extra (superfluous) civil treatment. Choice (A) has nothing to do with Robin's treatment. Instead, it refers to the affinity of the occupants toward alcoholic beverages. Choice (B) refers to a custom among the Turks of eating in their own small groups; it has nothing of great significance to add to the treatment that Robin received, and so choice (B) should be avoided. Choice (D) also seems to be a reference to the consumption of beverages in the tavern and is not germane to the question.

36. **(B)** Robin probably avoided eating at the tavern because he did not have the money and hoped that the Major would give him food. Choice (B) includes one of these answers and is the best choice. Food was not avoided simply because it was not served; choice (A) should not be selected. Since we already know the innkeeper was hospitable and he does invite Robin to stay (suggesting available places), both choices (C) and (D) are unacceptable answers.

37. **(C)** This fits the entire framework of the passage (i.e., first the statistics, then their effects). Though the passage tracks the gross national

product (B), this is by no means central to the entire passage. The passage nowhere degrades Hoover's presidency (A) nor does it monitor the actual *effects* of the banking system (D), though it does show how the banking system was *affected*; yet even so, this is by no means central to the passage.

38. **(C)** Due to the inherent logic of the sentence, (C) is correct. The diseases do make people immune to starvation (A) because the victims of the disease die before they can starve. The sentence nowhere implies that the diseases cause malnutrition (B); rather, it is the malnutrition that creates disease susceptibility. Although few died of starvation, many died of disease, which is indirectly caused by malnutrition; therefore, (D) is incorrect.

39. **(B)** The 1933 bar is highest, and the graph measures the percent of unemployment by the height of the bars. The bars for 1929 (A), 1938 (C), and 1944 (D) are all lower than the bar for 1933, the year in which unemployment was the highest.

40. **(D)** 1944 (the bar between 1943 and 1945) is the lowest bar on the graph. As previously mentioned, the graph measures the percentage of unemployment on the length of the bars. The bars for 1929 (A), 1933 (B), and 1938 (C) are all higher than the bar for 1944.

VOCABULARY

1. *Pungent* means being sharply painful or having a stiff and sharp point. It also means marked by a sharp incisive quality, or having a strong, foul smell.

2. *Condone* means to pardon or overlook voluntarily, especially to treat as if trivial, harmless, or of no importance.

3. *Finite* means completely determinable in theory or in fact by counting, measurement, or thought.

4. *Ruminate* means given to or engaged in contemplation.

5. *Facsimile* means an exact copy.

6. *Enamored* means inflamed with love or fascinated.

7. *Omniscient* means having infinite awareness, understanding, and insight of all things.

8. *Demise* means cessation of existence or activity.

9. *Palpable* means capable of being touched or felt. It also means easily perceptible by the mind.

Section 2 – Writing

WRITTEN SUMMARY

Essay 1

STRONG RESPONSE

Although there is some dispute over the validity of evidence for asserting that the world was once completely gaseous, there is some consensus in giving credence to the suggestion that the earth was once a self-luminous star.

Water existed in the form of a translucent vapor, as did most all of the earth's substances. This precluded the existence of animal and plant life, as well as water. The fiery orb that was earth probably did revolve on an axis and revolved in turn around the sun, while the moon, if the moon existed yet, would have pulled the ocean of fire in tidal waves that enveloped the whole planet.

The brightness of the fiery ocean's glare would have been far more stunning than the light given off by the sun today. Through a gradual process of thermal equilibrium, the earth cooled, allowing a solidification of portions of the globe's molten mass. Eventually this lead to the formation of a crust that sat upon the liquid mass covering most of the earth.

Some have argued that in such a scenario, the solid material would have sunk into the liquid. If this is true, then we would have to believe that the process worked in a different way, whereby the solidification would have commenced at the center of the globe, or there would have been a general cooling down that would have solidified the entire world. However, it is generally held that the center of the earth is molten, and if this is so, then the first solids could not have descended into the liquid mass. To further support this first theory, we also know that the solid parts that developed were less dense than the water and therefore could stay afloat.

Most evidence, therefore, suggests a theory of the earth's development that is predicated upon the formation of a crust.

ANALYSIS

The main points of the passage are recounted. The writer moves through a summary of the passage with thoroughness and clarity. The vocabulary and sentence structure is sophisticated and demonstrates proficiency in recounting complex scientific concepts.

Essay 2

STRONG RESPONSE

Many powerful figures wanted the United States to go to war with Spain, but we must also be mindful of the important role played by public opinion on President McKinley's decision to enter the war.

The end of the nineteenth century saw the birth of what was known as "Yellow Journalism," a competitive practice among competing newspapers to attract readers through sensational and sometimes inaccurate reporting. Famous newspaper publishers like William Randolph Hearst and Joseph Pulitzer continually tried to outdo each other in search of increased circulation.

One of the most significant effects of this struggle for control of the newspaper market was its influence on United States foreign policy. A Cuban revolt had recently been put down by the Spanish, and American newspapers had reported, often with distortions, of the brutality with which this revolt was handled by the Spanish. The American public began to feel responsible for helping a small and militarily weak country gain its independence. These sensationalized reports of Spain's treatment of Cubans, in particular in connection to the rebellion in Cuba against the Spanish government, lead to public outcry for U.S. intervention. When a United States ship, the U.S.S. *Maine,* blew up in the Havana harbor, newspapers immediately blamed the Spanish. The cause of the explosion has never been finally determined, but public furor over the incident was enough to influence the president's decision to enter a war with Spain.

In addition to seeking revenge for the *Maine*, the public also saw war with Spain as a chance to liberate Cubans from Spanish rule. This move was much in line with the wishes of many empire seekers in Washington, such as Roosevelt, but their influence alone could not have pushed the U.S. into war. In order to understand America's entry in a war with Spain, we must recognize the importance of Yellow Journalism and its effects on public opinion.

ANALYSIS

The writer covers the major points of the passage and is appropriately detail oriented in explaining concepts such as "Yellow Journalism" and the importance of the explosion of the U.S.S. *Maine*.

Essay 3

STRONG RESPONSE

While other countries were able to abolish slavery through legislative means, in the United States, this was not feasible. A legal solution to the problem of slavery required the willing participation of Southern states, a political force too large and powerful to be overruled in Congress. The South was bitterly opposed to any steps toward abolishing slavery, and war proved to be the only means to bring this about.

Controversy over slavery had a long history even before the Civil War era. Thomas Jefferson, in 1787, drafted the Northwest Ordinance to halt the spread of slavery into soon-to-be states Ohio, Indiana, Illinois, Michigan, and Wisconsin. Although a slave owner himself, Jefferson believed that slavery contradicted the spirit of America. He knew it would be too hard to abolish outright in places where it currently existed but hoped that preventing its spread would ultimately lead to its extinction.

The slave trade itself was abolished in 1808, and many Northerners devised elaborate plans to return slaves to Africa, although nothing much came of these. By the 1830s, a strong and persistent movement began in the North to end slavery without compromise or concession. The abolitionists, as the adherents to this radical anti-slavery position were known, saw slavery as a national sin that had to be done away with.

The question of slavery in new territories was what ultimately pushed the country into Civil War. Following Jefferson's rationale in the Northwest Ordinance, Northern legislators sought to prevent the spread of slavery into new territories. The South felt this was a challenge to the integrity and legality of the institution on which much of the Southern economy rested. Several compromises were made during the 1840s and 1850s to keep the South happy, but in 1861 a Republican was elected president on a platform that called for no slavery in new territories. It was this that finally led the South to secede from the Union, a move that provoked the Civil War.

ANALYSIS

The writer covers all the salient points and has a good grasp of the subtleties and nuances of the passage. The writing is clear, concise, and grammatically sound.

WRITTEN COMPOSITION

Essay 1

STRONG RESPONSE

On television the other day, I saw a story about teenagers gambling and piling up big debts with bookies. One of the male students interviewed had the typical clothing of a high-school student: baseball cap, tee-shirt, jeans, even an earring. The old saying "clothes make the man" came to mind when I saw that report. In this and other cases of teenagers wearing conforming clothing, especially if it differs from that worn by adults, clothing behavior follows the crowd rather than "making" the individual. In other words, young people conform almost blindly to the latest clothing trend in a desperate attempt to show that they are not like their parents and in an equally shallow attempt to be accepted rather than rejected by their peers. Perhaps their state of transition and their probing into the notion of who they are leads to wearing conforming clothing.

Conforming behavior in clothing among young people usually has some basis of rebellion in it. If their school has a code about skirt length, you can be sure that students will try to test it by wearing short skirts, if they are "in" that year, that is. Likewise, wearing torn jeans, whether torn at the knee or in different places, seems to signify that students are rejecting the middle-class value of having a wardrobe of nice clothes. The irony of the torn jeans reached its height in the 1980s when jeans makers started selling pre-torn clothing at very high prices. If manufacturers are selling products like that, no doubt they are trendy, and that trend finally represents the normal when large numbers of young people buy and wear these products.

Teenagers often rebel against their parents as much as they do against school rules. After all, teens are going through the period in their lives when they are maturing sexually, if not emotionally and mentally. Their identities may not yet be revealed to themselves or others. They are searching for something that sets them apart from their parents because they are trying to be their own person. Ironically, this searching usually leads to role playing in fashion rather than identity discovery. A young woman I know decided to cut a design into her wrist as an identifying mark like the members of her teen "tribe." Her parents pointed out to her that she already had a "tribe," her family, but she did not see it that way. She probably knew that the scarification would annoy her parents, just as her wearing Seattle "grunge" clothing to conform to her friends' tastes had already done so. Technically, piercings, scarifications, and tattoos are not clothing, but they serve some of the same purposes of "decoration" that clothes do. So I think they fit into my points about conforming clothing behaviors of young people.

Conforming clothing among teenagers also has the effect of gaining acceptance among their peers. Teenagers can be very cruel to each other at a time in their lives when their emotions are already in turmoil. Teens seem to need some sort of acceptance, not necessarily for sharing interests or for earning self-esteem. In fact, teenagers who stand out by making good grades or by not smoking marijuana or not drinking alcohol find themselves lacking in popularity. So they may make up for it by dressing the way other teens in a particular group dress in order to be perceived as a member of that group. If the "cool" group clothing of the moment in their school is khaki trousers and plaid shirts, some teens will wear those clothes to make others think they are in that group, even if that it is not true. Where does the individual "man" or "woman" reveal himself or herself in that kind of behavior?

Some conforming clothing can lead to the "un-making" of the person in a different and tragic way. Four years ago where I live, a fifteen-year-old was shot and killed because he would not give up his very expensive Boston Celtics team jacket to thieves. In other cities, similar stories involving expensive Nike or other brand athletic shoes have been in the news the last few years. Young people, even pre-adolescents, have been killed for their popular, but expensive, athletic clothing. These killings suggest the conforming power of those clothes (and shoes). Young people who can't afford them just kill someone who does have them if they can't steal them.

Young people, especially teenagers, are going through a very difficult time in their lives at the turn of the millenium. The pressures on them seem more weighty than in previous generations. Their bodies and feelings are telling them they are growing up, but their experiential knowledge, wisdom, and mental maturity still need developing. In a way, they are like boats thrown around in stormy seas. They see clothing and outer markings that identify them with celebrities in sports and music as a way of finding a calm port in that storm. They do not seem to recognize that reaching that port means compromising their developing individuality to an extent.

ANALYSIS

This essay has a score in the high range. It has an assertive thesis that controls the direction (structure) of the development. The subordinate ideas develop the main idea quite well, even though there seems to be a slight digression from discussing clothing to discussing scarifications, piercings, and tattooing. However, the writer does attempt to show that this digression is part of the same idea of conforming clothing being against the forming of the person's identity. It has few errors of any kind, and it uses specific examples to develop each subordinate idea. Both the introduction and the conclusion do their jobs well. The word choice and general language use are also quite good.

Essay 2

STRONG RESPONSE

Years ago, before formal education was available, everybody learned what they needed to know by experience. The prehistoric hunter-gatherers had assigned roles in the tribe or community, and each person learned their role by following an expert around and by practicing skills like hurling a spear or keeping a fire going. In a way, they were "learning on the job." Today, however, learning on the job no longer works for many of the technologically oriented jobs in the marketplace. People need some academic learning before or at the same time as experiential learning.

In the distant past of low technology, people learned how to do their work by practicing it under the direction of a parent or another experienced adult. Even the so-called primitive people had to learn how to hunt and what plants are edible in the process of becoming hunters and gatherers. There was no manual and no school of hunting or gathering. They learned skills at the knee of their elders. As technology advanced, more knowledge became necessary. And when agricultural life began to dominate, skills such as knowing when and what to plant were learned by experience, often harsh experience at that. As technology advances farther into the use of complex machinery, more people will need more formal training. An IBM television commercial a few years ago showed how farmers can be more productive when they use an IBM personal computer to help manage their business. You don't have to go to college to learn how to use a computer, but you probably need some specialized formal training.

Today, job recruiters constantly say that they need workers who can learn by experience, who are prepared by academic training to learn work skills. If you want to work in accounting, for instance, you need to learn the rules and practices of accounting before you can start working. Then you learn even more in the practice of auditing other people's books. Some jobs also require a lot of formal education before you can work in that job. Real estate sales, for example, requires a state license that can only be acquired after a certain number of hours of formal training. Even relatively skilled jobs that do not requiring college degrees may require some prior academic training. If you have little or no knowledge of applied mathematics, you will have a hard time doing carpentry or machinery work.

On the other hand, classroom training is often out of touch with the "real world." Part of that is by design. Most people will not use directly a subject like algebra in their work. They won't write essays or interpret poetry. These academic skills often are used to do other academic work, but they can contribute to the ability to learn by experience. Algebra and poetry interpretation both train us in abstract thinking and creative problem solving, which should make us more valuable to an employer. Essay writing skills can be adapted fairly easily to business writing requirements. In other words, a large part of our academic learning prepares us to learn academically at a higher level or to apply the skills we learn in schools and college to real jobs.

Even college graduates are often assigned to a person on the job who is supposed to help the new employee learn by experience. Sometimes, though, there is no such help and the school of experience becomes the school of "hard knocks." Each time the new employee makes an error, they can either learn from that error and adapt or, ultimately, lose their job. By the same token, the new employee can learn through success as well. If they find out how to enter data into a microcomputer software program like a spreadsheet in accounting, they can build on that success and try to use or write a macro (a sort of mini-program) to help them become even more productive.

So, it seems that both academic learning and learning by experience are valuable in a technologically advanced culture. The best and most satisfying jobs aren't learned overnight or just in school or college. They require a mixture of academic or formal training and experience that helps them build on the academic learning.

ANALYSIS

The introduction is well thought-out and presents a strong thesis. The body paragraphs are detailed and support the thesis clearly and completely. Their sound structure steps through the author's argument clearly and there are few grammatical or punctuation errors. The conclusion could be stronger, but based on the length and considering the time constraints, it is adequate. The author uses language well except for a persistent pronoun-antecedent agreement problem and a few grammatical errors.

Essay 3

STRONG RESPONSE

In today's society, many people continue to believe many common misconceptions about other groups that lead to derogatory stereotypes. Different ethnic and racial groups often believe negative stereotypes about other groups. People of both genders have unfavorable beliefs about the other sex. People of different social classes often have suspicious ideas about those who are not of the same class. But one of the most common misperceptions that leads to a negative stereotype is held by people of all races, genders, and social groups. Like all stereotypes, this one is based on fear and misunderstanding. The stereotype I am talking about is that all handicapped people are retarded and somehow contaminating to healthy people.

Some of the common misperceptions about handicapped people are: 1) all people who are in wheelchairs are mentally, as well as physically, handicapped; 2) a person who cannot speak clearly cannot think clearly either; 3) all handicapped people have trouble feeding themselves and need help to do everything; 4) all handicapped people are born that way; and 5) all handicapped people feel sorry for themselves and everyone else should feel sorry for them, too. Let's look at each of these beliefs individually, and determine the accuracy or inaccuracy of each.

First, consider the belief that all people in wheelchairs are mentally, as well as physically, handicapped. One can see this stereotype in action when waiters ignore the person in the wheelchair and ask that person's companion what the handicapped person would like to order. Or when people speak very slowly and loudly to someone in a wheelchair, as if they were talking to a deaf person or a child.

The second misperception, that a person who cannot speak clearly cannot think clearly, is also very pervasive. For example, a child who stutters is more likely to be labelled "slow" or "learning disabled," regardless of that child's actual performance. People who stutter or who cannot speak clearly because of paralysis or diseases that affect motor control, like Parkinson's disease, are treated as if they are deaf or as if they are retarded. People tend to finish their sentences for them, to suggest words when they cannot say what they want to say, to speak to them loudly and slowly, or to talk to them through other people.

The third misperception, that handicapped people are unable to do things for themselves, leads to people offering to perform even mundane tasks for handicapped people. Handicapped people are capable of controlling their own wheelchairs, dialing telephones, taking notes, opening doors and drawers, and most other everyday tasks. If a handicapped person is unable to do something, he or she will usually ask for help; if he or she does not ask, people should not presume to do these tasks for them. Handicapped people often undergo special therapy to learn to cope with their disabilities, and many have specially trained dogs and monkeys to help them with daily tasks. Many able-bodied people are annoyed when others presume to give them unsolicited help; most handicapped people feel the same way, and they deserve the same respect.

The fourth misunderstanding about handicapped people is that they are born that way. This is the most obviously false idea about people with physical challenges. Many people who grow up perfectly healthy suffer spinal injuries that leave them either partially or completely paralyzed and necessitate the use of a wheelchair. A car accident, a sports injury, or even a child's game can cause this kind of spinal damage, which affects a person's ability to control his or her movement, but has no effect on the person's brain. There are several debilitating illnesses that confine sufferers to wheelchairs. These diseases range from muscular dystrophy to cancer to diabetes to disorders of the nervous system, almost all of which leave the person's mental abilities unaffected. The important point that people need to understand is that when a person becomes handicapped, it is only their physical attributes that change. They are still the same person as before the accident or illness, with the same feelings and emotions. They might need more help to accomplish certain tasks, but they have not metamorphosed into some totally different person.

The last misperception, that handicapped people feel sorry for themselves and that other people should feel sorry for them, too, is probably the most damaging. While many people go through a period of self-pity after an accident or illness leaves them impaired, this is a normal part of the acceptance process, and eventually the person will get past the "why me?" feeling and will learn to cope with the disability. Handicapped people consider themselves just to be faced with different challenges; most of them realize that self-pity is a useless waste of time. When other people feel sorry for them and make it clear that they see the handicapped person as someone to be pitied, it is degrading. It implies that a person's physical capabilities define who that person is, rather than personality and ability.

Even persons who have mental handicaps, whether from a congenital problem like Down's syndrome or from disease or injury, are not less of a person than someone who is not mentally challenged. A mentally handicapped person may not be able to achieve the same intellectual goals as an unimpaired person, but they still experience needs and desires, emotions, and likes and dislikes. Most people who suffer from mental retardation are kind, gentle people who can provide a lot of joy to their families. They maintain lifelong the innocence and sweetness of very young children. Despite society's perceptions, the love and joy these people offer are just as valuable as any contributions a "normal" person can make.

Common misperceptions about the causes and needs of handicapped people, combined with the fear of the unknown and the misunderstood, lead to derogatory stereotypes about people who face physical and mental challenges. To many people, a handicapped person is somehow less human, but this idea and the actions it inspires are demeaning and false.

We need to educate ourselves about this issue, so that these stereotypes, and all stereotypes, can be eradicated and replaced with respect and understanding for those who are different.

ANALYSIS

The writer of this essay presents a clear thesis and expands that thesis in a logical manner. The arguments presented in support of the thesis are lucid and detailed. The writer offers a well-organized essay that informs the reader of the points to be examined and then proceeds to discuss each of those points rationally. The conclusion sums up the main argument of the essay and refers back to the central thesis. The writer makes very few mistakes in grammar, usage, and mechanics, and demonstrates a clear understanding of the rules of written English. This understanding allows the writer to communicate very effectively.

GRAMMAR AND USAGE

1. **(D)** Choice (D) is the logical transition between Sentence 2 which describes the composition of stucco and Sentence 3 which describes how the finish is applied. Choice (A) contradicts the thesis and breaks voice with "I." Choice (B) and choice (C), although true facts, introduce extraneous ideas.

2. **(C)** In choice (C), a comma is necessary to set off the introductory adverbial clause that begins with "Since." Choice (A) would create an incoherent sentence. Choice (B) is incorrect because the transition "In addition" can be placed at the beginning or the middle of a sentence, but not at the end. Choice (D) changes the meaning of the sentence since the cheapness is the main emphasis, not the weight.

3. **(A)** Choice (A) is correct because the plural verb "are" agrees with the plural subject "finishes." An intervening phrase, "applied with a trowel," does not affect the choice of verb, even if the phrase ends with a singular word, "trowel." Choice (B) is incorrect because future tense is not needed. Choice (C) would create a fragment. Choice (D) is conditional tense and inappropriate because the composition for a stucco finish is clearly defined, not subject to condition.

4.   **(A)**   Choice (A) is correct because it introduces the idea of recycling the trees. Choice (B) detracts from the thesis. Choice (C) introduces extraneous information. Choice (D) changes tone and detracts from support for the thesis.

5.   **(D)**   Choice (D) would move Sentence 11, which names the Artificial Reef Fund, before Sentence 9, which makes reference to "this self-sustaining program." Choice (A) deletes the topic sentence. Choice (B) would delete a vital piece of information, how the program works. Choice (C) incorrectly reverses the topic sentence, which introduces the topic, with the concluding sentence, which summarizes the usefulness of the rigs.

6.   **(B)**   Choice (B) is correct because present tense is needed to show this program is still operational. Choice (A) is incorrect because "who" can be used only for people, and "which" is used only for objects. Choice (C) changes the correct comparative degree used for two options to the superlative degree used for more than two options. Choice (D) would include an unnecessary comma, needed to form a compound sentence only if there were a subject after "and." Sentence 13 has a compound verb: "sport fishers and divers already know…and come."

7.   **(D)**   Choice (D) contains the idea of Dena's failing health, mentioned in Sentence 6, and the idea of captivity, followed up in Sentence 7. Choice (A) contradicts the author's point made in Sentence 7. Choice (B) is too formal in tone and does not fit logically. Choice (C) introduces irrelevant information.

8.   **(D)**   Choice (D) is correct because Sentence 15 contains an error in pronoun and antecedent agreement. The indefinite pronoun "everyone" is always singular and should be followed by the singular pronouns "his or her," not the plural pronoun "their." Choices (A), (B), and (C) all contain correct pronoun usage.

9.   **(B)**   The phrase "like in the movie *Orca*" not only disrupts the rhythm of the sentence, but the allusion itself is gratuitous and is not necessary to the author's point in this sentence, which is to ask rhetorically whether this particular killer whale should be released from captivity.

10. **(D)**   "From her natural habitat" is clearly an error, because what is being debated in this letter is the fact that Dena does *not* live in her natural habitat. Therefore, "into" is the best substitution for "from." "Under" in choice (C) makes no sense in this context. Choice (A) changes the verb to the past tense, which is clearly wrong, since what is being discussed is surely that Dena presently deserves to be released. Choice (B) makes a quasi-poetical

inversion, which is unnecessarily stylized for such a letter, and more importantly, the sentence retains the incorrect preposition "from."

11. **(D)**   In the original, the modifier "Sea Habitat, Inc." was in the wrong position to be modifying "owners." Both choices (A) and (C) correct this in acceptable ways. Only choice (B) is incorrect; "Since" emphasizes the incidental fact that "Sea Habitat, Inc." is Dena's owner and creates a misleading logical relation.

12. **(A)**   Choice (A) best follows Sentence 10 because it continues the theme of obstacles toward Dena's release. Choices (B) and (C) set up misleading logical relations with the phrases "As a matter of fact" and "As we all know," and would not follow well from Sentence 10. Choice (D) is as gratuitous and unnecessary as the *Orca* allusion in Sentence 4.

13. **(C)**   "Stayed" in Sentence 10 should be "stay" to agree with the present tense of the rest of the passage. (A) and (B) are correct as written and should not be changed. (D), which suggests errors in both (B) and (C), is also an incorrect choice.

14. **(D)**   Sentence 8 is simple in structure and direct in meaning; it is best with no punctuation.

15. **(B)**   Choice (B) clears up the pronoun usage problem, eliminating the ambiguous reference of "he"; it is clear that Dickens is delighted. Choice (A) does not clearly identify the antecedent of "he." Choice (C) incorrectly identified the "delighted" person as the giver, not Dickens. Choice (D) is unnecessarily lengthy.

16. **(A)**   Choice (A) combines all the elements correctly and uses parallel structure, creating a balanced sentence. In choice (B), the many commas create confusion. Choice (C) does not have parallel verbs: "wanted" and "being." Choice (D) incorrectly combines the two ideas, making it seem as if the children are blocking Grip's action.

17. **(D)**   Choice (D) keeps the formal tone of the essay and avoids passive voice. Choice (A) breaks the formal tone and uses another voice: "you." Choice (B) is perhaps too formal and not straightforward. Choice (C) uses the passive voice.

18. **(A)**   Choice (A) smoothly combines both major ideas as a cause-and-effect sequence. Choice (B) does not clarify the source of Poe's dissatisfaction. Choice (C) does not clearly present the idea that the prophetic use was Poe's, not Dickens'. Choice (D) is too fragmented.

19. **(A)** Choice (A) is correct; the paragraph gives information on the origin of the bird. Although the paragraph gives one or two humorous incidents, choice (B) cannot be the main intention. Choice (C) is unlikely; the bird's biting is presented as more humorous than tragic. Choice (D) would be a more effective label for Paragraph 2.

20. **(C)** Choice (C) clears up the confusion caused by the possessive pronoun "his," which in this sentence would incorrectly refer to "Dickens' children." "Their" would also be fine, but "the" is probably best, as it is clear from the context which family we are referring to. Choice (A) adds "it," which is unnecessary and redundant. Choice (B) replaces the past with the past progressive tense, which does not agree with the verb tense throughout the passage. Choice (D) replaces a neat prepositional phrase with an awkward clause.

21. **(C)** "Despite" best fits the relation between the religious and secular themes. Choice (A), "beyond," would be the next best choice, though it sounds a bit overzealous. Choice (B), "until," would be inappropriate since the rest of the passage does not suggest that the secular themes preceded the religious, but rather that they coexisted. "Unless" (D) is nonsensical in this context.

22. **(C)** "Craftsman" should be plural to agree with the other noun, "artisans." We assume that there were multiple "craftsmen working over many generations," so the singular would be nonsensical.

23. **(B)** Sentence 3, as it stands, introduces a wholly new subject without transition. Sentence 4 best carries this transition, and should follow Sentence 2. Sentence 3 introduces the spread of Gothic style throughout Europe, and this point is directly supported in Sentence 8.

24. **(C)** "Becomes" should be in the past tense ("became") to accord with the rest of the passage.

25. **(D)** Choice (D) sets the clause off with commas, and best clarifies the sentence. Choice (A) uses commas to disrupt the main idea of the sentence. Choice (B) sets the clause off well, but the colon is inappropriate and should be a comma. Choice (C) employs too many commas; the second and fourth should be eliminated, as they disrupt the flow of the sentence.

26. **(C)** Choice (C) continues to describe the internal physical characteristics of Gothic cathedrals, and best fits between Sentences 10 and 11. Choice (A) switches to the external aspect of the building. Choice (B)

introduces the author's opinion, which is not necessary at this part of the passage. Choice (D) is a relevant thought but would best be placed elsewhere: it describes the purpose of the architecture, where Sentences 10 and 11 are describing the physical qualities of the interior of the buildings.

27. **(A)** Choice (A) is the best condensation of the wordy portion. Choice (B) and choice (D) omit the time period. Choice (C) is redundant, using both the words "conflict" and "wars."

28. **(A)** Choice (A) reduces wordiness through two means: deleting a subordinate clause by eliminating "What" and deleting a prepositional phrase by converting it to a possessive. Choice (B) keeps the subordinate clause. Choice (C) creates an incorrect sentence structure. Choice (D) trivializes the serious conflicts by using the word "novelty," which has light connotations.

29. **(C)** Choice (C) is the best reduction of the wordy original. Choice (A) uses "alot," which should be split into two words as it is in choice (B). However, (B) is still unnecessarily wordy and choice (D) is almost wordier than the original.

30. **(D)** Choice (D) presents the ideas correctly and concisely. Choices (A) and (C) use the awkward phrase "because of." Choice (B) sounds as if the first part of the sentence is unrelated to the last part.

31. **(D)** Paragraph 4 is a conclusion (D), winding up the main idea, the good relationship between Crook and the Indian soldiers. Choice (A) is not correct as there is no specific incident given. Choice (B) could be a second choice, but the best features of the subject are more fully discussed earlier in the paper. Choice (C) has no bearing on this essay.

32. **(B)** The past progressive tense is best, as it expresses Crook's use of the scouts as a common occurrence, not as a single event, which may be implied by the past tense in the original. (A) eliminates "and" which further confuses the sentence and does not help the verb problem. (C) changes only the first verb to the progressive. (D) is not incorrect, but does not clarify the sentence any, and lets the verb tense stand.

33. **(A)** The phrase "at one time…" is a nonrestrictive unit that is not necessary to the basic meaning of the sentence; consequently, both commas are needed. The commas for (B) and (D) are necessary to set off introductory or qualifying phrases. No commas are needed in (C) since the phrase that follows is a direct adjectival qualification of what kind of rockets they are as we know them today. Thus, no comma of separation is needed.

34. **(B)** This is just a long phrase; it has no subject or verb. The other choices are standard subject/verb independent sentence units.

35. **(A)** This word is too general for such a specific informational context. (B) should remain because it is the exact, or first, phrase the writer discusses. (C) need not be changed because only a synonym such as "real" would be needed, but the meaning would remain the same. (D) is acceptable because the writer points not to any specific study, research, or development done, but to all that type of "work" in general.

36. **(C)** It is not the work force that is "for the better," but the situation for men. This is also supported by the rest of the evidence offered in the paragraph. The other sentences have their modifying phrases directly related to the idea they qualify.

37. **(B)** The writer is comparing only two things—before and after the appearance of women in management; therefore the comparative form, not the superlative, is correct: "greater." (A), (C), and (D) are all incorrect responses; they have no comparative adjectives and are used in a standard way.

38. **(B)** It is a run-on sentence, incorrectly punctuated with a comma after "families" instead of a period or a semicolon. The rest of the choices are all standard sentences.

39. **(D)** Choice (D) is the choice because we need to know if Alexander was a child, a teenager, or a young man. Choice (A) has an example in the sentence. Choice (B) is followed by several examples of Alexander's fearlessness and promise. Choice (C) is a very specific verb describing the behavior of horses.

40. **(B)** Choice (B) is correct because a comma is needed after introductory adverbial clauses. Choice (A) is incorrect because "who" is a personal pronoun to describe people, not animals or objects. Choices (C) and (D) do not make any appreciable improvements to the sentences.

SENTENCE CORRECTIONS

Sample Correct Responses

1. The new rule prohibits employees' smoking inside the building.

2. Australia is noted for its unique animals: koalas, platypuses, kangaroos, and emus.

3. Economics can effectively teach people to manage their own affairs and to be contributing members of society.

4. Growth stocks are those expected to increase in market value over a period of years.

5. The woman winner's voice had an excited tone, so it made her sound shrill.

6. On Monday the newspaper reported that Paul Radous would receive a scholarship grant of $1,000.

GRAMMATICAL VOCABULARY

1. An antecedent is a word or group of words to which a pronoun refers; it usually precedes the pronoun, but can follow it.

2. A compound sentence is composed of at least two independent clauses but no subordinate clauses.

3. An independent, or main, clause is a group of words—containing a subject and predicate—that can function as a free-standing unit.

4. Mood reveals the attitude of the speaker or the writer to the action or state shown by the verb.

5. The predicate, which includes the verb and any complement of the verb, embraces the action of the sentence or what is said about the state of the subject.

6. In the passive voice, the subject receives the action.

WRITTEN MECHANICS

Passage 1

Common errors

Students often confuse *its* and *it's*. *Its* is the possessive form, while *it's* is a contraction which stands in for it is. An easy way to make sure you write the correct one is to attempt to substitute *it is* for *its/it's*. If it makes sense, then you need the apostrophe; if not, do not add the apostrophe. Also easy to confuse are *sight* and *site: sight* is the sense and *site* is a place. *Ensured* and *insured* are another pair to keep in mind: *ensure* is a transitive verb which means to make sure while *insure* means to cover with insurance or to make sure or certain, as against loss. *Box-like* is another term that may be confusing: because it is a two-word modifier, it is hyphenated. Also, *New York City* is the official name of the city and therefore is capitalized.

Passage 2

Common errors

African American is preferred over *African-American*. Be sure you know the difference between *effect*, a noun meaning the result, and *affect*, a verb meaning to influence. Be aware that *self-conscious* is a hyphenated word. *Renaissance* is a frequently misspelled word; if you have trouble with it, you should be sure to memorize it. Titles of artistic works are often set off using either italics or quotation marks. The parenthetical punctuation of the title *Mary Turner (A Silent Protest Against Mob Violence)* is hard to detect by listening, but you should have heard that the second part of the title was somehow set off.

MTEL

Massachusetts Tests for Educator Licensure —
Communication and Literacy Skills Test

Practice Test 2

PRACTICE TEST 2

(Answer sheets appear in the back of this book.)

Section 1 – Reading

MULTIPLE CHOICE

> **DIRECTIONS:** Read each passage and answer the questions that follow.

Passage A

If we speak of deriving good from a story, we usually mean something more than the gain of pleasure during the hours of its perusal. Nevertheless, to get pleasure out of a book is a beneficial and profitable thing, if the pleasure be of a kind which, while doing no moral injury, affords relaxation and relief when the mind is overstrained or sick of itself. The prime remedy in such cases is change of scene, by which change of the material scene is not necessarily implied. A sudden shifting of the mental perspective into a fictitious world, combined with rest, is well known to be often as efficacious for renovation as a corporeal journey afar.

In such a case the shifting of scene should manifestly be as complete as if the reader had taken the hind seat on a witch's broomstick. The town man finds what he seeks in novels of the country, the countryman in novels of society, the indoor class generally in outdoor novels, the villager in novels of the mansion, the aristocrat in novels of the cottage.

The narrative must be of a somewhat absorbing kind, if not absolutely fascinating. To discover a book or books which shall possess, in addition to the special scenery, the special action required, may be a matter of some difficulty, though not always of such difficulty as to be insuperable; and it may be asserted that after every variety of spiritual fatigue there is to be found refreshment, if not restoration, in some antithetic realm of ideas which lies waiting in the pages of romance.

From Thomas Hardy, "The Profitable Reading of Fiction," 1888

1. The first sentence of this passage indicates that the author's purpose is to

   (A) suggest that people read only for pleasure.

   (B) analyze the benefits of reading stories.

   (C) defend the view that reading is a waste of time.

   (D) entertain the reader by telling a story.

2. In this passage the author shows bias in favor of

   (A) reading nonfiction.   (C) reading for relaxation.

   (B) reading thrillers.   (D) city life over country life.

3. The image in Paragraph 2 of the reader taking a ride on a witch's broomstick is used to illustrate

   (A) the frivolousness of reading merely for pleasure.

   (B) the complete change of scenery which reading can provide.

   (C) the wickedness of trying to escape reality.

   (D) the dangerous power of storytellers.

4. From this passage you could infer that the author

   (A) is a novelist trying to promote the reading of novels.

   (B) disapproves of pleasure reading.

   (C) believes there are other benefits to reading stories.

   (D) leads an unhappy life.

Passage B

I have noticed in the course of my psychoanalytic work that the state of mind of a man in contemplation is entirely different from that of a man who is observing his psychic processes. In contemplation there is a greater play of psychic action than in the most attentive self-observation; this is also shown by the tense attitude and wrinkled brow of contemplation, in contrast with the restful features of self-observation. In both cases, there must be concentration of attention, but, besides this, in contemplation one exercises a critique, in consequence of which he rejects some of the ideas which he has perceived, and cuts short others, so that he does not follow the trains of thought which they would open; toward still other thoughts he may act in such a manner that they do not become conscious at all—that is to say, they are suppressed before they are perceived. In self-observation, on the other hand, one has only the task of suppressing the critique; if he succeeds in this, an unlimited number of ideas, which otherwise would have been impossible for him to grasp, come to his consciousness. With the aid of this material, newly secured for the purpose of self-observation, the interpretation of pathological ideas, as well as of dream images, can be accomplished. As may be seen, the point is to bring about a psychic state to some extent analogous as regards the apportionment of psychic energy (transferable attention) to the state prior to falling asleep (and indeed also to the hypnotic state). In falling asleep, the "undesired ideas" come into prominence on account of the slackening of a certain arbitrary (and certainly also critical) action, which we allow to exert an influence upon the trend of our ideas; we are accustomed to assign "fatigue" as the reason for this slackening; the emerging undesired ideas as the reason are changed into visual and acoustic images. In the condition which is used for the analysis of dreams and pathological ideas, this activity is purposely and arbitrarily dispensed with, and the psychic energy thus saved, or a part of it, is used for the attentive following of the undesired thoughts now coming to the surface, which retain their identity as ideas (this is the difference from the condition of falling asleep). "Undesired ideas" are thus changed into "desired" ones.

The suspension thus required of the critique for these apparently "freely rising" ideas, which is here demanded and which is usually exercised on them, is not easy for some persons. The "undesired ideas" are in the habit of starting the most violent resistance, which seeks to prevent them from coming to the surface. But if we may credit our great poet-philosopher Friedrich Schiller, a very similar tolerance must be the condition of poetic production. At a point in his correspondence with Koerner, for the noting of which we are indebted to Mr. Otto

Rank, Schiller answers a friend who complains of his lack of creativeness in the following words: "The reason for your complaint lies, it seems to me, in the constraint which your intelligence imposes upon your imagination. I must here make an observation and illustrate it by an allegory. It does not seem beneficial, and it is harmful for the creative work of the mind, if the intelligence inspects too closely the ideas already pouring in, as it were, at the gates. Regarded by itself, an idea may be very trifling and very adventurous, but it perhaps becomes important on account of one which follows it; perhaps in a certain connection with others, which may seem equally absurd, it is capable of forming a very useful construction. The intelligence cannot judge all these things if it does not hold them steadily long enough to see them in connection with the others. In the case of a creative mind, however, the intelligence has withdrawn its watchers from the gates, the ideas rush in pell-mell, and it is only then that the great heap is looked over and critically examined. Messrs. Critics, or whatever else you may call yourselves, you are ashamed or afraid of the momentary and transitory madness which is found in all creators, and whose longer or shorter duration distinguishes the thinking artist from the dreamer. Hence your complaints about barrenness, for you reject too soon and discriminate too severely" (Letter of December 1, 1788).

And yet, "such a withdrawal of the watchers from the gates of intelligence," as Schiller calls it, such a shifting into the condition of uncritical self-observation, is in no way difficult.

Most of my patients accomplish it after the first instructions; I myself can do it very perfectly, if I assist the operation by writing down my notions. The amount, in terms of psychic energy, by which the critical activity is in this manner reduced, and by which the intensity of the self-observation may be increased, varies widely according to the subject matter upon which the attention is to be fixed.

From Sigmund Freud, "The Interpretation of Dreams," trans. A. A. Brill

5. Which are characteristics of contemplation, according to the author of this article?

   I. A greater play of psychic action than in the most attentive self-observation.

II.   A tense attitude, a wrinkled brow, and a concentration of attention.

III. A suppression of some thoughts before they are perceived.

IV.   A critique in which one rejects some of the ideas and cuts short others.

(A) I only.   (C) I, II, and III only.

(B) I and II only.   (D) I, II, III, and IV.

6.   Which are characteristics of self-observation?

I.   Restful features and a suppressing of the criticism.

II.   Less play of psychic action and a concentration of attention.

III. An interpretation of pathological ideas and dream images.

(A) I only.   (C) I, II, and III.

(B) I and II only.   (D) I and III only.

7.   In sleep

(A) no psychic energy is available for the attentive following of undesired thoughts.

(B) fatigue causes the slackening of a certain arbitrary and often critical action, according to most people's way of thinking.

(C) undesired and desired ideas are not modified.

(D) the watchers of the gates of intelligence have not withdrawn.

8.   The writer states that shifting into the condition of uncritical self-observation

(A) is impossible.

(B) can be done perfectly by the writer's patients.

(C) is difficult in many ways.

(D) is a feat the writer of the article maintains he can do perfectly.

9.   The lack of creativeness lies in the constraints imposed upon the imagination by the intelligence, according to

(A) Freud.   (C) Schiller.

(B) Rank.   (D) Koerner.

10. A trifling and very adventurous idea

    (A)   is usually important in itself.

    (B)   should be considered in isolation.

    (C)   should not be held long in the mind to make room for other ideas.

    (D)   may become important because of an idea which follows.

11. Uncritical self-observation

    (A)   is difficult to perform since we are all biased toward ourselves.

    (B)   should not be encouraged if creative thinking is to result.

    (C)   is inherent, not learned.

    (D)   requires one to be unashamed or unafraid of the momentary and transitory madness.

12. In a creative mind

    (A)   each idea is examined critically and individually as it is received.

    (B)   ideas enter in a systematic manner.

    (C)   a heap of ideas are examined critically at one time.

    (D)   rejection comes soon and discrimination must be severe at all times.

13. According to Schiller

    (A)   the tolerance of undesired ideas must be eliminated.

    (B)   freely rising ideas must be critically examined as they occur.

    (C)   the suspension of freely rising ideas is necessary.

    (D)   a tolerance for undesired ideas is a necessary condition.

14. The author notes that psychic energy, by which the critical activity is reduced and by which the intensity of the self-observation may be increased, varies according to

    (A)   the time of day at which the activity occurs.

    (B)   the subject matter upon which the attention is fixed.

    (C)   whether the intelligence has withdrawn its watchers from the gate.

    (D)   whether the idea is trifling or constructive.

Passage C

Vaulting played a great part—perhaps the greatest, though certainly not the only part in developing Gothic architecture; but it will not do to define it as simply the expression of scientific vaulting. The Romans were masters of the art of vaulting long before; they used—probably invented—the cross-vault, and understood the concentration of thrusts on isolated points. It was from them, and from Eastern Rome as well, that the Romanesque builders learned how to make their stone roofs, and they in their turn passed the art on to their Gothic successors, who improved and developed it in their own way, making in the end almost a new art of it. But it must be remembered that most of the problems of scientific vaulting had presented themselves before their time, and had been partially at all events solved by their predecessors, though not so completely.

Nor is it correct to regard vaulting as an essential feature of the style, however great its influence may have been on the structure of great churches. In England except on a grand scale it is exceptional; and yet if Westminster Hall with its stupendous timber covering, and the Fen churches with their glorious wooden roofs, and the splendid ceiling of the nave at St. David's are not Gothic what are they? And what else can we call the countless village churches, gems of modest art, that stud our country far and wide, and constitute one of its greatest charms, though it is only here and there that they aspire to the dignity of a vaulted ceiling?

Again if the test of Gothic is to be the logical expression of a vaulted construction what becomes of domestic architecture both here and abroad, in which vaulting certainly does not play an important part? Are the townhalls of Brussels, Ypres, and Louvain not Gothic, nor the Broletto of Como, the pontifical palace at Viterbo, or that of the popes at Avignon, or the ducal palace at Venice?

Still less is Gothic architecture, as it has appeared to the ordinary layman, a matter of quatrefoils and trefoils, of cusps and traceries, of crockets and finials, pinnacles and flying buttresses. These are but the accidents of the style, though no doubt they resulted naturally from the application of certain principles behind them. But they might all fly away and yet leave a Gothic building behind them. Many an old tithe barn of rough timber framework is as truly a piece of Gothic architecture as York Minster or Salisbury Cathedral.

If then none of these attempted definitions are really coextensive with the Gothic style of architecture, for a building may be Gothic and yet have none of these characteristics, how are we to define it?

The true way of looking at Gothic art is to regard it not as a definite style bound by certain formulas—for it is infinitely various—but rather as the expression of a certain temper, sentiment, and spirit which inspired the whole method of doing things during the Middle Ages in sculpture and painting as well as in architecture. It cannot be defined by any of its outward features, for they are variable, differing at times and in different places. They are the outward expression of certain cardinal principles behind them, and though these principles are common to all good styles—Gothic among them—the result of applying them to the buildings of each age, country, and people will vary as the circumstances of that country, that age, and that people vary.

From Sir Thomas Graham Jackson, "Gothic Architecture in France, England & Italy"

15. Which statement is most accurate?

    (A) The Gothic forms were predecessors to the Romanesque builders.

    (B) The Romanesque builders were successors to the Gothic builders.

    (C) The Romanesque builders had partially solved many of the problems of scientific vaulting before their Gothic successors.

    (D) In developing Gothic architecture, vaulting played only a minor role.

16. The author believes that

    (A) vaulting is an essential feature of Gothic architecture.

    (B) Gothic architecture had no influence in churches because, "…it is only here and there that they [the village churches] aspire to the dignity of a vaulted ceiling."

    (C) Gothic architecture might still exist even without quatrefoils, trefoils, cusps, traceries, pinnacles, flying buttresses, and finials.

    (D) Gothic architecture is a definite style bound by certain formulas.

17. Gothic art

    I.   is to be regarded as a definite style bound by certain formulas.

    II.   is the expression of a certain temper, sentiment, and spirit which inspired sculpture and painting.

    III.   cannot be defined by any one of its outward features since they are variable.

    (A)   I only.   (C)   II and III only.

    (B)   I and II.   (D)   I, II, and III.

18. The writer believes that Gothic art

    (A)   is a thing of the past.

    (B)   will be applied to buildings of each age and country exactly as in the past.

    (C)   will be applied with some variation to buildings of each age and country.

    (D)   does not follow the principles common to all good styles.

19. The central purpose of the article is to

    (A)   define Gothic architecture.

    (B)   give the characteristics of Gothic architecture.

    (C)   present "the true way of looking at Gothic."

    (D)   disparage Gothic architecture.

20. "Vaulting" in this article refers to

    (A)   a way of leaping high, as in popularity.

    (B)   a way of styling similar to that of vaults, or places where bodies are interred.

    (C)   a way of producing high ceilings without visible support.

    (D)   a way of drawing and producing plans on paper.

21. A "pontifical palace" may be best interpreted as

    (A)   a place of happiness and merriment.

    (B)   a place of rest and relaxation.

(C)   a place which seems friendly.

(D)   a place which seems dignified.

22. Quatrefoils, according to the article, are

(A)   not accidents of style.

(B)   not results of applications of principles.

(C)   essential to Gothic buildings.

(D)   results of the natural application of certain principles.

23. The author regards Gothic art as

(A)   a definite style bound by certain formulas.

(B)   having styles which are similar in all expressions.

(C)   the expression of infinitely various temper, sentiment, and spirit.

(D)   defined by outward features.

24. The author says Gothic art is NOT

(A)   a whole method of doing things during the Middle Ages.

(B)   an influence on architecture, painting, and sculpture.

(C)   defined by its features.

(D)   an outward expression of certain cardinal principles.

Passage D

The Slave Trade

The most significant demographic shift in these decades was the movement of blacks from the Old South to the new Southwest. Traders shipped servants by the thousands to the newly opened cotton lands of the gulf states. A prime field hand fetched an average price of $800, as high as $1500 in peak years. Families were frequently split apart by this miserable traffic. Planters freely engaged in this trade, but assigned very low status to the traders who carried it out.

Although the importation of slaves from abroad had been outlawed by Congress since 1808, they continued to be smuggled in until the 1850s. The import ban kept the price up and encouraged the continuation of the internal trade.

Blacks in bondage suffered varying degrees of repression and deprivation. The harsh slave codes were comprehensive in their restrictions on individual freedom, but they were unevenly applied, and so there was considerable variety in the severity of life. The typical slave probably received a rough but adequate diet and enjoyed crude but sufficient housing and clothing.

But the loss of freedom and the injustice of the system produced a variety of responses. Many "soldiered" on the job, and refused to work hard, or they found ways to sabotage the machinery or the crops. There was an underground system of ridicule toward the masters which was nurtured, as reflected in such oral literature as the "Brer Rabbit" tales.

BLACK SOCIAL STRUCTURE IN THE OLD SOUTH, 1860

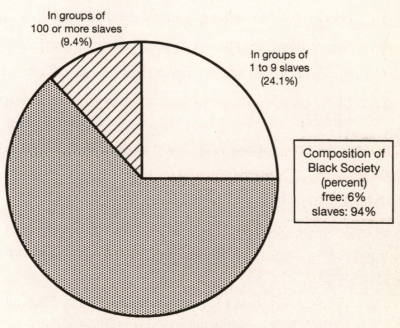

In groups of 100 or more slaves (9.4%)

In groups of 1 to 9 slaves (24.1%)

Composition of Black Society (percent) free: 6% slaves: 94%

In groups of 10 to 99 slaves (60.5%)

Violent reaction to repression was not uncommon. Gabriel Prosser in Richmond (1800), Denmark Vesey in Charleston (1822), and Nat Turner in coastal Virginia (1831) all plotted or led uprisings of blacks against their white masters. Rumors of such uprisings kept whites in a state of constant apprehension.

The ultimate rebellion was to simply leave, and many tried to run away, some successfully. Especially from the states bordering the North, an ever increasing number of slaves fled to freedom, many with the aid of the "underground railroad" and smugglers such as Harriet Tubman, who led over 300 of her family and friends to freedom after she herself had escaped.

Most of those in bondage, however, were forced simply to adapt, and they did. A rich culture was developed within the confines of the system, and included distinctive patterns of language, music, and religion. Kinship ties were probably strengthened in the face of the onslaughts of sale and separation of family members. In the face of incredible odds, the slaves developed a distinctive network of tradition and interdependence, and they survived.

25. The main idea portrayed in this passage is

 (A) Harriet Tubman and many slaves escaped bondage.

 (B) the oral literature of the underground ridiculed white slave-masters.

 (C) the slave market was run much the same way as other markets.

 (D) black society in the nineteenth century endured despite great hardship.

26. In what way is the word "soldiered" used in the second sentence of Paragraph 4?

 (A) Took up arms   (C) Undercut their labor

 (B) Labored   (D) Were uniformed

27. Which of the following best expresses the main idea of the third paragraph?

 (A) While a violation of human freedom, slave treatment did not always include inhumane living conditions.

 (B) Insufficient housing and diet were typical with slave treatment.

 (C) Most slaves received the same degree of abuse as their fellows.

 (D) Poor living conditions often forced escape attempts by slaves.

28. According to the graph,

    (A) 100% of all blacks in the Old South were slaves of some sort.

    (B) the majority of slave groups consisted of 100 or more persons.

    (C) more than half the slaves were in groups of 10 to 99 slaves.

    (D) more than half the slaves were in groups of 1 to 99 slaves.

Passage E

Great cities are levelling; they lift up the low and depress the high; they exalt mediocrity and abase superlativeness—the result of the action of the mass, as powerful in society life as in chemistry.

Soon after I came to this ancient city of Salamanca which has now become so dear to me, a city of some thirty thousand souls, I wrote to a friend and told him that if after two year's residence here he should be informed that I spent my time playing cards, taking siestas and strolling round the square for a couple of hours every day, he might give me up for lost; but if at the end of that time I should still be studying, meditating, writing, battling for culture in the public arena, he might take it that I was better off here than in Madrid. And so it has proved to be.

I remember that Guglielmo Ferrero's conclusion, based upon a review of ancient Greece, of the Italy of the Renaissance and of the Germany of a century ago, is that for the life of the spirit, small cities of a population like that of Salamanca are the best—better than very small towns or large ones of over a hundred thousand inhabitants.

This depends, of course, upon the quality of the spirit in question. I am convinced that the monastic cloister, which so often atrophies the soul and reduces the average intelligence to a lamentable slavery to routine, has in certain exceptional cases exalted the spirit by its arduous discipline.

Great cities are essentially democratic, and I must confess that I feel an invincible platonic mistrust of democracies. In great cities culture is diffused but vulgarized. People abandon the quiet reading of books to go to the theatre, that school of vulgarity; they feel the need of being together; the gregarious instinct enslaves them; they must be seeing one another.

From Miguel de Unamuno, "Large and Small Towns," 1917

29. From this passage, you could infer that

   (A)   the author believes that great cities are essentially democratic.

   (B)   given a choice, the author would prefer to live in a small city.

   (C)   the author has never lived in a small town or out in the country.

   (D)   the author believes that democracy is the best form of government.

30. Identify the statement below which gives the most accurate statement of the central idea of this passage.

   (A)   Great cities tend to reduce everyone to the same level and are therefore not conducive to the life of the spirit.

   (B)   The cloistered life of monks and nuns is perhaps the best way of life for the person interested in spiritual growth.

   (C)   Smaller cities are not conducive to spiritual and intellectual growth because they are too sleepy and inactive.

   (D)   As far as the spiritual life is concerned, great cities are superior both to small cities and to life in the country.

STOP

> The following additional multiple-choice questions have been provided to help you sharpen your skills. This section will not appear on the actual MTEL test. Please turn to "Vocabulary" on page 314 to resume the timed practice test.

Passage F

   The first thing that struck me on landing in America was that if the Americans are not the most well-dressed people in the world, they are the most comfortably dressed. Men are seen there with the dreadful chimney-pot hat, but there are very few hatless men; men wear the shocking shallow-tail coat, but few are to be seen with no coat at all. There is an air of comfort in the appearance of the people which is a marked contrast to that seen in this country, where, too often, people are seen in close contact with rags.

The next thing particularly noticeable is that everybody seems in a hurry to catch a train. This is a state of things which is not favorable to poetry or romance. Had Romeo or Juliet been in a constant state of anxiety about trains, or had their minds been agitated by the question of return-tickets, Shakespeare could not have given us those lovely balcony scenes which are so full of poetry and pathos.

America is the noisiest country that ever existed. One is waked up in the morning not by the singing of the nightingale, but by the steam whistle. It is surprising that the sound practical sense of the Americans does not reduce this intolerable noise. All art depends upon exquisite and delicate sensibility, and such continual turmoil must ultimately be destructive of the musical faculty.

From Oscar Wilde, "Impressions of America," 1882

31. The example of Romeo and Juliet in the second paragraph is introduced in order to

   (A)   criticize Americans for their ignorance of Shakespeare.

   (B)   suggest humorously that their poetic and romantic world would be impossible in America.

   (C)   underscore the need for silence if art is to thrive.

   (D)   contrast the drabness of American dress with Romeo and Juliet's exquisite dress.

32. The word "faculty," as used in the last sentence of the passage, means

   (A)   professors.   (C) instrument.

   (B)   a power of the mind.   (D) ease.

33. The first sentence of this passage ("The first thing...comfortably dressed.") indicates that the author's purpose is to

   (A)   give a comprehensive objective analysis of American society.

   (B)   compare the ways Americans dress with the ways Europeans dress.

(C)   offer some personal observations on America from a foreigner's perspective.

(D)   ridicule Americans for the way they dress, eat, and live.

Passage G

The rage for glitter—because its idea has become, as we before observed, confounded with that of magnificence in the abstract—has led us, also, to the exaggerated employment of mirrors. We line our dwellings with great British plates, and then imagine we have done a fine thing. Now, the slightest thought will be sufficient to convince any one, who has an eye at all, of the ill effect of numerous looking-glasses, and especially of large ones. Regarded apart from its reflection, the mirror presents a continuous, flat, colorless, unrelieved surface—a thing always and obviously unpleasant. Considered as a reflector, it is potent in producing a monstrous and odious uniformity; and the evil is here aggravated, not in merely direct proportion with the augmentation of its sources, but in a ratio constantly increasing. In fact, a room with four or five mirrors arranged at random is, for all purposes of artistic show, a room of no shape at all. If we add to this evil the attendant glitter upon glitter, we have a perfect farrago of discordant and displeasing effects. The veriest bumpkin, on entering an apartment so bedizened, would be instantly aware of something wrong, although he might be altogether unable to assign a cause for his dissatisfaction. But let the same person be led into a room tastefully furnished, and he would be startled into an exclamation of pleasure and surprise.

From Edgar Allan Poe, "Philosophy of Furniture"

34. The first sentence of this paragraph indicates that the author's purpose is to

(A)   define the abstract term "magnificence."

(B)   criticize the overuse of mirrors in decoration.

(C)   show how the use of mirrors has led to the popularity of "glitter."

(D)   compare the usefulness of mirrors with the usefulness of windows.

35. In this context, the word "augmentation" means

    (A) quality.   (C) variety.

    (B) decline.   (D) increase.

36. The author of this passage has created a tone that could be described as

    (A) critical.   (C) optimistic.

    (B) amused.   (D) nostalgic.

Passage H

The process of "creation"—one common to all men and therefore known to each of us by inner experience—occurs as follows: a man surmises or dimly feels something that is perfectly new to him, which he has never heard of from anybody. This something new impresses him, and in ordinary conversation he points out to others what he perceives, and to his surprise finds that what is apparent to him is quite unseen by them. They do not see or do not feel what he tells them of. This isolation, discord, disunion from others, at first disturbs him, and verifying his own perception the man tries in different ways to communicate to others what he has seen, felt, or understood; but these others still do not understand it as he understands or feels it. And the man begins to be troubled by a doubt as to whether he imagines and dimly feels something that does not really exist, or whether others do not see and do not feel something that does exist. And to solve this doubt he directs his whole strength to the task of making his discovery so clear that there cannot be the smallest doubt, either for himself or for other people, as to the existence of what he has seen, understood, or felt, others at once see, understand, and feel as he does and it is this effort to make clear and indubitable to himself and to others what both to others and to him had been dim and obscure, that is the source from which flows the production of man's spiritual activity in general, or what we call works of art—which widen man's horizon and oblige him to see what had not been perceived before.

From Leo Tolstoy, "On Art"

37. The main idea expressed in this passage is that

(A)   works of art arise from an individual's attempt to clarify a new perception or discovery.

(B)   society little appreciates the artists in its midst and is undeserving of their artistic creations.

(C)   society forces the creative individual into conformity to its commonplace perceptions of the world.

(D)   the artistic individual never doubts his own superior perceptions.

38.   The fact that the man tries first to communicate his discovery to others in ordinary conversation is used to show

(A)   how the impetus for creation arises from a need to communicate.

(B)   how little attention ordinary people pay to the artists in society.

(C)   that creative people are ordinary in every way.

(D)   the difficulty of being an artist these days.

Passage I

I have already intimated that my condition was much worse, during the first six months of my stay at Mr. Covey's, than in the last six. The circumstances leading to the change in Mr. Covey's course toward me form an epoch in my humble history. On one of the hottest days of the month of August 1833, Bill Smith, William Hughes, a slave named Eli, and myself were engaged in fanning wheat. Eli was turning, Smith was feeding, and I was carrying wheat to the fan. The work was simple, requiring strength rather than intelligence; yet, to one entirely unused to such work, it came very hard. About three o'clock of that day, I broke down; my strength failed me; I was seized with a violent aching of the head, attended with extreme dizziness...I nerved myself up, feeling it would never do to stop work. I stood as long as I could stagger to the hopper with grain. When I could stand no longer, I fell, and felt as if held down by an immense weight. The fan of course stopped; every one had his own work to do; and no one could do the work of the other, and have his own go on at the same time. Mr. Covey was at the house...On hearing the fan stop, he immediately...came to the spot where we were. He hastily inquired what the matter was. Bill answered that I was sick. I had by this time crawled away under the side of the post-and-rail fence, hoping to find relief by getting out of the sun. He then asked where I was. Told by one of the hands, he came to the spot, and, after looking at me for a while, asked me what the matter was. I told him as well as I could, for I scarce had the strength to speak. He then gave me a savage kick in the side, and told me to get up. I tried to do so, but fell back in the attempt. He gave me another kick, and again told me to rise. I again tried, and succeeded in gaining my feet; but I again staggered and fell. Mr. Covey took up the hickory slat with which Hughes had been striking off the half-bushel measure, and with it gave me a heavy blow upon the head, making a large wound, and the blood ran freely.

Mr. Covey had now left me to my fate. At this moment I resolved to go to my master, enter a complaint, and ask his protection. In order to do this, I must that afternoon walk seven miles; and this, under the circumstances, was truly a severe undertaking. I was exceedingly feeble by the kicks and blows I had received. While Covey was looking in the opposite direction, I succeeded in getting a considerable distance on my way to the woods, when Covey discovered me, and called after me to come back, threatening what he would do if I did not come. I disregarded both his calls and threats.

This battle with Mr. Covey was the turning point in my career as a slave. It rekindled within me a sense of my own manhood. It recalled the departed self-confidence, and inspired me again with a determination to be free. My long-crushed spirit rose, cowardice departed, bold defiance took its place; and I now resolved that, however long I might remain a slave in form, the day had passed forever when I could be a slave in fact. I did not hesitate to let it be known of me, that the white man who expected to succeed in whipping, must also succeed in killing me.

From Frederick Douglass, "Resurrection"

39. Define the word "epoch" as it is used in the first paragraph of this selection.

   (A)   Change of direction   (C)   Period of time

   (B)   Great event   (D)   A blot or stain

40. Which of the following best sums up the writer's main idea in this selection?

    (A)   Slavery was a more brutal thing than anyone who has never been a slave could know.

    (B)   What began as a conflict with Mr. Covey resulted in a slave's new understanding of his own manhood and self-esteem.

    (C)   Slavery made men out of people rather than crush their spirits.

    (D)   White slave owners were generally an insensitive lot.

VOCABULARY

DIRECTIONS: This section tests your vocabulary knowledge. Use the spaces below each word to write the definitions. Your responses will be marked as correct or incorrect based on the accuracy and adequacy of the definition provided.

1. ✓ Define *fundamental*.

_____

_____

_____

2. ? Define *tawdry*.

_____

_____

_____

3. ? Define *sedition*.

_____

_____

_____

4.   Define *pithy*.

_____

_____

5.   Define *awry*.

_____

_____

6.   Define *facade*.

_____

_____

7.   Define *lustrous*.

_____

_____

8.   Define *nullify*.

_____

_____

9.   Define *tribute*.

_____

_____

_____

Section 2 – Writing

WRITTEN SUMMARY

> **DIRECTIONS:** Read the following passages and then summarize, in your own words, their main points. Your responses will be scored according to the following characteristics: fidelity, conciseness, organization, sentence structure, word usage, and mechanical conventions.

Essay 1

The Civil Service Commission authorized tests and other forms of screening. Applicants are ranked according to test scores and other criteria, such as experience. Secretaries, plumbers, and other skilled laborers are required to take specialized tests. In earlier years professionals were given PACE examinations, but these exams are no longer administered. According to the ranking scale, the top three applicants become finalists who will compete for the job vacancy. Once on the job, the employee must deal with other forms of classification. For years, the Civil Service Commission made policy with regard to pay scales based on job descriptions. The procedure proved unwieldy. Currently, agencies handle their own classification systems. Controversies surface from time to time. After the Watergate scandal, Congress decided that change was in order. In 1978, Congress passed the Civil Service Reform Act. The legislators defined merit and cited nine principles that serve as guidelines today. Merit pay was initiated. New structural changes led to division of duties among the Office of Personnel Management, the Merit System Protection Board, the Office of Special Counsel, the Federal Labor Relations Authority, and the Senior Executive Services.

The new system was designed to improve working conditions. Proponents pointed to flexibility and rewards for excellent service. To protect the honest, hardworking civil servants from dishonest and/or unfair supervisors or fellow employees, the Merit System Protection Board promulgates rules and sees that they are administered by other agencies. Federal employees may bring their complaints to the Office of Special Counsel. After investigation and hearings, the case may go before the Merit System Protection Board. Cases that deal with violations of the law may be investigated by Congress, or the federal courts. Analyst Ronald D. Sylvia found that the Office of Special Counsel has not functioned well. Few cases have been appealed to the board or to court. Whistleblowers have experienced little protection in the way the Office functions.

Despite changes in laws, system, rules, procedures, and practices, federal government has yet to resolve many problems that beset both private and public sectors. For example, it has been hard to eliminate different kinds of discrimination in state and federal agencies: sex, age, race, religion, and members of ethnic groups. Policymakers are generally puzzled on how to deal fairly with employees who are pregnant, new parents, victims of sexual harassment, drug abusers, alcoholics, and AIDS victims. Proponents are calling for changes in philosophy with regard to employee rights on the job and as politically active citizens. If Congress and/or the president as chief executive fail to address the controversies, agency managers must rely on legal staffs to aid them on a case-by-case basis in developing rules or deciding employee complaints. Eventually, questionable personnel management policies are challenged in courts of law or in arbitration and mediation processes.

The values of the 18th century practitioners included striving for honest government manned by highly ethical, educated citizens. Public service was performed by capable persons whose loyalty to the constitution was seldom questioned. Although many other principles have become woven into the fabric of public administration today, Congress and recent presidents through their executive orders have tried to maintain these values and incorporate higher goals. As we have seen, the tasks have not been easy. Much remains to be envisioned, crafted, and implemented.

Essay 2

Life in colonial times was harsh, and the refinements of the mother country were ordinarily lacking. The colonists, however, soon began to mold their English culture into the fresh environment of a new land. The influence of religion permeated the entire way of life. In most Southern colonies, the Anglican church was the legally established church. In New England, the Puritans were dominant; and, in Pennsylvania, the Quakers. Especially in the New England colonies, the local or village church was the hub of community life; the authorities strictly enforced the Sabbath and sometimes banished nonbelievers and dissenters.

Unfortunately, the same sort of religious intolerance, bigotry, and superstition associated with the age of the Reformation in Europe also prevailed in some of the colonies, though on a lesser scale. In the last half of the seventeenth century, during sporadic outbreaks of religious fanaticism and hysteria, Massachusetts and Connecticut authorities tried and hanged a few women as "witches." Early in the seventeenth century, some other witchcraft persecution occurred in Virginia, North Carolina, and Rhode Island. As the decades passed, however, religious toleration developed in the colonies.

Because of the strong religious influence in the colonies, especially in New England, religious instruction and Bible reading played an important part in education. In Massachusetts, for example, the law of 1645 required each community with 50 households to establish an elementary school. Two years later the same colony passed the "Deluder Satan" law which required each town of 100 families to maintain a grammar school for the purpose of providing religious, as well as general, instruction. In the Southern colonies, only a few privately endowed free schools existed. Private tutors instructed the sons of well-to-do planters, who completed their educations in English universities. Young males in poor families throughout the colonies were ordinarily apprenticed for vocational education.

By 1700, two colleges had been founded: Harvard, established by the Massachusetts Legislature in 1636; and William and Mary, in Virginia, which originated in 1693 under a royal charter. Other cultural activities before 1700 were limited. The few literary products of the colonists, mostly historical narratives, journals, sermons, and some poetry, were printed in England. The Bay Psalm Book (1640) was the first book printed in the colonies. Artists and composers were few, and their output was of a relatively simple character.

Essay 3

All of Plato's philosophical writing was done in the form of dialogues, conversations in which almost always the principal speaker is Socrates. These are the first philosophical dialogues of the Western world. So far as we know, Plato himself invented the dialogue as a literary form, apparently from his actual experience of listening to Socrates in his characteristic conversations. Socrates wrote nothing, but all the philosophy Plato wrote is attributed to him, with the result that it is impossible to disentangle with complete certainty the Socratic from the Platonic element in the dialogues. Most scholars agree that aside from the very early dialogues in which Plato was seeking to present the true teaching of Socrates in order to defend him and to honor his memory, the dialogues represent Plato's own views. Plato wrote more than 20 dialogues, many of them of fine literary quality. Since they depict actual conversations, they are open-ended, flowing, informal, very different from the tight, systematic, rigorously deductive argumentation which we will find, for example, in Descartes. The persons who take part in the dialogues become three-dimensional as Plato sketches them—the pompous, blustering Thrasymachus; the polite reasonableness of Adeimantus and Glaucon; the handsome and clever Alcibiades; and Socrates himself, master of the put-down, making fools of those who ventured to offer their opinions in response to his prodding, and making enemies of those he disagreed with in politics and philosophy.

Most of the dialogues use the philosophic method which Socrates invented—the *Socratic Method*. It is a form of seeking knowledge by question and answer. The question is put by Socrates, and is usually a general question: What is courage? What is justice? The answer offered by the respondent takes the form of a definition: Courage is ——. Socrates then proceeds to refute each definition by offering a counterexample designed to show that the definition which was offered is too narrow, too restricted, or is biased or uninformed. Plato uses the Socratic Method superbly in Book I of the *Republic*. Socrates asks Cephalos, a wealthy and honorable old merchant, "What is justice?" Cephalos replies from the narrow point of view of the ethics of a businessman: Justice is speaking the truth and paying one's debts. But Socrates replies with a counterexample: "Sometimes paying one's debts may be unjust, as when you owe a friend a weapon, but since he has subsequently become insane, would it not be unjust to return it to him?" Cephalos agrees; his own definition is demolished. A new definition must be constructed to cover this type of case.

The Socratic Method uses the technique of the counterexample to mount a series of questions expanding the number of examples, cases, particulars, to be included in the definition. A definition must state what all the examples, cases, instances, particulars, have in common as examples of courage, justice, and so forth. Sometimes the definition arrived at shows the falsity of the original definition by completely reversing it. Sometimes, as at the end of Book I of the *Republic*, no definition is reached although many are rejected.

Under the influence of Socrates' emphasis upon the importance of universal and unchanging definitions, Plato's primary intention as a philosopher was to find definitions for the concepts of justice and of the state.

WRITTEN COMPOSITION

DIRECTIONS: Read the following statements and passages, as well as each set of directions; then write your response. Your compositions will be scored according to the following characteristics: appropriateness, mechanical conventions, word usage, sentence structure, focus and unity, organization, and development.

Essay 1

The rising cost of health care has been a hotly debated political topic in recent years. What are your opinions on this subject?

Essay 2

Many leaders have suggested over the last few years that instead of a military draft, we should require all young people to serve the public in some way for a period of time. The service could be military or any other reasonable form of public service.

Do you agree or disagree with this statement? Support your opinion with specific examples from history, current events, literature, or personal experience.

Essay 3

✓

Because of increased crime involving teenagers at area malls and other places of recreational activity, local city councils and many concerned citizens have recently proposed curfews, hoping to stem the tide of teen crime.

Write an essay, to be read by the city council and concerned citizens, approving or disapproving of the proposed curfews for teenagers.

GRAMMAR AND USAGE

DIRECTIONS: Read each passage and answer the questions that follow.

Passage A

[1]The Lincoln Cent was first struck in 1909 to celebrate the 100th Anniversary of the birth of Abraham Lincoln, our 16th President. [2]Designed by Victor D. Brenner, the coin carried the motto "In God We Trust"—the first time it appeared on this denomination coin. [3]It is interesting that the law for the motto was passed during Lincoln's administration as president. [4]Though we might not think so at first glance, the lowly Cent is a fitting memorial for the great man whose profile graces this most common coin of the realm and is a tolerable symbol for the nation whose commerce it serves.

[5]The obverse has the profile of Lincoln as he looked during the trying years of the War Between the States. [6]Faced with the immense problems of a divided nation, the prevention of the split between North and South was difficult. [7]"A house divided against itself cannot stand," he warned the nation. [8]With the outbreak of war at Fort Sumter. [9]Lincoln was saddened to see his beloved country caught up in the senseless war in which father fought against son, brother against brother. [10]Throughout America, war captured the attention of people: the woman who

saved the lives of the wounded, the soldier waiting to go into battle, the bewildered child trying hard to understand the sound of guns. [11]Lincoln stood on the broad, silent battlefield at Gettysburg in 1863 to dedicate the site as a national cemetery. [12]Gettysburg had been the scene of some of the most bitter fighting of the war and had ended in a Union victory. [13]In his special address at Gettysburg, he called upon the American people to end the war. [14]His words boomed out over the large audience before him:

[15]It is rather for us [the living] to be here dedicated to the great task remaining before us—that from these honored dead we take increased devotion to that cause for which they gave the last full measure of devotion; that we here highly resolve that these dead shall not have died in vain; that this nation under God, shall have a new birth of freedom; and that government of the people, by the people and for the people, shall not perish from the earth."

[16]Barely a month before the end of the war, Lincoln took the oath of office a secondly time as President. [17]With the war still raging, his inaugural address took on added meaning:

[18]With malice toward none, with charity for all, with firmness in the right as God gives us to see the right, let us strive on to finish the work we are in, to bind up the nation's wounds, to care for him who shall have borne the battle and for his widow and his orphan, to do all which may achieve and cherish a just and lasting peace among ourselves and with all nations.

1. Which of the following changes is needed in the fourth paragraph?

   (A) Sentence 16: Change "end" to "climax."

   (B) Sentence 16: Change "secondly" to "second."

   (C) Sentence 17: Change "With" to "Of."

   (D) Sentence 17: Change "on" to "in."

2. Which of the following changes is needed in the second paragraph?

   (A) Sentence 5: Change "has" to "had."

   (B) Sentence 6: Change "the prevention of the split between North and South was difficult" to "Lincoln found it difficult to prevent the split between North and South."

    (C)   Sentence 10: Change "waiting" to "waited."

    (D)   Sentence 11: Change "site" to "sight."

3.   Which of the following sentences is a nonstandard sentence?

    (A)   Sentence 2   (C)   Sentence 8

    (B)   Sentence 4   (D)   Sentence 12

Passage B

[1]Many people think of Ransom Eli Olds as the actual founder of the automobile industry. [2]He built the first automobile factory and was the first to mass produce cars with an assembly-line method. [3]In the late 1800s he experimented with steam engines; the first steam-powered four-wheeled vehicle came out in 1883. [4]This car was sold to a company in India. [5]In 1896 he built his first gasoline-powered car. [6]He helped found the Olds Motor Works in 1899, which produced gasoline engine automobiles.

[7]However, it was in 1901 that he introduced the method that turned out the "curved dash" Oldsmobile in an assembly-line or "stage" production. [8]Assembled in a process using jigs and machine tools, the vehicle was a light-weight, one-cylinder model. [9]This car sold for $650, about one-half the price of similar vehicles from competitors. [10]Many were sold by 1906. [11]In 1904, for example, 5,000 cars, more than three times that of its larger competitor, Peugeot.

[12]Later, in 1914, Henry Ford revolutionized the automotive industry at the Ford Motor Co. plant. [13]This plant used the first moving assembly production line and could turn out a complete vehicle in 90 minutes.

4.   Which of the following underlined words in the second paragraph should be replaced by more precise wording?

    (A)   assembly-line   (C)   about one-half

    (B)   process   (D)   Many

5. Which of the following is a nonstandard sentence?

    (A) Sentence 3   (C) Sentence 11

    (B) Sentence 7   (D) Sentence 12

6. Which of the following is least relevant to the main idea of the first paragraph?

    (A) Sentence 1   (C) Sentence 3

    (B) Sentence 2   (D) Sentence 4

Passage C

[1]Sandra Davis and her two children are finding out just how cold life can be when you're poor. [2]It's the beginning of fall, and a chill wind briskly tosses red and gold leaves into a pile by the front door of the Davis home on Rand Street. [3]But, the inside of the house is cold, too, because the gas has just been turned off for non-payment of the bill. [4]Sandra is out of a job. [5]She suffers, but her children will suffer as much or more.

[6]In fact poor children across America are suffering. [7]According to the stereotype, we believe that poor children are born into large families in big cities, and these families are headed by minority, welfare mothers. [8]Nothing could be further from the truth. [9]More poor children live outside cities. [10]Nearly two-thirds of all poor families have only one or two children. [11]Most poor families' income comes from the wages of one or more workers. [12]Most shocking of all is that even if every single-parent family was to disappear, the United States would still have one of the highest child poverty rates among industrialized nations. [13]This problem is a disgrace in a country as great as ours, but the government cannot legislate a solution. [14]The people of the United States must become concerned about child poverty and commit to a personal involvement before there can be an effective solution.

7. Which of the following, if added between Sentences 6 and 7, is most consistent with the writer's purpose and audience?

    (A) Who can blame Sandra for being angry about being laid off her job?

    (B) However, many of the stereotypes about poor children to which most Americans subscribe are not on target.

(C)   A study on child poverty made newspaper headlines on the front pages of American newspapers.

(D)   Frankly, I am shocked by the poverty that still exists in the United States.

8.   Which of the following is needed?

   (A)   Sentence 1: Delete the word "out."

   (B)   Sentence 3: Change the comma after "too" to a semicolon.

   (C)   Sentence 6: Place a comma after the phrase "In fact."

   (D)   Sentence 7: Place a colon after the word "stereotype."

9.   Which of the following uses a nonstandard verb form?

   (A)   Sentence 11   (C)   Sentence 13

   (B)   Sentence 12   (D)   Sentence 14

Passage D

[1]A French composer, the bolero inspired Anton Ravel to create the ballet *Bolero*. [2]The sister of the legendary Russian dancer Vaslav Nijinsky choreographed the ballet created by Ravel. [3]A popular and well-known folk dance in Spain, the bolero as we know it is credited to Anton Bolsche and Sebastian Cerezo around the mid 1700s. [4]Although almost no one has seen the ballet, the music from *Bolero* has retained immense popularity and is performed on a regular basis around the world.

[5]The center and driving force of it is a snare drum. [6]The percussionist begins by playing a rhythmic pattern lasting two measures and six beats, the rhythm of the bolero dance, as quietly as possible. [7]At the beginning, other instruments pick up the rhythm as the frenzy builds. [8]The first flute then introduces the melody, the second important part of *Bolero*; different instruments play individual parts, such as the clarinet, bassoon, and piccolo. [9]The buildup of the music occurs in two ways: the individual musicians play their instrument louder and louder, and more and more instruments beginning to play together. [10]For most of the 15 to 17 minutes of the performance, *Bolero* is played in a relenting harmony of C Major. [11]The end is signaled by a brief shift to E Major and then a strong return to C Major.

10. Which of the following is least relevant to the main idea of the first paragraph?

   (A) Sentence 1   (C) Sentence 3

   (B) Sentence 2   (D) Sentence 4

11. Which of the following, if added between Sentences 6 and 7 of the second paragraph, is most consistent with the writer's purpose and audience?

   (A) Doesn't that sound kind of boring?

   (B) It's pretty obvious why this piece is not currently popular.

   (C) It would be helpful to see the ballet, as bolero dancers use facial expressions and wave their arms to express emotions.

   (D) This rhythm does not change during the entire performance, but the music becomes gradually louder until the final crescendo.

12. Which of the following contains a misplaced modifier?

   (A) Sentence 1   (C) Sentence 6

   (B) Sentence 3   (D) Sentence 10

13. Which of the following revisions would best improve Sentence 1?

   (A) The bolero inspired Anton Ravel to create the ballet *Bolero*, a French composer.

   (B) The bolero, a French composer, inspired Anton Ravel to create the ballet *Bolero*.

   (C) The bolero inspired Anton Ravel, a French composer, to create the ballet *Bolero*.

   (D) The bolero inspired Anton Ravel to create the ballet, a French composer, *Bolero*.

14. Which of the following would best replace "it" in Sentence 5?

   (A) this musical composition

   (B) the folk dance

   (C) them

   (D) Anton Bolsche and Sebastion Cerezo

STOP

The following additional multiple-choice questions have been provided to help you sharpen your skills. This section will not appear on the actual MTEL test. Please turn to "Sentence Corrections" on page 336 to resume the timed practice test.

15. Which of the following best improves Sentence 8?

    The first flute then introduces the melody, the second important part of *Bolero*; different instruments play individual parts, such as the clarinet, bassoon, and piccolo.

    (A) the clarinet, bassoon and piccolo and other different instruments play individual parts.

    (B) different instruments, such as the clarinet, bassoon, and piccolo, play individual parts.

    (C) individual parts are played by the clarinet, bassoon and piccolo, as well as other different instruments.

    (D) different instruments play different parts, like clarinet, bassoon and piccolo.

16. Which of the following verbs is used incorrectly?

    (A) "inspired" in Sentence 1

    (B) "credited" in Sentence 3

    (C) "pick up" in Sentence 7

    (D) "beginning" in Sentence 9

17. Which of the following corrections should be made?

    (A) Change "choreographed" to "composed" in Sentence 2.

    (B) Change "retained" to "remained" in Sentence 4.

    (C) Change "individual" to "total" in Sentence 9.

    (D) Change "relenting" to "unrelenting" in Sentence 10.

18. Which of the following would be the best way to punctuate Sentence 11?

    (A) The end, is signaled by a brief shift, to E Major and then a strong return to C Major.

    (B) The end is signaled, by a brief shift to E Major, and then a strong return, to C Major.

(C)   The end is signaled by a brief shift to E Major, and then a strong return to C Major.

(D)   The end is signaled by a brief shift, to E Major, and then a strong return, to C Major.

Passage E

[1]In the past thirty years, television has become a very popular past time for almost everyone. [2]From the time the mother places the baby in her jumpseat in front of the television until the time the senior citizen in the retirement home watches Vanna White turn the letters on "Wheel of Fortune," Americans spend endless hours in front of the "boob tube."

[3]When my mother was a little girl, what did children do to entertain themselves? [4]They played. [5]Their games usually involved social interaction with other children as well as imaginatively creating entertainment for themselves. [6]They also developed hobbies like woodworking and sewing. [7]Today, few children really know how to play with each other or entertain themselves. [8]Instead, they sit in front of the television, glued to cartoons that are senseless and often violent. [9]Even if they watch educational programs like "Sesame Street," they don't really have to do anything but watch and listen to what the answer to the question is.

[10]Teenagers, also, use television as a way of avoiding doing things that will be helping them mature. [11]How many kids does much homework anymore? [12]Why not? [13]Because they work part-time jobs and come home from work tired and relax in front of the television.

19. Which of the following sentences uses a nonstandard verb form?

(A)   Sentence 3   (C)   Sentence 7

(B)   Sentence 6   (D)   Sentence 11

20. Which of the following sentences in the passage is nonstandard?

(A)   Sentence 2   (C)   Sentence 9

(B)   Sentence 6   (D)   Sentence 13

Passage F

Dear Senator Simon,

[1]I am writing in support of your bill that, if passed, will be instrumental in getting legislation which will put a warning label on violent television programs. [2]Violence needs to be de-glamorized. [3]One must detest and deplore violence of excess and other such excesses in one's viewing choices.

[4]Unfortunately, violence sells. [5]One of the main reasons is because violent shows are easily translated and marketed to other countries. [6]Network executives have actually requested their script writers to include more violence in certain shows with a steady audience, as well as to create new violent shows for the late evening slot just before the news.

[7]The National Institute of Health did a study. [8]In this study children viewed violent scenes. [9]After this, children are more prone to violent acts. [10]Maybe parents will pay more attention to their children's viewing if this labeling system is enacted. [11]Maybe commercial sponsors will hesitate to sponsor programs that are labeled violent, so these programs will diminish in number and children will have fewer such programs to view.

[12]Yes, I think people need to be aware of violent events happening around the world and within our own country. [13]We need to know what is happening in the Balkans, Somalia, and South Africa, as well as in Los Angeles riots and the bombings in New York, are just to name two examples. [14]However, these are real events, not glamorizations.

[15]Please keep up your campaign to get rid of excessive violence!

Sincerely,

Sue Chan

21. Which of the following is the best revision of the underlined portion of Sentence 1 below?

I am writing in support of your bill <u>that, if passed, will be instrumental in getting legislation which will put</u> a warning label on violent television programs.

(A)   in order to pass legislation in order to put

(B)   passing legislation which will require putting

(C)   to pass a law that will legislate putting

(D)   for a law requiring

22. In the context of the sentences preceding and following Sentence 3, which of the following is the best revision of Sentence 3?

(A)   One should agree with me that excessive violence should be detested and deplored.

(B)   I detest and deplore excessive violence.

(C)   You can see that I think wanton violence should be detested and deplored.

(D)   Detesting and deploring wanton violence and other such excesses is how I feel.

23. In relation to the passage as a whole, which of the following best describes the writer's intention in Paragraph 2?

(A)   To present background information

(B)   To contradict popular opinion

(C)   To provide supporting evidence

(D)   To outline a specific category

24. Which of the following is the best revision of the underlined portion of Sentence 5 below?

One of the main reasons is because violent shows are easily translated and marketed to other countries.

(A)   is being that violent shows

(B)   being that violent shows are

(C)   is that violent shows are

(D)   is due to the fact that violent shows seem to be

25. Which of the following is the best way to combine Sentences 7, 8, and 9?

(A)   After doing a study, the children viewing violent scenes at the National Institute of Health were more prone to violent acts.

(B)   Children viewing violent scenes at the National Institute of Health were more prone to violent acts.

(C)   After viewing violent scenes, children at the National Institute of Health were more prone to doing violent acts themselves.

(D)   The National Institute of Health did a study proving that after viewing violent scenes, children are more prone to violent acts.

26. Which of the following would be the best revision of the underlined portion of Sentence 13?

We need to know what is happening in the Balkans, Somalia, and South Africa, <u>as well as in Los Angeles riots and the bombings in New York, are just to name two examples</u>.

(A)   as well as in Los Angeles riots, and the bombings in New York just to name two examples.

(B)   as well as, to name two examples, the Los Angeles riots and the bombings in New York.

(C)   as well as riots in Los Angeles and the bombings in New York.

(D)   as well as events such as the riots in Los Angeles and the bombings in New York.

Passage G

[1]Actually, the term "Native Americans" is incorrect. [2]Indians migrated to this continent from other areas, just earlier then Europeans did. [3]The ancestors of the Anasazi—Indians of the four-state area of Colorado, New Mexico, Utah, and Arizona—probably crossed from Asia into Alaska. [4]About 25,000 years ago while the continental land bridge still existed. [5]This land bridge arched across the Bering Strait in the last Ice Age. [6]About A.D. 500 the ancestors of the Anasazi moved onto the Mesa Verde a high plateau in the desert country of Colorado. [7]The Wetherills, five brothers who ranched the area, is generally given credit for the first exploration of the ruins in the 1870s and 1880s. [8]There were some 50,000 Anasazi thriving in the four-corners area by the 1200s. [9]At their zenith A.D. 700 to 1300, the Anasazi had established widespread communities and built thousands of sophisticated structures—cliff dwellings, pueblos, and kivas. [10]They even engaged in trade with Indians in surrounding regions by exporting pottery and other goods.

27. Which of the following best corrects the grammatical error in Sentence 7?

(A) The Wetherills, a group of five brothers who ranched in the area, is generally given credit for the first exploration of the ruins in the 1870s and 1880s.

(B) The Wetherills, five brothers who ranched in the area, are generally given credit for the first exploration of the ruins in the 1870s and 1880s.

(C) The Wetherills are generally given credit for the first exploration of the ruins in the 1870s and 1880s, five brothers who ranched in the area.

(D) The Wetherills, generally given credit for the first exploration of the area, is five brothers who ranched in the area.

28. Which of the following sentences would best fit between Sentences 9 and 10 of the passage?

(A) Artifacts recovered from the area suggest that the Anasazi were artistic, religious, agricultural, classless, and peaceful.

(B) By 12,000 to 10,000 B.C., some Indians had established their unique cultures in the southwest.

(C) The Navaho called their ancestors the Anasazi, the Ancient Ones.

(D) I think it is unfortunate that such a unique and innovative culture should have disappeared from the country.

29. Which of the following is an incomplete sentence?

(A) Sentence 4   (C) Sentence 6

(B) Sentence 5   (D) Sentence 7

30. Which of the following best corrects the underlined portion of Sentence 9?

At their zenith A.D. 700 to 1300, the Anasazi had established wide-spread communities and built thousands of sophisticated structures— cliff dwellings, pueblos, and kivas.

(A) At their zenith which was from A.D. 700 to 1300

(B) At their zenith B.C. 700 to 1300

(C) At their zenith, from A.D. 700 to 1300,

(D) At their zenith, being A.D. 700 to 1300,

31. Which of the following would be the best way to punctuate Sentence 6?

(A) About A.D. 500, the ancestors of the Anasazi moved onto the Mesa Verde a high plateau, in the desert country of Colorado.

(B) About A.D. 500 the ancestors of the Anasazi moved, onto the Mesa Verde: a high plateau in the desert country of Colorado.

(C) About A.D. 500 the ancestors of the Anasazi moved onto the Mesa Verde: a high plateau, in the desert country of Colorado.

(D) About A.D. 500, the ancestors of the Anasazi moved onto the Mesa Verde, a high plateau in the desert country of Colorado.

32. Which of the following sentences contains a spelling/grammatical error?

(A) Sentence 1   (C) Sentence 3

(B) Sentence 2   (D) Sentence 10

Passage H

[1]The dismissal of Dr. Dennis Ruoff is a travesty of justice. [2]It is not a good feeling to know that a tenured professor can be hounded out of his post just because he disagrees with the board of regents. [3]True, his was the only negative vote on the curriculum issue pushed by the university board of regents. [4]However, since when has a dissenting opinion been the catalyst for persecution of faculty members on this campus? [5]_____. [6]English professors, especially, have traditionally had the reputation of fighting courageously against blockhead thinking and against lockstep decision making. [7]They have also historically been the school's champions against injustice.

[8]There cannot be an issue closer to the basis of America's founding principles than this one because the foundation of America is based on freedom of speech. [9]The students of this university need to know whose to blame for the loss of Dr. Ruoff. [10]He is a stimulating speaker, an engaging person, and one of the finest teachers. [11]Where will this issue come to a halt? [12]Will other tenured professors now be even more intimidated and hesitate to express any view not consistent with the general consensus of opinion? [13]Will students receive a quality education from a university that infringes on freedom of speech?

33. Which of the following requires revision for unnecessary repetition?

   (A)   Sentence 3   (C)   Sentence 8

   (B)   Sentence 6   (D)   Sentence 12

34. Which of the following, if added between Sentences 4 and 6, best supports the writer's purpose and audience?

   (A)   We should allow teachers to express their own opinions regardless of what we ourselves think.

   (B)   This university has always prided itself on teachers who are rather maverick in their thinking, to say the least.

   (C)   Don't you think this is a pitiful way to treat a fine teacher?

   (D)   One must acknowledge that university professors, as a whole, should support the opinions of fellow faculty members.

35. Which one of the following changes is needed?

   (A)   Sentence 8: Change "closer" to "closest."

   (B)   Sentence 9: Change "whose" to "who's."

   (C)   Sentence 10: Change "finest" to "finer."

   (D)   Sentence 11: Change "Where" to "When."

Passage I

[1]By the end of the decade, it will be common for manufacturers to be more concerned about the environment. [2]Consumers are putting increasing pressure on manufacturers to emphasize environmentally safe products. [3]In making their concerns known, consumers are influencing the corporate world to transform the way it produces and markets goods. [4]There are people who are not concerned with production and care only that the product be cheap and reliable.

[5]Soon, it will be the rare business that does not use "being green" as a promotional device. [6]Its impossible to know with any certainty if the product is recyclable or environmentally safe. [7]Some companies are now beginning to display a seal that purports to verify their claims of being environmentally safe. [8]These "seals of approval" are being given by non-profit or volunteer organizations, not the federal government, so there are

problems with this system. [9]For example, the degree of safety and protection of the environment *varies*. [10]Although the government polices deceptive advertising claims, there are no set standards to which a company must comply before meriting a seal of approval.

36. Which of the following focuses attention on the main idea of the first paragraph?

   (A) Delete the phrase "By the end of the decade" from Sentence 1.

   (B) Change Sentence 2 from a declarative sentence to an interrogative sentence by beginning with "Why are consumers..."

   (C) Change the pronoun in Sentence 3 from "their" to "our."

   (D) Delete Sentence 4.

37. Which of the following changes makes the sequence of ideas in the second paragraph clearer?

   (A) Reverse the order of Sentences 5 and 6.

   (B) Place Sentence 6 after Sentence 9.

   (C) Reverse the order of Sentences 7 and 8.

   (D) Delete Sentence 10.

38. Which of the following is needed in the second paragraph?

   (A) Sentence 5: Change "does not use" to "uses."

   (B) Sentence 6: Change "its" to "it is."

   (C) Sentence 7: Change "now beginning to display" to "beginning to now display."

   (D) Sentence 8: Change "not" to "as well as."

Passage J

[1]Consumers who believe a company is well run and shows promise of doing well in the stock market will invest in that company's stock. [2]If the company shows a profit, the investor will receive a dividend check. [3]Buying United States Savings Bonds is another well-known way of investing money. [4]Some companies offer a dividend reinvestment plan: the profits, instead of being sent to the investor in the form of a check, can be rein-

vested automatically in the company's stock. ⁵To encourage this practice, companies offer several incentives. ⁶For example, if the dividend is too small to buy a whole share, most companies allow the investor to purchase part of a share until enough dividends accumulate for a whole share. ⁷In addition, some companies offer shareholders a discount off the market price of their stock, usually at about a five percent discount. ⁸About 70 percent of companies charge no fee if the stockholder wishes to purchase more shares for cash.

⁹There are several advantages to reinvestment in this manner. ¹⁰There are no brokerage commissions or service fees for most dividend reinvestment plans. ¹¹Further, there is the benefit of compounding the profits, similar to earning interest from a traditional savings account. ¹²Also, dividend reinvestment enables the consumer to dollar-cost average. ¹³By steadily purchasing stock at fixed intervals, the investor ends up buying more shares when the price goes down and fewer shares when the price goes up.

39. Which of the following, if added between Sentences 10 and 11, best fits the writer's purpose and intended audience?

   (A)   Therefore, the system is a relatively inexpensive way to build a strong portfolio of stock in reliable companies.

   (B)   Doesn't this form of investment sound like a smart idea?

   (C)   Some people question the fiscal policy of reinvesting and prefer to have control over when to buy and sell extra stocks.

   (D)   Personally, I think automatic reinvestment of dividends is a sound idea.

40. Which of the following draws attention away from the first paragraph?

   (A)   Sentence 1   (C)   Sentence 3

   (B)   Sentence 2   (D)   Sentence 4

SENTENCE CORRECTIONS

DIRECTIONS: The sentences in this section contain grammatical errors. Rewrite them using the correct grammatical form.

1. The restrictive diet prohibited the inclusion of animal fats, salt, nor any dairy products.

    _____

    _____

    _____

2. Preparing for the tax season, the leisure time of many young people is lost until after April 15.

    _____

    _____

    _____

3. Totalling more than she had anticipated, the bride was shocked by the costs of flowers, food, and entertainment.

    _____

    _____

    _____

4. In the summer I usually like swimming and to water-ski.

    _____

    _____

    _____

5. I found five dollars eating lunch in the park.

    _____

    _____

    _____

6. Janet is one of those people who you can't really describe with words.

    _____

    _____

    _____

GRAMMATICAL VOCABULARY

DIRECTIONS: This section tests your knowledge of grammatical vocabulary. Use the space below each statement to provide the correct definitions. Your responses will be graded as correct or incorrect based on their accuracy and adequacy.

1. Define *direct object*.

2. Define *infinitive*.

3. Define *abstract noun*.

4. Define *third person*.

5. Define *indefinite pronoun*.

6. Define *comma splice*.

7. Define *superlative*.

WRITTEN MECHANICS

Passage 1

Vegetarianism is a rapidly growing lifestyle among Americans. In fact, the first of October is World Vegetarian Day. Today, seven percent of Americans describe themselves as vegetarian, up from just one percent twenty years ago. Almost half of these vegetarians cite health reasons for their choice. Other popular reasons given include concern for animal welfare and for the environment. Types of vegetarians include ovo-lacto vegetarians who eat eggs and dairy products and vegans who eat neither. While the first vegetarians in the United States were a nineteenth-century fringe religious group and vegetarians of the twentieth century were often seen as health or moral extremists, today vegetarianism is becoming a mainstream choice.

Passage 2

What we know about Celtic mythology today comes from the written records made by monks who preserved the ancient sagas despite their own project of furthering Christianity. The poetic tales were viewed as entertainment by the monks and therefore posed no threat of paganism. Irish myths are characterized by their inclusion of fighting battles and their emphasis on reincarnation. The underworld in Celtic mythology is a pleasant place where the dead await reincarnation. Later Celtic mythology is concerned with Christianity. Christianity is central to the Arthurian myths, for example, in which the knights are often sent on quests.

Communication and Literacy Skills Test

PRACTICE TEST 2

ANSWER KEY

MULTIPLE CHOICE

1.	(B)	11.	(D)	21.	(D)	31.	(B)
2.	(C)	12.	(C)	22.	(D)	32.	(B)
3.	(B)	13.	(D)	23.	(C)	33.	(C)
4.	(C)	14.	(B)	24.	(C)	34.	(B)
5.	(D)	15.	(C)	25.	(D)	35.	(D)
6.	(C)	16.	(C)	26.	(C)	36.	(A)
7.	(B)	17.	(C)	27.	(A)	37.	(A)
8.	(D)	18.	(C)	28.	(C)	38.	(A)
9.	(C)	19.	(A)	29.	(B)	39.	(C)
10.	(D)	20.	(C)	30.	(A)	40.	(B)

GRAMMAR AND USAGE

1.	(B)	11.	(D)	21.	(D)	31.	(D)
2.	(B)	12.	(A)	22.	(B)	32.	(B)
3.	(C)	13.	(C)	23.	(A)	33.	(C)
4.	(D)	14.	(A)	24.	(C)	34.	(B)
5.	(C)	15.	(B)	25.	(D)	35.	(B)
6.	(D)	16.	(D)	26.	(D)	36.	(D)
7.	(B)	17.	(D)	27.	(B)	37.	(B)
8.	(C)	18.	(C)	28.	(A)	38.	(B)
9.	(B)	19.	(D)	29.	(A)	39.	(A)
10.	(C)	20.	(D)	30.	(C)	40.	(C)

DETAILED EXPLANATIONS OF ANSWERS

Section 1 — Reading

MULTIPLE CHOICE

1. **(B)** (B) is correct because the author refers to gaining pleasure from reading stories without himself telling a story (D). Because the author clearly indicates that he does not believe reading is a waste of time, (C) is incorrect; he also suggests the possibility of benefits beyond reading only for pleasure, so (A) is incorrect.

2. **(C)** (C) is correct because the author describes reading as a pleasant means of relieving spiritual fatigue. (B) is more specific than the author is. (A) is incorrect because the author specifically refers to reading stories, a form of fiction. (D) refers only to one particular example used to illustrate the relaxing effect reading can have.

3. **(B)** (B) is correct because the following sentence clearly describes examples of scenery changes. (A) contradicts the main point of the passage; (C) and (D) have more negative meanings than the author intended.

4. **(C)** (C) is correct because although the author advocates the relaxing effects of reading, he refers to the possibility of "something more than the gain of pleasure…" (B) contradicts the main point of the passage. There is no evidence that the author is himself a novelist or that he leads an unhappy life, so (A) and (D) are incorrect.

5. **(D)** All the statements given in the question are true and are taken from the passage, but only (D) allows one to select I, II, III, and IV; therefore it is the correct answer. The passage states that in contemplation there is a greater play of psychic action than in the most attentive self-observation (I), a tense attitude, a wrinkled brow, and a concentration of attention (II), a suppression of some thoughts before they are perceived (III), and a critique in which one rejects some of the ideas and cuts short others (IV).

6. **(C)** (C) is the best answer since it includes three correct statements. The passage includes the statements that self-observation involves restful

features and a suppressing of the criticism (I), less play of psychic action and a concentration of attention (II), and an interpretation of pathological ideas and dream images (III). Answers (A), (B), and (D) do not allow the reader to include all the correct choices.

7. **(B)** The best answer is (B); according to the passage, most people believe that fatigue causes the slackening of a certain arbitrary and often critical action. According to the reading passage, even in sleep there is psychic energy available for the attentive following of undesired thoughts; (A) is false and should not be chosen. At the end of the first paragraph of the reading passage, Freud refers to undesired ideas being changed into desired ones during sleep; therefore, (C) is incorrect. Since in sleep the watcher of the gates of intelligence may be withdrawn, (D) is not correct.

8. **(D)** The feat the writer, Freud, mentions is that he can perform self-observation perfectly; therefore, (D) is the correct answer. Because the writer states that self-observation is possible, (A) is incorrect. The writer maintains that he, not the patients, can perform self-observation perfectly; hence, (B) should not be chosen. The writer believes that self-observation can be taught; he does not make the statement that self-observation is difficult in many ways, so (C) should not be selected.

9. **(C)** The passage states that the lack of creativeness lies in the constraints imposed upon the imagination by the intelligence, according to Schiller; therefore (C) is the best answer choice. It is neither Freud (A), Rank (B), nor Koerner (D) who is directly quoted in the reading passage and credited with this statement.

10. **(D)** (D) is the best choice because, according to Schiller's correspondence, a trifling, very adventurous idea may become important because of another idea which follows it. The trifling idea is not usually important in itself; it is when the idea is followed by another that it may become important; hence, (A) should not be chosen. The trifling idea should not be considered in isolation in most cases, but rather it should be considered in connection with others; (B) is not the best selection. The trifling, adventurous idea should be held in the mind for a while; (C) suggests the opposite and is not acceptable.

11. **(D)** Uncritical self-observation requires one to be unashamed or unafraid of the momentary madness; (D) is the best answer. The writer tells the reader that uncritical self-observation is in no way difficult. Since (A) states that such self-observation is difficult, (A) should not be chosen. (B) states that self-observation should *not* be encouraged; (B) is an incorrect

choice. The author of the passage states that uncritical self-observation can be learned; (C), which suggests the opposite, should not be selected.

12. **(C)**   In a creative mind, a heap of ideas will be collected and examined critically at a later time; (C) is the best choice. A creative mind collects the ideas; it does not try to examine each critically and individually at the time they are collected; therefore, (A) is an incorrect answer. Because ideas enter in random order at times, there may not be a systematic way of collecting the ideas; (B) is not a good choice. According to Schiller's letter, it is the "withdrawal of the watchers (i.e., rejection and discrimination) from the gates of intelligence" which identifies the creative mind; since (D) suggests the opposite, it is another incorrect choice.

13. **(D)**   Schiller suggests that in order to be creative, one must learn to accept even undesired ideas as a possibility; (D) suggests this very idea and is, therefore, the best answer. (A) suggests that the tolerance must be eliminated, which is the opposite of what Schiller states, and, thereby, causes (A) to be incorrect. According to Schiller's letter in the reading passage, one should not critically examine freely rising ideas as they occur; (B) should be rejected. Schiller states that one must allow freely rising ideas to occur and the suspension of these ideas is not acceptable; therefore, (C) should not be selected.

14. **(B)**   In the last sentence, the author suggests that the subject matter upon which the attention is fixed can affect psychic energy and intensity; (B) is the best answer. Neither time of day (A), watchers from the gate (C), nor the idea being trifling or constructive (D) can be the answer since none of these choices is supported in the passage as being the cause of variation in psychic energy. While (C) and (D) are mentioned in the passage, it is in reference to the creative mind, rather than psychic energy.

15. **(C)**   Since the Romanesque builders had partially solved many of the problems of scientific vaulting before their Gothic successors, (C) is the best answer. Since the Romanesque builders were predecessors to the Gothic forms (not the other way around), (A) is false. The Romanesque builders were predecessors (not successors) to the Gothic builders; therefore, (B) should not be chosen. In the first sentence, it is stated that vaulting played a great part in Gothic architecture; (D) is false.

16. **(C)**   Gothic architecture might still exist even without quatrefoils, trefoils, cusps, traceries, pinnacles, flying buttresses, crockets, and finials; therefore, (C) is the best answer. Since vaulting is not essential to Gothic architecture, (A) is false. Gothic architecture had an influence in churches

even if only here and there the village churches "…aspire to the dignity of a vaulted ceiling." (B) should not be chosen. Gothic architecture cannot be described as a definite style with certain formulas; (D) is incorrect.

17. **(C)**   (C) is the best answer since it includes both II (Gothic art is the expression of a certain temper, sentiment, and spirit which inspired sculpture and painting) and III (Gothic art cannot be defined by any of its outward features since they are variable). Both II and III are correct, but I, which states that Gothic art is bound by certain formulas, is not true. Since (A), (B), and (D) all include I, only (C) is correct.

18. **(C)**   The best answer is (C); it states that the writer believes Gothic art will be applied with some variation to buildings of each age and country. (A), which states that Gothic art is a thing of the past, is false. Choice (B) states that Gothic art will be applied to buildings of each age and country exactly as in the past; (B) is inaccurate due to the inclusion of the words "exactly as in the past." Gothic art follows the principles common to all good styles; (D) states that Gothic art does not follow the principles common to all good styles. Since (D) is refuted by the last sentence of the passage, it is incorrect as an answer.

19. **(A)**   The best choice is (A); it states that the central purpose of the article is to define Gothic architecture, which is an accurate statement. Since the characteristics of Gothic architecture vary so much, (B) should not be chosen since a comprehensive analysis of the article does not give character-istics of Gothic architecture. (C) is incorrect since there is no true way of viewing Gothic architecture. (D) is inaccurate since the writer seems to value Gothic architecture and this answer suggests the opposite.

20. **(C)**   Vaulting is a way of producing high ceilings without visible support; (C) can be inferred from reading the passage. (A) is incorrect since no mention of leaping is made in the passage. (B) is also incorrect since vaulting is part of a style rather than a style. (D) is incorrect since neither drawing nor producing plans on paper is mentioned or alluded to in the reading passage.

21. **(D)**   (D) is the best answer since "pontifical" is used to describe palaces in this reading passage; "pontifical" means dignified. Such a place is not necessarily a happy, merry place; (A) should not be chosen. A "pontifical palace" is not necessarily a place of rest and relaxation; (B) should not be selected. (C) should not be chosen since it suggests that a "pontifical palace" necessarily involves a place which is friendly.

22. **(D)**   Quatrefoils are the result of the natural application of certain principles; (D) is the best answer. By referring to the passage, it can be

ascertained that (A), (B), and (C) are all opposites of what the author writes; therefore, all are incorrect.

23. **(C)**   Gothic art is the expression of infinitely various temper, sentiment, and spirit; (C) is the best choice. It is perhaps easier to define, first of all, what Gothic architecture is not. It is not bound by formulas (A); it is not characterized by similar styles (B); and it is not defined by outward features (D).

24. **(C)**   Choice (C)—Gothic art is not defined by its features—is stated in the last paragraph of the passage. Since the reader is searching for a statement which is not true, (C) should be selected. In perusing the passage, statements (A), (B), and (D) will be found; the author says that Gothic art is a whole method of doing things during the Middle Ages (A), an influence on architecture, painting, and sculpture (B), and an outward expression of certain cardinal principles (D). None of these answers should be chosen.

25. **(D)**   This message either underlies or is explicitly stated in every part of the passage. Though the statements regarding Harriet Tubman (A), the oral literature (B), and the slave market (C) are all true, they are only important in the respective paragraphs in which they appear.

26. **(C)**   This is evident from the results of "soldiering" in the rest of the sentence (i.e., refusing to work hard, sabotaging the machinery and crops). It could not mean "labored" (B), because this is incompatible with the remainder of the sentence. The sentence does not imply armed resistance to oppression (A), nor certainly does it mention anything to do with uniforms (D).

27. **(A)**   Both the violation of human freedom and the less severe living conditions experienced by some slaves are emphasized in the paragraph. (B) is incorrect because "adequate diet" and "sufficient housing" are both mentioned in the paragraph as being afforded to typical slaves. (C) is incorrect because the paragraph clearly states the varying degrees of slave hardship. Although (D) may be true, it is not mentioned in the paragraph.

28. **(C)**   The dark area labeled "In groups of 10 to 99 slaves (60.5%)" is larger than half the circle graph and therefore clearly greater than 50% (60.5%). (B) is clearly not correct because the 9.4% slice of the circle graph hardly represents the majority of slaves. (D) is incorrect because the group representing 1 to 9 slaves is 24.1%, obviously less than a half of the slaves represented on the graph. (A) is incorrect because, as stated on the key to the graph in the center, only 94% of Black Society in the Old South consisted of slaves. The total percentages of the graph itself only equal 94%.

29. **(B)** (B) is correct because the author in lines 14–16 praises small cities, and throughout the passage is critical of great cities. (A) is incorrect because the author directly states this point. (D) is incorrect because the author clearly indicates that he mistrusts democracies. There is no evidence in the passage indicating (C).

30. **(A)** (A) summarizes points the author makes in the first and last paragraphs. Because the author refers to cloisters but doesn't consider them best for spiritual growth, (B) is incorrect. (C) contradicts the point he makes in lines 8–11; (D) contradicts the main point of the passage.

31. **(B)** (B) is correct. The author does not mention either ignorant Americans or Romeo and Juliet's dress, so (A) and (D) are incorrect. (C) is incorrect because the example of Romeo and Juliet is introduced to highlight the American people's anxiety to catch the trains, not to advocate the need for silence.

32. **(B)** (B) is correct; the third paragraph describes noise and hearing and uses the word "sensibility," all of which are abstract ideas related to the power of people's minds to perceive things. (D) is incorrect because while "ease" is an abstract idea, it does not relate to how people perceive things; (A) and (C) are not abstract ideas.

33. **(C)** (C) is correct. The author is not ridiculing Americans but rather praising, among other things, their "sound practical sense"; (D) is incorrect. (B) is incorrect because the author never mentions how Europeans dress. (A) is incorrect not only because the author's tone is not objective but also because his treatment of American society is not comprehensive; it is very specifically focused on dress, hurry, and noise.

34. **(B)** (B) is correct because it refers to the overuse of mirrors implied by "exaggerated employment." (A) is incorrect because the author refers to "magnificence" only in passing; (C) is incorrect because it switches the causal order the author suggests—the author suggests that the popularity of glitter led to the use of mirrors, not the other way around. (D) is incorrect because the author never mentions windows.

35. **(D)** (D) is correct because the sentence contains the word "increasing" and appears to be about something getting larger; also, the author is referring to large mirrors. (B) is incorrect because "decline" suggests something getting smaller. (A) and (C) are incorrect because they do not refer to size changes.

36. **(A)** (A) is correct because the tone of the passage is clearly negative; (B) and (C) both suggest a positive tone, and (D) suggests bittersweetness.

37. **(A)** (A) is correct because the passage describes the process an artist goes through as he works to communicate his new perceptions. The passage refers to the difficulties and self-doubt artists experience only as they are unable to communicate their ideas, making (D) incorrect; because the artist suggests that in overcoming those difficulties, the artist creates a work of art, (B) and (C) are incorrect.

38. **(A)** (A) is correct because the passage describes the ways in which the need to communicate ideas leads to the creation of art. (B) and (C) are incorrect because the author is not seeking to describe ordinariness or the responses of ordinary people, but to show what leads to actual creation of art. Because the author never refers directly to the difficulties of being an artist, now or at any other time, (D) is incorrect.

39. **(C)** The context in which this word is used at the beginning of the paragraph suggests this meaning. (A) is incorrect; there exists no indication that the change in Mr. Covey refers to "epoch." (B) is incorrect; the selection doesn't imply that the event is a great event as such; the term would then contradict the writer's "humble history." (D) is incorrect; the writer gives no indication that what follows is a demeaning thing.

40. **(B)** The writer expresses this in the last paragraph. (A) is incorrect; this may be a true assertion, but this point is never made or hinted at by the writer. (C) is incorrect; this statement would be an unfair generalization about a singular incident about one man. (D) is incorrect; the writer speaks of a single owner and makes no inferences about slave owners as a whole.

VOCABULARY

1. *Fundamental* means one of the minimum constituents without which a thing or a system would not be what it is.

2. *Tawdry* means cheap or gaudy in appearance or quality.

3. *Sedition* means incitement of, resistance to, or insurrection against lawful authority.

4. *Pithy* means having substance and point, tersely cogent.

5. *Awry* means in a turned or twisted position or direction. It also means off the correct or expected course.

6. *Facade* means a false, superficial, or artificial appearance or effect. It also means the front of a building.

7. *Lustrous* means reflecting light evenly and efficiently without glitter or sparkle.

8. *Nullify* means to make of no value or consequence.

9. *Tribute* means something that indicates the worth, virtue, or effectiveness of the one in question, such as material evidence or a formal attestation.

Section 2 – Writing

WRITTEN SUMMARY

Essay 1

STRONG RESPONSE

The Civil Service Commission makes use of tests to ensure that the most qualified people will obtain government jobs. Applicants are ranked according to test results, and one of the top three applicants will be selected. Once working, employees are then ranked in other ways that define their position and payscale. The Commission itself used to administer pay scales, but this proved to be too inefficient, so that responsibility for such determinations has shifted to the agencies themselves.

Government reform after Watergate included a restructuring of the Civil Service system. The Civil Service Reform Act of 1978 made merit a principle guideline for salary and promotion, and several duties were divided up among the Office of Personnel management, the Merit System Protection Board, the Office of Special Counsel, the Federal Labor Relations Authority, and the Senior Executive Services.

In line with the ideals of the new system, the Merit System Protection Board sets up rules governing the fair treatment of honest, hard working civil servants and oversees their enforcement. There is a system wherein employees can bring complaints against their employers through the Office of Special Counsel. The Merit System Protection Board makes decisions on such cases. More serious cases go on to be considered by Congress or the federal courts. However, this system has not been entirely successful according to analyst Ronald D. Sylvia. Whistleblowers, for instance, have not always been given adequate protection by the Office of Special Counsel.

Despite, then, all the reform that has been undertaken, many problems still persist. An important one is job discrimination in federal and state agencies, making it difficult for women and minorities to have equal opportunities for employment and advancement.

There is much confusion about how to best deal with an increasingly diverse workforce with needs ranging from maternity leave to access for people with disabilities.

Eighteenth-century civil servants followed a philosophy of public service that is currently in decline. Congress has failed to make such ideals a cornerstone of the Civil Service System, so that there remains a great deal of work to be done to create a fair and efficient government workforce.

ANALYSIS

The writer manages to include adequate coverage of the major points of the essay and pays sufficient attention to important details, such as the various agencies named and their particular responsibilities. The writing is strong and expressive and the contours of the passage's argument are reproduced with a great degree of accuracy.

Essay 2

STRONG RESPONSE

The living conditions in colonial America were not as comfortable as they were in Europe, but colonialists soon set about creating a new country where they could prosper. Religion was at the center of their lives, although religious affiliation differed according to region. In the south, most of the colonialists were Anglicans, while in the North, most were Puritans. Religious authorities, especially in New England, tended also to be political authorities, and strictly regulated the lives of the settlers, enforcing church attendance, for instance.

This religious fervor lead to many tragic deaths, though. As an off-shoot of a wider European phenomena in the seventeenth century, many women in New England were accused of witchcraft, tried, and hanged. It was not until decades later that religious tolerance began to develop and gain wide acceptance.

Elementary schools were founded throughout the colonies, with an emphasis on religious training and instruction. This was more common in New England, though, where religious fervor was stronger. In the South, there tended to be fewer schools that were privately funded and not necessarily designed for religious instruction. Wealthy families sent their sons to England to study at the university level, while poorer young men learned trades.

Two colleges were eventually formed in the colonies. Harvard was founded in Massachusetts in 1636, while in Virginia, William and Mary was founded in 1693. Literary production began in the colonies at this time as well, but mainly consisted of sermons and historical narratives.

ANALYSIS

The writer covers all of the passages salient points. The writing is clear and expressive and mostly free from error. There is careful attention paid to the trajectory of the passage's narrative as the writer manages to neatly reproduce the main ideas and themes.

Essay 3

STRONG RESPONSE

The dialogue as a literary form was developed by Plato. It is in the form of the dialogue that his philosophy survives today. Plato developed this method from his teacher Socrates, who is normally the principal speaker in his dialogues. Socrates himself never wrote anything, so that all we know of his philosophy comes to us through Plato. This makes it hard to always uncouple the one from the other, and know with any certainty which ideas in a given dialogue originate with Plato and which with Socrates. However, most scholars agree that, with the exception of his earliest writings, the philosophy of most of Plato's works represents Plato's own ideas. The structure of the dialogue form allows for conversations to emerge that are informal and open-ended. This is a far cry from the rigorous and tightly organized work of later philosophers such as Descartes. Characters actually emerge from these dialogues, so that we can attribute specific qualities like bombastic speech to the figure Thrasymachus or polite and reasonable speech to Adeimantus and Glaucon. Socrates himself dominated, though, by pointing out the deficiencies in the others' thinking. This could often become dangerous, as he was not afraid to make enemies of those he disagreed with in matters of both politics and philosophy.

The Socratic Method is a method of philosophy that is foregrounded in most of Plato's dialogues. This method is a form of learning and teaching that takes on the structure of a question and answer. Socrates will put forth a question that will be open and general, such as: what is justice? The answer will inevitably take the form of a declarative definition, i.e. "Justice is x." Socrates will then proceed to demonstrate the shortcomings of any attempt to define such a concept. Sometimes the definitions offered are too narrow; other times they are too clearly based on the speaker's own self-interest. An excellent example of this occurs in the Republic, when a wealthy merchant named Cephalos believes justice to be a matter of business ethics—paying one's debts is justice. Socrates finds examples, though, where this is not always the case. Is it just, for instance, to return a borrowed weapon to a man who has become insane? Cephalos sees that this would not be justice, and a new definition must be sought.

Socrates' main tool in the Socratic method is the counter example. Through using counter examples, Socrates forces a series of further questions and answers that help to expand the definition of any given concept. At times, like the end of Book I of the Republic, no exact definition is arrived at, but, importantly, many false ones are rejected.

Plato used the Socratic Method primarily as a philosophic tool to arrive at definitions of such important and complex concepts as justice and good government.

ANALYSIS

The passage is written clearly and correctly. The writer faithfully reproduces the main points of the passage and is sufficiently detailed in his or her summary. The major thematic points are reproduced and the mode of exposition is reiterated accurately.

WRITTEN COMPOSITION

Essay 1

STRONG RESPONSE

The rising cost of health care in the United States has become more than a national concern; it is now a national crisis. The situation has become so grave that the President made health care costs a major issue in his campaign and has appointed a task force to investigate ways of providing equitable health care for all Americans. One of the most pressing problems the task force is addressing is health insurance.

The cost of health insurance in this country has skyrocketed in the last two decades. Many middle class Americans cannot afford to insure themselves and their families, despite earning relatively large incomes, and for the working class, health insurance is completely out of reach. The result is that these people literally cannot afford to get sick. An illness means lost work and wages, as well as exorbitant medical bills. Those who can afford to buy health insurance often find that their policy is inadequate for anything beyond rudimentary care. An unexpected surgery can involve thousands of dollars in out-of-pocket expenses, and a chronic disease like cancer or diabetes can eat up a policy's maximum allowable benefits in a matter of weeks or months.

The cost of providing group insurance has become so high that many employers, especially smaller companies, are trying to either cut benefits or find some cheaper way of providing coverage, while many prospective employees accept or reject job opportunities on the basis of benefits rather than salary.

Health-maintenance organizations (HMOs) and preferred-provider organizations (PPOs) are two common means that many employers have turned to in their attempts to regulate costs. HMOs and PPOs provide coverage for routine and preventive health care while keeping costs down by limiting benefits on certain types of care or by not covering certain expenses at all. However, these programs have serious limitations. Yearly out-of-pocket deductibles are generally high, and annual maximum benefits can be quite low. This means that for people who are in good overall health, these plans are beneficial, but if a family has an unexpected health emergency, whether it be a serious injury or a debilitating illness, these plans provide little assistance. It is also possible for a person with a rare illness not to be diagnosed because of the limitations on testing imposed by these plans.

One solution is to set national limits on how much certain procedures and tests can cost. By standardizing costs and then standardizing how much of the cost is covered by the government health care plan, costs can be managed. Many insurance companies already try to control costs by standardizing how much they will pay for various tests and procedures, but there are no regulations that restrict physicians or medical facilities from charging more than this standard rate. A national health care plan that did regulate fees would prevent some doctors and hospitals from overcharging for services. This type of fee schedule, combined with a sliding scale based on income for the amount of the fee that is covered by the government, could go far to easing this country's health care crisis. Other options are to base national health care on the plans already instituted in other countries. Canada and England are among the other countries that have instituted national health care and managed to control health care costs. A recent study showed that drug costs in Canada (for the same medications produced by the same companies) were less than half what they are in this country.

The health care problem in this country has reached crisis proportions. Many people who hold good jobs cannot afford to insure themselves or their families, and the working class and the poor cannot afford to get sick at all. Even those people who can afford health insurance find that the policies they buy do not cover catastrophic illnesses or injuries. Many employers have tried to provide health care coverage for their employees, but escalating costs have made it harder to provide comprehensive coverage. The only thing that can be said for certain is that health care reform is desperately needed, but the president's task force does not have an easy job ahead of it.

ANALYSIS

This essay provides a clear thesis and develops that thesis in a clear and logical manner. The body of the essay expands on various aspects of the thesis, and provides concise and reasonable support. The few usage, structural, and mechanical errors do not interfere with the writer's ability to communicate effectively, and the writer demonstrates a solid understanding of the rules of written English. The essay is well-thought-out and the conclusion relates the various points raised in the essay to the general argument made throughout.

STRONG RESPONSE

The cynic in me wants to react to the idea of universal public service for the young with a reminder about previous complaints aimed at the military draft. These complaints suggest that wars might never be fought if the first people drafted were the adult leaders and lawmakers. Still, the idea of universal public service sounds good to this concerned citizen who sees everywhere—not just in youth—the effects of a selfish and self-indulgent culture.

One reads and hears constantly about young people who do not care about the problems of our society. These youngsters seem interested in money and the luxuries money can buy. They do not want to work from the minimum wage up but want instead to land a high paying job without "paying their dues." An informal television news survey of high school students a few years ago suggested that students had the well-entrenched fantasy that with no skills or higher education they would not accept a job paying less than $20 an hour. Perhaps universal service helping out in an urban soup kitchen for six months would instill a sense of selflessness rather than selfishness and provide the perspective necessary to demonstrate the flaw in this perception.

The shiny gleam of a new expensive sports sedan bought on credit by a recent accounting student reflects self indulgence that might be toned down by universal service. That self indulgence may reflect merely a lack of discipline, but it also may reflect a lack of purpose in life. Philosophers, theologians and leaders of all types suggest throughout the ages that money and objects do not ultimately satisfy. Helping others—service to our fellow human beings—often does. Universal public service for that accounting student might require a year helping low income or senior citizens prepare income tax forms. This type of service would dim that self indulgence, give the person some experience in the real world, and also give satisfaction that one's life is not lived only to acquire material things.

Universal service might also help young people restore faith in their nation and what it means to them. Yes, this is the land of opportunity, but it is also a land of forgotten people, and it is a land that faces outside threats. Part of the requisite public service should remind young people of their past and of their responsibility to the future.

ANALYSIS

This essay uses a traditional structure: the first paragraph states the topic; the second and third present development with specific examples from personal observation. The fourth ends the essay, but it is not as strong a conclusion as it could be. The writer probably ran out of time. The essay as a whole is unified and uses pertinent examples to support the opinion stated. The sentence structure varies, and the vocabulary is effective. Generally, it is well done within the time limit.

Essay 3

STRONG RESPONSE

Life, Liberty, and Curfews

In a way we all are subject to a variety of curfews. Some curfews are self-imposed while others are imposed on us by others. Parents, for example, sometimes impose their own curfews on us and even themselves, especially if they have young children that they can't find babysitters for. Students who participate in extra-curricular activities and attend out of town functions have curfews imposed upon them by chaperons and coaches. Curfews like these are okay because they are enforced by relatives or by people standing in for relatives. But city-wide curfews that will be imposed on teenagers not even known by these officials are unfair and unconstitutional.

Local support of these curfews stereotype all teenagers as participants in crimes such as theft, harassment, loitering, and drug abuse, and although supporters state that curfews actually protect teenagers from being victims themselves and therefore do not lump all teens into one category, the majority of citizens first think about teenagers as juvenile delinquents. As a result every teenager at area malls who is not accompanied by a parent or guardian generally represents, to the curfew supporter, a potential act of violence about to occur.

Stereotyping is not the only negative result that occurs from imposed curfews. Class and race stereotyping also occur. Kids who dress differently, wear their hair differently, or are of a minority race are most often targets for adult harassment, especially at malls. Some managers and security guards at these places like Red Bird Mall or West End Marketplace say that they really aren't discriminating against any class or race, but the kids who are most often asked to leave or are even ticketed are kids from lower socio-economic levels and/or a minority. Curfews would not only make this problem worse, but it would punish many teens who fit these physical and social categories but not the crime-related one.

Since America functions on the idea that all people are created equal, with equal rights and protection under the law, instituting any type of curfew, regardless of how well-intentioned, represents an unconstitutional act targeted at an entire group of people—teenagers. Just as our government has always been there to stop unlawful acts against a group or race of people, it should be here now for teenagers. We are just like the African-Americans of the Civil Rights movement, the women of the suffragist/feminist movement, the Hispanic, Asians, and any other group or culture seeking fairness, equality, and respect. Just because we are under the age of 21, though, adults sometimes think that they don't have to ask us how we feel, what solutions we could recommend, or how we'd handle certain situations.

So what is the best solution? Rather than instituting city-wide curfews that would punish, stereotype, and alienate all teenagers—criminals and victims—I suggest that if teenagers find themselves in trouble, their parents should bear the responsibility. If, for example, I am creating a disturbance at a mall and am reprimanded by the manager, the manager should notify the police, and they in turn will notify and fine my parents. Needless to say, my parents will not long abide my getting into trouble, especially since they have to pay. By using this plan instead of a city-wide curfew, only those teens who are committing the crime or disturbance will actually pay the consequences. The tide of teen crime, consequently, would decrease considerably. Teens who work late or whose dates run later than the curfew will not be punished. And most importantly, parents will have to take an active and responsible role in their children's actions.

ANALYSIS

The essay topic is clearly introduced in the first paragraph. The language fits the writer's perspective: one teen speaking for many. Though the style is informal, it reflects maturity and rationality in its author. The essay systematically addresses the question in mind, without unnecessary tangents. The appeal to using family-centric authority to impose curfews is suggested in the first paragraph and neatly completed in the conclusion. The examples given, though centering frequently on mall activity, all coordinate with the main topic. The author is careful about leaping to conclusions and controls the limits of forceful language. Each paragraph builds upon the argument with appeals to government and local authorities for justice, and the conclusion ends with a suggestion for improvement, which helps soften the otherwise negative drift of the argument.

GRAMMAR AND USAGE

1. **(B)** The adjectival form "second," not the adverbial form "secondly," is appropriate here, since it modifies a noun, not a verb.

2. **(B)** The opening verbal phrase is a dangling modifier. "Prevention" is not "faced" with anything; Lincoln is. All the other choices are standard English sentences.

3. **(C)** "With the outbreak..." is a prepositional phrase that is stopped with a period[.]. It has no subject or verb and is not a standard English sentence. All the rest are correct English.

4. **(D)** Choice (D) should be made more precise. It would add a needed specific, concrete detail to bolster the interest of the passage. Choice (A) is readily understood as it is. Choice (B) does not really need clarification because it can be inferred that the "process" is an assembly-line method. Choice (C) is a common and simple concept.

5. **(C)** Choice (C) is a fragment lacking a verb for the apparent subject, "5,000 cars." Sentence 11 should probably be combined with Sentence 10. Choices (A), (B), and (D) are all standard sentences.

6. **(D)** In choice (D), although it is interesting to note that India bought steam-powered vehicles from Ransom Eli Olds, the information is really not essential and is the least relevant. Choice (A) is the topic sentence. Choice (B) and choice (C) are proof to substantiate what the pioneering Olds did in the automobile industry.

7. **(B)** Choice (B) contains the continuation of the topic "poor children" with the addition of "stereotype." Therefore, choice (B) would be the logical sentence to tie together Sentences 6 and 7. Choice (A) is a question best asked in the first paragraph. Choice (C) might be a logical choice, but there is no transition included to tie together Sentences 6 and 7. Choice (D) shifts voice with "I."

8. **(C)** In choice (C), a comma is indicated for the introductory phrase "In fact." Choice (A) creates no difference. Choice (B) would create a

fragment in the second half of the sentence by isolating the subordinate clause beginning with "because." Choice (D) is incorrect because no colon should be used after the introductory phrase.

9. **(B)** Choice (B) has an incorrect verb form. The subjunctive mood "were" is needed in conditions contrary to fact. Thus, the sentence should read, "even if every single-parent family were to disappear" because the clause beginning with "if" signals a condition contrary to fact. Choices (A), (C), and (D) are all correct.

10. **(C)** Choice (C) indicates that information about the originators of the folk dance is not necessary in a paragraph about the ballet. Choice (A) introduces the topic of the ballet and its composer. Choice (B) tells who choreographed the ballet. Choice (D) gives further information on the ballet and its music.

11. **(D)** Choice (D) is the only choice containing information about the rhythm discussed in Sentences 6 and 7. Choice (A) and choice (B) both break the formal tone and use contractions. Choice (C), although a possible choice, has nothing to do with rhythm and introduces new information on the folk dance.

12. **(A)** Choice (A) contains the phrase, "A French composer," which does not modify "the bolero." The phrase should be placed after "Anton Ravel" to correct the error. Choices (B), (C), and (D) are all correct sentences.

13. **(C)** The clause "a French composer" modifies Anton Ravel. In the original, it would appear to modify "the bolero." Choice (C) best corrects this ambiguity. Each of the other choices places the modifier in an incorrect place.

14. **(A)** "This musical composition" should replace "it" in Sentence 5 because the paragraph should not start off with a pronoun that lacks a clear antecedent. Choice (B) ("the folk dance") may look right, but since the rest of the passage concerns the music and not the dance, it would be inappropriate. Choices (C) and (D) are clearly the wrong antecedents for "it" in this sentence.

15. **(B)** In the original, "clarinet, bassoon, and piccolo" would appear to modify "parts." Choice (B) best clears up this confusion by placing the clause so as to modify "instruments." Choices (A) and (C) are both technically correct, but are less clear in the structure of the sentence than choice (B).

16. **(D)**   The word "beginning" in Sentence 9 is in the present progressive tense. It should be changed to "begin" to accord with the present tense used in the rest of the sentence and throughout the passage.

17. **(D)**   The word "relenting," in this context, is wrong; if the harmony remains in the same key for 15 to 17 minutes, this is surely "unrelenting."

18. **(C)**   Choice (C) separates the temporal relation of the shift in key nicely with a single comma, where the unpunctuated original was too jumbled. Choices (A), (B), and (D) all use too many commas in awkward positions.

19. **(D)**   (D) has an incorrect agreement between "kids" and "does." Kids (they) do (something). All the other sentences use standard English syntax.

20. **(D)**   The sentence is a rhetorical clause that begins with a subordinating conjunction, "because." Consequently, it cannot stand alone as a complete standard sentence. The rest are standard.

21. **(D)**   Choice (D) is the clearest and most concise rewording of the sentence portion. Choice (A) unnecessarily repeats the phrase, "in order to." Choice (B) and choice (C) both contain unnecessary wordiness in the clauses beginning with "which will" and "that will."

22. **(B)**   Choice (B) keeps the first person voice and states the main point using parallel structure and concise language. Choices (A), (C), and (D) are still excessively wordy; in addition, choice (A) changes the voice to "one."

23. **(A)**   Paragraph 2 provides background information, choice (A), to explain why there is so much violence on television. Choice (B) is incorrect because the argument in Paragraph 2 is not a contradiction to anything. Choice (C) would be correct if the paragraph contained support for the main argument. While the paragraph does give some specifics, choice (D) cannot be considered as categorizing anything.

24. **(C)**   Although choice (C) employs two forms of the verb "to be," it is the best wording. Choices (A) and (B) both use the weak phrase "being that" and create fragments. Choice (D) is far too wordy and uses the weak wording "seem to be"; use of the word "seem" makes the writer appear uncertain and tentative, not precise.

25. **(D)**   Choice (D) is the most concise combination, one which clearly shows time sequence and cause and effect. Choice (A), because it has a misplaced modifier, implies that the children conducted the study. Choice (B)

implies that the children were prone to violence only while they were viewing the violent acts, a slight distortion of the correct finding. Choice (C) subtly suggests that only the children at the Institute were affected by this condition, with the implication that other children are not. This failure to indicate an extension of the findings subtly distorts the original meaning.

26. **(D)**   (D) would be the best revision; the phrase "are just to name two examples," besides being grammatically incorrect, is unnecessary, and the structure of (D) sets up the parallel best. (B) is the next best, but "to name two examples" is awkward and unnecessary. (A) and (C) are not specific about any particular riots. [These would at least need the article "the" as in (B) and (D).]

27. **(B)**   "The Wetherills" is plural, and the verb must agree. Choice (B) correctly changes "is" to "are"; the rest of the sentence is fine. (A) adds the singular "a group" which may make the verb "is" seem right, but it still modifies "The Wetherills" and must agree accordingly. (C) corrects the verb problem but misplaces the clause "five brothers who ranched in the area." (D) fails to correct the verb disagreement and places the clause at the end of the sentence, which alters the sense.

28. **(A)**   Choice (A) best continues the topic of Sentence 9, which concerns the cultural achievements of the Anasazi and provides a nice transition toward the final sentence. (B) concerns an entirely different historical epoch, and is clearly irrelevant. (C) may fit somewhere in this essay but not between Sentences 9 and 10, where this new fact would seem obtrusive. (D) introduces the personal voice of the author which is contrary to the expository tone in the passage thus far and which would not fit between the factual content of Sentences 9 and 10.

29. **(A)**   Sentence 4 is a dependent prepositional clause and would be best added onto Sentence 3.

30. **(C)**   The years of the Anasazi's zenith are best set off by commas and turned into a prepositional phrase; of the two choices that do this, (C), which uses "from," is more appropriate than (D), which uses "being." Without the punctuation, choice (A) is awkward; if the phrase were set off by commas, it would be acceptable, though (C) is more concise. (B) is just wrong; from the context of the passage, it is clear that the Anasazi thrived in the years A.D and not B.C.

31. **(D)**   Choice (D) best utilizes commas to clarify the sense of the sentence. Choice (A) places the second comma incorrectly. (B) and (C) both incorrectly use a colon, and each has an unnecessary comma.

32. **(B)** Sentence 2 uses "then," a temporal reference, instead of "than," which should be used for the comparison in this sentence.

33. **(C)** Choice (C) unnecessarily repeats the words "basis," "based," "founding," and "foundation." These forms need not be repeated and the sentence should be condensed. Choice (A) repeats the phrase "board of regents," found in the previous sentence, but it is needed for transition of thought. Choice (B) and choice (D) are well-worded sentences.

34. **(B)** Choice (B) fits between Sentence 4 and Sentence 6. Sentence 4 mentions the topic of dissenting opinion, and Sentence 6 elaborates by stating the position that English professors have always been outspoken. This idea is continued in Sentence 7. Choice (A) changes voice to "we," which is out of place in this letter. It also does not provide as smooth a transition to Sentence 6 as choice (B) does. Choice (C) is too casual. Choice (D) directly contradicts the thesis of the letter.

35. **(B)** Choice (B) contains an inappropriate use of words. The contraction for "who is" should be used to make the sentence correct. The possessive "whose" is not correct in this context. Choice (A) correctly uses the comparative degree. Choice (C) correctly uses the superlative degree. Choice (D) does not make a needed change.

36. **(D)** Sentence 4 directly contradicts the thesis and should be eliminated. Since the author of the essay is promoting business concerns for recycling brought about by consumer pressure, it does not benefit the essay to include a sentence about consumers who do not care about recycling. Choice (A) contains a clause necessary for time frame reference. Choice (B) creates an illogical sentence. Choice (C) would create an informal tone by changing "their" to "our." Although the author may be a concerned consumer, the tone of the article is formal and should not be broken.

37. **(B)** In choice (B), Sentence 6 logically fits after Sentence 9. This sequence is marked by the continuation of the subject of not knowing the safety of any product due to the lack of government standards of labeling. Choice (A) would move the topic sentence, Sentence 5, to an unsatisfactory position. Choice (C) reverses the logical order of ideas: first, the seals are introduced in Sentence 7; then, the seals are referred to in Sentence 8 with the transition "These seals." Choice (D) completes the idea of lack of government standards and, therefore, should not be deleted.

38. **(B)** In choice (B), the correct form of the subject and verb combination is "it is" or "it's." The form "its" is a possessive pronoun. Choice (A)

creates a negative statement that contradicts the thesis. Choice (C) forms a split infinitive, "to now display." The adverb "now" should be placed before or after the infinitive "to display," because infinitives should never be split by an adverb. Choice (D) would form an inaccurate sentence.

39. **(A)** Choice (A) shows a clear cause and effect sequence begun by Sentences 10 and 11. The tone of choices (B) and (D) are far too casual because they introduce the contraction "doesn't" and the personal pronoun "I." Choice (C) directly contradicts the thesis.

40. **(C)** Choice (C) introduces an extraneous topic: another form of investment savings—savings bonds. Choice (A) is necessary because it is the topic sentence. Choice (B) reinforces the topic by explaining the reason people buy a company's stock. Choice (D) is essential because it introduces the next part of the paragraph, dividend reinvestment.

SENTENCE CORRECTIONS

Sample Correct Responses

1. The restrictive diet prohibited the inclusion of animal fats, salt, or any dairy products.

2. Preparing for the tax season takes up the leisure time of many young people until after April 15.

3. Totalling more than she had anticipated, the costs of food, flowers, and entertainment shocked the bride.

4. In the summer I usually like to swim and water-ski.

    I usually like to swim and water-ski in the summer.

    I usually like swimming and water-skiing in the summer.

5. I found five dollars while I was eating lunch in the park.

6. Janet cannot be described with words.

    You cannot describe Janet with words.

GRAMMATICAL VOCABULARY

1. A *direct object* is a word that receives a direct action from the subject of a sentence.

2. An *infinitive* is the basic form of the verb, usually preceded by the preposition "to."

3. An *abstract noun* is a noun that names a quality or mental concept; something intangible that exists only in our minds.

4. The *third person* indicates "he," "she," "it," or "they" as the subject of a sentence.

5. An *indefinite pronoun* is a pronoun that has an unknown or ambiguous antecedent.

6. A *comma splice* is an incorrect sentence construction in which two independent clauses are fused together with a comma.

7. A *superlative* compares three or more persons, places, or things.

WRITTEN MECHANICS

Passage 1

Common Errors

World Vegetarian Day, *United States*, *Americans* and *October* are capitalized because they are proper nouns. *Nineteenth-century* is hyphenated because it is used as an adjective while *twentieth century* is not hyphenated because it is used as a noun. In formal writing, words are not abbreviated but spelled out, such as *the first of October*, *one percent*, *seven percent* and *twentieth century*. Also, make sure the word *cite* (to quote) is spelled correctly, and not confused with *site* (a location) or *sight* (to see).

Passage 2

Common Errors

Celtic, *Christianity*, and *Arthurian* are all proper nouns so they should be capitalized. Be sure not to confuse *inclusion* with *exclusion*, or *emphasis* with *emphasize*. The phrase *for example* is often set off by commas. If you misspelled any of the words above, be sure to memorize them before the test.

MTEL

*Massachusetts Tests for Educator Licensure —
Communication and Literacy Skills Test*

Practice Test 3

PRACTICE TEST 3

(Answer sheets appear in the back of this book.)

Section 1 – Reading

MULTIPLE CHOICE

> **DIRECTIONS**: Read each passage and answer the questions that follow.

Passage A

An ancient Sage boasted, that, tho' he could not fiddle, he knew how to make a *great city* of a *little one*. The science that I, a modern simpleton, am about to communicate, is the very reverse.

I address myself to all ministers who have the management of extensive dominions, which from their very greatness are become troublesome to govern, because the multiplicity of their affairs leaves no time for *fiddling*.

In the first place, gentlemen, you are to consider, that a great empire, like a great cake, is most easily diminished at the edges. Turn your attention, therefore, first to your *remotest* provinces; that, as you get rid of them, the next may follow in order.

That the possibility of this separation may always exist, take special care the provinces are never incorporated with the mother country; that they do not enjoy the same common rights, the same privileges in commerce; and that they are governed by *severer* laws, all of *your enacting*, without allowing them any share in the choice of the legislators. By carefully making and preserving such distinctions, you will (to keep to my simile of the cake) act like a wise gingerbread-baker, who, to facilitate a division, cuts his dough half through in those places where, when baked, he would have it *broken to pieces*.

Those remote provinces have perhaps been acquired, purchased, or conquered, at the *sole expence* of the settlers, or their ancestors, without the aid of the mother country. If this should happen to increase her *strength*, by their growing numbers, ready to join in her wars; her *commerce*, by their growing demand for her manufactures; or her *naval power*, by greater employment for her ships and seamen, they may probably suppose some merit in this, and that it entitles them to some favour; you are therefore to *forget it all, or resent it*, as if they had done you injury. If they happen to be zealous Whigs, friends of liberty, nurtured in revolution principles, *remember all that* to their prejudice, and resolve to punish it; for such principles, after a revolution is thoroughly established, are of *no more use*; they are even *odious* and *abominable*.

However peaceably your colonies have submitted to your government, shewn their affection to your interests, and patiently borne their grievances; you are to *suppose* them always inclined to revolt, and treat them accordingly. Quarter troops among them, who by their insolence may *provoke* the rising of mobs, and by their bullets and bayonets *suppress* them. By this means, like the husband who uses his wife ill *from suspicion*, you may in time convert your *suspicions* into *realities*...

If, when you are engaged in war, your colonies should vie in liberal aids of men and money against the common enemy, upon your simple requisition, and give far beyond their abilities, reflect that a penny taken from them by your power is more honourable to you than a pound presented by their benevolence; despise therefore their voluntary grants, and resolve to harass them with novel taxes. They will probably complain to your parliaments, that they are taxed by a body in which they have no representative, and that this is contrary to common right. They will petition for redress. Let the Parliaments flout their claims, reject their petitions, refuse even to suffer the reading of them, and treat the petitioners with the utmost contempt. Nothing can have a better effect in producing the alienation proposed; for though many can forgive injuries, *none ever forgave contempt*...

Lastly, invest the General of your army in the provinces, with great and unconstitutional powers, and free him from the controul of even your own Civil Governors. Let him have troops enow under his command, with all the fortresses in his possession; and who knows but (like some provincial Generals in the Roman empire, and encouraged by the universal discontent you have produced) he may take it into his head to set up for himself? If he should, and you have carefully practised these few *excellent rules* of mine, take my word for it, all the provinces will immediately join him; and you will that day (if you have not done it sooner) get rid of the trouble of governing them, and all the *plagues* attending their *commerce* and connection from henceforth and for ever.

From Benjamin Franklin, "The Ambassador of Political Reason"

1. The author's purpose is

   (A) to communicate the wisdom of an ancient sage.

   (B) to advise ministers of churches who do not take time for fun and fiddling.

   (C) to describe how a little country can make itself a great one.

   (D) to tell how a great city may be reduced to a small one.

2. The author compares

   (A) an empire to a cake.

   (B) a country to a gingerbread baker.

   (C) a minister to a cake.

   (D) a religious minister to a gingerbread baker.

3. The passage was

   (A) to give advice to all rulers of small countries.

   (B) a tongue-in-cheek article.

   (C) from the viewpoint of a religious minister.

   (D) to inspire ministers to take time to "fiddle," or smell the roses.

4. The best interpretation of the clause, "Let him [the General] have troops enow under his command..." is

   (A) let the General keep the troops in tow.

   (B) let the General have enough soldiers to command.

(C)   let the General have troops endowed with skill under his control.

(D)   let the General have captured troops to control.

5.   The author's reason for writing this passage is that he

(A)   hopes to help the ministers rid themselves of the trouble of governing the provinces.

(B)   hopes to help the ministers build their powers and increase the provinces.

(C)   is proposing new ideas on increasing the provinces of a country since this article was written only a few years ago.

(D)   is presenting the viewpoint of the colonies and the provinces to the mother country.

6.   Which of the following actions is least advisable in order to keep a large country intact?

(A)   Limit the General of the army of the large country to constitutional powers.

(B)   Give the citizens of the provinces the same rights as the citizens of the mother country.

(C)   Suppose the provinces to be always ready to revolt and treat them as if you expect revolt.

(D)   Do not require taxation without representation.

7.   Which of the following actions by Parliaments toward the provinces is most advisable?

(A)   Flaunt their claims.

(B)   Allow petition for redress.

(C)   Refuse to suffer the reading of claims.

(D)   Take the necessary monies from your colonies by requisition and not benevolence.

8.   How can one expect a great empire to be diminished most easily?

(A)   From within   (C)   At the edges

(B)   From without   (D)   From the ministers

9. To ensure separation of the provinces:

    (A) incorporate the provinces with the mother country.

    (B) do not give common rights.

    (C) allow them the right to enact their own laws.

    (D) allow them to choose legislators.

10. If there are zealous Whigs and friends of liberty in the provinces, the empire will be least likely to be reduced to a small one if

    (A) they are remembered in their prejudice by the empire.

    (B) they are punished for their principles by the empire.

    (C) they are punished by the empire after a revolution is already established.

    (D) the mother empire remembers that after the revolution is already established it may be too late to change.

Passage B

Though it is generally recognized from philosophic investigations extending over many years that heat is one manifestation of energy capable of being transformed into other forms such as mechanical work, electricity, or molecular arrangement, and derivable from them through transformations, measurements of quantities of heat can be made without such knowledge, and were made even when heat was regarded as a substance. It was early recognized that equivalence of heat effects proved effects proportional to quantity; thus, the melting of one pound of ice can cool a pound of hot water through a definite range of temperature, and can cool two pounds through half as many degrees, and so on. The condensation of a pound of steam can warm a definite weight of water a definite number of degrees, or perform a certain number of pound-degrees heating effect in water. So that taking the pound-degree of water as a basis the ratio of the heat liberated by steam condensation to that absorbed by ice melting can be found. Other substances such as iron or oil may suffer a certain number of pound-degree changes and affect water by another number of pound-degrees. The unit of heat quantity might be taken as that which is liberated by the condensation of a pound of steam, that absorbed by the freezing of a pound of water, that to raise a pound of iron any number of degrees or any other quantity of heat effect. The heat unit generally accepted is, in metric measure, the calorie, or the amount to raise one kilogram of pure water one degree centigrade, or the B.T.U., that is necessary to raise one pound of water one degree Fahrenheit.

All the heat measurements are, therefore, made in terms of equivalent water heating effects in pound-degrees, but it must be understood that a water pound-degree is not quite constant. Careful observation will show that the melting of a pound of ice will not cool the same weight of water from 200° F to 180° F, as it will from 60° F to 40° F, which indicates that the heat capacity of water or the B.T.U. per pound-degree is not constant. It is, therefore, necessary to further limit the definition of the heat unit, by fixing on some water temperature and temperature change, as the standard, in addition to the selection of water as the substance, and the pound and degree as units of capacity. Here there has not been as good an agreement as is desirable, some using 4° C = 39.4° F as the standard temperature and the range one-half degree both sides; this is the point of maximum water density. Others have used one degree rise from the freezing point 0° C or 32° F. There are good reasons, however, for the most common present-day practice which will probably become universal, for taking as the range and temperatures, freezing-point to boiling-point and dividing by the number of degrees. The heat unit so defined is properly named the mean calorie or mean British thermal unit; therefore,

Mean calorie = (amount of heat to raise 1 Kg. water from 0° C to 100° C)

Mean B.T.U. = (amount of heat to raise 1 lb. water from 32° F to 212° F)

From Charles Edward Lucke, "Engineering Thermodynamics"

11. According to the author, which of the following is NOT true?

(A) Heat is capable of being transformed into mechanical work.

(B) Heat is derivable from molecular arrangement.

(C) Heat should be regarded as a substance.

(D)   Measurements of quantities of heat can be made without knowledge of heat being derivable from mechanical work, electricity, or
molecular arrangement.

12.   The calorie and the B.T.U. are similar in that they both relate to

(A)   one pound of water.

(B)   the amount of heat necessary to raise the temperature one degree.

(C)   the metric system.

(D)   a pound of iron.

13.   The author denies which of the following?

(A)   The equivalence of heat effects proves proportional to quantity.

(B)   The melting of one pound of ice can cool a pound of hot water
through a definite range of temperature and can cool two pounds
through twice as many degrees.

(C)   The melting of one pound of ice can cool a pound of hot water
through a definite range of temperature and can cool two pounds
through half as many degrees.

(D)   The condensation of a pound of steam can warm a definite weight
of water a definite number of degrees.

14.   The author states that

(A)   a water pound-degree is constant.

(B)   the melting of ice will cool the same weight of water from 60° to
40° Fahrenheit as it will from 200° to 180° Fahrenheit.

(C)   the heat capacity of water or the B.T.U. per pound-degree is
constant.

(D)   the heat capacity of water or the B.T.U. per pound-degree is not
constant.

15.   The author indicates a point of disagreement among scientists; this point
of contention is

(A)   whether the melting point of ice will not cool the same amount of
water from 200° to 180° Fahrenheit as it will from 60° to 40°
Fahrenheit.

(B)   whether the heat capacity of water is constant.

(C)   whether the equivalence of heat effects proved effects proportional to quantity.

(D)   how to best limit the definitions of the heat unit.

16.   The author appears to

(A)   be a proponent of the metric system.

(B)   be a proponent of the customary system.

(C)   be an opponent of the use of the mean calorie.

(D)   suggest that there are good reasons for taking the freezing-point to boiling-point as the range.

17.   The purpose of the passage is to

(A)   advocate mean calories.

(B)   advocate mean British thermal units (B.T.U.).

(C)   oppose mean calories and B.T.U.

(D)   advocate both mean calories and mean B.T.U.

18.   The author predicts

(A)   the universal adoption of the B.T.U.

(B)   the universal adoption of the calorie.

(C)   the universal acceptance of the mean B.T.U. and the mean calorie.

(D)   the demise of the calorie and the universal adoption of the mean B.T.U.

19.   The author would like to limit the definition of the heat unit by

I.   fixing on some water temperature.

II.   fixing on some temperature change.

III.   selecting water as the substance.

IV.   using the pound and degree as the units of capacity.

(A)   I only.   (C)   IV only.

(B)   II only.   (D)   I, II, III, and IV.

20. The author's argument for limiting the definition of the heat unit is

   I.   to create an agreement within the scientific community regarding the heat unit.

   II. to explain the inconsistencies found when melting a pound of ice to cool the same weight of water that has been heated to different temperatures.

   III. not fully explained in this passage.

   (A) I only.   (C) I and II only.

   (B) II only.   (D) I, II, and III.

Passage C

What, then, is the cause of the difference between Japanese painting and that of the Occident? Some say that the difference in the colouring matter and the brushes used has caused a wide divergence in the tone of Oriental and of Occidental painting. This opinion is, however, far from conclusive. For, looking deeper into the matter, the question arises, "What has brought about all these differences in the pigments and the brushes, as well as in the technique adopted by artist of the East and of the West?" In my opinion here lies the key to the whole problem. In the first place, Eastern and Western painters hold somewhat different views concerning the primary object of art, and from these results their disagreement in technique and other details. In order to understand the real source of the differences between Eastern and Western painting it is therefore requisite to study closely their contents, which differ to some extent in essentials.

Painting should have for its object the expression of ideas, and as such "it is invaluable, being by itself nothing." In art an idea may be expressed in ways which differ, principally according to the two modes, the subjective and the objective. To state the matter more explicitly, a painter may use the object he delineates chiefly for expressing his own thought, instead of revealing the idea inherent in the object itself. On the contrary, another painter strives to bring out the spirit of the object he portrays, rather than to express ideas of his own that may arise in association with the object. In general, Western painters belong to the latter class, while those of Japan to the former; the one laying stress on objective, and the other on subjective ideas. This distinction discloses the fundamental differences between Eastern and Western painting, which causes wide dissimilarities in conception and execution.

Take for instance their subjects. Here one cannot fail to notice a marked contrast between Japanese and European pictures. In Western painting, where special importance is attached to objective qualities, the portraiture of human figures naturally receives the foremost attention, as though it were nobler and grander than other themes. Is it not because in man, unlike the lower creations, there exists a spirit, the interpretation of which, in its different manifestations, affords a rare scope for the artist's talent? Accordingly, in Occidental painting in which the expression of the spirit externally manifest in the object is made the chief point, human portraiture necessarily claims the first consideration. The same holds true not only of painting, but almost every other art. Conversely in Japanese pictures, flowers, birds, landscapes, even withered trees and lifeless rocks, are esteemed as highly as God's highest creation—human being. The reason is not far to seek; it is simply this: landscapes, birds, flowers, and similar things may be devoid of soul, but the artist may turn them into nobler objects, as his fancy imparts to them the lofty spiritual attributes of man.

Anyone with an extensive knowledge of our pictures cannot fail to discern this common characteristic of composition, namely, that the centre of a picture is not found in any single individual object, for the guiding principle of the synthesis is expressed in the mutual relations of all the objects treated. In other words, in Japanese painting no serious attempt is made to give all-exclusive prominence to any one particular object, but, instead, the effect of the whole is considered the point of prime importance. Hence in the minds of our painters, not each and every portion of a picture need be accurate, but the picture as a whole should be microcosmically complete. Such is but the inevitable outcome of stress laid almost exclusively on subjective ideas.

From Sei-ichi Taki, "Three Essays on Oriental Painting"

21. The term "Occidental art" refers to

    (A)   accidental, or unintentional, art.

    (B)   Western art.

    (C)   non-Western art.

    (D)   Oriental art.

22. The purpose of the article is to

    (A)   contrast the paintings of the Japanese and the Occident.

    (B)   compare the paintings of the Japanese and the Occident.

    (C)   compare the contents of the paintings of the Occident and of the Japanese.

    (D)   compare the composition of the paintings of the Japanese and the Occident.

23. A main difference between the Occidental and the Japanese paintings is

    (A)   differing views concerning the primary object of art.

    (B)   differing views on technique.

    (C)   differing views of details.

    (D)   differences in pigments and brushes.

24. The author's area of expertise appears to be primarily

    (A)   Occidental painting.   (C)   Oriental painting.

    (B)   Japanese painting.   (D)   Asian painting.

25. The Japanese painter can be said to

    (A)   use the object he delineates to express his own thoughts.

    (B)   express ideas of his own that may arise in association with the object.

    (C)   stress objective ideas.

    (D)   stress the spirit of the object being portrayed.

26. The painters of the pictures in Western art

    (A)   give foremost attention to the human figure.

    (B)   do not believe the human figure is grander than other themes.

    (C)   accept the expression of the spirit.

    (D)   esteem God's creations highly.

27. Japanese artists

    (A)   esteem rocks, trees, and flowers on the canvas as highly as human beings.

    (B)   see birds and flowers as having a soul.

    (C)   are not able to give landscapes, birds, and flowers lofty spiritual attributes.

    (D)   are not able to impart, through their fancy, spiritual attributes to non-human matter.

28. The author explains that in

    (A)   Japanese art the viewer can find a single individual object in the center of a picture.

    (B)   Japanese art there are mutual relations of all objects treated in a picture.

    (C)   Western art no one particular object receives all-exclusive prominence.

    (D)   Japanese painting a serious attempt is made to give all-exclusive prominence to any one particular object.

29. The author's primary purpose is to

    (A)   persuade the reader that Japanese art is superior to Western art.

    (B)   persuade the reader that Western art is superior to Japanese art.

    (C)   explain objectively some differences between Japanese and Western art.

    (D)   present the points in favor of Japanese art over Occidental art.

30. The reader should interpret the phrase, "…the picture as a whole should be microcosmically complete…" to mean

   (A) Japanese paintings should be complete in every detail.

   (B) every portion of the canvas should be completely covered with pigment so that, even if examined under a microscope, no area is without cover.

   (C) everything on a canvas does not have to be accurate but rather the relations should be complete.

   (D) the emphasis is placed on completion in objective terms.

STOP

The following additional multiple-choice questions have been provided to help you sharpen your skills. This section will not appear on the actual MTEL test. Please turn to "Vocabulary" on page 384 to resume the timed practice test.

Passage D

Professor Hostead, in his article "Modern Agnosticism Justified," argues that a) religion is basically belief in God and immortality, b) most religions consist of "accretions of dogma and mythology" that science has disproven, c) it would be desirable, if it were possible, to keep the basic religious belief without those accumulations of religious notions and legends, but that d) science has rendered even the basic elements of religion almost as incredible as the "accretions." For the doctrine of immortality involves the view that man is a composite creature, a soul in a state of symbiosis with a physical organism. But science can successfully regard man only monastically, as a single organism whose psychological characteristics all arise from his physical nature; the soul then becomes indefensible. In conclusion, Professor Hostead asserts that our only hope rests in empirical, observable evidence for the existence of the soul; in fact, in the findings of psychical research.

My disagreement with Professor Hostead starts at the beginning. I do not consider the essence of religion as simply the belief in God and immortality. Early Judaism, for example, didn't accept immortality. The human soul in Sheol (the afterworld) took no account of Jehovah, and God in turn took no account of the soul. In Sheol all things are forgotten. The religion revolved around the ritual and ethical demands of God and on the blessings people received from him. During earthly life these blessings were usually material in nature: happy life, many children, good health, and such. But we do see a more religious note also. The Jew hungers for the living God; he obeys God's laws devoutly; he considers himself as impure and sinful in Jehovah's presence. God is the sole object of worship. Buddhism makes the doctrine of immortality vital, while we find little in the way of that which is religious. The existence of the gods is not denied, but it has no religious significance. In Stoicism again both the practice of religion and the belief in immortality are variables, not absolute traits of religion. Even within Christianity itself we find, as in Stoicism, the subordinate position of immortality.

From C. S. Lewis, "Religion Without Dogma"

31. Which of the following best defines the phrase "accretions of dogma and mythology" as it is used in the first paragraph?

    (A) Combinations of fact and fiction

    (B) Conflicts of sound principles and unsound theories

    (C) Implications and ideas of religion

    (D) Religious ideas and fables that have gradually accumulated to form accepted religious belief

32. What is the main idea of the entire passage?

    (A) Belief in God is scientifically valid.

    (B) Professor Hostead's assumption that the essence of religion is the belief in God and immortality is incorrect.

    (C) Neither Judaism, Buddhism, Stoicism, nor Christianity fit into Hostead's definition of religion.

    (D) Judaism, Buddhism, Stoicism, and Christianity are all valid ideologies in their regard for immortality and belief in God.

33. The writer's purpose in this passage is to

    (A) outline the basic tenets of Judaism, Buddhism, Stoicism, and Christianity.

    (B) establish the scientific credibility of four ideologies so as to undermine Hostead's positions.

(C)   attack Hostead's views by establishing the vulnerability of Hostead's first position.

(D)   define the essence of religion.

Passage E

Intelligence and will support a man. Man relies not merely on physical existence, for something beyond the physical resides within him. This "something" transcends the physical; it is a more rewarding existence. Through knowledge and love man has a "spiritual superexistence" which creates him more than a part of a whole but instead creates a microcosm, containing within himself the elements of the entire universe through knowledge. And the characteristic of love enables him to give freely to others whom he regards as other selves. Nowhere in the physical environment can we find such a unique relationship as this.

At the root of this phenomenon is the concept of the soul, which Aristotle described as the first principle of life in any organism and which he thought contained a superior intellect in man. Christianity maintains that the soul is the dwelling place of God and is therefore created for eternity. The human soul exists within our physical framework, amidst all the bones and tissue and internal organs, and has greater value than the entire universe. Though a man is subject to the slightest material accidents, his soul dominates time and death. The soul is the root of personality.

From Jacques, "The Aims of Education"

34. According to this selection, how could we best define the term "spiritual superexistence"?

(A)   That quality that makes man more than simply another part of the universe

(B)   That quality that lives forever

(C)   Supreme intelligence

(D)   Knowledge and love

35. Which of the following statements best sums up the central idea of this selection?

(A)   Man's knowledge and love separate him from the lower animals.

(B) The human soul is the key factor that makes man a microcosm instead of simply another part of our universe.

(C) Both Aristotle and Christianity have placed tremendous importance on the human soul.

(D) The value of the soul is greater than that of the physical universe.

36. Which of the following statements represents an opinion of the writer rather than a fact?

(A) Christians maintain that the soul is the dwelling place of God.

(B) Aristotle dismissed the idea of the soul.

(C) Intelligence and will support a man.

(D) Man is subject to accidents.

Passage F

A rock-solid consensus of opinion exists in urban-industrial society regarding the correct means of measuring our progress beyond the primal, the period when human civilization was in its infancy. The prevailing conclusion is that we measure progress by examining how artificial our environment becomes, either by ridding ourselves of nature's presence or by controlling natural forces. Without much doubt, human environment must always maintain an artificial flair about it. In fact, we might almost say that the human space is destined to possess an "artificial naturalness" in that people spontaneously fill their universe with artifacts and man-made, non-natural institutions. Humans invent and scheme, devise and intricately thread a finished product: culture, a buffer zone conceived by and intended for man where man may live legitimately as plant and animal inhabit their environment of instinct, reflex, and roteness. But as we acknowledge human culture, we must also acknowledge natural environment—the mountain and the shore, the fox and its flora, the heavenly bodies—and the close relationship primitives had with this natural habitat for millennia. These people used as their clocks the seasonal rhythms, timing their own activities to these smooth organic cycles. They learned from the plants and animals that surrounded them, spoke with them, worshipped them. Primitives considered their destiny tied inherently to the non-humans, allies and foes alike, and created places of honor for them in their culture.

We cannot possibly exaggerate the importance of this intimacy between human and nature to the growth of human awareness. This inadequate, sterile term "nature" that we use to categorize the non-human world has regretfully lost its impact through the simple connotation we give it today: a designated area of random physical things and events outside and other than ourselves. We may think of "nature poetry" as poems that touch on daisies and sunsets, one possible topic out of myriad possibilities, many of which are irrelevant to polluted city streets and the asphalt aura of modern life. We overlook the universal view of nature, which includes us. Nature, however, has brought us into existence and will outdistance us; from it we have learned of our destiny. It mirrors who we are. Whatever our culture produces that severs humans from a vibrant tie with nature, that removes us from or alienates nature is—strictly speaking—a sick delusion. What culture produces unmindful of the natural world doesn't merely lack ecological soundness; more alarmingly it lacks psychological completeness. It remains devoid of a truth our primitive counterparts learned from an infant world of nature: the reality of spiritual being.

From Theodore Roszak, "The Human Environment"

37. Which of the following best defines "culture" as the writer uses the term?

    (A) The result of mankind changing his otherwise natural environment to an artificial one

    (B) The condition of being destructive to the forces of nature

    (C) The condition of being literate and articulate in the ways of human life

    (D) Man's recognition of nature's elements

38. For what purpose does the writer use the phrase "artificial naturalness"?

    (A) To show how man should treat nature

    (B) To suggest an insincere attitude on man's part

    (C) To suggest man's integral tie to nature

    (D) To demonstrate man's natural tendency to create an artificial environment

39. According to this passage, what caused primitive peoples to place importance on elements of nature?

    (A) The belief that their fates were intricately entwined with the natural world

    (B) Simply their primitive, superstitious ignorance

    (C) Their lack of an artificial environment

    (D) Their ecological concerns

40. The first means used to tell time, according to the passage, was

    (A) plants and animals.

    (B) human instinct, reflex, and roteness.

    (C) the awareness of spiritual being, which man derived from his awareness of nature.

    (D) seasonal rhythms.

VOCABULARY

1. Define *prodigal*.

   _____

   _____

   _____

2. Define *virulent*.

   _____

   _____

   _____

3. Define *meretricious*.

   _____

   _____

   _____

4. Define *elusive*.

_____

_____

5. Define *incessant*.

_____

_____

6. Define *tedious*.

_____

_____

7. Define *endorse*.

_____

_____

8. Define *prevalent*.

_____

_____

9. Define *obscure*.

_____

_____

Section 2 – Writing

WRITTEN SUMMARY

> **DIRECTIONS:** Read the following passages and then summarize, in your own words, their main points. Your responses will be scored according to the following characteristics: fidelity, conciseness, organization, sentence structure, word usage, and mechanical conventions.

Essay 1

The eruption of Mount Katmai in June, 1912, was one of the most tremendous volcanic explosions ever recorded. A mass of ash and pumice whose volume has been estimated at nearly five cubic miles was thrown into the air. In its fall this material buried an area as large as the state of Connecticut to a depth varying from 10 inches to over 10 feet, while small amounts of ash fell as much as 900 miles away.

Great quantities of very fine dust were thrown into the higher regions of the atmosphere and were quickly distributed over the whole world, so as to have a profound effect on the weather, being responsible for the notoriously cold, wet summer of that year.

The comparative magnitude of the eruption can be better realized if one should imagine a similar eruption of Vesuvius. Such an eruption would bury Naples under 15 feet of ash; Rome would be covered nearly a foot deep; the sound would be heard at Paris; dust from the crater would fall in Brussels and Berlin, and the fumes would be noticeable far beyond Christiania, Norway.

Fortunately the volcano is situated in a country so sparsely inhabited that the damage caused by the eruption was insignificant—very much less than in many relatively small eruptions in populous districts, such as that of Vesuvius, which destroyed Pompeii and Herculaneum. Indeed, so remote and little known is the volcano that there were not any witnesses near enough to see the eruption, and it was not until the National Geographic Society's expeditions explored the district that it was settled definitely which of several near-by volcanoes was really the seat of the disturbance.

The most important settlement in the devastated district is Kodiak, which, although a hundred miles from the volcano, was buried nearly a foot deep in ash. This ashy blanket transformed the "Green Kodiak" of other days into a gray desert of sand, whose redemption and revegetation seemed utterly hopeless. When I first visited it, a year later, it presented an appearance barren and desolate. It seemed to every one there that it must be many years before it could recover its original condition.

From National Geographic, 1917

Essay 2

Not only does music have the ability to entertain and enthrall, but it also has the capacity to heal. The following passage illustrates the recent indoctrination of music therapy.

Music's power to affect moods and stir emotions has been well known for as long as music has existed. Stories about the music of ancient Greece tell of the healing powers of Greek music. Leopold Mozart, the father of Wolfgang, wrote that if the Greeks' music could heal the sick, then our music should be able to bring the dead back to life. Unfortunately, today's music cannot do quite that much.

The healing power of music, taken for granted by ancient man and by many primitive societies, is only recently becoming accepted by medical professionals as a new way of healing the emotionally ill.

Using musical activities involving patients, the music therapist seeks to restore mental and physical health. Music therapists usually work with emotionally disturbed patients as part of a team of therapists and doctors. Music therapists work together with physicians, psychiatrists, psychologists, physical therapists, nurses, teachers, recreation leaders, and families of patients.

The rehabilitation that a music therapist gives to patients can be in the form of listening, performing, taking lessons on an instrument, or even composing. A therapist may help a patient regain lost coordination by teaching the patient how to play an instrument. Speech defects can sometimes be helped by singing activities. Some patients need the social awareness of group activities, but others may need individual attention to build self-confidence. The music therapist must learn what kinds of activities are best for each patient.

In addition to working with patients, the music therapist has to attend meetings with other therapists and doctors who work with the same patients to discuss progress and plan new activities. Written reports to doctors about patients' responses to treatment are another facet of the music therapist's work.

Hospitals, schools, retirement homes, and community agencies and clinics are some of the sites where music therapists work. Some music therapists work in private studies with patients who are sent to them by medical doctors, psychologists, and psychiatrists. Music therapy can be done in studios, recreation rooms, hospital wards, or classrooms, depending on the type of activity and needs of the patients.

Qualified music therapists have followed a four-year course with a major emphasis in music plus courses in biological science, anthropology, sociology, psychology, and music therapy. General studies in English, history, speech, and government are other requirements for a Bachelor of Music Therapy. After college training, a music therapist must participate in a six-month training internship under the guidance of a registered music therapist.

Students who have completed college courses and have demonstrated their ability during the six-month internship can become registered music therapists by applying to the National Association for Music Therapy, Inc. New methods and techniques of music therapy are always being developed, so the trained therapist must continue to study new articles, books, and reports throughout his/her career.

Essay 3

Unjust laws exist: shall we be content to obey them, or shall we endeavor to amend them, and obey them until we have succeeded, or shall we transgress them at once? Men generally, under such a government as this, think that they ought to wait until they have persuaded the majority to alter them. They think that, if they should resist, the remedy would be worse than the evil. But it is the fault of the government itself that the remedy *is* worse than the evil. *It* makes it worse. Why is it not more apt to anticipate and provide for reform? Why does it not cherish its wise minority? Why does it cry and resist before it is hurt? Why does it not encourage its citizens to be on the alert to point out its faults, and *do* better than it would have them? Why does it always crucify Christ, and excommunicate Copernicus and Luther, and pronounce Washington and Franklin rebels?

One would think that a deliberate and practical denial of its authority was the only offence never contemplated by government; else, why has it not assigned its definite, its suitable and proportionate, penalty? If a man who has no property refuses but once to earn nine shillings for the State, he is put in prison for a period unlimited by any law that I know, and determined only by the discretion of those who placed him there; but if he should steal ninety times nine shillings from the State, he is soon permitted to go at large again.

If the injustice is part of the necessary friction of the machine of government, let it go, let it go: perchance it will wear smooth—certainly the machine will wear out. If the injustice has a spring, or a pulley, or a rope, or a crank, exclusively for itself, then perhaps you may consider whether the remedy will not be worse than the evil; but if it is of such a nature that it requires you to be the agent of injustice to another, then, I say, break the law. Let your life be a counterfriction to stop the machine. What I have to do is to see, at any rate, that I do not lend myself to the wrong which I condemn.

Under such a government which imprisons any unjustly, the true place for a just man is also prison. The proper place today, the only place which Massachusetts has provided for her freer and less desponding spirits, is in her prisons, to be put out and locked out of the State by her own act, as they have already put themselves out by their principles. It is there that the fugitive slave, and the Mexican prisoner on parole, and the Indian come to plead the wrongs of his race should find them; on that separate, but more free and honorable ground, where the State places those who are not *with* her, but *against* her—the only house in a slave State in which a free man can abide with honor. If any think that their influence would be lost there, and their voices no longer afflict the ear of the State, that they would not be as an enemy within its walls, they do not know by how much truth is stronger than error, nor how much more eloquently and effectively he can combat injustice who has experienced a little in his own prison. Cast your whole vote, not a strip of paper merely, but your whole influence. A minority is powerless while it conforms to the majority; it is not even a minority then; but it is irresistible when it clogs by its whole weight. If the alternative is to keep all just men in prison, or give up war and slavery, the State will not hesitate which to choose. If a thousand men were not to pay their tax-bills this year, that would not be a violent and bloody measure, as it would be to pay them, and enable the State to commit violence and shed innocent blood. This is, in fact, the definition of a peaceable revolution, if any such is possible. If the tax-gatherer, or any other public officer, asks me, as one has done, 'But what shall I do?' my answer is, 'If you really wish to do anything, resign your office.' When the subject has refused allegiance, and the officer has resigned his office, then the revolution is accomplished. But even suppose blood should flow. Is there not a sort of blood shed when the conscience is wounded? Through this wound a man's real manhood and immortality flow out, and he bleeds to an everlasting death. I see this blood flowing now.

From Henry David Thoreau, "Civil Disobedience"

WRITTEN COMPOSITION

DIRECTIONS: Read the following statements and passages, as well as each set of directions; then write your response. Your compositions will be scored according to the following characteristics: appropriateness, mechanical conventions, word usage, sentence structure, focus and unity, organization, and development.

Essay 1

"The end justifies the means."

Write an essay in which you either agree or disagree with this statement. Be sure to support your opinion with examples of illustrations from history, current events, or your personal experience.

Essay 2

There are growing problems in the American judicial system.

Write an essay in which you agree or disagree with this statement.

Essay 3

"There is a wonderful, mystical law of nature that the three things we crave most in life—happiness, freedom, and peace of mind—are always attained by giving them to someone else."

Write a composition in which you either agree or disagree with this statement. Be sure to support your opinion with specific examples or illustrations from history, current events, literature, or personal experience.

GRAMMAR AND USAGE

> **DIRECTIONS**: Read each passage and answer the questions that follow.

Passage A

[1]Summer is upon us, and many students are going out to "catch some rays." [2]In order to keep themselves beautiful and healthy, these sun worshipers should show respect for the power of old Sol. [3]Frequent or prolonged exposure to the sun can cause skin cancer, the deadliest form of which is malignant melanoma, and incidences of this disease are rising faster than any cancer. [4]Ninety percent of skin cancer is caused by overexposure to the sun.

[5]While most Americans believe application of sun screen helps prevent cancer, less than ten percent of us use it when we go out. [6]Also, we tend to go out during the most dangerous part of the day, between 10 a.m. and 2 p.m. in the summer. [7]This is

the time when the sun emits peak ultraviolet radiation in the Northern Hemisphere. [8]Even hiding under an umbrella near a pool or beach is insufficient to protect us from the damaging effects of the sun because the UV rays are reflected off the surface of sand and water.

[9]Wearing sunscreen may protect us a little, but sweat or swimming washes the lotion off, so the sunscreen really doesn't help protect us very much. [10]It's hard to use self-control in a nation that worships the rich, the thin, and the tan, but the burning rays of the sun can give cancer to anyone who wants a dark tan every summer. [11]We'd be better off just trying to get rich and thin.

1. Which of the following is needed?

(A) Sentence 3: Add "other" between "any" and "cancer."

(B) Sentence 5: Change "application" to "applying."

(C) Sentence 8: Change "to protect us" to "in protecting us."

(D) Sentence 9: Delete "off."

2. Which of the following requires revision for unnecessary repetition?

(A) Sentence 2   (C) Sentence 8

(B) Sentence 3   (D) Sentence 9

Passage B

[1]When interest rates decrease, home mortgage rates also drop. [2]Homeowners who bought a house when rates were high seek to refinance their mortgage loans in order to take advantage of the cheaper rates. [3]Lower interest rates <u>results</u> in lower monthly payments.

[4]A person who owns a $100,000 home with a fixed interest rate of 11 percent for 30 years pays almost $1,000 in monthly principal and interest. [5]However, there is a fee of $1,800 to $2,400 for refinancing. [6]The same home with a 30 year loan, but with a 9 percent loan, pays about $850 a month. [7]Obviously, it is to the consumer's advantage to refinance his home. [8]The "rule of thumb" in the mortgage industry is that the homeowner is wise to refinance if he or she can get a loan at two or more

percentage points lower than his or her current rate. [9]Therefore, if the homeowner is planning to move within a year or two, refinancing is not considered a wise choice of action.

3. Which of the following should be used to replace the underlined word in Sentence 3?

    (A) result

    (B) resulted

    (C) is resulting

    (D) had resulted

4. Which of the following makes the sequence of ideas clearer in the second paragraph?

    (A) Place Sentence 5 between Sentences 8 and 9.

    (B) Reverse the order of Sentences 4 and 5.

    (C) Reverse the order of Sentences 7 and 9.

    (D) Delete Sentence 6.

5. Which of the following is a nonstandard sentence?

    (A) Sentence 4

    (B) Sentence 6

    (C) Sentence 8

    (D) Sentence 9

Passage C

[1]One of the world's most valuable gems, pearls are valued for their luminous beauty. [2]Pearls are formed when an irritant, like a few grains of sand or a parasite, enters a mollusk. [3]Nacre-forming cells begin to cover the intruder with smooth layers of calcium carbonate until the irritant assumes the same appearance as the inside of the mollusk. [4]Only rarely, and after many years, do the layers of nacre form a pearl.

[5]When a cut pearl is examined under a microscope, concentric layers of nacre are revealed. [6]Tiny crystals of the mineral aragonite, held in place by a cartilage-like substance called conchiolin, reflects light in an iridescent rainbow effect. [7]Jewelers call this iridescence *orient*. [8]Most mollusks do not make iridescent pearls because their aragonite crystals are too large. [9]Perfectly round pearls are quite rare in natural occurrence. [10]Most pearls now are cultured. [11]A young oyster receives both a

piece of mantle from a donor oyster and a seeding bead of mussel shell. [12]These are tucked into a carefully-made incision in an oyster. [13]Which is then lowered into the ocean in a wire cage so it can be cleaned and periodically x-rayed to check on progress. [14]Because the oyster is a living organism and not a machine in a factory, the oyster may choose to spit out the introduced nucleus or the resulting pearl may be full of lumps and stains. [15]Minor stains and imperfections, however, may be eliminated by carefully grinding down the surface of the pearl in order to produce a smaller, but more valuable, perfect pearl.

6.   Which of the following is needed in the first paragraph?

   (A)   Sentence 1: Delete "One of."

   (B)   Sentence 2: Change "like" to "such as."

   (C)   Sentence 3: Change "until" to "because."

   (D)   Sentence 4: Change "and after" to "and then."

7.   Which of the following is needed in the second paragraph?

   (A)   Hyphenate "Perfectly round" in Sentence 9.

   (B)   Combine Sentences 12 and 13 by changing the period after "oyster" to a comma.

   (C)   Delete Sentence 14.

   (D)   Add a sentence between Sentences 14 and 15 to give examples of defects.

8.   What change needs to be made to paragraph 2?

   (A)   Sentence 6: Change "reflects" to "reflect"

   (B)   Sentence 8: Change "too" to "to."

   (C)   Sentence 12: Delete the hyphen in "carefully-made."

   (D)   Sentence 15: Change "minor stains and imperfections" to "minor stains or imperfections."

Passage D

[1]One thing is certain: Christopher Columbus was a real person who left real logs of his journey from Spain on August 3, 1492, to the Bahamas and back. [2]_____. [3]To the Spanish he is Cristobal Colon, but the Italians call him Cristoforo Colombo. [4]The Italians insist he is a native of Genoa, but some claim he was a Jew born in Spain, or born in Spain but not a Jew. [5]One version has touted Columbus as a Norwegian.

[6]Contrary to the popular myth, most educated people of the 1400s believed the world was round. [7]Columbus didn't have to sell almost anyone on that idea. [8]What he was trying to sell was a faster route to India. [9]Trade with India went by the centuries-old overland routes or the newer route by ship around the southern tip of Africa. [10]Also, another common myth is that Isabella had to sell her jewels in order to provide financing; actually, her husband had to approve all expenses, and funding was taken from the royal treasury.

[11]Even the original landing site is not known for certain, but most scholars agree that it is probably San Salvador Island in the Bahamas. [12]After his voyage, Columbus sent his handwritten logs to Isabella. [13]The copy the queen had made is known as the Barcelona log. [14]The original handwritten one has disappeared, as has all but a fragment of the Barcelona log copied by a Dominican friar named Bartolome de las Casas.

9. Which of the following changes is needed?

    (A) Sentence 6: Change "Contrary to" to "Opposing."

    (B) Sentence 7: Delete the word "almost."

    (C) Sentence 9: Change "by" to "around."

    (D) Sentence 11: Change "probably" to "probable."

10. Which of the following sentences would best be added between Sentences 1 and 3?

    (A) Columbus was very adventurous.

    (B) However, many details about Columbus's life are unknown.

    (C) These logs provide many details of his journey to the Bahamas.

    (D) He is known by different names in different countries.

11. What change would best improve this passage?

   (A) Sentence 6: Delete the comma between "myth" and "most."

   (B) Sentence 8: Insert a comma between "sell" and "was" in Sentence 8.

   (C) Place Sentence 11 after Sentence 5.

   (D) Sentence 10: Change the semicolon to a comma.

12. What change would best improve Paragraph 2?

   (A) Sentence 6: Add an apostrophe to "1400s."

   (B) Sentence 7: Delete the word "almost."

   (C) Sentence 9: Delete the hyphen in "centuries-old."

   (D) Sentence 10: Delete the word "also."

Passage E

^{1}The recent contretemps over the _proposed_ hike in the student parking fee has provided a test for the new administration. ^{2}After a proposed doubling of the current $40 per semester parking fee, students threatened a walkout and planned demonstrations. ^{3}The fees were intended to cut down on the incidents of vandalism and potential assaults in campus parking lots. ^{4}Faced with these threats, the director of student services, the provost, and several other administrators met with the president of the student body and heads of several student organizations. ^{5}The increased fees, already approved by the board of regents, were to pay the salary of additional parking lot attendants. ^{6}_Some_ students viewed the rate increase as a means of subsidizing more campus minor bureaucrats and petty disciplinarians. ^{7}Although our university has not had much trouble with vandalism in the past, and no reported incidents of assault, such incidents are rising in surrounding areas and are a growing problem in universities across the United States.

^{8}_After_ the two groups met, complaints and fears were exchanged. ^{9}The administration listened _attentively_. ^{10}Rather than just paying "lip service" to the process of negotiation, the administration agreed to a compromise on the service fee in exchange for a well-organized student patrol which will be trained and monitored by the town's police force. [11]It is hoped that the presence of these students, who will wear an identifying arm band, will deter potential criminal activity.

13. Which of the following makes the sequence of ideas clearer in the first paragraph?

    (A) Reverse the order of Sentences 1 and 2.

    (B) Delete Sentence 2.

    (C) Place Sentence 3 after Sentence 6.

    (D) Delete Sentence 7.

14. Which of the following, underlined in the previous passage, should be replaced by a more precise word?

    (A) proposed   (C) After

    (B) Some   (D) attentively

STOP

The following additional multiple-choice questions have been provided to help you sharpen your skills. This section will not appear on the actual MTEL test. Please turn to "Sentence Corrections" on page 408 to resume the timed practice test.

Passage F

[1]Consultative teaching models have gained much popularity lately. [2]The Content Mastery program is one such model designed to assist students who have been identified as learning disabled to achieve their maximum potential in normal classroom environments. [3]Learning disabled students are intelligent but need extra skills in order to overcome their disabilities. [4]A learning disabled student who is mainstreamed may have difficulties in a class where the teacher may not have the training necessary to help students with different disabilities. [5]The student who needs extra help can go to the Content Mastery classroom and work on an individualized basis under the guidance of the special programs teacher with the materials available there. [6]Students needing the Content Mastery program exhibit the fol-

lowing characteristics: consistently low grades, poor performance, and gaps in skills.

[7]Contrary to popular belief, Content Mastery is not just "a little extra help." [8]It also is not designed to "give" students the answers to worksheets and tests. [9]What Content Mastery does is offer increased stimulus variation in the form of many different strategies. [10]For example, the Content Mastery materials include taped textbooks, hi-lighted books and worksheets, and supplementary materials (such as laminated charts to practice labeling), as well as small study groups, individual counseling, sessions on test-taking strategies, and other types of problem-solving skills.

15. Which of the following, if inserted between Sentences 4 and 5, is most consistent with the writer's purpose and audience?

(A) Also, since class sizes vary, some classes may be too large for the teacher to give individualized instruction necessary for the success of these students.

(B) I think some students use the Content Mastery classroom as a cop-out for getting out of work.

(C) It has been clearly demonstrated that students below grade level in their psychomotor development benefit most from practicing tactile kinesthetic skills activities in Content Mastery.

(D) Even though it is a problem-solving model, Content Mastery is not successful with all students.

16. Which of the following changes is needed?

(A) Sentence 1: Change "much" to "a lot."

(B) Sentence 3: Change "their" to "his or her."

(C) Sentence 6: Add a colon after "characteristics."

(D) Sentence 7: Remove the quotation marks around "a little extra help."

17. What change would best improve Paragraph 1?

(A) Sentence 2: Insert a comma between "model" and "designed."

(B) Sentence 3: Insert a comma after "intelligent."

(C) Sentence 5: Change "work" to "works."

(D) Sentence 6: Change the commas to semicolons.

Passage G

¹Born Domenikos Theotokopoulos in Crete in 1541, El Greco became one of the world's great painters. ²He earned the name *El Greco,* meaning "The Greek," when he moved to Spain around 1577 after several frustrating years in Venice and Rome. ³Probably because El Greco was unable to obtain important commissions during his years in Italy, he left for Spain in his mid-30s. ⁴However, he had no better luck in Spain. ⁵At that time, paintings were supposed to inspire prayer and teach religious doctrine, but El Greco did not always adhere to scripture. ⁶For example, he put three Marys in *The Disrobing of Christ,* set biblical scenes in Toledo, Spain, and painted Roman soldiers in Sixteenth-Century armor. ⁷As a result, he lost the patronage of the Toledo Cathedral. ⁸Later, he was able to gain the respect and patronage of Toledo's intellectuals, who admired and supported El Greco. ⁹This wide audience probably left the artist more freedom in developing his own style.

¹⁰El Greco's painting style is based on his early Venetian training. ¹¹The Venetian style, called *mannerism,* characterized by elongated forms, graceful lines, and metallic colors with white highlights. ¹²El Greco's works show humans and animals such as horses extremely elongated, and his landscapes distorted. ¹³Although some critics attribute these characteristics to a peculiar brand of mysticism, probably they show more freedom of experimentation, a freedom not allowed those artists painting politically correct scenes. ¹⁴With loose brushstrokes and sharp contrasts in light and shadow, he anticipated the Expressionist style and profoundly influenced those painters in the 1900s.

18. Which of the following, if placed between Sentences 4 and 5, best supports the writer's purpose and audience?

    (A) He sought work under King Philip of Spain, the most powerful monarch in Europe at that time.

(B) El Greco sought to show the difference between the mundane and the supernatural by making his figures seem to glow with an inner radiance.

(C) In his masterpiece, *The Burial of Count Orgaz*, El Greco created a realistic lower, earthly half to contrast with abstract forms and distorted proportions in the upper, heavenly half.

(D) The painter from Crete failed to win King Philip's favor with the painting *Martyrdom of St. Maurice*.

19. Which of the following is a nonstandard sentence?

(A) Sentence 3   (C) Sentence 11

(B) Sentence 8   (D) Sentence 13

20. What change would best improve Paragraph 1?

(A) Sentence 1: Delete the apostrophe in "world's."

(B) Sentence 3: Delete the hyphen in "mid-30s."

(C) Sentence 6: Insert an apostrophe before the "s" in the word "Marys."

(D) Sentence 6: Make "Sixteenth-Century" all lowercase.

Passage H

[1]A growing number of businesses are providing day care facilities for the children of their employees. [2]Some companies charge a standard fee, but most provide the day care free or at a nominal cost. [3]These care programs provide services that continue through the early teens of the children. [4]If they should help with day care at all is what many companies are trying to decide. [5]In the event parents need to work overtime, centers are even open on weekends, and some companies <u>showing</u> special initiative in building company loyalty of each employee by making arrangements for special field trips to zoos and museums. [6]Is this kind of care really necessary? [7]Should businesses really be in the business of day care.

^{8}Experts in the field cite many advantages for this system. ^{9}Therefore, loyalty to the company is built, so morale climbs. ^{10}Studies show that when a company helps its employees blend parent and worker roles, absenteeism and tardiness drop. ^{11}In addition, workers feel the company has taken more of a personal interest in them. ^{12}Most companies also provide various health care programs for their employees. ^{13}Turnover becomes a much less significant factor for managers. ^{14}Human resource managers also estimate that every $1 spent on these programs returns $2 or more in increased productivity.

21. Which of the following best improves the underlined portion of Sentence 3?

    These care programs provide services that <u>continue through the early teens of the children.</u>

    (A) continue, through the early teens, of the children.

    (B) continue through the children and their early teens.

    (C) continue through the children's early teens.

    (D) continue on through the early teens of the children.

22. Which of the following would be a better way to structure Sentence 4?

    (A) What many companies are trying to decide is if they should help with day care at all.

    (B) Unsure if they should help with day care at all, many companies are trying to decide.

    (C) Many companies, unsure if they should help with day care at all, are trying to decide.

    (D) Many companies are trying to decide if they should help with day care at all.

23. Which of the following would be an acceptable substitution for the underlined word in Sentence 5?

    (A) show   (C) showed

    (B) will show   (D) (A), (B), and (C)

24. Which of the following contains a punctuation error?

    (A) Sentence 1   (C) Sentence 7

    (B) Sentence 3   (D) Sentence 10

25. Which of the following sentences is irrelevant in the second paragraph and should be eliminated?

    (A) Sentence 8   (C) Sentence 12

    (B) Sentence 10   (D) Sentence 14

26. Which of the following best improves the sequence of ideas in the second paragraph?

    (A) Reverse the order of Sentences 8 and 9.

    (B) Place Sentence 9 after Sentence 14.

    (C) Delete Sentence 11.

    (D) Place Sentence 9 after Sentence 11.

Passage I

[1]Polar bears, so named because they lived near the North Pole, are called "Nanook" by the Eskimo. [2]Living along the cold waters and ice floes of the Arctic Ocean, some polar bears spend time along the coastal areas of northern Canada, Alaska, Norway, Siberia, and Greenland, although some bears live on the islands of the Arctic Ocean and never come close to the mainland. [3]Most of these areas lie north of the Arctic circle and about 85% of Greenland is always covered with ice. [4]To protect them from the arctic cold and ice, polar bears have water-repellant fur and a pad of dense, stiff fur on the soles of their snowshoe-like feet. [5]In addition, the bears have such a thick layer of fat that infrared photos show no detectable heat, except for their breath.

[6]Polar bears are the largest land-based carnivores. [7]Because their fur is white with a tinge of yellow, they are difficult to spot on ice floes, their favorite hunting ground. [8]Polar bears have a small head, a long neck, and a long body, so they make efficient swimmers. [9]Polar bears have no natural enemy except humans. [10]Increased human activity in the Arctic region has put pressure on polar bear populations. [11]The Polar Bear Specialist Group was formed to conserve and manage this unique animal. [12]An

increase in the number of polar bears is due to cooperation between five nations. [13]In 1965, there were 8,000 to 10,000 bears reported, but that population is estimated at 25,000 at the present.

27. Which of the following verbs is used in an inappropriate tense?

    (A) "lived" in Sentence 1

    (B) "Living" in Sentence 2

    (C) "is covered" in Sentence 3

    (D) "conserve" in Sentence 11

28. Which of the following sentences is not necessary to the first paragraph, and would be best eliminated?

    (A) Sentence 1   (C) Sentence 3

    (B) Sentence 2   (D) Sentence 4

29. Which of the following would be the best way to improve the structure of Sentence 5?

    (A) In addition, except for their breath, the bears have such a thick layer of fat that infrared photos show no detectable heat.

    (B) The bears have such a thick layer of fat that, in addition, infrared photos show no detectable heat except for their breath.

    (C) Except for their breath, infrared photos show no detectable heat, the bears have such a thick layer of fat.

    (D) Best as it is.

30. Which of the following sentences would best fit the writer's plan of development, and would fit between Sentences 6 and 7?

    (A) Full-grown polar bears may be about nine feet long and weigh between 1,000 and 1,600 pounds.

    (B) These bears have keen eyesight and are not sensitive to snow blindness.

    (C) In the winter the female polar bear enters a cave in an iceberg and gives birth to one or two cubs.

(D)   Polar bears can swim great distances with a speed of approximately six miles an hour.

31.   How would Sentences 9, 10, and 11 be properly combined to better effect?

(A)   Polar bears have no natural enemy, except humans: increased human activity in the Arctic region has put pressure on polar bear populations, while the Polar Bear Specialist Group was formed to conserve and manage this unique animal.

(B)   Since polar bears have no natural enemy except humans, the Polar Bear Specialist Group has formed to conserve and manage this unique animal because increased human activity in the Arctic region has put pressure on polar bear populations.

(C)   Polar bears have no natural enemy except humans, and though increased human activity in the Arctic region has put pressure on polar bear populations, the Polar Bear Specialist Group was formed to conserve and manage this unique animal.

(D)   Polar bears have no natural enemy except humans, and since increased human activity in the Arctic region has put pressure on polar bear populations, the Polar Bear Specialist Group was formed to conserve and manage this unique animal.

Passage J

[1]In the poem "The Raven" by Edgar Allan Poe, a man has nodded off in his study after reading "many a quaint and curious volume of forgotten lore." [2]His mood is melancholy. [3]He is full of sorrow. [4]He is grieving for "the lost Lenore."

[5]When he hears the tapping at his window, he lets in a raven. [6]The raven perches on the bust of Pallas Athena, a goddess often depicted with a bird on her head by the Greeks who believed that birds were heralds from the dead. [7]At first, the man thinks the bird might be a friend but one who would leave soon, but the raven says, "Nevermore," an affirmation which makes the man smile. [8]However, the bird's repetition of "Nevermore" leads the speaker to the realization that Lenore will never return, the bird becomes an omen of doom and is called "evil" by the mournful speaker. [9]He becomes frantic, imploring the raven to let him know if there is comfort for him or if he will ever again

hold close the sainted Lenore. [10]To both questions, the bird replies, "Nevermore." [11]Shrieking with anguish, the bird is ordered to leave, but it replies, "Nevermore." [12]At the end of the poem, the man's soul is trapped in the Raven's shadow "that lies floating on the floor" and "shall be lifted—nevermore."

[13]Thus, the bird evolves into an ominous bird of ill omen. [14]Some argue that the bird deliberately drives the speaker insane. [15]While others feel the bird is innocent of any premeditated wrong doing, and I think the bird doesn't do anything but repeat one word. [16]One thing is certain, however. [17]The poem's haunting refrain is familiar, one which students of American literature will memorize and forget "nevermore."

32. Which of the following is the best way to combine Sentences 2, 3, and 4?

    (A) He is melancholy and sorrowful and grieving for "the lost Lenore."

    (B) He is grieving for "the lost Lenore," full of melancholy and sorrow.

    (C) Melancholy and sorrowful, he is grieving for "the lost Lenore."

    (D) Melancholy and full of sorrow, he is grieving for "the lost Lenore."

33. Which of the following is the best revision of the underlined portion of Sentence 8 below?

However, the bird's repetition of "Nevermore" leads the speaker to <u>the realization that Lenore will never return, the bird becomes an omen of doom and is called "evil" by the mournful speaker</u>.

    (A) realize the following—Lenore will never return, the bird is evil and an omen of doom.

    (B) the realization of Lenore's failure to return, the evil and omen of doom of the bird.

    (C) realize that Lenore will never return, so the bird, called "evil" by the mournful speaker, becomes an omen of doom.

    (D) Best as it is.

34. Which is the best revision of the underlined portion of Sentence 11 below?

Shrieking with anguish, <u>the bird is ordered to leave, but it</u> replies, "Nevermore."

(A)   the bird is ordered to leave but

(B)   the man orders the bird to leave, but it

(C)   the order is given for the bird to leave, but it

(D)   the bird, ordered to leave,

35.   In the context of the sentences preceding and following Sentence 15, which of the following is the best revision of Sentence 15?

(A)   Others feel the bird is innocent of any premeditated wrongdoing because it does not do anything but repeat one word.

(B)   Innocent and not doing anything, the bird repeats one word.

(C)   Innocent of any premeditated wrongdoing, the bird does not do anything.

(D)   One may argue that, innocent of any premeditated wrongdoing, the bird does not do anything but repeat one word.

36.   Which of the following would be a better way to end the passage, combining Sentences 16 and 17?

(A)   One thing is certain, however: the poem's haunting refrain is a familiar one which students of American literature will memorize and forget "nevermore."

(B)   One thing is certain, however, that the poem's haunting refrain is familiar, one which students of American literature will memorize and forget "nevermore."

(C)   One thing is certain, however; the poem's haunting refrain is familiar, one which students of American literature will memorize and forget "nevermore."

(D)   One thing is certain, however: the poem's haunting refrain is familiar, one which students of American literature will memorize and forget "nevermore."

Passage K

[1]The Dead Sea Scrolls are considered the archaeological find of the century. [2]_____. [3]The manuscripts are believed to have

been written between 200 B.C. and A.D. 50 by the Essenes, members of an ascetic Jewish sect. [4]Most of the Old Testament books (except Esther) appear in the scrolls, and some of the scrolls are multiple copies of these books written by different scribes. [5]Other scrolls are books of the Apocrypha, such as Jubilees, Tobit, and the Wisdom of Solomon, as well as hymns, prayers, prophecies, and biblical commentaries.

[6]For nearly 2,000 years this priceless cache of sacred writings lay hidden in the desert of Judah along the Dead Sea. [7]The first find was in 1947 when a Bedouin shepherd boy discovered the scrolls in a rocky cave of Qumran, ten miles from Jerusalem on the edge of the Dead Sea. [8]Shortly after, other manuscripts were uncovered nearby in different caves. [9]The larger group of scrolls was found in 1952.

[10]Four photographic copies of the scrolls were distributed, and these photographic copies were kept under the strict supervision of a group of 40 scholars dedicated to studying the photographs and analyzing the copies. [11]In December 1990, however, Huntington library in San Marino, California, began granting access to anyone who wants to view and study the photographs. [12]This move is hailed by those who have felt left out of the elite cadre of 40 scroll scholars.

37. Which of the following changes is needed?

    (A)   Sentence 3: Change "between" to "among."

    (B)   Sentence 6: Change "lay" to "have lain."

    (C)   Sentence 9: Change "larger" to "largest."

    (D)   Sentence 11: Change "who" to "whom."

38. Which of the following requires revision for unnecessary repetition?

    (A)   Sentence 4   (C)   Sentence 7

    (B)   Sentence 6   (D)   Sentence 10

39. Which of the following would best fit between Sentences 1 and 3?

    (A)   Some people claim that these scrolls are actually forgeries.

    (B)   There are probably many ancient scrolls that have yet to be discovered.

    (C)   The scrolls, about 800 different documents, are written on leather and papyrus.

    (D)   The Dead Sea is a salt lake that lies between Israel and Jordan.

40. Which of the following changes is needed?

    (A)   Sentence 7: Insert a comma after "1947."

    (B)   Sentence 10: Change "studying" to "study."

    (C)   Sentence 11: Insert a comma between "December" and "1990."

    (D)   Sentence 11: Capitalize "library."

SENTENCE CORRECTIONS

> **DIRECTIONS:** The sentences in this section contain one or more grammatical errors. Rewrite them using proper grammatical form.

1.   The climate of the small island is quite variable and the most unique of any place in the world.

_____

_____

2.   Eleven states out of 50 housing nuclear facilities which must be monitored by the Department of Energy.

_____

_____

3.   One of every two students in the class say that they have used marijuana.

_____

_____

4.   The memories of when I last saw James and she are not ones I am proud of.

_____

_____

_____

5. When the police stopped James and Dan on the highway, he asked him for his license.

_____

_____

_____

6. In order to qualify for the job, an applicant must be 21 or older, have their own transportation, and pass a simple test.

_____

_____

_____

GRAMMATICAL VOCABULARY

DIRECTIONS: This section tests your knowledge of grammatical vocabulary. Use the space below each statement to provide the correct definitions. Your responses will be graded as correct or incorrect based on their accuracy and adequacy.

1. Define *transitive verb.*

_____

2. Define *idiom.*

_____

3. Define *relative pronoun.*

_____

4. Define *declarative statement.*

_____

5. Define *preposition.*

_____

6.　Define *active voice sentence.*

7.　Define *nominative case.*

WRITTEN MECHANICS

DIRECTIONS: This portion of the Communication and Literacy Skills Test will be dictated on audiotape. You will be expected to write down the passage exactly as it is spoken on the audiotape; use correct spelling, punctuation, and capitalization. Each passage will be read three times: the first time at a normal speed, the second time more slowly, and the third time, again at a normal speed. (There will be a two-minute break between the second and third readings in order to revise what you have written.) Your responses will be assigned a score based on the following scale:

4　6 or fewer errors

3　7 to 12 errors

2　13 to 18 errors

1　19 or more errors

For this practice test, we advise that you have someone read the passage out loud to you (three times as described above). Use the scale to determine your score and refer to this section in the Detailed Explanations of Answers, provided at the end of each practice test, for a review of potential problems.

Passage 1

The early history of knitting is uncertain; although there are theories that place knitting earlier, the first examples of knitting are thirteenth-century Egyptian fragments. The dry climate of Egypt preserved patterned sandal socks worn by Egyptians. Also surviving are early ecclesiastical pieces throughout Europe. When a better method of producing knitting needles was developed in Europe during the Renaissance, knitting increased and knitting guilds were created. Incidentally, the members of these guilds were exclusively male. The development of better yarns at the beginning of the nineteenth century led to a knitting explosion among middle-class women. In the twentieth century, knitting has become both an industry for the rural poor and a leisure activity for wealthier classes.

Passage 2

Art nouveau is a movement in the arts popularized at the end of the nineteenth century in Europe and the United States. Philosophically, the movement was a reaction against increasing industrialization and the accompanying ideology of progress. Poets, painters, musicians, graphic designers, craftspeople, and architects all took part in the movement to bring art into everyday life. Art nouveau attempted to break with the past by utilizing new materials and technologies as well as by seeking to create a new style. The art nouveau style approaches abstraction in its streamlined lines, yet maintains a recognizable resemblance to natural forms. Practitioners of art nouveau also emphasized the value of beautiful and well-wrought items in an increasingly mechanized age.

Communication and Literacy Skills Test

ANSWER KEY

MULTIPLE CHOICE

1. (D)	11. (C)	21. (B)	31. (D)
2. (A)	12. (B)	22. (A)	32. (B)
3. (B)	13. (B)	23. (A)	33. (C)
4. (B)	14. (D)	24. (B)	34. (A)
5. (D)	15. (D)	25. (D)	35. (B)
6. (C)	16. (D)	26. (A)	36. (C)
7. (B)	17. (D)	27. (A)	37. (A)
8. (C)	18. (C)	28. (B)	38. (D)
9. (B)	19. (D)	29. (C)	39. (A)
10. (D)	20. (D)	30. (C)	40. (D)

GRAMMAR AND USAGE

1. (A)	11. (C)	21. (C)	31. (D)
2. (D)	12. (D)	22. (D)	32. (C)
3. (A)	13. (C)	23. (A)	33. (C)
4. (A)	14. (C)	24. (C)	34. (B)
5. (B)	15. (A)	25. (C)	35. (A)
6. (B)	16. (C)	26. (D)	36. (D)
7. (B)	17. (A)	27. (A)	37. (C)
8. (A)	18. (D)	28. (C)	38. (D)
9. (B)	19. (C)	29. (D)	39. (C)
10. (B)	20. (D)	30. (A)	40. (D)

DETAILED EXPLANATIONS
OF ANSWERS

Section 1 — Reading

MULTIPLE CHOICE

1.   **(D)**   (D) is the best answer. The author is actually advising empires of the causes of revolutions and unrest. Even though the first sentence refers only to the wisdom of an ancient sage, more recent information is also imparted. Therefore, (A) is not the best answer. The advice is offered to rulers, not church ministers, so (B) should not be selected. Even though the first sentence states the passage is about how to make a little city into a great one, the second sentence clearly states the author is going to explain how to do the reverse. Therefore, (C) should not be chosen.

2.   **(A)**   The best answer is (A). The author compares an empire to a cake. (B) is incorrect because it is a minister, not the country, who is compared to a gingerbread baker. It has already been ascertained that it is a minister being compared to a gingerbread baker so (C) is not the best answer. (D) is incorrect because it is not a religious minister who is compared to a gingerbread baker, but rather, a minister who has the "management of extensive dominions."

3.   **(B)**   The best answer is (B) because the article is tongue-in-cheek. Even though the suggestion is that Franklin is going to tell the reader how to make a little city of a great one, the author (who is not a simpleton) is actually giving advice. (A) is incorrect because Franklin addresses himself to ministers of "extensive" or large dominions rather than small countries. (C) is incorrect because the advice is being given to governmental ministers rather than being received from religious ministers. (D) is also incorrect because the word "fiddle" is used only as a vehicle for the satire of the passage and is not to be taken literally.

4.   **(B)**   In the last paragraph of the reading passage, the writer states that the General needs enough troops under his command. Therefore, (B) is the best choice. The writer is not suggesting that troops need to be kept in tow, so (A) should not be chosen. Even though the General should certainly be lucky to have troops endowed with skill under his control, there is no support in the

passage for this answer; (C) should not be chosen. Because the clause has nothing to do with captured troops, (D) should not be chosen.

5. **(D)**   (D) is the best choice because the article is written by Benjamin Franklin, who was a friend of the colonists and is writing to advise the mother country on how to behave. Franklin is not writing to help rid the ministers of their troubles; therefore, (A) should not be selected. The writer is not hoping to help the ministers build their powers and increase their provinces, so (B) should not be chosen. Because the article was written by Benjamin Franklin, it could not have been written only a few years ago nor does it contain new ideas to help increase the provinces; (C) should not be chosen.

6. **(C)**   The reader should note that the answer looked for is the one which is *least* advisable. (C) is the answer which is least advisable because a minister should *not* treat the provinces as if he or she expects them to revolt and as if he or she supposes them to be always ready to revolt. To keep a large country intact, the General of the army should be limited to the constitutional powers, so (A) is *not* an answer which is *least* advisable. The provinces should be given the same rights as those in the mother country; thus, (B) is an advisable answer and should not be chosen. A mother country should not require taxation without representation, just as (D) says. Since (D) is true, it should not be selected. (A), (B), and (D) are incorrect because they are extremely advisable actions to take for keeping a large country intact and the question asks for the least advisable action.

7. **(B)**   The reader should note that in this case he or she is to give the answer which is *most* advisable. (B) is the best answer because the Parliaments should allow petition for redress and (B) is the only advisable action offered among the choices. Flaunting claims (A), refusing to read the claims (C), and allowing taxation without representation (D) are not to be chosen because they all are *not* advisable.

8. **(C)**   One can expect a large empire to be diminished (according to the author of this article) from the edges, therefore, (C) should be selected. In the third paragraph of this reading passage, Franklin warns the ministers to "Turn your attention, therefore, first to your remotest provinces…" The remotest provinces are those at the edges of the country. Once the information concerning the remotest provinces is located in the passage, it is clear that (A), (B), and (D) cannot be the answer.

9. **(B)**   The reader is asked to give the answer which is most likely to ensure *separation* from the mother country. (B) is the answer most likely to ensure separation since if the mother country does not give common rights,

separation is ensured, according to the fourth paragraph of the passage. On the other hand, incorporating the provinces (A), allowing them to enact their laws (C), and allowing them to choose legislators (D) are all actions which can unite or draw the provinces to the mother country. Therefore, they should not be accepted.

10. **(D)**   The question asks which answer will *least* likely reduce an empire to a small country. The best answer is that if the revolution is already established, it may be too late to change. Therefore, (D) should be chosen. If the mother country remembers their prejudice (A), punishes provinces for their principles (B), and punishes the provinces after the revolution is already established (C), the empire may likely be reduced. Therefore, the reader should not select the incorrect answers (A), (B) and (C).

11. **(C)**   The item that the writer contends is *not* true is (C) because the first sentence of the reading passage uses the words "even when," implying that heat is no longer regarded as a substance. The other items (A), (B), and (D) are all items the writer states as being true in the first paragraph. None of them should be chosen.

12. **(B)**   The best answer is (B) because the calorie and B.T.U. both relate to the amount of heat necessary to raise the temperature one degree. Because one unit relates to a kilogram (2.2 pounds) and one relates to a pound of water, (A) should not be chosen; it relates to one pound of water only. One unit relates to the customary system and one to the metric system, not both to the metric system. Thus, (C) cannot be chosen. Only the B.T.U. relates to a pound of iron, so (D) is also incorrect.

13. **(B)**   The best answer is (B) because the melting of one pound of ice can cool a pound of hot water through a definite range of temperature and can cool two pounds of water through *half* as many degrees (C). (B) is therefore denied by the author. Neither (A) nor (D) can be the correct answer because they are stated, not denied, by the author in the first paragraph of the reading passage.

14. **(D)**   The author states that the heat capacity of water or the B.T.U. per pound-degree is not constant, so (D) is the best answer. The author does not state that a water pound-degree is a constant; therefore, (A) should not be chosen. Because the temperature does make a difference, (B) should not be chosen. (C) is exactly opposite of the correct answer (D) and should not be selected.

15. **(D)**   The best choice is (D). The disagreement concerns how to limit and define the heat unit. Since the passage states without any indication of

doubt or negation that the melting of a pound of ice will not cool the same weight of water from 200° Fahrenheit to 180° Fahrenheit as it will from 60° Fahrenheit to 40° Fahrenheit, (A) is not the best answer. As the opening sentence of the second and last paragraph states, there is general agreement that a water pound-degree is not quite constant; thus, (B) should not be chosen. There is no point of disagreement among scientists as to whether the equivalence of heat effects proved effects proportional to quantity. Consequently, (C) is not the correct answer.

16. **(D)**   The best answer is (D). The author appears to suggest that there are good reasons for taking the freezing-point to the boiling-point as the range by including the words "which will probably become universal"—interesting, but not totally necessary, information that leads the reader to believe the author readily accepts this as a range. Both the metric and the customary systems are mentioned without preference for either system. Therefore, neither (A), which indicates a predilection for the metric system, nor (B), which indicates a predilection for the customary system, is the correct answer. Because the author precedes his mention of the mean calorie with the words "properly named," he is indicating his approval of, rather than his opposition to, the mean calorie; hence, (C) is another incorrect choice.

17. **(D)**   The phrase "properly named" is applied to both the mean calorie and the mean British Thermal Unit in the last sentence of the reading passage and makes (D), which includes both mean calories and mean British Thermal Units, the correct choice. Neither (A) nor (B) is correct because each of these answers is only one-half of the correct answer. Because we already know that (D) is the correct answer, we can see that (C) is incorrect; there is no support for such opposition in the passage.

18. **(C)**   The author predicts the universal acceptance of the mean B.T.U. and the mean calorie as mentioned toward the end of the reading passage; hence, (C) is the best answer. (A) should not be selected since it mentions the universal adoption of the B.T.U. alone. (B) mentions the universal adoption of the calorie alone and should not be accepted. Because the author predicts not the demise but the universal adoption of the calories, (D) is incorrect.

19. **(D)**   Statements I, II, III, and IV are all necessary parts of the definition of the heat unit. Only (D) allows for all these parts. (A), (B), and (C) are all incorrect since each omits some part or parts of the correct four-part answer.

20. **(D)**   According to the passage, the author seems to be striving toward a "universality" of the heat unit (I), and would also like to find an explanation for the inconsistencies found when melting a pound of ice to cool the same

weight of water when heated to different temperatures (II). The passage does end, however, before the author has completely stated his argument (III). (A), (B), and (C) only allow the reader to choose part of the complete answer and are incorrect. Only (D) allows the reader to select all the correct statements.

21. **(B)** The best answer is (B) because, in the first sentence, the author opposes the terms "Japanese" and "Occident." Later in the same paragraph, he opposes the terms "Oriental" and "Occidental," which effectively eliminates (D). Because there is no support for (A) in the passage, the reader is able to infer that this is incorrect. Assuming the reader knows that both Japan and the Orient are part of the East, (C) is incorrect; the term "non-Western" implies "Eastern." By a process of elimination, the reader can determine that only (B) can be the correct choice.

22. **(A)** The best answer is (A); the author contrasts, or shows the differences between, the paintings of the Japanese and the Occident. The author discusses differences, rather than similarities (comparisons), between the two types of painting, so (B) is an incorrect answer. (C) and (D) are incorrect because the author writes about contrasts, rather than comparisons. In addition, (C) mentions only content whereas the author also mentions the stress—objective or subjective ideas—in the painting styles.

23. **(A)** The best answer is (A) because the main difference between Occidental and Japanese painting is the differing views concerning the primary object of art, as is explained toward the end of the second paragraph of the reading passage. While (B), (C), and (D) are mentioned, there is no in-depth analysis of any of these answers. The question asks for the *main* difference, so (B), (C), and (D) are all incorrect answers.

24. **(B)** Sei-ichi Taki refers to Oriental and Occidental art in general and to Japanese art in particular; therefore, (B) is the best answer. (A) is incorrect because the writer's area is not Occidental (Western) painting but Oriental painting, although he is able to make many comparisons between the two. The article does not cover the broad expanse of Oriental painting (C) or Asian painting (D), but concentrates on Japanese painting. Hence, (C) and (D) should not be selected.

25. **(D)** (D) is the best choice. The Japanese painter can be said to bring out the spirit of the object being portrayed, as stated by the author in the second paragraph. Because the correct answer (D) refers to the spirit of the object being portrayed, it is logical that neither the painter's own thoughts, ideas, or objective ideas can be the answer. Consequently, (A), (B), and (C) are incorrect choices.

26. **(A)** (A) is the best answer because the reader is asked to identify what the painters of Western art do. The author states near the beginning of the third paragraph that the painters of Western art give their foremost attention to the human figure. Because of this (B) should not be chosen; it is exactly the opposite of what the author states. The painters of Western art are not greatly concerned with the expression of the spirit but rather with the human figure; (C) should not be chosen. The painters in Western art are not always concerned with showing high esteem for God's creations, but rather with objective qualities; (D) should not be chosen.

27. **(A)** As discussed by the author in the third paragraph, Japanese artists are different from Western artists in that they esteem rocks, trees, and flowers on the canvas as highly as they do human beings; therefore, (A) is the correct answer. Because the author states that birds and flowers may be devoid of, rather than possess, souls, (B) is incorrect. Japanese artists do give landscapes, birds, and flowers lofty spiritual attributes; thus, (C) is false and should not be selected. (D) is incorrect; the author states precisely the opposite of the answer choice, as was also the case with (C).

28. **(B)** The author explains that in Japanese art mutual relations of all objects treated in a picture are important; this makes (B) the best answer. As the author explains in the last paragraph, there is no one individual object in the center of Japanese pictures; consequently, (A) should not be chosen. In Western art, one particular object receives all-exclusive prominence. (C) says just the opposite and should not be chosen. (D) directly opposes the author's statement that in Japanese painting no serious attempt is made to give all-exclusive prominence to any one particular object and should not be chosen.

29. **(C)** The writer objectively presents information about Western and Japanese art. He is not seeking to put one form above the other. Therefore, (C) is the best answer. Since the author is being objective in his writing, neither (A) nor (B) can be the answer as both contain the words "persuade" and "superior." (D) cannot be chosen since it suggests, by using the word "favor," that the writer presents one type of art as superior to another type.

30. **(C)** The best answer is (C); the author states in the first sentence of the last paragraph that the relations should be complete. "Microcosmically complete" does not mean that every detail must be in order. (A) should not be selected because it states the opposite of that which the author explains. The amount of pigment on the canvas is not mentioned anywhere in the passage; (B) is incorrect. (D) is incorrect because the emphasis is placed on completion in subjective, not objective, terms.

31. **(D)**   Item (D) in the first paragraph refers to this term with a correct definition: "those accumulations of religious notions and legends." (A) is incorrect; the first paragraph doesn't suggest that these "accretions" are anything but "incredible" and fiction. (B) is incorrect; the first paragraph maintains that Hostead's position rejects any soundness in such accretions. (C) is incorrect; again, "accretions," according to contextual clues, doesn't mean "implications," but rather "accumulations."

32. **(B)**   Hostead's first assumption makes that statement about the essence of religion while the second sentence in paragraph two disputes it. (A) is incorrect; paragraph one defines Hostead's position, while the second paragraph addresses the first position, which doesn't deal with scientific validity of any belief in God. (C) is incorrect; these four ideologies are simply used to illustrate that immortality is not necessarily the essence of a religion, but the central idea of the passage is not the defense of these ideologies. (D) is incorrect; again the writer is not defending the validity of those ideologies, but using them to attack one of Hostead's points.

33. **(C)**   The first two sentences of the second paragraph state this purpose exactly. (A) is incorrect; the writer only touches on one aspect of each of these beliefs to disprove Hostead's first point. (B) is incorrect; the writer touches only the first position, which does not deal with scientific credibility. (D) is incorrect; the writer disputes Hostead's definition of essence of religion rather than provide his own definition.

34. **(A)**   The fourth sentence of the selection states this. (B) is incorrect; the selection does not say that "spiritual super-existence" lives forever; the soul does. (C) is incorrect; the writer doesn't say man has "supreme" intelligence; he says that Aristotle felt the human soul had a superior intellect. (D) is incorrect; man has spiritual super-existence through his knowledge and love, but the writer doesn't say knowledge and love are the essence of spiritual super-existence.

35. **(B)**   The first paragraph establishes man as a microcosm while the second paragraph attributes that condition to the human soul. (A) is incorrect; perhaps this is a statement with which the writer would agree, but it's only by inference that this statement would be considered true. (C) is incorrect; this true statement doesn't summarize the central idea of the passage; it only supports it. (D) is incorrect; this statement, which reflects the writer's opinion, doesn't constitute the main idea of the selection.

36. **(C)**   This is not a factual statement; many would argue that man has no more will than any other creature. (A) is incorrect; while not all agree with this

statement, it is a fact that Christians believe this. (B) is incorrect; this is the opposite of what the writer says. (D) is incorrect; we can all agree that man is indeed subject to accidents, as the writer maintains; this is not an opinion.

37. **(A)** The writer says humans make their environment artificial and the result of their efforts is culture. (B) is incorrect; the writer does not suggest that culture in and of itself is a bad or destructive thing. (C) is incorrect; the writer doesn't allude to erudition or intelligence; even primitive, illiterate man had culture. (D) is incorrect; culture is an artificial element while nature's elements are not.

38. **(D)** Sentences 3 and 4 say this outright. (A) is incorrect; the writer introduces this term early in the passage before he even touches on man's relationship with nature. (B) is incorrect; the word "artificial" doesn't connote lack of sincerity; it suggests "not occurring in nature." (C) is incorrect; the passage does say man is inherently a part of nature, but this term is not used by the writer to describe that relationship.

39. **(A)** This is stated in the final sentence of the first paragraph. (B) is incorrect; the writer calls them primitive but not ignorant; in fact, the passage suggests enlightenment on their part. (C) is incorrect; the writer doesn't suggest that primitive man had no culture; their worship of nature didn't take the place of an artificial environment. (D) is incorrect; their concerns were not ecological but more theological; they may have acted in an "ecologically correct" fashion, but the writer doesn't emphasize any ecological concerns.

40. **(D)** The sentence that begins with this phrase in Paragraph 1 makes this statement. (A) is incorrect; while one may infer that organic cycles prompt plants and animals to act in clock-like fashion, the writer does not say that early humans used them as clocks. (B) is incorrect; these are qualities that the writer ascribes to nonhuman aspects of nature and animals. (C) is incorrect; the writer's reference to the spiritual being is not related to his discussion of primitive man's methods of telling time.

VOCABULARY

1. *Prodigal* means recklessly extravagant or characterized by wasteful expenditure.

2. *Virulent* means able to overcome bodily defense mechanisms, extremely poisonous, or full of malice.

3.   *Meretricious* means of, relating to, or having the nature of prostitution. It also means tawdrily and falsely attractive.

4.   *Elusive* means hard to comprehend, define, isolate, or identify.

5.   *Incessant* means continuing or following without interruption.

6.   *Tedious* means tiresome because of length or dullness.

7.   *Endorse* means to express support and approval publicly and definitely.

8.   *Prevalent* means generally or widely accepted, practiced, or favored.

9.   *Obscure* means not readily understood or clearly expressed. It also means shrouded in or hidden by darkness.

Section 2 – Writing

WRITTEN SUMMARY

Essay 1

STRONG RESPONSE

In 1912, Mount Katmai was the seat of one of the most powerful volcanic eruptions in recorded history. Its explosion was so massive its debris would cover an area as large as Connecticut, and its range was so vast that ash fell as far as 900 miles away.

The explosion had a large impact on the world, contributing, through throwing fine particles of dust into the atmosphere, to the cold, wet summer of that year.

To understand exactly how great the eruption was, we might imagine a comparable event taking place at Mount Vesuvius. In such an instance, great cities such as Naples would be covered by 15 feet of ash while Rome would get up to a foot of ash.

In the case of Mount Katmai, though, the surrounding region was underpopulated enough that no one even witnessed the eruption. In fact, it took an expedition from National Geographic to determine exactly which of the region's volcanoes had erupted.

The most significant area to have been directly impacted by the eruption of Mount Katmai was Kodiak. Although a hundred miles from the volcano, the region was buried in a foot of ash. It would take years for this area, once known as the "Green Kodiak," to have any hope of a return to its former condition.

ANALYSIS

The writing is clear, concise and expressive. It is faithful to the original passage and sufficiently reproduces the passage's mode of exposition.

Essay 2

STRONG RESPONSE

Using music as a tool for healing is a very old notion that dates back to the ancient Greeks. Even if we no longer agree with the hyperbolic assertion that if music could heal, the music of Mozart's age would raise the dead, today we still look for an ameliorative effect from music. However, our expectations have shifted, so that the emphasis now is on music as a means specifically to help the emotionally ill.

This practice is known as music therapy, and there are professionals called music therapists who work in conjunction with other health care professionals to administer to the mentally ill. The therapy will differ for different patients but could include listening as well as performing. Some patients are even encouraged to try to compose music.

The music therapist must work closely with the patients' other doctors. This takes the form of attending meetings and submitting written reports. Music therapy takes place in a variety of locations, including retirement homes, hospitals, community centers, clinics and even schools.

Goals for treatment vary on a case by case basis. For instance, singing lessons can be useful for someone with a speech defect, while learning to play an instrument can help someone regain coordination they may have lost as the result of an illness or injury. Oftentimes, a patient may simply need to learn to be comfortable in group situations, for which group singing, performing, or music appreciation lessons can be helpful.

To become a music therapist, one must attend a four-year college and earn a Bachelor's degree in Music Therapy. This course of study includes, in addition to a heavy concentration on music, other courses in biology, science, and psychology. In addition to that, anyone studying to be a music therapist can expect to participate in an internship with a registered music therapist. Once this training is completed, interested and qualified candidates can become registered with the National Association For Music Therapy.

ANALYSIS

The sentences are smooth and syntactically correct. The writer thoroughly covers the major points and most of the subtleties of the original passage's mode of exposition.

Essay 3

STRONG RESPONSE

The passage advocates various forms of civil disobedience as nonviolent measures to enact large scale social changes. The existence of immoral laws calls for more drastic action than trying to work for change within the system. According to the author, a system that has produced immoral laws is itself inherently corrupt. Any attempt to bring about change from within a corrupt system will be limited in how much good it can really bring.

Thoreau sees the lack of stable and clearly defined laws and sentences for crimes against state authority as indicative of the fact that governments do not know how to deal with conscientious objections to their practices and ideologies. The state's unwillingness to consider the possibility of significant changes initiated by a "wise minority" demonstrates its reluctance to consider alternatives to immoral laws and customs. Thoreau believes that when the government imprisons citizens unfairly, all truly moral people belong in jail. He offers the example of slavery. According to his logic, in a slave state, the only just house for an honorable person to dwell is prison. In a place where slavery is supported by the law, the law is a bankrupt concept, and breaking the law a sign of one's justness.

The passage offers examples of non-violent resistance that include refusing to pay taxes that support violent and oppressive policies and resigning your post if that post somehow lends support to oppressive governments. Such actions may seem relatively tame compared to more extreme forms of resistance, but for Thoreau, such non-violent forms of resistance can truly bring about revolution more peaceably and efficiently.

ANALYSIS

The passage is clear and direct. The vocabulary is sophisticated and the sentence structure is sound. The salient points from the passage are covered and a precise understanding of the passage is demonstrated.

WRITTEN COMPOSITION

Essay 1

STRONG RESPONSE

The primary figure associated with the philosophy of "the end justifies the means" is Machiavelli. His treatise, *The Prince*, is a study in cynicism. He outlines methods a sensible prince will take in order to maintain a stable, and thus prosperous, state; these methods include military conquest, bribery, large (rather than minor) insults and threats, and so on. During the Elizabethan times, his infamous reputation earned him the dubious honor of having his Christian name be a synonym for the devil; however, Machiavelli's methods are studied and employed by many leaders.

The military establishment has always employed somewhat less than total honesty in order to win. The Greeks are a notable example of a people who accepted bribery and trickery as an honorable battle tactic. Themistocles sent his personal slave with a message that the Greek general secretly supported the Persian invaders and the retreating Greeks could easily be trapped in the narrow waters at the exit to the Bay of Salamis. The Persians deployed their troops accordingly, and the devastating defeat of Xerxes at Salamis is a textbook study in military brilliance.

Giving false intelligence to the enemy and concealing one's own numbers, position, and plans are intelligent tactics; wars are not won with honesty.

Politics is another arena for less than honorable dealings. Spies ferret out secrets useful in applying leverage to another nation's position. Russia and the United States maintain a constant stream of information about each other through the use of secret intelligence; even supposed allies such as the United States and Israel spy on each other. A recent survey of Americans showed politicians are considered less trustworthy than used car dealers. However, compromising ideals is inherent in the politician's job: a person who never bends or looks the other way will never be a chairman of the military or budget committee.

Even a "gung-ho" patriot can be excused the methods if the job gets done effectively. During the Iran-Contra hearings it became painfully obvious that the intent of the law was circumvented, but Oliver North has emerged a national hero. His testimony, as well as the testimony of others, shows him to have been a "can-do" kind of person, one who can even supply within two days a ship for the CIA that the government agency could not attain for itself through normal channels.

The American public overlooks the methods if the person achieves goals no one else can—or will. Machiavelli and Themistocles knew the business of statesmanship and war. So do modern government officials. They are all judged by their accomplishments.

ANALYSIS

With fluid transition of ideas, depth of thought, and good vocabulary, this essay has a clear thesis in the introductory paragraph, three body paragraphs with a specific focus for each, and a conclusion that sums up the main points without exactly repeating the thesis or topic sentences. Each body paragraph begins with a clear topic sentence which is supported either with an extended example or with several examples. There is a good variety of sentence length and structure. Although not perfect, this essay shows clarity and purpose.

Essay 2

STRONG RESPONSE

There are many growing problems in our judicial system. Rising crime rates, over-crowded jails, an increase in juvenile crime, and a lack of standard sentencing guidelines are all difficulties that inhibit our country's ability to maintain an effective judicial system. Perhaps the most pressing problem our judicial system faces is the disparity between the treatment of those who have money and those who don't. Our constitution mandates that those who cannot afford legal representation shall have a court-appointed attorney to defend them. This right is supposed to guarantee that all citizens have access to legal coverage, and the representation provided by a public defender is supposed to be as good as that afforded by a private attorney. Unfortunately, this is usually not the case.

Public defenders work for the state, and like many other state employees who handle a large number of clients, these lawyers are often significantly overworked. A public defender in a large city might represent hundreds of clients every week. Often case loads are so large that the attorneys only meet their clients a few minutes before going into court. This burden of work has serious consequences for the defendant.

Most importantly, the quality of the defense a public defender can provide his client is necessarily poorer than that of a private attorney. The limited contact with the defendant before going into court means that the public defender has little time to search for precedents that could help the client. It also means that there is little opportunity for the attorney and the client to become acquainted with one another, which makes it difficult for the defendant to trust the attorney. Many of the people forced to rely on public defenders are poorly educated and do not understand the repercussions of intricate legal procedures or the consequences of plea bargaining. If these people do not trust the public defender assigned to their case, they are often uncooperative because they cannot believe that their lawyer really has their best interests at heart. Public defenders are commonly perceived as more concerned with settling the case quickly rather than fairly.

Even if the attorney and his client manage to establish a trusting relationship, time constraints and staff limitations make it difficult for the public defender thoroughly to research the case. Private law firms have large research staffs to search out precedents and to investigate the facts of a case. Public defenders' offices often lack these resources, or else the research staff is overwhelmed by the demands of many attorneys with many cases. In difficult economic times, research staffs are often the first to suffer from budget cuts.

Another factor of this problem is that there is little incentive for public defenders to continue with a case after a client has been convicted. Case loads often dictate that, rather than attempting to establish their client's innocence, public defenders are forced to try to negotiate the most favorable plea bargain. If the client chooses to go to trial and is found guilty, an overworked public defender is less likely to urge the client to appeal the conviction. If the defendant does appeal the conviction, he or she is often forced to deal with a different public defender for the appeal because the case loads can interfere with the attorney's ability to stay with the case.

The problems between the public defender and the defendant are exacerbated by the lack of trust on both sides. Unlike private attorneys, who can choose whom they represent, public defenders must represent everyone assigned to them. They do not have the luxury of selecting only those clients whom they believe to be innocent. Because so many of the clients they represent really are guilty of the crimes with which they are charged, it is all too easy for public defenders to become cynical and assume that *all* of their clients are guilty. This presumption of guilt makes it harder for the defendant to place his confidence in the public defender, and it contributes to the antagonistic relationship that is so common between public defenders and their clients.

Those defendants who can afford to hire their own attorney, on the other hand, can provide themselves with an attorney who believes in them and who is committed to making the best defense possible. Because the private attorney and his client have much more time to spend before the client goes into court, the lawyer has more time to prepare an adequate defense and to prepare plans for an appeal in the case of a conviction.

The most important growing problem in our judicial system is the difference in legal representation afforded by public defenders and private attorneys. Those people who are forced to accept a public defender do not receive the most competent legal care because their lawyers are overworked and understaffed, and are under pressure to settle as many cases as quickly as possible. Time constraints that dictate that many clients do not even meet their attorneys until minutes before going into court insures that, no matter how well-meaning, public defenders are just not equipped to provide their clients with competent legal advice and representation. Americans are supposed to enjoy equality under the law, but until we invest more money into public defense, that equality will remain out of reach of our poorer citizens.

ANALYSIS

This essay provides a clearly defined thesis in the introductory paragraph. The writer then presents logical and convincing supporting arguments throughout the remainder of the essay. The arguments are presented in a rational order and reflect a well-thought-out approach to the topic. The conclusion sums up the major arguments presented in the essay, and cleanly closes the discussion. The writer makes few grammar, spelling, or usage mistakes and demonstrates an ability to communicate effectively in written English.

Essay 3

STRONG RESPONSE

Happiness, freedom, and peace of mind are goals that we all want in life, yet they are very abstract and difficult to measure. Happiness is a frame of mind that means we enjoy what we do. Freedom is the ability to do what we want although it is limited to not doing anything that takes away freedom from other people. Peace of mind is a feeling that we are all right and that the world is a good place. How do we achieve these important goals? They can best be acquired when we try to give them to other people rather than when we try to get them ourselves.

The people who feel happiest, experience freedom, and enjoy peace of mind are most often people who are concentrating on helping others. Mother Theresa of Calcutta is an example. Because she took care of homeless people, she probably didn't have time to worry about trivial matters and was therefore happy, free, and peaceful.

There are other people in history who seem to have attained the goals we all want by helping others. Jane Addams established Hull House in the slums of Chicago to help other people, and her life must have brought her great joy and peace of mind. She gave to the mothers in the neighborhood freedom to work and know that their children were being taken care of; Jane Addams apparently had the freedom to do what she wanted in order to help them.

On the other hand, there are people in literature who directly tried to find happiness, freedom, and peace of mind; they were often miserable. The two people who come to mind are Scrooge and Silas Marner. Scrooge had been selfish in the past, and he wouldn't give anything to the poor. Only later when he began helping others did he become satisfied with his life. Silas Marner was another very selfish character; he hoarded his money and thought it would make him happy. It was not until he adopted his daughter, whom he loved more than money, that he found true happiness.

If we want to achieve happiness, freedom, and peace of mind, we should get involved in helping others so much that we forget ourselves and find joy from the people we are helping. When we try to give away the qualities we want, we find them ourselves.

ANALYSIS

This essay is well-organized, with the opening paragraph serving as the introduction and stating the thesis of the paper in its last sentence. Defining the terms serves as an effective way to introduce the paper. The last paragraph concludes the essay and restates the thesis. The three middle paragraphs support the thesis with specific examples that are adequately explained and have a single focus. Transitions effectively relate the ideas. The sentence structure varies, and the vocabulary is effective. There are no major errors in sentence construction, usage, or mechanics. Although the essay would benefit from some minor revisions, it is well done considering the time limit imposed upon the writer.

GRAMMAR AND USAGE

1.   **(A)**   Choice (A) is correct because any time one item is being compared or contrasted with other items in the same category or group, it is necessary to include the words "other" or "else." Choice (B) creates an awkward construction, "applying of." Choice (C) creates a bit of an awkward wording and does not improve the sentence. In choice (D), the word "off" is necessary to the meaning of Sentence 9.

2.   **(D)**   Choice (D) has unnecessary repetition of the phrase "protect us." Choices (A), (B), and (C) are tightly worded sentences.

3.   **(A)**   Choice (A) shows correct use of present tense. Choices (B) and (D) incorrectly use past tense. Choice (C) is the incorrect use of present progressive.

4.   **(A)**   Choice (A) places Sentence 5 before Sentence 9. This creates a logical flow of ideas because Sentence 9 is the explanation of the drawback of the refinancing fee mentioned in Sentence 5. Choice (B) is incorrect because a sentence beginning with "However," needs to follow a contrasting idea. Choice (C) is incorrect because Sentence 7 is a sentence concluding the advantages and train of thought presented in Sentences 4 and 6. Choice (D) would delete a vital piece of information.

5.   **(B)**   Choice (B) is missing a clear subject, a person paying the money. It is obvious that a home cannot pay a loan. Choices (A), (C), and (D) are clear sentences.

6.   **(B)**   Choice (B) is correct because "such as" is used to introduce an example; "like" signals unequal comparisons. Choice (A) changes the meaning of the sentence; pearls are not the most valuable gems. In choice (C) the change would omit the correct transition "until" which shows time sequence. Choice (D) would create an incoherent sentence.

7.   **(B)**   Choice (B) combined the fragment in Sentence 13 with the complete sentence in Sentence 12. Choice (A) is not a necessary addition. Choice (C) would delete a necessary sentence, one which provides the lead into the idea of grinding down imperfections. Choice (D) is unnecessary because examples of defects ("lumps and stains") have already been listed in Sentence 14.

8.   **(A)**   The plural noun "crystals" needs the verb "reflect." Choices (B) and (C) are correct as they are. Choice (D) would not make an appreciable difference.

9.   **(B)**   Choice (B) would delete the unnecessary adverb "almost." Choice (A) creates a poorly worded transition. Choice (C) creates a sentence that is self-contradictory, making the traders appear to avoid the route they actually took. Choice (D) changes the correct adverb "probably," meant to modify the verb "is," to the incorrect adjective "probable."

10. **(B)**   Choice (B) provides a smooth transition from Sentence 1 to Sentence 3. Choice (C) continues the subject of Sentence 1 but does not mention that of Sentence 3. Choice (D) does not provide a smooth transition between the two sentences and does not allow for the other inconsistencies such as Columbus's country of birth. Choice (A) begins a new topic and should not be chosen.

11. **(C)**   Sentence 11 continues the topic of the uncertain details of Columbus's life and voyage. Choices (A), (B), and (D) are all incorrect answers and should not be chosen.

12. **(D)**   In Sentence 10, the words "also" and "another" are redundant. They both imply that a new example will follow. Choices (A), (B), and (C) are incorrect answers; the sentences are correct in the passage.

13. **(C)**   Choice (C) would move the sentence that discusses the reason for the fees to the end of the paragraph. Sentence 5 introduces the use for the fees, and Sentence 6 presents student objections to the attendants. Sentence 3 should be placed before Sentence 7, which further explains the problem of vandalism and assaults. Choice (A) would move Sentence 2, introducing the idea of threatened demonstrations and walkouts, away from Sentence 4, which contains reference to "these threats." Choice (B) would eliminate the crucial cost of the fees. Choice (D) would eliminate the overriding reason for the fee hike.

14. **(C)**   In choice (C) the incorrect word "After" should be replaced with the correct word "When." It is unlikely that fears and complaints were not exchanged until after the meeting between administration and students. Choice (A) is shown with concrete details in Sentence 2. Choice (B) is not necessary; inclusion of the protestors' names would be irrelevant and coun-terproductive to the conciliatory tone of the article. Choice (D) needs no elaboration because the administration has shown its responsiveness with a compromise.

15. **(A)**   Choice (A) contains the transition word "Also" and another reason why the pull-out program, Content Mastery, is necessary. Choice (B) contains slang, "cop-out," as well as a negative attitude not displayed in the rest of the passage. Choice (C) is far too formal in tone. Choice (D) refutes the thesis of the passage and the reason for instituting a Content Mastery program.

16. **(C)**   In choice (C) a colon is necessary before a list introduced by "the following." Choice (A) is an unnecessary change. Choice (B) would change a correct plural pronoun "their," referring to a plural antecedent "students," to an incorrect singular one. Choice (D) would incorrectly remove necessary quotation marks around a commonly repeated phrase that breaks the tone of the essay.

17. **(A)**   In Sentence 2, a comma is needed to distinguish the attributes of one of the many models mentioned in Sentence 1. Choice (C) is an incorrect

answer; the passage refers to "the student," who works. Choices (B) and (D) are best left as they are.

18. **(D)**　Choice (D) is logical because it gives a specific example of El Greco's failure to win the patronage of an influential person, the king. Choice (A) may appear logical at first, but it does not show the result of the attempt to become employed by the king; therefore, it does not continue the idea of "no better luck in Spain." Choices (B) and (C), although true, deal with El Greco's style, not his failure to seek employment in Spain.

19. **(C)**　Choice (C) is a fragment. The subject "Venetian style" needs to be completed by the verb phrase "*is* characterized by." Choices (A), (B), and (D) are complete sentences.

20. **(D)**　Choice (D) is the correct answer; there is no reason to capitalize "sixteenth-century." Choices (A), (B), and (C) are all incorrect answers. In Sentence 1 [Choice (A)], "world's" is a possessive noun and therefore needs an apostrophe. "Mid-30s" in Sentence 3 [Choice (B)] requires a hyphen because it is a compound word in which the second element is a numeral. Choice (C) should not be chosen because "Marys" is a plural noun; it does not require an apostrophe.

21. **(C)**　"Children's early teens" is much neater and clearer than "the early teens of the children." (A) introduces unnecessary punctuation. (B) is nonsensical ("continue through the children"). (D) adds "on" which does nothing but further convolute the original sentence.

22. **(D)**　(D) makes a clear and simple sentence out of the clumsy original. The structures of (A), (B), and (C) duplicate the confusions of the original.

23. **(A)**　"Showing" in the original sentence is clearly wrong, and "show" (A) is the only acceptable answer. The other choices are not in the present tense and are therefore not parallel to the verbs in the rest of the passage.

24. **(C)**　Sentence 7 is a rhetorical question, like Sentence 6, and needs a question mark.

25. **(C)**　Sentence 12 introduces a new issue in the middle of the paragraph and would best be eliminated.

26. **(D)**　The idea in Sentence 9 about company morale and employee loyalty would be best placed in support of the ideas in Sentence 11, which states that the workers feel that the company has taken interest in them.

"Therefore" sets up a logical relation which is not present between Sentences 8 and 9.

27. **(A)**   Polar bears continue to live near the North Pole so the past tense is inappropriate.

28. **(C)**   Sentence 3 digresses from the main topic, which is the polar bear and its habits, to a geological account of the Arctic region in general. This is irrelevant to the progression of this passage, and would best be eliminated.

29. **(D)**   Sentence 5 is best as it is; the punctuation is correct and the modifiers are properly placed. (A), (B), and (C) all scramble the sense of an otherwise clear sentence.

30. **(A)**   Choice (A) is best because it continues the physical description of the polar bear. (B) is not wholly irrelevant, but it does not provide a clear transition and would be best placed elsewhere. (C) introduces a new subject. (D), like (B), is somewhat relevant but would also be best placed elsewhere.

31. **(D)**   Choice (D) combines the sentences best and uses commas to separate the thoughts. Choice (A) introduces a colon, which could work if the end of the sentence were altered. "While" in the last portion of the sentence, though, is absolutely wrong. (B), as it stands, would best be changed back to three sentences. Choice (C) is similar to (D), except that "though" confuses the relationship between the two ideas.

32. **(C)**   Choice (C) correctly and smoothly combines the two adjectives while providing sentence variety. Choice (A) is not correct; "grieving" is not parallel with the other two adjectives. In choice (B), the adjectives appear to modify the dead Lenore instead of the grieving man. In choice (D) the idea of melancholy and grief are not stated in concise parallel structure.

33. **(C)**   Choice (C) is the most concise expression of the major ideas. Choice (A) is too abrupt and states that the bird "is evil" instead of being "called 'evil'. " Choice (B) contains awkward wording: "the realization of" and "the evil and omen of doom of the bird." The wording of choice (D) creates a run-on sentence.

34. **(B)**   Choice (B) correctly identifies who is doing what. Choices (A) and (C) do not indicate the man as the subject. Choice (D) implies the bird is shrieking with anguish.

35. **(A)**   Choice (A) correctly uses the cause-and-effect construction; in addition, this choice uses a transition word at the beginning of the sentence

in order to indicate contrasting ideas. Choices (B) and (C) leave out a transition word and present as fact what is considered opinion. Choice (D) is too verbose and also omits the transition word.

36. **(D)**   The colon is the most appropriate way to unify the closing thoughts into a single sentence. (A) also utilizes the colon, but the elimination of the comma to create the phrase "is a familiar one" is more clumsy than the original. (B) adds a comma between the two sentences, which creates a run-on. (C) uses a semicolon which is inappropriate.

37. **(C)**   Choice (C) is the correct answer. The comparative degree is used for comparing two things, so "larger" should be changed to the superlative degree, "largest," because more than two caves were discovered containing scrolls. Choice (A) correctly uses "between" to indicate something falling between two dates; "among" is used for more than two things. In choice (B) the use of "lay" is correct; the past tense is required for a condition no longer in effect. In choice (D) "who" is correct as the subject of the subordinate clause with the verb "wants." "Whom" is the objective case and cannot be a subject.

38. **(D)**   Choice (D) should be revised to eliminate unnecessary repetition of "photographic" and "copies." Choices (A), (B), and (C) are concise sentences.

39. **(C)**   Choices (A) and (C) are the only answers that continue the discussion of the discovery of these specific scrolls (the Dead Sea scrolls). Choice (A), however, mentions an irrelevant fact about them, one that is discussed nowhere else in the passage; (A) is therefore not the best choice.

40. **(D)**   Choice (D) is the correct answer. "Library" needs to be capitalized because it is part of a specific name. Only if it stood alone, independent of "Huntington," would it be in lowercase. All of the other choices are incorrect; they are best left alone.

SENTENCE CORRECTIONS

Sample Correct Responses

1.   The climate of the small island is variable and unique to any place in the world.

2. Eleven out of 50 states house nuclear facilities which must be monitored by the Department of Energy.

3. One of every two students in the class says that he or she has used marijuana.

4. The memories I have of my last meeting with James and her are not ones of which I am proud.

5. The police asked James for his license when they stopped Dan and him on the highway.

6. In order to qualify for the job, applicants must be 21 or older, have their own transportation, and pass a simple test.

GRAMMATICAL VOCABULARY

1. A *transitive verb* is a verb that takes an object to complete its meaning.

2. An *idiom* is an expression that is characteristic of a particular language.

3. A *relative pronoun* is a pronoun that relates one part of a sentence to a word in another part of the sentence.

4. A *declarative statement* is a sentence that makes a statement.

5. A *preposition* is a word that demonstrates the relationship between its object and another word in the sentence.

6. An *active voice sentence* is a sentence in which the subject performs the action.

7. The *nominative case* is when a noun or pronoun is the subject of the verb.

DICTATION

Passage 1

Common Errors

Again, *thirteenth-century* and *middle-class* are hyphenated because they are used as adjectives while *nineteenth century* and *twentieth century* are not hyphenated because they are used as nouns. The punctuation of the first sentence is complicated; if two independent clauses are related, they may be joined by a semicolon or be made into two separate sentences. Differentiating between the two possibilities requires careful attention on the part of the listener.

Passage 2

Common Errors

Everyday is used as an adjective here so it should be written as one word. *Well-wrought* is hyphenated because it forms an attributive modifier before the noun. *Nineteenth century* is not hyphenated because it is used as a noun. Many of the words in the referenced passage are commonly misspelled; if you found some of them difficult, be sure to memorize them for the test. When a sentence gives a list (such as poets, painters, musicians, graphic designers, craftspeople, and architects), it is acceptable either to include or disclude the comma before the word "and."

MTEL Practice Test 1
ANSWER SHEET

MULTIPLE CHOICE

#		#		#	
1.	A B C D	15.	A B C D	28.	A B C D
2.	A B C D	16.	A B C D	29.	A B C D
3.	A B C D	17.	A B C D	30.	A B C D
4.	A B C D	18.	A B C D	31.	A B C D
5.	A B C D	19.	A B C D	32.	A B C D
6.	A B C D	20.	A B C D	33.	A B C D
7.	A B C D	21.	A B C D	34.	A B C D
8.	A B C D	22.	A B C D	35.	A B C D
9.	A B C D	23.	A B C D	36.	A B C D
10.	A B C D	24.	A B C D	37.	A B C D
11.	A B C D	25.	A B C D	38.	A B C D
12.	A B C D	26.	A B C D	39.	A B C D
13.	A B C D	27.	A B C D	40.	A B C D
14.	A B C D				

GRAMMAR AND USAGE

#		#		#	
1.	A B C D	15.	A B C D	28.	A B C D
2.	A B C D	16.	A B C D	29.	A B C D
3.	A B C D	17.	A B C D	30.	A B C D
4.	A B C D	18.	A B C D	31.	A B C D
5.	A B C D	19.	A B C D	32.	A B C D
6.	A B C D	20.	A B C D	33.	A B C D
7.	A B C D	21.	A B C D	34.	A B C D
8.	A B C D	22.	A B C D	35.	A B C D
9.	A B C D	23.	A B C D	36.	A B C D
10.	A B C D	24.	A B C D	37.	A B C D
11.	A B C D	25.	A B C D	38.	A B C D
12.	A B C D	26.	A B C D	39.	A B C D
13.	A B C D	27.	A B C D	40.	A B C D
14.	A B C D				

MTEL Practice Test 2
ANSWER SHEET

MULTIPLE CHOICE

1. Ⓐ Ⓑ Ⓒ Ⓓ
2. Ⓐ Ⓑ Ⓒ Ⓓ
3. Ⓐ Ⓑ Ⓒ Ⓓ
4. Ⓐ Ⓑ Ⓒ Ⓓ
5. Ⓐ Ⓑ Ⓒ Ⓓ
6. Ⓐ Ⓑ Ⓒ Ⓓ
7. Ⓐ Ⓑ Ⓒ Ⓓ
8. Ⓐ Ⓑ Ⓒ Ⓓ
9. Ⓐ Ⓑ Ⓒ Ⓓ
10. Ⓐ Ⓑ Ⓒ Ⓓ
11. Ⓐ Ⓑ Ⓒ Ⓓ
12. Ⓐ Ⓑ Ⓒ Ⓓ
13. Ⓐ Ⓑ Ⓒ Ⓓ
14. Ⓐ Ⓑ Ⓒ Ⓓ

15. Ⓐ Ⓑ Ⓒ Ⓓ
16. Ⓐ Ⓑ Ⓒ Ⓓ
17. Ⓐ Ⓑ Ⓒ Ⓓ
18. Ⓐ Ⓑ Ⓒ Ⓓ
19. Ⓐ Ⓑ Ⓒ Ⓓ
20. Ⓐ Ⓑ Ⓒ Ⓓ
21. Ⓐ Ⓑ Ⓒ Ⓓ
22. Ⓐ Ⓑ Ⓒ Ⓓ
23. Ⓐ Ⓑ Ⓒ Ⓓ
24. Ⓐ Ⓑ Ⓒ Ⓓ
25. Ⓐ Ⓑ Ⓒ Ⓓ
26. Ⓐ Ⓑ Ⓒ Ⓓ
27. Ⓐ Ⓑ Ⓒ Ⓓ

28. Ⓐ Ⓑ Ⓒ Ⓓ
29. Ⓐ Ⓑ Ⓒ Ⓓ
30. Ⓐ Ⓑ Ⓒ Ⓓ
31. Ⓐ Ⓑ Ⓒ Ⓓ
32. Ⓐ Ⓑ Ⓒ Ⓓ
33. Ⓐ Ⓑ Ⓒ Ⓓ
34. Ⓐ Ⓑ Ⓒ Ⓓ
35. Ⓐ Ⓑ Ⓒ Ⓓ
36. Ⓐ Ⓑ Ⓒ Ⓓ
37. Ⓐ Ⓑ Ⓒ Ⓓ
38. Ⓐ Ⓑ Ⓒ Ⓓ
39. Ⓐ Ⓑ Ⓒ Ⓓ
40. Ⓐ Ⓑ Ⓒ Ⓓ

GRAMMAR AND USAGE

1. Ⓐ Ⓑ Ⓒ Ⓓ
2. Ⓐ Ⓑ Ⓒ Ⓓ
3. Ⓐ Ⓑ Ⓒ Ⓓ
4. Ⓐ Ⓑ Ⓒ Ⓓ
5. Ⓐ Ⓑ Ⓒ Ⓓ
6. Ⓐ Ⓑ Ⓒ Ⓓ
7. Ⓐ Ⓑ Ⓒ Ⓓ
8. Ⓐ Ⓑ Ⓒ Ⓓ
9. Ⓐ Ⓑ Ⓒ Ⓓ
10. Ⓐ Ⓑ Ⓒ Ⓓ
11. Ⓐ Ⓑ Ⓒ Ⓓ
12. Ⓐ Ⓑ Ⓒ Ⓓ
13. Ⓐ Ⓑ Ⓒ Ⓓ
14. Ⓐ Ⓑ Ⓒ Ⓓ

15. Ⓐ Ⓑ Ⓒ Ⓓ
16. Ⓐ Ⓑ Ⓒ Ⓓ
17. Ⓐ Ⓑ Ⓒ Ⓓ
18. Ⓐ Ⓑ Ⓒ Ⓓ
19. Ⓐ Ⓑ Ⓒ Ⓓ
20. Ⓐ Ⓑ Ⓒ Ⓓ
21. Ⓐ Ⓑ Ⓒ Ⓓ
22. Ⓐ Ⓑ Ⓒ Ⓓ
23. Ⓐ Ⓑ Ⓒ Ⓓ
24. Ⓐ Ⓑ Ⓒ Ⓓ
25. Ⓐ Ⓑ Ⓒ Ⓓ
26. Ⓐ Ⓑ Ⓒ Ⓓ
27. Ⓐ Ⓑ Ⓒ Ⓓ

28. Ⓐ Ⓑ Ⓒ Ⓓ
29. Ⓐ Ⓑ Ⓒ Ⓓ
30. Ⓐ Ⓑ Ⓒ Ⓓ
31. Ⓐ Ⓑ Ⓒ Ⓓ
32. Ⓐ Ⓑ Ⓒ Ⓓ
33. Ⓐ Ⓑ Ⓒ Ⓓ
34. Ⓐ Ⓑ Ⓒ Ⓓ
35. Ⓐ Ⓑ Ⓒ Ⓓ
36. Ⓐ Ⓑ Ⓒ Ⓓ
37. Ⓐ Ⓑ Ⓒ Ⓓ
38. Ⓐ Ⓑ Ⓒ Ⓓ
39. Ⓐ Ⓑ Ⓒ Ⓓ
40. Ⓐ Ⓑ Ⓒ Ⓓ

MTEL Practice Test 3
ANSWER SHEET

MULTIPLE CHOICE

1. Ⓐ Ⓑ Ⓒ Ⓓ	15. Ⓐ Ⓑ Ⓒ Ⓓ	28. Ⓐ Ⓑ Ⓒ Ⓓ
2. Ⓐ Ⓑ Ⓒ Ⓓ	16. Ⓐ Ⓑ Ⓒ Ⓓ	29. Ⓐ Ⓑ Ⓒ Ⓓ
3. Ⓐ Ⓑ Ⓒ Ⓓ	17. Ⓐ Ⓑ Ⓒ Ⓓ	30. Ⓐ Ⓑ Ⓒ Ⓓ
4. Ⓐ Ⓑ Ⓒ Ⓓ	18. Ⓐ Ⓑ Ⓒ Ⓓ	31. Ⓐ Ⓑ Ⓒ Ⓓ
5. Ⓐ Ⓑ Ⓒ Ⓓ	19. Ⓐ Ⓑ Ⓒ Ⓓ	32. Ⓐ Ⓑ Ⓒ Ⓓ
6. Ⓐ Ⓑ Ⓒ Ⓓ	20. Ⓐ Ⓑ Ⓒ Ⓓ	33. Ⓐ Ⓑ Ⓒ Ⓓ
7. Ⓐ Ⓑ Ⓒ Ⓓ	21. Ⓐ Ⓑ Ⓒ Ⓓ	34. Ⓐ Ⓑ Ⓒ Ⓓ
8. Ⓐ Ⓑ Ⓒ Ⓓ	22. Ⓐ Ⓑ Ⓒ Ⓓ	35. Ⓐ Ⓑ Ⓒ Ⓓ
9. Ⓐ Ⓑ Ⓒ Ⓓ	23. Ⓐ Ⓑ Ⓒ Ⓓ	36. Ⓐ Ⓑ Ⓒ Ⓓ
10. Ⓐ Ⓑ Ⓒ Ⓓ	24. Ⓐ Ⓑ Ⓒ Ⓓ	37. Ⓐ Ⓑ Ⓒ Ⓓ
11. Ⓐ Ⓑ Ⓒ Ⓓ	25. Ⓐ Ⓑ Ⓒ Ⓓ	38. Ⓐ Ⓑ Ⓒ Ⓓ
12. Ⓐ Ⓑ Ⓒ Ⓓ	26. Ⓐ Ⓑ Ⓒ Ⓓ	39. Ⓐ Ⓑ Ⓒ Ⓓ
13. Ⓐ Ⓑ Ⓒ Ⓓ	27. Ⓐ Ⓑ Ⓒ Ⓓ	40. Ⓐ Ⓑ Ⓒ Ⓓ
14. Ⓐ Ⓑ Ⓒ Ⓓ		

GRAMMAR AND USAGE

1. Ⓐ Ⓑ Ⓒ Ⓓ	15. Ⓐ Ⓑ Ⓒ Ⓓ	28. Ⓐ Ⓑ Ⓒ Ⓓ
2. Ⓐ Ⓑ Ⓒ Ⓓ	16. Ⓐ Ⓑ Ⓒ Ⓓ	29. Ⓐ Ⓑ Ⓒ Ⓓ
3. Ⓐ Ⓑ Ⓒ Ⓓ	17. Ⓐ Ⓑ Ⓒ Ⓓ	30. Ⓐ Ⓑ Ⓒ Ⓓ
4. Ⓐ Ⓑ Ⓒ Ⓓ	18. Ⓐ Ⓑ Ⓒ Ⓓ	31. Ⓐ Ⓑ Ⓒ Ⓓ
5. Ⓐ Ⓑ Ⓒ Ⓓ	19. Ⓐ Ⓑ Ⓒ Ⓓ	32. Ⓐ Ⓑ Ⓒ Ⓓ
6. Ⓐ Ⓑ Ⓒ Ⓓ	20. Ⓐ Ⓑ Ⓒ Ⓓ	33. Ⓐ Ⓑ Ⓒ Ⓓ
7. Ⓐ Ⓑ Ⓒ Ⓓ	21. Ⓐ Ⓑ Ⓒ Ⓓ	34. Ⓐ Ⓑ Ⓒ Ⓓ
8. Ⓐ Ⓑ Ⓒ Ⓓ	22. Ⓐ Ⓑ Ⓒ Ⓓ	35. Ⓐ Ⓑ Ⓒ Ⓓ
9. Ⓐ Ⓑ Ⓒ Ⓓ	23. Ⓐ Ⓑ Ⓒ Ⓓ	36. Ⓐ Ⓑ Ⓒ Ⓓ
10. Ⓐ Ⓑ Ⓒ Ⓓ	24. Ⓐ Ⓑ Ⓒ Ⓓ	37. Ⓐ Ⓑ Ⓒ Ⓓ
11. Ⓐ Ⓑ Ⓒ Ⓓ	25. Ⓐ Ⓑ Ⓒ Ⓓ	38. Ⓐ Ⓑ Ⓒ Ⓓ
12. Ⓐ Ⓑ Ⓒ Ⓓ	26. Ⓐ Ⓑ Ⓒ Ⓓ	39. Ⓐ Ⓑ Ⓒ Ⓓ
13. Ⓐ Ⓑ Ⓒ Ⓓ	27. Ⓐ Ⓑ Ⓒ Ⓓ	40. Ⓐ Ⓑ Ⓒ Ⓓ
14. Ⓐ Ⓑ Ⓒ Ⓓ		

REA's Test Prep Books Are The Best!

(a sample of the <u>hundreds of letters</u> REA receives each year)

(more on front page)